SEPARATED AND DIVORCED WOMEN

Recent Titles in Contributions in Women's Studies

SEPARATED AND DIVORCED WOMEN

LYNNE CAROL HALEM

CONTRIBUTIONS IN WOMEN'S STUDIES, NUMBER 32

Greenwood Press

WESTPORT, CONNECTICUT • LONDON, ENGLAND

Library of Congress Cataloging in Publication Data

Halem, Lynne Carol.
    Separated and divorced women.

    (Contributions in women's studies, ISSN 0147-104X ;
no. 32)
    Bibliography: p.
    Includes index.
    1. Divorcees—United States. I. Title. II. Series.
HQ834.H33   306.8'9   81-13178
ISBN 0-313-23160-5 (lib. bdg.)   AACR2

Library of Congress Catalog Card Number: 81-13178
ISBN: 0-313-23160-5
ISSN: 0147-104X

First published in 1982

Greenwood Press
A division of Congressional Information Service, Inc.
88 Post Road West, Westport, Connecticut 06881

Printed in the United States of America

10 9 8 7 6 5 4 3 2 1

TO STEPHEN, ADAM, AND SAMANTHA WITH LOVE

CONTENTS

PREFACE

As the title indicates, this is a book about separated and divorced women —about their experiences, their feelings, and their thoughts. As the title does not indicate, this is also a book about one woman—about her experiences, her feelings, and her thoughts. 'Sheila Ash,'* the only individual in the book whose identity is revealed, has much in common with her anonymous sisters: They all live in the same suburban community; they all have dependent children; they all have postsecondary education; they all are members of that large and indeterminate grouping known as the middle class. But the one bond, above all else, which aligns Sheila with these other women is that she has just separated from her husband.

Sheila Ash is, however, not a real woman. She has no parents, no history, no present, no future, not even a social security number. She is a figment of my imagination. I am her creator; I am also her being. Like Geppetto, I am responsible for her transformation from an inanimate being to an animate one—in short, for her materialization. For, you see, it was I, using the pseudonym of Sheila Ash[1] and assuming the identity of a separated woman, who became the person whose story is retold in this book.

Yet in 1975 when I first conceived of the idea of roleplaying a separated woman, I planned to maintain the pseudo-identity of Sheila Ash for three months and three months only. In that time frame I had to design and execute a research project on single-parent women. To accomplish the task by simulation, that is, by attempting to understand some of the problems and needs of a particular population by roleplaying, appealed to my dramatic sensibilities and my hitherto unfulfilled thespian aspirations. It seemed so simple. Sheila would be a facsimile of myself: She would have the same date of birth, the same socioeconomic background, live in the same community, have two small children, and so on. The one difference, of

*All pseudonyms or coded names are identified through the use of single quotation marks the first time the name appears in the text.

course, was that Sheila would be separated from her husband. Perhaps I was too consumed by the theatrics of the plot to foresee the difficulties inherent in actualizing my proposal. It was one thing to imagine oneself as another individual, that is the stuff of which dreams are made; it was quite another thing to duplicate experiences about which you have no intimate knowledge. Realizing that Sheila's materialization would have to be stayed until I learned more about single-parent women, I developed a three-phase game plan. First came an in-depth review of the literature on separation and divorce; second, with the help of a friend and colleague a questionnaire was developed on the basis of the problems identified in the literature; and third, a sample of individuals was selected for open-ended interviews (see Appendixes A and B). In the course of compiling these data, I assumed no identity other than my own. I told all participants what I was doing and why. Sheila Ash was known to these people only as what she was—a fictitious woman to be used as an investigatory tool.

Still, Sheila was not ready to make her appearance. For my creation, I finally had to admit, needed an artistic overhauling. If initially I had assumed that Sheila's birth could be occasioned merely by substituting her name for mine on a résumé, I now knew that she could not and should not be my alter ego. The could nots in themselves were substantial. Because my educational and professional references on file at a university placement office could not be tampered with, I would have to contact numerous individuals, explain my project, and request that they rewrite my references using Sheila's name. Even if they agreed to become accomplices in this venture, the time involved and the mechanics of tracking down these people were sufficient dissuasions to cause me to abandon the idea. In addition, for the last nine years I had been employed in the state. As such, all individuals for whom I had worked would have to be forewarned in the event that employers approached by Sheila might routinely follow up her job application with personal inquiries. Without prior notification these individuals would be hard pressed to provide any information on a Ms. Sheila Ash, a person who existed solely on paper.

The should nots furnished equally compelling reasons for revising my plans. For one, my background was not truly representative of my sample. While 52% worked (25% part-time and 27% full-time), only two had graduate education past a master's degree and, for the group as a whole, those with graduate degrees were in the minority. Because my objective was to simulate the experiences of respondents, not to perform a trial run of my own life as a divorcee, it was more important that Sheila be a replica of the sample than of myself. This meant that she would have to have many of the same liabilities and advantages as sample members,[2] not all of which would be related directly to her status as a separated woman. In fact, her employment search or her investigation of day care, housing, and credit might also reveal obstacles faced by women in general or at least single-parent women. If, however, Sheila was to don my background, the investigation would not even touch on the problems of displaced homemakers and other areas of concern voiced by many interviewees.[3]

If both the project and character of Sheila underwent a series of major and unanticipated metamorphoses during the three months of research, my interest in the subject, as well as in roleplaying, never waned. Indeed, it grew more intense. To my surprise I was unable to let go, to relinquish that part of me who had been (and probably always will be) Sheila. Learning to respond to a different name was but a minor part of my transformation. More significantly, I had actually experienced anxiety, anger, disgust, and even self-pity while ostensibly performing under the guise of a fictitious persona. It was not, however, only my overidentification with Sheila which kept her alive. Even prior to Sheila's materialization, I had spoken to many people like Sheila individually and in groups; their concerns, comments, and ideas also lingered, haunting me. I had listened as they spoke of the complexities of their new lives, their sense of bewilderment, loss, guilt, and loneliness. I had attended meetings where questions posed to guest lawyers, court officials, and educators were artfully evaded. I had observed disappointment, anger, and helplessness in the audience. I had heard their requests for support, direction, and services rebuffed. To all these experiences I had reacted with sympathy and concern. But perhaps there was always in the back of my mind the nagging thought that just possibly I could supply some answers, even provide some help. Perhaps this was one reason why I chose not only to retain the identity of Sheila Ash but also to expand my investigation into a more detailed examination of the community in which respondents lived and in which the roleplaying was conducted. For another seven months Sheila and I continued to research the community I call 'Westside.'[4] My efforts to convince others to redirect existing community resources into a support network for the separated and divorced were received with enthusiasm and died in obscurity—funding was unavailable; people who supported the idea lost their positions; priorities were assigned to other projects. The message was clear: Sheila could be no more.

Although I finally did let go of Sheila, I continued to research the subject of divorce, first completing a doctoral dissertation, "Divorce and the Law: Pathology, Policy, and Practice" (1977), and then a book, *Divorce Reform: Changing Legal and Social Perspectives* (1980). Friends and colleagues fondly dubbed me, "The Divorce Lady," still thinking about me more as Sheila than about my social-historical research on divorce. Maybe they knew, as I should have known, that I would return to Sheila again. Now, as I

begin to write in 1980, after five years of compiling data on Westside (fortu-
nately I never did stop looking for information in local papers and probing
friends and neighbors for their observations and experiences) and two years of
actual roleplaying, I wonder if there ever would have been a Sheila if I
had realized in 1975 where an inspiration to assume another name and
identity would lead me.

With Sheila's help I have updated the material on the community, because there have been changes. I have interviewed more individuals both to
obtain a larger sample and to ascertain whether in the intervening years the
community had become more attuned to the needs of this population and/
or whether the requirements of the population itself had changed. Moreover, I have altered the focus of my presentation. Whereas before, the
information compiled from roleplaying was used to supplement questionnaire and interview data, it has now assumed a more primary function.
Sheila moved closer to center stage as her feelings and anecdotal recounts
of her experiences omitted from the two previous papers appear in this
book not only because they lend flavor to the story but, more importantly,
because they provide the reader with a more detailed and intimate view of
the problems confronted by separated and divorced women.

The book presents qualitative and some quantitative data on the subject
of separation and divorce, but it is also very much a story of Sheila and, by
extension, of myself. The difficulty presented to the writer becomes obvious:
The line between scholarly research and a personalized account needs to be
clearly drawn. Hopefully after five years of studying a subject I can differentiate the two components without marring the validity of either.
Hopefully this book provides more information about an important topic
through the presentation of data and through the more private reflections
of one, who although not a member of the sample population, has attempted to use identification and empathy as tools for understanding her
subject. To the many people who have wondered for so long whether my
marriage was a second or even a third one, the answer remains no. An
autobiography, in the true sense of the term, this is not. But if Sheila were
real, as she might well be, so clearly is she mirrored in the comments and
actions of respondents, then this is both her story and theirs.

NOTES

1. The last name of Ash was selected because of its simplicity and the absence of
any association with a specific ethnic or religious group.

2. That interviewees and Sheila had much in common was therefore no accident.

3. This was because my own employment history was an uninterrupted one,
without time lapses for childbearing or periods of unemployment.

4. "Separation in Westside: An Analysis of Patterns of Interaction Between
Separated Single-Parent Women and Their Community," Doctoral qualifying
paper, Harvard University, 1976.

ACKNOWLEDGMENTS

To the women and men whose stories appear on the pages of this book I will always be grateful. Anonymous though they must remain, each and every one of them will always be remembered as both a teacher and a muse.

To Bill Gum for his special brand of editorial oversight, his friendship, and his everlasting good humor. To my mother, Muriel Hessel, for her conscientious and painstaking proofreading. That she viewed it only as a labor of love says more about her contribution than I can express in words. To my father, Benjamin Hessel, for his encouragement and love. To my brother, Paul Hessel, for being my lawyer, my brother, and my friend.

To my husband, Stephen, I am especially indebted, not only for his assistance in outlining the logistics of the research, nor only his patience and love, but also for welcoming Sheila Ash into the family. If at times it seemed amusing to be married to *and* separated from the same woman with two different names, it was never easy and always confusing. Both Sheila and I are grateful. Last but never least, I thank my children, Adam and Samantha, for the parts they performed in the roleplaying, but most of all for the parts they play in my life.

SEPARATED AND DIVORCED WOMEN

INTRODUCTION

For centuries divorce has been a subject of interest and concern. Clerics, scholars, social commentators, and civil authorities have written, spoken, and argued about divorce; but for the most part their discourses remained hidden from the eyes and ears of the public. This, of course, is no longer true. Today not only has the public become privy to dialogues on divorce, but they have joined in the debates as active participants. As the divorce controversy has, in a manner of speaking, gone public, a nation of experts has been spawned. If knowledge on divorce was once primarily the preserve of the few, now just about everyone and anyone seem to have an opinion warranting expression. Perhaps we can attribute this collective wisdom to escalating divorce rates. As the national divorce rate rose, more and more individuals joined the ranks of those with inside information on the causes and consequences of marital dissolution. Concurrently, the interest of others was aroused. Some were motivated to generate new data, theories, and solutions; others responded out of a concern for the institutions of marriage and the family, individual well-being, or social solidarity; and still others were simply moved by the prospects of monetary gain.

One result of this awakened and rising sense of public awareness and involvement was the proliferation of books, articles, and data on divorce. The media played no small role in fostering this "knowledge" explosion. Beginning in the mid-1960s and sustaining the momentum throughout the 1970s and into the decade of the 80s, the media have engaged in a massive "hype" of the divorce controversy, sometimes to the point of sensationalism. Undoubtedly the dramatic increase in popular literature and, to a lesser but still notable degree, the stepped-up output of scholarly analyses and findings have served a purpose. We know more about divorce and its ramifications than we ever have. New programs and services for the divorced and their families have been created, although by most indicators the supply has lagged far behind the demand. Self-help manuals, fictionalized and personalized accounts of marital dissolutions, and the "I'm Okay, You're

Okay'' genres have responded to the needs of some who find in these offerings guidance, reassurance, and even company in their "misery."

On the downside both academic and lay literature as well as demographic data on divorce have been used to support the thesis that the American family is an endangered species. Coincidentally, or perhaps not so coincidentally, rising public interest in divorce and in the family occurred at about the same time. While we can pose the proverbial chicken and egg question, the reasons for the tie-in seem less important than the association itself. Here there is cause for concern. Because the literature and data on divorce focus primarily on the pathological effects of marital dissolution as it pertains to adults, children, and even the nation, this dolorous prognosis gives substance to the belief that the family is critically, if not terminally, afflicted (Halem, 1980). And unfortunately there is no shortage of individuals willing and able to corroborate the "truth" of this deduction. Indeed, it may be that we have progressed past the state of being a nation of experts and are becoming a nation of judges. If so, the trial of the American family is to be adjudged by a jury of many. Regardless of the verdict, it is apparent that the evidence presented at the trial will influence the future direction of public policy, thereby impinging on all our lives and the lives of our children and our children's children.

It is also apparent that much of the evidence will relate to divorce and to the divorced. There will be demographic data on divorce, social and psychological data on divorce, economic data on divorce, legal data on divorce, and whatever other data on divorce that can be amassed. The publicity accorded to information presented in national forums is not easily ignored. Even if we were to closet ourselves in a Thoreauvian sanctuary away from blaring televisions and radios and the printed "truth" published in newspapers, magazines, and books, we may succeed in muting the hullabaloo but not in silencing it.

I say all this because I am writing about divorce and the lives of the separated and divorced, and I am concerned. Already the statistics, the media's hype, and increased public interest in divorce and the family have taken their toll; for one cannot speak to the mothers or fathers of children in single-parent or reconstituted families without noting the undercurrents of guilt. "My children fight so much because of my divorce." "My daughter has headaches because of the divorce." "My son dresses up in women's clothes because there is no man in the house." "My daughter's grades are slipping because her mother doesn't discipline her the way I did when I was home." While some of these inferences may be correct, others may not. Most siblings fight; children can have headaches or do poorly in school for many reasons; boys can dress up in their mothers' clothes in homes where fathers are active participants and models of masculinity.

I say all this as a cautionary preamble, for by relating the needs and concerns of the separated and divorced, the book exposes many of their problems and some of their fears. But my intention is to highlight the practical aspects of divorce, not its pathological ones. The fact that divorce can be a problematic occurrence or that it can have negative repercussions does not mean that the act itself is inherently detrimental, destructive to individuals and society. Such an explanation does a disservice to man and to science, for neither the causes nor the consequences of divorce can be explained by scientific axioms. While others may sit in judgment of the divorced or take it upon themselves to forecast their destiny and that of their families, I have no such ambition. I am neither a judge nor a soothsayer. This, of course, says more about what I will not and cannot do than about the research I have conducted and the book I have written. In order that the reader understand both my purpose and my methods from the outset, the following overview is presented.

THE FOCUS OF THE STUDY

In novels, autobiographies, and academic studies authors have probed, pondered, and exposed the agonies and even some of the ecstasies of separation and divorce. In more abbreviated formats, journalists have done likewise. Some accounts begin at the moment of discovery, that dramatic (and traumatic) instant when the individual first learns or realizes that his or her marriage is to end. Others begin with the life of the married couple, providing glimpses of togetherness or strife, a background, if you will, against which life after marriage can be contrasted. Not all accounts are this theatrical, and certainly not all are as moving as Ingmar Bergman's "Scenes from a Marriage"; but all, whether they be fact or fiction or somewhere in between, portray the movement from marriage to life as a single person (and/or parent) as a period of transition and change.

Although my book differs in tone and in theory from most other books, particularly if the comparison is limited to the field of nonfiction, I too view separation and divorce as occurrences requiring adjustment and at times even the restructuring of one's goals and lifestyle. For this reason I chose to concentrate on the processes of decision making that follow a marital separation. I wanted to learn not only more about the different decisions which women who separate and divorce make, be they out of necessity or choice, but also more about the obstacles—personal, situational, or institutional—which impede action and growth as well as the supports which facilitate coping and adaptation.

This meant that the needs and concerns that women confront upon, during, or after separation would constitute a major component of this book. This also meant that the focus of the book would have to extend beyond the individuals themselves, beyond their families, friends, and homes; it would have to follow them into the larger world, the world where they work, go to school, obtain services, socialize, and, in short, go about the business of living. Within the limitations imposed by time and space I have tried to present the reader with a realistic depiction of the many worlds in which these women live, albeit the names of people, institutions, and places are often coded. Nonetheless, the community I call Westside is the true focal point of this book. Because it is the community in which the respondents lived and in which Sheila Ash's investigation was mostly conducted, it provides a nexus for integrating the data compiled from questionnaires and interviews with that of roleplaying. It also provides a point of reference for the discussion of change strategies, enabling the reader to envisage the transitions that have occurred in one community during a five-year period as well as to consider the community's potential for future adaptation and reform.

By viewing separation and divorce as a time of transition and decision making, it became evident that the major problems and needs faced by these women, the major changes which occurred in their lives and the lives of their families, and the major decisions which they made as they set about reordering their lives could be categorized into four substantive areas: legal, economic, social, and psychological. In a sense each of these classifications represents a different side of separation and divorce, albeit a side of multi-faceted dimensions. In another sense the sides cannot be separated, for the interrelationships are often more manifest than the distinctions. Recognizing that the effort to classify data may serve to confuse more than it does to clarify, the reader should realize that with respect to time and substance all four areas are in actuality intertwined.

Chapters 1, 3, 5, and 7 relate the material compiled from questionnaire and interview respondents, incorporating direct quotations with discussions of various aspects of the legal, economic, social, and psychological areas of concern. Chapters 2, 4, 6, and 8 are companion chapters, covering the same subjects, but this time from the perspective of Sheila Ash's exploration. Anecdotal recounts of Sheila's experiences are supplemented by comparisons to questionnaire and interview data. As such, the book presents two chapters in sequence for each of the four areas of concern. In all eight chapters references are made to the lay and scholarly literature as they pertain not only to separation and divorce but also to the broader topical areas. In addition, wherever possible I have tried, by referring to different studies, places, and statistical data, to illustrate the similarities between Westside and other locales, as well as between the women (and men) in this study and other groups of separated and divorced individuals.

Lastly, in Chapter 9 the subject of change and reform is broached. Using Westside as an example and the data compiled from both respondents and roleplaying as a basis for analysis, I suggest guidelines for change and note implications for future research and the creation of social policy.

THE SETTING: A COMMUNITY CALLED WESTSIDE

To my knowledge there is no community called Westside, yet the community is not a figment of my imagination. Westside does exist, and in all probability the curious and discerning reader will have no difficulty in uncovering its identity. Nonetheless, in deference to the many individuals who shared their ideas and concerns with me, who spoke openly and freely but confidentially, a pseudonym, if only as a means of offering some anonymity, is in order.[1]

Westside is a city of 83,000, located near a major metropolitan area in the northeast United States. Its population is approximately 20% Roman Catholic, 40% Jewish, and 40% Protestant. Less than 1% of the residents are nonwhite. By charter it is a city; by character it is a suburb. Indeed, one can even conceptualize Westside as 13 separate suburbs, for, not uncommonly, when residents are asked where they live, they respond by citing the name of one of the 13 villages that comprise the city. To many Westsidians their village is their community. At first blush the differences among the villages seem to justify this identification as a natural one. A visitor touring the village centers could not help but notice the contrasts— the contrasts between restored and antiquated architecture, between urban and rural atmospheres, between contemporary and historic settings, between planned design and random growth. But these are only the centers; it is upon closer inspection that the dissimilitudes within each village become as evident as the likenesses. If there are, as in any community, better and best sections, in Westside it might be more accurate to say better and best blocks. The streets intersect and intertwine in sometimes unfathomable patterns, but it is hard to imagine any resident losing his way because of the sameness of the dwellings. Drunk or sober, Westside is visibly not a development. Each village is in itself a potpourri—an economic, social, cultural, and physical mixture.

Technically the city is middle class, with a median income of $15,381 (Kravitz, 1977). The majority of its housing units are single-family dwellings with a median value of $33,600 (ibid.). Demographics can, however, be deceiving. There are homes with sprawling, manicured grounds which rival the grandeur of Beverly Hills, California, and Kings Point, New York; there are others which could sit comfortably and unnoticed in the deteriorated sectors of a metropolis. In this sense Westside is a city—a city with ethnic enclaves, with residents who are rich and poor, educated and uneducated, liberal and conservative, and those who belong to neither extreme. For the most part the city wears its diversity with pride, taking pleasure in its schizoid nature. It keeps its problems very much within its borders, with the result that most outsiders see Westside as a predominantly affluent, aspiring community, a place in which to escape urban poverty and its accomplices of crime, vice, and unemployment.

Still, many residents persist in forming their own classifications. Some make distinctions between villages, while others differentiate the city into two sides—a rich one and a poor one. Hence a move from one village to another, or across town, is often perceived as a sign of upward mobility. To a large extent the school system has perpetuated these misconceptions by accentuating the individuality of each school—an individuality so salient that special curriculums and programs are deemed necessary to meet the *unique* needs of each school's student and parent clientele. The trouble with this philosophical approach is that it is based on a faulty premise—the homogeneity of a school's clientele. In actuality, each school's population mirrors the differences as much as the likenesses of the subsections and villages in which it is situated, despite the existence in 1979 of 20 elementary schools, five junior high schools, and two high schools. This has led to the charge, by some, that the central administration's dichotomization of schools is a subtle instrument of stigmatization and a rationale for the unequal distribution of resources. Yet the discrepancies continue, and so does the myth that a move across town will mean far more than a bigger house and more land. And at times, at least in respect to education, it does.

While the school system has been the subject of some controversy, its local and national reputation has remained intact—a rather notable achievement at a time when confidence in public education and educators appears to be declining at a greater rate than even student enrollment.[2] But the schools are not the only source of pride. Westsidians boast of the city's cosmopolitan environment—its numerous cultural and social institutions and facilities—and the willingness of the citizenry to assume civic responsibilities. Many of Westside's residents are involved in political and consumer activities; liberal church groups were in the forefront of the civil rights and peace movements; and advocacy groups have been instrumental in mobilizing citizen action on issues ranging from violence on children's television programming to property reevaluation.

Westside is thus a bit of city, suburbia, and small town. Its uniqueness can be ascribed not to the sum of its parts but rather to the distinctiveness of each minuscule part. It lacks the cohesiveness and homogeneity of smaller communities and the excitement of larger cities. Its appeal can probably be best attributed to its conveniences—proximity to a major northeastern city, to colleges and universities, and to a variety of industries and businesses, a well-known public school system, adequate transportation, parks and recreational areas—or maybe simply to the fact that it is a pleasant place to live.

Westside is not, metaphorically speaking, "every community." That its residents are primarily middle-class, that only 1% of its population is nonwhite, that it is located in the northeastern United States, that it has not suffered unduly from high unemployment rates, urban unrest, or the devaluation of property are only some of the characteristics that set Westside apart from some other towns and cities. Demographic breakdowns with respect to religious affiliations, political preferences, and the number of years of schooling of its population are also atypical. And the list could be expanded further. Yet we should not become overly obsessed with disparities, even when addressing the question of the applicability of data from one locale to another. If Westside does not meet all the criteria necessary for receiving a middle-American certificate, it also would not qualify for certification as an anomalous community—neither markedly lower nor upper crust according to economic, social, or cultural indices. This suggests that there are indeed limitations to how far one can go in generalizing the information compiled on this community to the nation as a whole or even to suburbia. But this also suggests that there are similarities, as I will note, between Westside and other communities, be they urban or suburban.

Moreover, the utility of information cannot be assessed solely upon its value as a tool for making statistical inferences. Surely a case can be made for conducting a systematic and in-depth look at one community if it provides even a glimpse of how that community responds to the needs of a specific resident population. I would, however, maintain that the information from this study can also be useful in another way, namely, by helping policy makers and concerned citizens to become more knowledgeable about the kind and nature of services which the separated and divorced use and/or need. By comparing Westside to their own communities, and its resources to their own resources, they can selectively extrapolate relevant findings.

Thus in this book the setting is more than a backdrop for a narrative about separated and divorced women or even for Sheila's roleplaying experiences. The symbiotic relationship between a community and some of its residents is central to the book. The resources a community possesses and its decision on how to channel and allocate these resources are also central to the book. For those in marital transition, I suggest that they consider, as I have considered, the various options available to them in any community, for in this way they may come to realize that there are in fact alternatives and they do have a voice in shaping their lives. For those who plan to use the information to examine their own community, I suggest that they consider, as I have considered, some hard questions: How can communities outreach to special groups without stigmatizing and alienating their members? How can communities maximize the utility and effectiveness of existing resources? Are new services necessary for meeting the needs of the separated and divorced and their families? And if so, how can a community justify the creation of services and resources in a time of increasing budgetary constraints and pressures?

THE METHODS OF THE STUDY

This book looks at separation and divorce and the importance of community from two different perspectives: the perspective of separated and divorced women and that of a married woman attempting to simulate the experiences of women in marital transition through roleplaying. As a consequence the study depends on a multiple-method research approach. In order that the reader understand the methods used in the compilation of data as well as their limitations, a synopsis is herein presented.

THE SAMPLE: SEPARATED AND DIVORCED WOMEN SPEAK OUT

In the first exploratory study (see Appendix A for a description of the study design and methodology) I focused exclusively on the separation phase of divorce for three reasons: First, the period preceding the granting of the divorce decree was generally depicted in the separation and divorce literature as the most psychologically and socially disruptive phase of the divorce process (Marris, 1974; Weiss, 1975). Secondly, there was (and is) a paucity of research on separation as compared to that on divorce. And thirdly, researchers often failed to differentiate the separation period from the period following the divorce. This becomes particularly troublesome and confusing if one takes into account those among the separated who reconcile or obtain a legal separation. While these reasons provide a compelling rationale for studying separation, in this book I have expanded the scope of my research to include divorced as well as separated women.

If the differences between the stages in the divorce process warrant special attention, so too do the similarities. Not only do the separated and divorced share common concerns, but they also experience common problems. Difficulties occurring in the initial stage of a marital dissolution do not necessarily vanish upon the finalization of a divorce decree. A judicial award is not a magical potion. Patterns of adjustment and coping are influenced by many factors, ranging from practical issues relating to money, employment, and child care to the more emotional dimensions of the dissolution (e.g., who initiated the separation, whether there was a third party involved, whether the rejected partner suspected a problem or was caught unaware, and the reactions of children, family, and friends). In part, then, the circumstances surrounding the split determine the ease or difficulty with which individuals make the transition from marriage to separation or divorce. But people differ, as do situations and circumstances, some adjusting more readily than others. My point, simply put, is that the problems encountered by the separated are neither unique to these individuals nor to separation.[3]

Moreover, as a result of my interest in this subject, I became a logical person to talk to about divorce. More and more frequently as time passed friends and even friends of friends spoke to me about their problems and experiences. Perhaps they came and came back again because I was a sympathetic listener, because I was a source of information, or because talking is in itself a kind of therapeutic experience. I too benefited from these conversations. They added greatly to my knowledge of separation and divorce, in part corroborating my previous research and in part furnishing new data.

For these reasons and also because I was, at the time, writing a social-historical book on divorce and the law (Halem, 1980), interview material collected for this book was not confined to separated, single-parent women, although for each direct quotation I have noted whether the respondent was separated or divorced and for how long a period of time. In addition, I chose not to limit the study to women between the ages of 28 and 38. The increasing rate of divorce among the middle-aged justifies, I believe, more attention to this population. However, because of my interest in single parenthood, I have retained the requirement that interviewees have dependent children residing at home. Perhaps as a result of this prerequisite, all respondents were under 50 years of age.

Nonetheless, this book, like my preliminary research, is about middle-class women. (Data on men of like socioeconomic status are used for comparison purposes.)[4] The selective process was and is largely motivated by the tendency in marital separation and divorce research to bypass these individuals. The decision to study and target recommendations for further research and social policy to low-income (especially urban) groups has long been supported by the population's high divorce rate. While it is still true that the poor outrank the middle classes in the number of divorces, John (and Jane) Q. Public is fast advancing. In recent decades, as the middle classes have noticeably contributed to the nation's escalating divorce rate (not to mention trends toward later marriages and decreasing first marriage rate as well as the declining birth rate), it is no longer accurate to portray divorce as a lower-class phenomenon. Furthermore, whether divorce is experienced by a middle-income or a lower-income person, it appears that both encounter similar problems in adjusting to life as a single parent and person (albeit they vary in kind and in degree).

In all, 50 interviews with separated and divorced women (see footnote 4) were intermittently conducted over a period of four years (1975-1979).[5] If time had permitted, I could have interviewed hundreds more. Indeed, there was nary a person—woman or man—to whom I spoke who did not volunteer to be interviewed. But time did not permit, particularly since the interviews had to be widely spaced, allowing four to six hours per session.[6]

Admittedly, some sessions centered almost exclusively on the foibles of ex-spouses. In these interviews I often found it hard to convince the respondent that she (or he) did not have to justify the dissolution, that the whys and wherefores of the separation were not my primary interest. In general, the more recent the separation, the greater the need to build an adequate defense, to be vindicated. In part this may be ascribed to the legal system's emphasis on fault,[7] but it also seems to be a stage through which many individuals must pass. At the beginning one's identity is so closely tied to that of another that the act of weaning is exceedingly difficult and painful. In order to look ahead to a new life, a life apart from a former spouse, each person must first expunge her (or his) misgivings and come to terms with feelings of personal failure and guilt. Sometimes this takes the form of self-defamement: the "if only I had" or "if only I had not" statements express regret for past transgressions, real or imaginary. At other times or with other people, the ignobility of the ex-spouse is the focus of attention.

The placement of blame upon one's ex-spouse or self-incrimination may, however, continue well past the initial months of separation. Especially in divorces involving children, continued interaction between parents can be a bitter experience. Stormy visitation sessions, absent or delayed support or alimony payments, the courting of the children, the deprecation of one parent by another, and, of course, remarriage are some examples of incendiary episodes and occurrences which can rekindle or perpetuate anger and conflict between spouses.

I soon realized that interviews which began in this way and in which individuals were permitted to dwell too long on their anguish or indignation were almost impossible to turn around. Accordingly, I found it necessary to initiate each session with a description of the kinds of information I was seeking. I would explain my interest in learning the needs and concerns (legal, economic, social, and psychological) of individuals who had experienced a marital dissolution, how their lives had changed since the separation (e.g., with respect to employment, child care, living arrangements, credit), and their utilization and assessment of community resources as well as their recommendations for change (informing them at this point about Sheila Ash and the role she was to play in the research).

In short, although the interviews remained open-ended and informal, I introduced some structure by outlining my goals and specifying the particular areas I hoped to cover. I did not always succeed. Occasionally the psychic dimensions of the divorce were so all consuming that any attempt to redirect the dialogue (actually, a monologue) was either ignored by the individual or interpreted as an affront, an unwillingness to hear her out. Yet in most cases I was able to extrapolate information on the practical aspects of separation and divorce, while still providing an opportunity for the respondent to vent her spleen or relive a regretted past.

The women whose stories supply the inspiration for my book and much of its substance are alike in several respects: They all live in Westside, have dependent children, are educated members of the American middle class, and have experienced a marital dissolution. Such information, however, does not reveal the subtleties of personality, those intricacies of the self that distinguish one person from another. It helps little to add that 18% of the participants were Roman Catholic, 38% Protestant, and 44% Jewish; all participants were white; they ranged in age from 28 to 49; politically the vast majority were Democrats or liberals; most were involved in some way with a community organization or organizations; prior to separation 40% had been unemployed for a minimum of five years, 8% had never had a job, and the remaining 52% had either part-time (25%) or full-time (27%) jobs; and lastly, after separation their incomes, based upon earnings and monies received from child support and alimony, ranged from $8,000 to $30,000, as compared to $15,000 to $50,000 before the separation.[8] Still, this is not the stuff of which people are made. While it is regrettable that the uniqueness of each individual is not only concealed but lost in the preponderance of data, it may also be unavoidable. As researchers, we often promise to protect the anonymity of our participants, and in so doing we classify people into categories, as if they were objects. Instead of individual actors, these women become known in studies like mine, for example, as single parents, female heads of households, separated women, divorced women, or even women in transition. And that is not all we do. In our effort to identify likenesses among members of the group—common patterns of reaction, concerns, needs, and problems—we further disembody our subjects.

All of the above constitutes both an apology to each individual whose distinctiveness I shall not forget and a rationale for the manner in which I have chosen to present her story. This is not a book of case histories, for I have selectively excerpted segments of stories, classifying them under the broad headings of legal, economic, social, and psychological areas of concern and using subdivisions for further clarification and specificity.

These women of Westside, then, appear on the pages of the book as sources of information. Their responses tell much about how they coped with separation and divorce, what they perceived to be the areas of greatest difficulty and of triumph, who helped them, and how they helped themselves. These data also formed the basis for Sheila's exploration of Westside. As such, much like a building depends upon the strength of its foundation, my research depended upon the accuracy of respondents' information.

From the outset I was well aware that these recollections would reflect the perceptions and personal situations of a limited population and that perceptual and psychological defenses might operate unintentionally to distort or conceal more fundamental or disparate needs. But as individual after individual focused on the same problematic issues (which, by the way, were also the ones most frequently identified in the literature on separation and divorce), I became increasingly confident of the validity of the information I was compiling. After five years of research I have not changed my mind. This is not to say that I have compiled an exhaustive list of all the needs and concerns of separated and divorced women, nor that I have devised solutions for redressing their problems. Neither was my intent. Rather I have sought to stimulate thought on the subject of separation and divorce through a better understanding of not only the problems of some women but also of the different options they have. All women do not go down the same path as they make the transition from marriage to life as a single person, and this is as it should be. But they all make choices; they all have alternatives; and they all change, in some way, to some degree. Whether one is the instigator of a divorce action or the surprised spouse (it does not necessarily follow that the first becomes the plaintiff and the latter the defendant) or whether the separation is welcomed or dreaded, a marital dissolution necessitates a reorganization of the lives of both partners. It is a time of adaptation, or in Gail Sheehy's jargon, a "passage." That every woman and man have at least some control over the kind of lives they create for themselves is perhaps most significant.

THE CREATION OF A CHARACTER: MS. SHEILA ASH

Name: Sheila Ash
Age: 33
Name of spouse: Michael Ash
Address: 26 Barron Road, Westside
Marital Status: Separated
Number of children: 2
Occupation: Homemaker

Sheila Ash, as the reader knows, is not real. She is a fictional composite of the women interviewed for this study. But Sheila is not a character in a novel or an actress in a play; her milieu is not a contrived setting but the real world. And thus I, who was to assume her identity, to become Sheila Ash, had to make sure that her veracity would not be questioned. The creation of the character was the easy part; the transformation of the character into a woman realistic enough to convince employers, providers of services, and landlords, among others, of her needs and goals was the difficult part. Not only did my performance as a separated woman have to be a credible one, but I also had to make sure that I (Sheila) had the necessary credentials and information to gain access to people and places. In addition, the entire scenario was to be acted out in the community in which I lived. Somehow I had to function simultaneously as myself and as Sheila. But I am going too quickly. The problems of roleplaying and living in the same community will become clearer as the story unfolds. For now, let us concentrate on the tasks involved in bringing about Sheila's materialization.

The Props

Sheila Ash (nee George), as it turned out, was very much her own person. If we shared the same date and place of birth, attended the same public schools through high school, lived in the same communities during childhood and adolescence, and even had some of the same interests and hobbies, after high school we parted ways. In 1960 Sheila attended the University of Michigan, where she majored in elementary education and English literature. It was there that she met Michael, whom she married in 1963 (coincidentally, the same year in which I was married).[9] Sheila returned to New York City in 1964 and taught for one year before moving out-of-state. Upon relocation, she secured a job as a nursery schoolteacher, remaining at the same school for three years (until 1968). Peter was born in 1969 and Laurie in 1972 (coincidentally, the same years in which my children were born).[10] For a year before Peter was born and for six years after his birth, Sheila tutored children with learning disabilities. Concurrently she joined the ranks of those invaluable and undervalued individuals known as volunteer workers, performing supervisory and administrative tasks. In addition, as a resident of Westside, she became involved in various community projects and activities (see Appendix D for Sheila's résumé).

If this was Sheila's history, it was a history for which I had very little documentation. I could neither manufacture a college transcript nor obtain scholastic references for a fictitious student, even one who was graduated with honors. This meant that, despite Sheila's degree in education, her employment search could not include school systems, as it is their practice to require job applicants to submit college transcripts. Nonetheless, I was able to do better in the job reference department, since I had already compiled my "evidence" for the rest of this bogus résumé. Indeed, Sheila's salaried and nonsalaried employment experience, with the sole exception of one year's teaching in a public school, had been determined more by whom I knew than by any planning or rational motives on my part.

In the interests of science and/or friendship I had persuaded a friend who owned a private nursery school to add Sheila to her list of past employees. Besides writing a particularly glowing reference for her former employee, she also agreed to answer any inquiries from prospective employers—hence Sheila the nursery schoolteacher.

Perhaps references from administrators in school systems would have been more impressive, and I did know individuals with such positions. Yet I had abandoned the idea, concluding that the workings of bureaucracies were too unpredictable and uncontrollable to use as sites for "fraud." In short, the risk would be too great—not for Sheila or me but for her sponsor(s). Looking elsewhere for suitable employers to support Sheila's candidacy for jobs and finding none, I finally decided that unpaid experience would be preferable to no experience. (Unfortunately, it is not by much. Money in the form of salaries pays more than the bills; it also buys status.) However, without much effort I was not only able to locate some friends who were active in volunteer organizations and others in charge of community projects but, more importantly, to help them "remember" Sheila's contributions to different projects and programs they had directed—hence Sheila the volunteer and community worker.

I had also obtained several letters from friends who praised Sheila's patience, ability, and ingenuity as a private tutor for their children—hence Sheila the learning disability tutor.

Call it inspiration or "hokum," I made one last effort to justify Sheila's seven years of unemployment (1968-1975) and to enhance her salability in fields outside of education. Ms. Sheila Ash, I proclaimed, would be a woman with artistic talents—indeed, a woman whose drawings and paintings were sufficiently proficient to be exhibited at a local amateur showing. This finishing touch was made possible by a friend who had arranged just such a showing—hence Sheila the amateur artist.

This, then, is the capsulization of Ms. Sheila Ash's educational and professional background. Perhaps not an imposing history, but for a so-called "displaced homemaker" it had at least a modicum of pluses.

Besides a résumé and references, Sheila's dossier included a library card and a community recreation card. She did not have a social security number, a driver's license, or even a birth certificate. At best her identification portfolio was several credentials short of being described as "meager." She did, however, have an address—courtesy of a friend who posted Sheila's name on her mailbox and informed the post office of her new roommate.

For a telephone number I had little choice but to use my own, since it was necessary that I be available to speak to employers, landlords, or other individuals approached during the roleplaying investigation.

To complete my metamorphosis I purchased two wigs, both styled differently and of a slightly darker hue than my own hair, several scarves, a few hats, clear nonprescription glasses, and large sunglasses. Before anyone jumps to the conclusion that this was a reenactment of a grade B movie, the reader should recall that, even though Westside is a city with a population of approximately 83,000, for a roleplayer who is also a resident the risk of detection is far greater than in a large urban center. It was impossible to predict whether a prospective employer, landlord, or provider of services would be someone I knew, even casually. Admittedly, the disguises were not particularly good; I was neither as talented a costume designer as Edith Head or as daring a roleplayer as John Griffin who, the reader will recall, colored his skin in order to gain personal insight into the problems of blacks in the south (*Black Like Me*). But I hoped that, if necessary, they would provide enough concealment to permit a quick exit. As it turned out, this was not always possible.

One last detail: My children had to be prepped for the roleplaying, as they too were to be participants. Not only did they sometimes answer the telephone and therefore had to be aware that callers who asked for Sheila Ash had not dialed the wrong number, but some nursery schools and day care centers requested that a child accompany his or her parent(s) when visiting the school. And lastly, because they were only 2½ and 5½ (albeit they, as well as I, grew older as time passed), mishaps, such as no-show babysitters, at times left me with little choice but to bring them along. Unexpectedly, they never questioned the project. Perhaps they were too young or perhaps they accepted the entire ruse as a game that adults play. They laughed at my attempts to disguise my identity, particularly when I wore a wig, but never did they say anything in public about my acting or changing my hair or using a pseudonym. Even more surprisingly, they actually seemed to enjoy the ploy of having their own names changed. Admittedly, they made mistakes. People called them and they did not respond. But overall their performances were admirable.

And so Sheila I became. In a matter of one and a half month's time, the children had been coached and the props secured. Sheila was ready to make her debut.

The Assignment

Sheila Ash's assignment was to check legal resources and obtain information on the state's divorce law and divorce proceedings without retaining legal counsel, to seek employment, to identify and investigate alternative forms of child care, to explore new places to live in Westside, to ascertain as far as possible her creditworthiness, and to survey local resources for separated and divorced persons and/or single parents. The questions to be answered were complex: Were there adequate services available in the community despite respondents' claims to the contrary? What kinds of services did the community offer separated and divorced individuals and their families? How difficult was it for an unemployed but educated home-maker to obtain a job and arrange care for her children? Was the separated (or divorced) woman hampered by a lack of knowledge of what was available and of how to negotiate in her own behalf? Or was there simply no system or relatively none through which to proceed? These, of course, were the more technical questions on the number and kind of community re-sources. In the course of the research other issues surfaced, raising ques-tions related to both overt and covert discrimination and stigmatization, be it to women, single parents, or children.

Moreover, examination of the social service system(s) in Westside was conducted from a different perspective and for a different purpose. Here an effort was made to learn how different organizations in the community functioned and whether organizations which were currently not servicing the separated and divorced did in fact have such a potential.

Thus Sheila was to be two people and in effect carry out two assignments. As a separated woman and a single parent she shared with respondents their problems and concerns. She knew separation to be a time of emotional confusion as well as one of critical decision making. But knowing and being are not the same. The second Sheila, the researcher, could reconstruct experiences with a detachment and freedom unknown to the women whose images she was trying to mirror. The advantages of creating such a fictitious identity are numerous. Sheila could compile information on the number and nature of existing resources; she could evaluate their visibility and accessibility to the target population; and to some extent she could assess, on the basis of her knowledge of organizational management and behavior, potential for reform and change.

In short, the creation of Sheila Ash was used as a mechanism for achiev-ing three objectives: first, to understand the problems identified by respon-dents through the simulation of their searches for legal information, jobs, child care, housing, and credit, as well as for various psychosocial services; second, to learn more about the kinds of public and private resources in Westside; and third, to stimulate thought on how communities could better address the needs of the separated and divorced and their families.

Nonetheless, I recognized from the outset that my research would not produce definitive answers. At most I hoped to uncover some clues that would help others and myself to appreciate both the problems confronted by the separated and divorced and their relationship to, and even dependency upon, the community in which they live for services and support.

Further, I realized that despite a conscientious effort to reproduce real-life experiences, there was bound to be a certain artificiality to the project which I could not eliminate. For Sheila there would be no litigation proceedings or legal negotiations; there would be no disputes over custody or visitation, over child support or over property division or alimony. Moreover, she would not have to explain the separation to her children (or family), answer their questions, or try to allay their fears.

There were other gaps in the study which were in part attributable to monetary and time constraints and in part to rather personal reasons. For example, with respect to the former there was a limit to the number of lawyers I could afford to consult. With respect to the latter I did not role-play Sheila during visits to groups for single parents, nor did I frequent dating bars, social clubs, or other "in" spots for singles. These decisions were swayed far more by my own beliefs and feelings than by the exigencies of time or circumstance. I felt that deceiving members of the population I was studying or partaking in activities such as dating would constitute unconscionable behavior; indeed, it would violate that already fragile partition that separates research from intrusion. I did attend meetings for single parents and separated and divorced persons, but not as Sheila. On such occasions Sheila the researcher had a companion, namely Lynne Halem, who performed tasks and participated in the investigation when the assignment and the situation called for more traditional methodological approaches. In the following presentation I have stated whenever the pseudo-identity of Sheila Ash was abandoned and my own substituted.

Lastly, I would be less than honest if I failed to reveal that this was a project involving the viscera as much as the intellect. Roleplaying places two contradictory demands upon the researcher. It requires that you perform in an identity other than your own—that, in a sense, you become another human being. Concurrently, it requires that you retain the ability to act and think dispassionately, for a researcher must, after all, be able to employ scientific techniques in compiling and analyzing data. Yet the more adept you are as a performer, the more difficult is the task of functioning as a scientist. I do not claim, therefore, that I was at all times a scholar, that is, detached and objective. As Sheila Ash, I experienced anger and joy; there were even momentary lapses when I actually thought of myself as Sheila and other times when I thought of her as someone I knew—someone who was real. In recounting Sheila's experiences I have taken pains to relate my feelings as well as my findings so that the reader is aware of my on-again, off-again propensity for overidentification.[11]

The Execution

Prior to Sheila's field research I had to determine specifically which of the legal, economic, social, and psychological concerns and needs identified by the respondents could and would be investigated. My interest in the community as a place in which separated and divorced women (and men) obtain help and/or encounter disappointment and frustration expanded the scope of the study. But it also meant that issues with little or no bearing on the relationship between these residents and their community had to be eliminated from consideration. This constituted the first step in identifying the areas to be investigated. The second step was to rank all remaining items according to two indices: the frequency with which they were cited and the respondents' assessment of their importance as communicated to the interviewer. The final refinement was even more subjective, based as it was on my evaluation of the feasibility of using field research techniques and role-playing for the analysis of specific problems and systems.

The stacks of outlines began to multiply as I planned the methods of execution, compiled the necessary materials, identified key individuals, and selected the organizations to be analyzed. Much of the assignment's difficulty was attributable to the necessity of having to initiate numerous projects at the same time. The research could not be separated into discrete categories so that, for instance, the exploration of legal questions and resources would be completed before the search for employment was begun. The reason for this overlap was twofold. One, in order to recreate an honest portrayal of the problems facing many separated and divorced women, different issues had to be addressed simultaneously. It is not uncommon for a separated woman to have to seek legal counsel while also in the process of looking for a new residence and employment, as well as surveying child-care services. In fact, the number of demands placed upon her and the number of decisions to be made at any one time can be shockingly high. Even if this were not the case, as some women do proceed more or less in a planned order, waiting until or after the divorce decree before they consider employment, schooling, relocation, or other critical life changes, the time restrictions on the collection and analysis of data prohibited a more leisurely course of action. This, then, was the second reason for the selected research design.

Nevertheless, for clarity and ease of comparison the presentation of Sheila's experiences and findings follows the same format used for the recount of questionnaire and interview data, with a separate chapter devoted to each of the four areas of concern.

NOTES

1. All references specifying geographic locations, institutions, and individuals have been coded to protect the anonymity of the community and study participants.

2. In one census survey after another residents cite the schools as their primary reason for moving to the community. (Whether disappointment also motivates

exits from the city or enrollment in private schools is, of course, not known.) Even more interesting is the fact that the residents have developed an almost umbilical attachment to their neighborhood school. When declining enrollment and rising educational costs surfaced the issue of school closings, the response from the citizenry was instantaneous and volatile. In principle, everybody supported school closings, so long as the school in question was not "their" school. That the school system managed to weather even this storm without losing the support—personal or financial—of the majority of the residents attests to both the commitment of the citizens to public education and the political sagacity of the central administration.

3. This becomes especially apparent if researchers do not categorize individuals according to the length of time for which they have been separated or divorced. Since time is often the most potent healer, an individual who has been separated for one year may have more in common with an individual who, although divorced, has lived apart from a spouse for one year than one who has been separated for, say, two months.

4. Formal interviews were conducted with 15 men and informal interviews with another ten. In addition, questionnaire data from the exploratory study (see Appendix A) are also included.

5. Questionnaires were not administered to the 25 women interviewed after the 1975 exploratory study.

6. A far greater number of informal interviews were conducted over the four-year period. Undoubtedly these interviews influenced the nature and focus of the research. The statistics cited in this book, however, pertain only to the data from the 50 interviews and the larger sample of questionnaire respondents.

7. Even the widespread passage of no-fault legislation has not resulted in the elimination of issues of fault and wrongdoing from divorce proceedings. Most notably in the areas of custody, alimony, property settlement, and child support, there is ample opportunity for the presentation of evidence of misconduct.

8. Because interviews were conducted over a four-year period, a tabulation of median incomes, either before or after separation, is of dubious value. Obviously, an income of $8,000 in 1979 is far less than the same income in 1975. Suffice it to say that in general these women's incomes after separation were 25 to 33% less than their joint incomes had been prior to dissolution.

9. By retaining at least some overlap between Sheila's background and mine, I did not have to memorize a totally different history. The possibility of erring during roleplaying was naturally also reduced.

10. Because my children had to take part in the roleplaying scheme, it was necessary for Sheila's children to be of the same age and sex as mine. The decision to change their names I cannot explain beyond a vague sense of superstition.

11. There was also a technical problem in recording conversations which took place during roleplaying. The question of whether to use "I said" or "Sheila (or she) said" has puzzled me ever since I began writing this book. In the first draft I used "she said" or "Sheila said," but in revising the book I changed to the personal pronoun "I." Concomitantly, I have used phrases such as "in Sheila's search for a job." I hope that these transitions between personal and impersonal pronouns and allusions to myself and Sheila do not overly confuse the reader.

CHAPTER 1

WOMEN FACING
THE LEGAL SYSTEM

Bob Woodward and Scott Armstrong wrote *The Brethren*, a gossipy exposé on the U.S. Supreme Court; the book was a best-seller before its official publication release. The California Supreme Court granted Michelle Triola Marvin the right to institute suit against her former cohabitant, actor Lee Marvin; the decision received headline billing from coast to coast and feature-story coverage in popular magazines two years and four months before a verdict was issued. Columbia pictures produced *Kramer vs. Kramer*, a cinematic version of a no-win custody suit; the motion picture broke box office records, won Academy Awards, and is likely to be followed by a sequel.

Neither the public's fascination with legal subjects and issues nor the media's ability to capitalize on its cash value is new. The novelty lies in the quantity of recent offerings—the commercial deluge of fiction and non-fiction books, newspaper and magazine articles, television programs, and movies on the law. Still the majority of women know little or nothing about legal statutes or the system designed to dispense liberty and justice for all. The same cannot be said for men, at least not to the same degree. Were this only true for those who had been denied, for one reason or another, social and educational opportunities, this discrepancy between the sexes would be easier to understand and accept. But the evidence contradicts this conclusion. Women who have been educated at prestigious institutions of higher learning, women who have been the recipients of academic honors, and women who have professional careers are members of the majority of which I speak. Indeed, they are the women with whom I spoke.

These articulate and educated women remain largely removed from the legal system. Few own businesses; few hold executive positions in the private or public sector; and few are members of professions that require knowledge of the law or contact with its providers. This should not be surprising. Women's advancement in the marketplace has been far from meteoric. While some have succeeded in infiltrating male-dominated bastions, the majority has not been so fortunate, remaining in the low status and poorly paid "female" occupations (Laws, 1979; "Increase Foreseen in Wives at Work," 1979; Rosen and Aneshensel, 1978). For women, then, on-the-job legal training is rarely an employment-related benefit.

Nor should it be surprising that many women have come to accept as "natural" their ignorance of legal and, for that matter, financial matters. They have learned their lessons well. In childhood and adolescence, parental and social pressures reinforce the notion that ladies, even little ladies, are to be unaggressive and nonassertive, avoiding confrontations and conflicts in the home, playground, or schoolhouse. Rewarded again and again for their docility, they are trained and encouraged to be dependent upon others.

In contrast, although grounded in analytical and reasoned precepts, the legal process operates within an adversary system. And by any definition the term "adversary" implies opposition and combat, rational and calculated as it may be. This is not a role that most women assume easily. Without having been reared or educated in the lore of combat, the law is to many a mysterious and unfathomable labyrinth, even an alien and hostile world in which they fear to tread.

Yet, fearful or not, the women whose experiences are recounted on the following pages did become consumers in the legal sector. They had no other choice. Divorce is a civil action instituted for the purpose of dissolving a marriage contract. The issuance of the divorce decree constitutes a judicial declaration that the marriage is terminated. Even in the simplest of divorces there are legal procedures to be followed, papers to be filed, decisions to be made. From the statements of these separated and divorced women we learn not only how they proceeded through the divorce system but also about their problems and accomplishments. Their perceptions, feelings, and observations provide a vivid illustration of the divorce process.

SEARCHING FOR LEGAL INFORMATION

I guess I did not know all the technical terms or all the steps I had to go through to get my divorce. But I had read many articles which mentioned the grounds for divorce in the state. Of course I also had friends who were divorced. They answered some of my questions, and the lawyer I knew at work was also helpful.

(47-year-old woman, 2 years divorced)

I had read about the divorce law before the idea of divorce ever entered my mind. I knew the different grounds and about how long it took to get the divorce. I really surprised my divorced friends with how much I knew, although they did answer questions for me.

Do you think I was really thinking about getting a divorce all along?

(38-year-old woman, 3 years divorced)

These women stand apart from the others I interviewed. They alone did not experience any difficulty obtaining legal information. Both were familiar with the state's divorce law prior to the decision to separate, and both had personal and professional contacts to whom they could turn for legal assistance. Significantly, the other 48 women expressed (in different ways and to different degrees) a profound and disturbing sense of anxiety when recalling their attempts to obtain information on legal processes and their own entitlements. While all agreed that the first and most important step in the divorce process is to secure legal counsel, over 50% of the women had not proceeded in this fashion. Any description of their actions must include words such as erratic, haphazard, searching, and bewildered. There was little indication of a systematic approach to the collection of information. They spoke to friends and relatives, but their conversations often centered on their feelings rather than on substantive issues.

Some wanted to run.

I had so many questions that I wanted to ask, but just did not know anyone to go to. I wanted to take the kids to New York, but did not know if that would ruin my case. I finally had to hire a lawyer to make sure I did not do the wrong thing.

(36-year-old woman, 5 months separated)

Some tried to avoid the reality of the situation, hoping each night that they would awaken in the morning to find it had all been a bad dream.

I couldn't believe he wanted a divorce after 12 years of marriage. We went out together often. We never took separate vacations. I knew so many who had bad marriages, so unlike mine, that I couldn't understand why my husband chose to break up our family. You see, we didn't fight. So I hoped and even prayed a little, although I'm not religious. I was afraid that if I hired a lawyer it would be all over. When he said he wanted custody of the children, I knew I couldn't wait any more. Anger replaced my dream world.

(39-year-old woman, 3 years divorced)

Others waited for their husbands to initiate the proceedings, prepared to react according to the demands placed upon them.

He had always taken care of running the business aspects of the house. He decided when we should invest money, when we should buy a house, and when we could afford to go on vacation. It's not that I didn't do anything. I taught school and kept the house clean. But I had never been interested in paying bills or studying the *Wall Street Journal*, and he never asked me to behave differently. One day I realized that there was something wrong with our marriage. We didn't talk much or really care about each other. I was the one who first mentioned a divorce and he was surprised at first. Then, I guess, the idea grew on him and he agreed. I did not get a lawyer; he did. I waited until he told me the settlement that he had worked out with his lawyer. He was even the one who told me I needed my own lawyer.

(42-year-old woman, 1 year divorced)

Still others tried to ascertain their rights and learn about the procedures involved in securing a divorce, but discovered that without a lawyer their efforts were largely futile.

I wasn't sure how to file divorce proceedings against my husband. I called Legal Aid, but they would not answer my questions without proof that I was poor. I even called three law schools. Finally a friend told me that her mother had just gotten a divorce. It was her mother who told me what I had to do. Naturally it involved getting a lawyer.

(32-year-old woman, 8 months separated)

Questions without answers was my main problem. Everyone gave me advice, but it was all different. Some said to just walk out and then file. Others said to file papers and make him leave the house. I finally went to my husband and together we sought legal advice. Luckily we are still friends today because I did not seek an underhanded divorce.

(30-year-old woman, 2½ years divorced)

Even women who did speak to lawyers reported having problems in obtaining information.

I spoke to three lawyers before I learned anything. One talked nonstop for 45 minutes without once explaining the jargon he was using. The other avoided my questions. The third was okay.

(45-year-old woman, 2 years divorced)

If you want to learn about the law, you have to be very aggressive. Lawyers don't answer questions directly or give advice unless they have to.

(37-year-old woman, 3 years divorced)

Interestingly, these women did not look to the literature on divorce for information. Popular manuals (Krantzler, 1973; Moffett and Scherer, 1976; Sherisky and Mannes, 1972; Sherwin, 1969; Women in Transition, Inc., 1975) which explain legal terminology and procedural steps, as well as determinations of child custody, child support, alimony, and property division, to mention a few issues, were virtually ignored by all women in the first stage of separation, although later many became avid readers of divorce books.

Because the women who did not initially seek legal counsel were unable to account for their inaction, any interpretation of their behavior is purely speculative. It is conceivable, for example, that these women, confused and disoriented by a personal crisis, were simply unable to amass sufficient energy to act in a knowledgeable and decisive manner. This does not, however, explain why men, who were similarly affected, behaved so differently. Of the 25 men with whom I spoke, only a few waited before seeking legal advice.[1] Women respondents corroborated this pattern when reporting the activities of their husbands. While there were some men who at first ignored reality and others who sought advice from friends, the time lag between the recognition of the impending dissolution and contact with a lawyer varied dramatically between women and men. This is one reason why I believe that the irresolute and floundering behavior exhibited by over 50% of these women is in part traceable to their social roles as reactors instead of actors. Long accustomed to following the standards set by others, be it parents, society, church, school, or spouses, they falter when confronted with situations requiring direct and forceable action. Trained to be dependent, it is hard to be independent, especially if this requirement is foisted unwillingly or suddenly upon them. Related to and coupled with this behavior, learned and reinforced over time, is the fact that they often do not have the connections or knowledge needed for this kind of decision making. While they were all aware that divorce was a legal process, they did not have the same access as did their spouses to legal resources. Many of their husbands could call their lawyers and set the legal wheels in motion, or at least have a better understanding of their rights and the procedures involved in obtaining a divorce. In contrast, even after the decision to retain counsel was made, most women had to invest more time and effort in finding a legal representative. It was also evident that the overwhelming majority of men were neither intimidated by lawyers nor uncomfortable in their dealings with them. The same could not be said for many of the women.

SELECTING A LAWYER

The experiences of these women suggest that the law is very much a closed system. The search for information or the attempt to negotiate within the legal sector without the benefit of an attorney may be at best difficult and at worst hazardous. While two of the women I interviewed had tried to handle their own suits, both ended up hiring a lawyer. One merely flirted with the notion of being her own counsel, giving up after three weeks.

I became so annoyed with the fees quoted me by attorneys that I decided to be my own lawyer. I bought one of those divorce kits, but I couldn't understand half of the terms or the forms. I gave up. Expensive as they are, lawyers are cheaper than losing your sanity.

(33-year-old woman, 10 months separated)

'Marion,' the second do-it-yourself enthusiast, worked over four months on the project. The circumstances of the case seemed to support her decision: The divorce was uncontested; both husband and wife earned compatible salaries and were on good terms; child support and custody of their 12-year-old son were to be shared; agreement on an equitable division of property had been reached; and neither was requesting alimony. In addition, they planned to remain in the community so that their son could continue to attend the neighborhood school and still spend time with both parents.

Everything was proceeding smoothly. I had compiled all the forms and researched the no-fault law until I could recite it in my sleep. Then 'Chris' blew it all! He hired a lawyer who claimed that cruel and abusive treatment was the way to go—less time consuming and easier. Worse than that, he hinted that because remarriage was always a possibility, he could not agree to stay in the community. But the bastard still wanted joint custody. I could have killed him! Suddenly I wondered whether there had been another woman all along. My femininity, my pride, and all that were wounded. I never expressed any of these things. I have always been defensive when my ego is at stake. Instead, I played on his vulnerability. I charged him with unfairness to our son. I pointed out the difficulty of split custody—our son would have two homes apart from his friends; he would be confused, torn; he would not see each of us whenever he wanted; he'd have to call and plan his visits. I went on and on, but though taken back, he remained resolute.
  Maybe I should have gone ahead with my plans to handle the divorce, but I feared the custody issue would be a problem. Anyway, I was angry, really angry! I hired a lawyer.

(37-year-old woman, 1 year divorced)

The subject of do-it-yourself divorce is a charged one. Beginning with Charles Sherman's much publicized book *How to Do Your Own Divorce in California* (1972), a network of advisory offices called WAVE was established in California for disseminating information to those interested in handling their own divorces. Although California is often viewed as a petulant sister state, the capital of divorce, and the inventor of no-fault divorce law, it soon became clear that do-it-yourself divorce was by no means a California phenomenon. Following on the heels of no-fault, the idea gained in popularity, circulating beyond the borders of its home state. Based upon the argument that no-fault had reduced legal actions to routine formalities, the advantages of the do-it-yourself divorce seemed to be supported in theory and practice. There are, however, certain facts which cast doubt on the validity of this assumption.

First, no-fault is not synonymous with easy divorce. Indeed, at times the legal terminology and requirements are purposively obtuse, and at other times the inclusion of counseling stipulations or prolonged separation periods actually lengthens the divorce process. What's more, even in the most liberal states, marital misconduct remains a consideration in determinations of custody, child support, property division, and alimony. The bottom line is that no-fault can expedite the divorce process, *if* the case is one in which there are no children, no request for alimony, and no disagreement over property. Alternatively, in suits, contested and uncontested, in which these qualifications are absent, the road to dissolution is significantly more complex, irrespective of fault or no fault.

Secondly, in all but the simplest cases a do-it-yourself divorce may not be the fiscally sound investment that its proponents claim. Not only do some kits cost hundreds of dollars, but citizen counsels are often unaware (as are, unfortunately, many lawyers) of the financial implications and conditions of their settlements (Foote et al., 1976). Failure, for instance, to consider taxes, education of the children, health insurance, and the like can be expensive oversights. Not surprisingly, the bar has been especially vocal about warning people of the pitfalls of handling their own cases. Moreover, their opposition has not been limited to the dissemination of consumer protection information. Bar associations have instituted a number of suits against do-it-yourself agencies and vendors of kits for practicing law without a license. These actions suggest that agencies precariously positioned at the intersection of the law and education must exercise caution, lest they be accused of trespassing on the law's domain. For example, when Divorce Services of Colorado was charged by the Colorado Bar Association with the unauthorized practice of law, Judge Robert T. Kingsley of the Denver District Court concurred, ruling against Divorce Services. This was in spite of their advertisements which accentuated the educational component of their services, replete with disclaimers of dispensing legal advice ("Halting Colorado's Do-It-Yourself Divorce," 1977).

Like do-it-yourself divorce, lawyer sharing, where one lawyer represents both parties, has been suggested as a way to reduce the high cost of divorce. Even more appealing than the economic consideration is the assumption that one-lawyer divorces encourage, and even require, a strong commitment by both spouses to planning and cooperation before, during, and after divorce. The "Catch 22" is that few lawyers will agree to accept such a case. While some commentators attribute such refusals to state codes of professional ethics, which by and large prohibit lawyers from representing both parties to a divorce action, others claim that lawyer sharing is not in the best interests of clients or lawyers, particularly in the 60% of divorce cases occurring in families with children (Glick, 1979). The data on these families, which involve over one million children per year (Plateris, 1976; Reinhold, 1979), lend credence to this argument. In approximately one-third of these families, according to lawyers Freed and Foster (1974), the divorce is followed by more litigation. In a recent Wisconsin study the figure was higher, with 52% of the divorced couples with children returning at least once to court, as compared to 5% of the childless couples. Moreover, in cases where postdivorce litigation does not materialize, the number of confrontations between divorced parties requiring legal intervention on issues related to visitation, child support, and child-rearing practices appears to be considerable. Thus the lawyer representing a divorced couple with children can reasonably expect that there will be a need for his or her services in the future. And it is the future that is of concern to the many lawyers who maintain that two contending parties can never be effectively represented by the same person.

'Joan,' one of the women I interviewed, and her husband knew nothing about the bar's position on shared-lawyer divorces. Having worked out the particulars of their agreement, they believed that their case was straightforward enough to be handled by one lawyer. Three of the four attorneys they spoke to disagreed, refusing to accept their case. The one attorney who was willing to represent them was found to be unsatisfactory.

We thought we had devised a fair and workable settlement. I was to stay in the house with the children, since the girls were only three and six then. We divided up our property equally and were going to share child support. 'Bruce' agreed that I would have custody,[2] and I agreed to liberal visitation rights. But we could not find a lawyer whom we both liked and who would take our case. Only one of the four was acceptable to us both, but he refused our case. He was concerned, or so he said, that our friendship before divorce might vanish if one or both of us remarried or wanted to move out of state. The children would always be a problem between us, he told us. The effort became too bothersome. We had paid consultation fees to four attorneys and were afraid that there might be four more before we found a satisfactory one. And the time involved was costly too. We were fighting over it and that also seemed unproductive. So we went ahead with a two-lawyer divorce.

I still think that our initial plan could have worked if the law was more realistic. They put stumbling blocks in the way of people who prefer to do things simply.

While Joan and her husband's difficulty in finding a lawyer can be attributed to their decision to employ one attorney, 80% of the respondents considered the selection of legal counsel to be a major problem. Upon examining their comments it becomes apparent that these women were looking for more than legal counsel and representation. Especially in the early stages of divorcing, the matrimonial lawyer is also frequently expected to function as a friend, even a therapist.

There's a terrific lady in _____. She used to be only an attorney, but is now also a psychologist. I was feeling very trapped as both a woman and a woman seeking a divorce. She hears me as a person and as a client.

(38-year-old woman, 10 months separated)

It is not uncommon for individuals to change lawyers several times during the divorce process and even after finalization of the decree (Molinoff, 1977a; Weiss, 1975). Rarely was the decision to fire or to retain counsel based solely on competence or fees. Personal characteristics such as warmth, interest, compatibility, and availability were at least equally as important.

I selected my lawyer by his reputation. He is supposed to be the best divorce lawyer in the city. The problem started when I tried to call him to ask some questions. I never got further than his rude secretary. I didn't know anyone to ask about hiring another lawyer, so by trial and error I finally managed to locate someone who was able to handle my case and me. In all, I spoke to four different lawyers and paid all of them for consultations. Had somebody understood what I was looking for, I could have saved a lot of time and money.

(34-year-old woman, 4 months separated)

I had to change lawyers in the middle of the negotiation period. He kept trying to turn my husband into an unnatural monster. Neither I nor my children viewed him in this way.

(30-year-old woman, 8 months separated)

There is a noticeable intensity and consistency in the manner in which women, as well as men, emphasize the interpersonal aspects of their relationship with their lawyers. Even if this observation is not unique to divorce or to lawyer-client interaction, it is a factor we cannot easily dismiss. Those who praised their attorneys' skills often added parenthetical comments on their sensitivity, patience, and availability. Some credited their attorneys with helping them to reorganize their lives. Significantly, none of these traits was viewed as mutually exclusive.

'Tom's' skill at retaining evidence and using it later to his advantage is truly remarkable. The final settlement was far from exorbitant. But without Tom I don't think I'd have gotten much of anything, because my husband was trying to conceal his wealth. Tom also made me get out of the house. I decided to go back to school and get a master's in business. It's been great for me.

(32-year-old woman, 1 year divorced)

'Alvin's' perseverance was admirable. He followed every lead, pursued every possible angle. Without him I would probably be penniless. But throughout all this and with all the hostility and deceit, he never ignored my ideas or dismissed my fears. He was available and sensitive to my needs at all times.

(43-year-old woman, 2 years divorced)

Over 70% of the women and 90% of the men expressed disappointment and anger over the way their cases were handled. Many harped on their lawyer's inability to represent them effectively; the women spoke of paltry settlements and the men of excessive ones. They also spoke of phone calls that were never returned and of being tricked out of suing for custody, increased child support, or alimony. They felt helpless and unimportant, victimized by their ex-spouses and their *own* attorneys.

My lawyer told me that I did not need to contest child support payments. He said the court would serve as my advocate. But the judge, in his great wisdom, quickly looked at the papers and said, "No change; you have enough and forget about back payments." The judge then asked the bailiff to lunch and dismissed the case and me.

(28-year-old woman, 3 years divorced)

What a settlement! He walks away rich and the kids and I have to take it. Why didn't my lawyer stand up and tell the judge how much my husband earned and could earn if he worked more than three days a week? You'd think the case was fixed. The divorce was not my idea; he walked out on me.

I thought for a long time that my lawyer was a nice guy. In court and after I realized that he had never listened to anything I told him. I guess I should have hired one of those nasty attorneys you hear so much about instead of trying to make the divorce as pleasant as possible.

(35-year-old woman, 1½ years divorced)

If the divorce proves to be a contentious one, the ability of the lawyer to negotiate and maneuver through the system increases in value.

I've got the best lawyer in town. Damn trouble is that he's never available to talk to me. If I were a man, he'd answer my phone calls. But what can I do? I need the best lawyer in town.

(45-year-old woman, 2 months separated)

It is not that the personal dimension ceases to be important; it never does. But a prolonged divorce or the prospect of an inequitable settlement or of loss of custody or alimony can serve as an incentive for retaining a "tougher" lawyer.

Admittedly, lawyers who are inaccessible, intimidating, and who do not respect the wishes and needs of their clients leave much to be desired. Alternatively, the demands of the client can be unintentionally excessive and suffocating. As one lawyer recalled,

'Mrs. Johnson' was a lonely, frightened woman. I felt sorry for her and sympathized with her position, but this did not mean that I had the time or ability to be on constant call. Somehow her capacity to cope ended with the sunset. She would call me at home, once, twice, and sometimes three times a night. I finally had to charge her for the time. Although this curtailed the calls, I'm sure it hasn't helped her.

While most individuals recognized that there were constraints on the time and energy of their lawyers, they argued repeatedly that the present delivery of legal services was inadequate.[3]

No one would deny or forget that you are not the only client your attorney has. But there are limits to how often and how much you can take being treated as a case number. There has to be a balance between law and humanity.

(41-year-old man, 10 months separated)

This schism between clients' and lawyers' perceptions of the attorney's role contributes not only to the phenomenon of legal musical chairs, where clients successively hire and fire lawyers, but also to the impersonal and rigid professional façade donned by many lawyers to shield themselves from "bothersome" clients. The difficulty of matching lawyer with client is not to be underestimated. Attorney Dan Molinoff (1977a) advises that "before attorneys are retained, they ought to be interviewed—no, cross-examined—as to the depths of their convictions, the nature of their anger" (p. A21).

Molinoff places a high value upon a lawyer's competence, but he also stresses the fact that expertise is not enough. To him "anger" is necessary to wage a victorious battle, whether it be against the injustices of the legal system or in combat with the other party. This anger shared by lawyer and client is the essence of the relationship. Perhaps in a difficult divorce anger is important; it constitutes a tangible bond between lawyer and client and is certainly preferable to indifference or negligence. While the separated and divorced women and men with whom I spoke also rated lawyers by their ability and conviction, the attribute that most sought after and few found in their attorneys was not anger but compassion—compassion in the sense of understanding. Still, Molinoff's point on the necessity for matching lawyer and client is well taken. Lawyer-client compatibility in terms of personality, time commitments, and goals may be crucial to the structuring of a good relationship as well as to the outcome of the suit.

This also pertains to the negotiation of fees. Costs for obtaining a divorce varied greatly depending upon the issues, the financial status of the client, whether the divorce or some aspect of the suit was contested, and the reputation of the lawyer or firm. Rarely did anyone believe that the fee was a reasonable one. Indeed, some suspected subterfuge—padded bills and kickbacks from contending attorneys. Others denounced exorbitant retainers and consultation fees. Members of single-parent groups, who routinely invited lawyers and court representatives to their meetings, complained that speakers guarded their fee scales as if they had been classified top secret by the CIA. Still, it was not uncommon for individuals to equate high fees with competence.

Anyone who charges $100 an hour has to be good. I'm unhappy about the expense, but my wife would have taken everything that I had if I didn't have a good lawyer. And good lawyers cost big dollars.

(32-year-old man, 3 years divorced)

I looked for the most expensive lawyer in town and I found him. There is no way that I can walk away from this divorce with anything but the clothes on my back without a high-class lawyer.

(38-year-old woman, 6 months separated)

The problems involved in obtaining legal information and in locating a lawyer are repeatedly confirmed in the recounts of individual users of the legal system.[4] There are, however, two different issues here that need to be distinguished: One is related to securing legal information and advice, the other to retaining legal counsel. The second is more complex, since interview data reveal that a major difficulty in choosing a lawyer has to do with the conflicting expectations of client and professional as to the role of the attorney. Thus statements on the problems of locating legal counsel cannot be taken at face value. Lawyers are not a rare commodity; indeed the supply of lawyers exceeds the demand for services. These women (and men) were speaking of the difficulty of matching lawyer and client, not of securing a legal representative. Further, if we put these observations together, we can conclude that divorce petitioners may not only encounter serious obstacles in attempting to learn about the divorce process without a lawyer, thereby being virtually forced into retaining an attorney, but they may also find the selection of legal representation to be a psychologically and economically taxing process.

PLAYING THE LEGAL GAME

Some divorces are relatively uncomplicated, legally and personally; others are harrowing experiences. The plot varies from couple to couple, but all divorce petitioners, including those who are their own counsels, must comply with procedural formalities and requirements set by law.

NEGOTIATIONS

While negotiation between spouses is not a prerequisite for a court hearing, it is generally agreed that of all the aspects of the divorce process negotiation is the most important.

If successful, the pretrial negotiations will culminate in the production of a separation agreement that will "govern the future relations between the parties in such detail and with such precision as to minimize the danger of controversy" (Felder, 1971, p. 202). This can be accomplished in different ways. The parties may, for example, work out their own agreement; they may employ a mediator or a lawyer to assist them; or they may retain attorneys to negotiate in their behalf. Although any of these approaches or a combination of them may result in a satisfactory agreement, negotiations do not necessarily end with the production of a written separation contract. Because negotiation refers to the discussion and settlement of terms and issues and because disagreements cannot always be avoided, negotiations between the parties and/or their lawyers may take place after as well as before divorce. In contentious divorces involving legal assistance and/or repeated litigation the costs in time and money can be considerable. Furthermore, as described by the following individuals, the negotiation process can be personally disruptive, if not destructive.

My husband and I had pretty much arranged everything—custody, child support, property division, and alimony. We hired lawyers and told them about our arrangement. My lawyer protested. He said the property settlement was too low, and the idea of temporary alimony was like playing with fire. His philosophy was to ask for everything, because we would never get all we asked for. My husband's lawyer had the same opinion, only in reverse. The negotiations were time consuming. But in the end their agreement was almost identical to the one we had from the start. This would be comical if it weren't that all this time and arguing affected my relationship with my husband. We too began to disagree, threaten each other, and even use the children as go-betweens. It worked out all right in the end, but it cost us a hell of a lot more money than we expected and almost destroyed the friendship we had for each other.

(31-year-old woman, 1½ years divorced)

I blame the lawyers for everything. They make you feel that only by fighting can you get a fair shake. The whole thing is an ugly game, with the lawyers holding all the trump cards. Each fight costs money. You gain one thing to lose another.

Once upon a time we loved each other enough to get married. When we decided to separate, it wasn't because of hatred. Now I think when the lawyers get through with us we may really hate each other.

(29-year-old woman, 5 months separated)

The attorneys made us paranoid. The negotiations made us bitter. We read between and under the lines of everything we said to each other or the children. It was awful! I guess it wasn't until a year after the divorce that we noticed the effect of our fighting on the children. Things are calmer now, but it is in spite of our lawyers.

(39-year-old man, 3 years divorced)

It is clear that individuals who blame their lawyers for the animosity and contention which come to characterize their relationships are objecting to the adversary nature of the divorce process (see also Spanier and Anderson, 1979). They are not alone in voicing this criticism. Divorce reformers have been advocating extralegal approaches for mediating agreements and settling disputes since the late 19th century (Halem, 1980; Wheeler, 1980a).

THE TRIAL

Depending primarily on whether the divorce is uncontested or contested, the trial can seem like an anticlimax or a legal melodrama. In uncontested suits the trial may last no more than five or ten minutes. Judges rarely deny divorces if the parties have presented the court with a signed agreement that includes provisions for children, finances, and property. It is even unusual for judges to question, let alone challenge, the agreement. This routinized exercise of the law has led antidivorce factions to charge the courts with complicitous acquiescence to divorce upon demand and petitioners to express shock, frustration, and, at times, anger over the casualness of the proceedings.

My lawyer told me the trial would be short and uncomplicated, but I never imagined it would be like a traffic court. My husband was not there and I just answered my lawyer's questions, sort of in a trance. I kept waiting for the judge to interrupt, for someone to do something. But nothing happened. When it was all over, I was numb. I couldn't believe 20 years had ended without any trumpets.

(42-year-old woman, 5 months divorced)

Shouldn't there be some mourning, some reverence for a marriage that has just died? I felt like I was at a funeral, and the judge acted like it was a schoolroom.

(48-year-old woman, 2 years divorced)

If a settlement has not been reached prior to the trial, the courtroom can become the arena in which the battle is fought. A contested divorce doesn't necessarily mean that one spouse is objecting to the divorce; more likely it is a dispute over custody, alimony, child support, or division of property (Benzaquin, 1975). In addition to the parties, their lawyers, and the judge, adjunct court personnel (e.g., social workers, guardians *ad litem*), lay witnesses, and outside experts (e.g., psychiatrists and psychologists) can all become actors in the courtroom drama.

Similar to pre-op preparations, lawyers frequently prime their clients for the trial by counseling them on dress, demeanor, and the art of answering questions. The rehearsal of stories is not uncommon. Attorney Charles Rothenberg (1974) explains the importance of legal coaching: "The demeanor of the party on the witness stand bears not only on the issue of credibility but on the very issue which is being tried" (p. 11). Moreover, Rothenberg advises the client to wear her wedding ring, to be tastefully but expensively dressed, to avoid too much makeup, and to recount the story (in a fault divorce) in such vivid detail that the judge will be able to conjure up a visual picture of the offense(s) (ibid.). (Note that in all Rothenberg's references to clients, the pronoun is feminine.)

Still, even in contested suits the trial may be unexpectedly speedy.

> The trial was a farce. The lawyers had never been able to agree on a separation agreement and so we were prepared for a fight. The judge asked a few questions of each lawyer and my husband, but ignored me. I told my lawyer I wanted to speak, but he said it was better to keep silent. The silence was costly. I got $120 a week in child support, no alimony, and our summer home, which was mainly a mortgage, since the down payment was only $2,000. I couldn't believe I got so little. The whole trial took 15 minutes. Fifteen minutes for eight years of marriage!
>
> (32-year-old woman, 2 years divorced)

Trials infrequently provide an opportunity for personal catharsis. In suits where one party feels that he or she has been treated unfairly by the other, due process appears to have been denied.

> One day he came home and announced he no longer loved me and wanted a divorce. No warning, no fights, no nothing. I never contested the divorce, but I did object to the financial settlement. I thought I'd be able to tell how unjust this all was in court, but all we spoke about was how much money he earned, I earned, and our savings and property. An accountant would have been a better arbitrator than a judge.
>
> (37-year-old woman, 10 months separated)

This woman expected to be able to "air the dirty linen," as the saying goes, in court, thereby proving herself to be the victim of injustice. Yet few who desire this kind of trial achieve satisfaction. While the injured party, especially in "genuine" adultery or cruelty suits, may be awarded a higher cash settlement, alimony, or custody on the basis of the other's misconduct, the trial, no matter how ugly, cannot redress feelings of failure or erase pain and anxiety. It is not a therapeutic experience. Neither the judge nor the lawyer will openly engage in mourning for the marriage or in public commiseration with the "defendant." Some who seek retribution do find an opportunity to exact a pound of flesh or their rightful dues by fighting over children and finances.

DISPUTES OVER CUSTODY

The number of custody disputes that actually end up in court constitutes about 10% of the contested suits (Molinoff, 1977b). But battles for custody, whether staged for effect, profit, or genuine motives, can be searing experiences for all concerned parties. Consider the following case.

'Howard and Sandy Towes' were married 15 years ago. Howard is an electrical engineer and Sandy a nurse practitioner. They have two children: 'Alice,' nine, and 'Tom,' six. By all indications they have been active, caring parents. In short, both are "fit" parents and both want sole custody.

At times the court, as in this case, will make a special point of stating that fitness is not being questioned. Judging both parties fit, the court proceeds on the "affirmative standard" of which party is " 'better fit' to guide the development of the children and their future" [*Salk v. Salk*, 393 N.Y.S. 2d 841 (1975)]. Legal mumbo jumbo aside, the case still boils down to a contest in which the presentation of evidence is directed toward proving the parental virtues of one and exposing the liabilities of the other.

Howard's lawyer claimed that Sandy was frequently strong-willed and stubborn, that she tended to order the children around instead of listening to them. Howard, on the other hand, was gentle and responsive; he listened and reasoned, rarely being argumentative. Sandy's lawyer pointed to Howard's long working hours, his trips out of town, and his career which was likely to become more demanding as time progressed. He argued that Sandy's hours were flexible; she was the one who stayed home when the kids were sick, took them to their appointments with doctors and to their lessons.

The psychiatric testimony ordered by the court confirmed that the children loved both of their parents and really wished for them to stay married. They were well-adjusted children, revealing no signs of instability. It also confirmed the obvious—Sandy and Howard were both well qualified and fit custodians for the children.

Still Sandy won on the basis that her work hours were more flexible than Howard's, permitting the children more opportunity to spend time with a parent. Howard was granted liberal visitation rights. (Undoubtedly, although unstated, being a woman and therefore also a mother played a decisive role in Sandy's victory. The woman, at least in custody disputes, does have a built-in advantage.)

In custody suits the parade of witnesses can seem endless. Psychiatrists may be retained by the parties to testify in their behalf. The court may request that the parties and/or their children be examined by a court-appointed specialist(s).[5] Character and eye witnesses—friends, relatives, neighbors, employers, employees, clergymen—can be summoned to appear. A guardian *ad litem* may be appointed to represent the children, and/or a court investigator, usually a social worker, may be asked to submit a written report on his or her recommendation for custody.

In addition, children ten years or older may be asked, probably in the judge's chambers, to state their preference for placement. Some psychiatrists and lawyers caution against relying too heavily on the child's choice: It may be attributable to parental "seduction" (Hatherley, 1973); it may reflect the permissiveness or generosity of one parent; and/or it may be a momentary or temporary expression of hostility toward one parent. Others believe that the child, if older than ten, may be able to provide an answer that the courts, parents, and experts cannot.

Age and sex are other factors considered by the court. Generally, children under seven and girls are awarded to mothers. The father's chances for custody increase if the children are older and are boys. These legal axioms have benefited from their association with clinical studies on maternal deprivation and father absence, but in the last decade and a half social scientists and lay critics have begun to strip away the veneer of scientific certitude. In the process they have exposed the small and narrow sampling procedures, the retrospective methodology (Ellsworth and Levy, 1969; Herzog and Sudia, 1971; Walters and Stinnett, 1971), and the practice of generalizing findings to populations only tangentially related to the subjects of the study. If maternal preference and the tender years presumption have not become historical artifacts, increasingly statutory law has deviated from this pattern, declaring mothers and fathers to be equal contenders for child custody. Thus, in theory, the law has begun to endorse egalitarian precepts, even as many courts continue to follow the precepts of old.

Howard Towes' pursuit of custody, like Dustin Hoffman's in *Kramer vs. Kramer*, is illustrative of a relatively new phenomenon—fathers who, by objecting to sex-based verdicts against the man as child caretaker, are challenging the 20th-century precedent for maternal guardianship. The numbers of such cases are relatively low, but there is evidence of a recent upswing both in the percentage of men who sue for custody[6] and of women who agree to paternal custody awards. The stigma of the "runaway" mother is still too strong to encourage more women to relinquish custody, but there are indications, even among custodial mothers, of changing attitudes.

If I had gotten my divorce today, I might be more than willing to be the weekend visitor.

(44-year-old woman, 6 years divorced)

If you were using my name, I'd never admit that I would have preferred my husband to have had custody. How can I explain how guilty it makes me feel to admit this, and how ashamed I am in telling you this? It is not only that he can afford the kids better than I can, but he has more patience than I do. I love them dearly, but loving and being on constant call is not the same thing.

(37-year-old woman, 1 year divorced)

The number of articles and books on paternal custody have increased (Baum, 1976; Droppler, 1973; Mendes, 1979; Metz, 1968; Molinoff, 1977b; Victor and Winkler, 1977). Some, such as Droppler and Metz, approach the subject with the assumption that women are the enemy to be fought by whatever means necessary to achieve victory. For example, Metz (1968), who, by the way, is not nearly as venomous as Droppler, counsels men to do the following.

Use visitations for the express purpose of letting potential witnesses see you with the children under the most favorable possible circumstances. . . .A custody fight is a deadly game that must be played out to the finish. Your only moral justification is that you love your children enough to work intelligently for their ultimate good (p. 94).

And Molinoff (1977b) offers this advice.

There's no such thing as a halfhearted war over who gets the kids. . . . [The father] should sue for divorce and custody (and support, if need be) first. There are practical and psychological advantages to being the plaintiff in the action. The very term "defendant" connotes wrongdoing and blame. . . . He should not leave home, no matter how difficult it is to stay there. Moving out . . . can be construed as abandonment later on . . . but even worse, he would be leaving the children in the care and custody of his wife (p. 14).

Also, the literature on and interest in joint custody have been on the rise (Baum, 1976; Dancey, 1976; Haddad and Roman, 1978; Milne, 1979). Both developments are manifestations of changing norms, patterns of child rearing, and lifestyles, transitions in thought and practice to which the law has not been immune. While the courts look askance at split custody unless the parents (and children) are especially persuasive in presenting a case for separating siblings, joint custody, once equally repugnant to courts (and child development specialists), is today being viewed with increased favor. In a sense it is the law's way of resolving the unresolvable. While all authorities agree that custody suits are among the most difficult cases facing the judiciary, the bench has received much bad press. Publicity of suits in which verdicts have been determined on the basis of relatively unimportant factors such as "cleanliness," "good or bad grandparents," and the professional status of one parent (Alter, cited in Molinoff, 1977b, p. 17) has not gone unnoticed by those outside and inside the legal system. Moreover, critics argue that a case may be influenced by the superior ability of one party's legal counsel, rather than by the merit of the party, and that dissatisfaction with a verdict can increase hostility between parents, leading to repeated litigation and even child kidnapping. By comparison, joint custody appears to be a benign choice.

Most supporters of joint custody, however, believe that its success is dependent upon a good postdivorce relationship between the spouses. This implies that the idea should originate within the family and not be court imposed. As Judge Shea (1978) stated in response to a father's request for joint custody and the mother's wish for sole custody:

When one parent resists joint custody and refuses to be persuaded that it is workable, what will be the result for the children when it is ordered by the court? There appear to be no social science studies that will answer this question. The most ardent professional proponents of joint custody assume cooperation between parents and agreement about child rearing practices as basic requirements for joint custody. It is hardly surprising that joint custody is generally arrived at by consent. . . .

The fact seems to be that court decreed joint custody often comes back to court for modification [*Dodd v. Dodd* (pseud.), *New York Law Journal*, February 27, 1978, p. 13].

Predictably, not all experts approve of joint custody. Goldstein, Freud, and Solnit (1973) even question the noncustodial parent's right to visitation. Others, less radical, object to two-parent custody, declaring it psychologically disruptive and unworkable. They maintain that arrangements made when children are young and neither spouse is remarried will require continuous adaptation as circumstances change; that the divorce is relived over and over; and that the child loses all benefit of continuity and security as each tomorrow necessitates the mobilization of new coping mechanisms and the reorganization of lifestyles.

Obviously, the entire question of custody is complicated and confused by the differences in expert and lay opinion and by the advent of new trends, further taxing the ingenuity and capacity of the bench to move with the times. Legal reformers and social scientists have called for more investigation in this area, particularly for longitudinal studies of alternate custody arrangements; but despite much public interest, research on custody of any kind remains sparse. That the judge's position in custody adjudication is not enviable is clear. Nor is that of either parent, one of which must be judged by the law to be superior to the other. Of all cases, custody suits may be among the most acrimonious and unsettling for parents and children alike.

I wanted custody of the children and so did my husband. The judge recommended a psychiatric evaluation, and my lawyer said it would be harmless. He told me that mothers always get custody of children unless they are insane or brazenly promiscuous. My husband spent two months prior to the evaluation bribing the children, telling them of the great times they would have together. The psychiatrist said we were both fit to have custody, but the children's preference for their father was an important factor. Without ever meeting me, he said I was given to bouts of depression and was an inconsistent disciplinarian. My husband was awarded custody. I hired another lawyer and instituted suit. The second time around I was awarded custody. It is still not over, as my husband keeps threatening to reopen the case.

(37-year-old woman, 4 years divorced)

While originally we had no trouble deciding who would get custody, after two years 'Alan' wanted to live with his father. I believed that the summer in Maine had made him feel that every day would be like that; but my husband felt differently and so did my son. Neither I nor my husband wanted to divide our sons, so we argued back and forth over whom they would live with. We never thought of joint custody. We lived too many miles apart and, besides, we had enough problems working out small, unimportant details to suggest that the larger ones would be impossible. 'Alan' [my husband] took me to court.

As much as I feared the trial and thought I was prepared for it, I never imagined anything could be so terrible. There were our lives dangling out in public for all to see; only, it was distorted. It seemed as if every foible of either of us was exposed and exaggerated. Meanwhile the kids waited, wondering what would happen. My son Alan must have felt very guilty. He kept saying he loved me but also loved his father. Both boys begged us to remarry. But we did not and I was awarded custody. The experience changed me. I agreed to much more liberal visitation rights, and my husband accepted the new agreement. Although our case was by no means disastrous and has in fact improved our relationship, I wouldn't wish a custody suit on anyone. To tell you the truth, I have to catch myself sometimes from lashing out at my son. Somehow no matter how much I can understand his love for his father, I still feel he betrayed me.

(46-year-old woman, 4 years divorced)

In effect, a custody suit means that the parents have abrogated their right to decide the guardianship of their children. The court becomes the decision maker, even though the verdict can be appealed and reversed. It also means that the private lives of all the family members will be scrutinized and that they will have no control over the time involved in resolving the suit or over the disposition of temporary custodianship pending the final outcome. They will be at the mercy of crowded court dockets, the schedules of witnesses, investigators, and lawyers. No matter what the final decision, it is hard to escape the infliction of some pain upon at least one of the family members.

For these reasons it is always preferable for the couple to resolve the issue of custody placement themselves. It is economically and emotionally less costly, even if they have to seek professional guidance (legal or clinical), than subjecting themselves and their children to the rigors and capriciousness of court-ordered decrees. It also forces parents to acknowledge that their own individual differences and disagreements are of secondary importance. The decision to divorce releases them, at least in theory, from dependency upon and allegiance to each other, but it does not free them from their responsibilities to their children. It is this shared interest and commitment which supposedly motivate both to seek custody and which should also motivate both to work out a new relationship in the "best interests of the children."

Big as the custody problem is, it is not the only area in which the law has been accused of malfeasance. The legal system's handling of the financial aspects of divorce is also under attack.[7]

DISPUTES OVER CHILD SUPPORT AND ALIMONY

Noncompliance with support and alimony orders is one major reason listed by sample members (questionnaire and interview) for instituting suit against former spouses.[8]

'John' paid his support payments fairly regularly until he remarried. When he and his wife had a baby, the payments became almost nonexistent. He claimed poverty —new wife, new baby, no raises at work. Since there was no way I could support the kids by myself, I took him to court. The judge reduced the payments because of my job and his other obligations, but even now he hardly ever pays. I can't afford to keep taking him to court, and I'm tired of begging.

(39-year-old woman, 4 years divorced)

Nonpayment of child support or requests by the husband for reduced support obligations or termination of the agreement often follow the remarriage of *either* spouse (Eckhardt, 1968). Divorced men frequently complain that the cost of contributing to the maintenance of two households becomes more burdensome (economically and psychologically) after they remarry, particularly if the new couple has children of their own.

My second wife complains all the time about how much money the children from my first marriage cost us. She says our child will not be able to enjoy special privileges because of it.

(37-year-old man, 5 years divorced)

My husband instituted suit to have the support payments lowered after he remarried. The judge denied my husband's petition, yet he still doesn't honor the agreement. The payments are few and far between.

(31-year-old woman, 2 years divorced)

Moreover, the wife's remarriage may be regarded by her former spouse as a monetary bonanza.

She's been on my back too long already. Next month it will all be over. I'm sure the judge will see how ridiculous it is for her not to share in supporting the children, now that she has remarried and is working. For Christ's sake, the woman lists rent as part of her expenses for the children and her husband owns the house outright!

(41-year-old man, 3 years divorced)

Not all disputes over support end up in court. Some are settled privately, through legal negotiations, or arbitration, and others are dropped because of fear of the repercussions of suit and/or the cost of litigation.

The support payments are always late, and when they do come, there are deductions made for all sorts of things like presents, dinner out, entertainment. My lawyer says it isn't worth the money to go back to court. He has called my husband's lawyer, but the lawyer tells him my husband is planning to return to court to get custody of the kids. I'm afraid to push him too far. Meanwhile he has a gorgeous apartment downtown, and I can't pay my monthly bills.

(34-year-old woman, 1 year divorced)

My wife asked for a raise in the support payments to coincide with my increased income. My lawyer said she'd have no trouble getting it, and so we settled out of court for a 10% hike, even though our agreement had no stipulations for increases.

(38-year-old man, 4 years divorced)

Alimony, cited as another source of conflict between ex-spouses, is a thorny and misunderstood subject. It is confused with property divisions, child support, and cash settlements. It is believed to be the automatic entitlement of all divorced wives and the albatross of all divorced husbands.[9] Still, approximately 10% of women are awarded alimony, temporary or permanent, and the number who receive such payments is lower due to the high figure on noncompliance (Weitzman, 1974). Further, of the 4.5 million divorced and separated women surveyed in 1975 by the U.S. Bureau of the Census and the National Center for Health Statistics, only 4% received alimony (Reinhold, 1979). The factual data on alimony have not dispelled mythical conceptions on the subject. The cover of the Committee for Fair Divorce and Alimony Laws (CFDAL) depicts a blind lady justice holding two scales: In the bottom scale is a dollar sign labeled "alimony" and in the other, high above, a chained man. The message in the picture and in the literature is far from subtle: Women, like fat cats, are getting fatter by living off husbands who are forced to maintain them in the style of the indolent rich.

Alternatively, even many feminists support alimony, albeit they suggest other appellations (e.g., reparations, entitlements, pensions), as a repayment for the woman's contribution to the marriage; they view alimony somewhat as a pension for work performed without compensation. Others maintain that alimony balances the inequities of the marketplace, where women earn substantially less than men; still others argue that displaced homemakers, who find themselves in middle age without money, a job, or marketable skills, would be subjected to undue hardship without alimony.

In reality, the statistics on alimony can be deceiving. Large cash settlements or generous property divisions can be an equitable compensation for alimony. Child support payments are sometimes categorized as alimony because the ex-wife pays taxes on the latter, and the ex-husband deducts payments from his income. This may be mutually beneficial, as long as the woman has a written stipulation that the "hidden" child support will continue if she remarries. In addition, we cannot overlook the fact that many divorced men do not earn sufficient money to pay alimony.

One female respondent who had been awarded alimony by the court spoke of her problem.

I received $45 a week in alimony until I began to live with 'Richard.' My husband took me to court on the grounds that he was supporting another man. How anyone could support two people on $45 a week is too ridiculous to argue. But the judge said it was Richard or the alimony. I wasn't about to ruin my life for $45 a week, so there went the alimony.

(47-year-old woman, 3 years divorced)

The notion of alimony as a form of reparation paid by the guilty to the innocent has a long history. It is therefore not surprising that chastity may be associated with the "right" to receive such payments. Raoul Felder (1971), a divorce lawyer, expresses this opinion: "Payments to an ex-wife should be conditioned on her chastity," elsewise she might choose to live "in sin" instead of remarrying (p. 236).[10] Another way of phrasing this might be the following: If alimony is conditioned upon a life of chastity, the probability is high that most women will forego such payments rather than become closet nuns.

'Margaret' also had an alimony provision in her divorce agreement.

Our lawyers agreed that I was to receive alimony for two years until I completed my master's. This was, in a way, payment for the years I had worked when 'Stan' was in school. But full-time school and assuming the roles of mother and father were physically and emotionally draining. I started to go part-time. Stan accused me of welching on my half of the bargain, but the judge sided with me. Once this was settled I was able to relax enough to work out a better relationship with Stan.

(32-year-old woman, 4 years divorced)

Temporary alimony is far more prevalent than permanent awards. Unless the wife has no marketable skills and is past the age of realistically acquiring job training, alimony awards are generally limited to a specified period of time or to the accomplishment of a specific goal (e.g., the completion of school, the obtainment of a suitable job, or the children's entrance into elementary school or graduation from high school).

As with support payments, a husband may agree to alimony at the time of divorce and then change his mind.

My ex-wife is bright and personable. She has a profession and some work experience, but instead of helping out she suddenly claims that she has to be a full-time mother. The kids are in school most of the day anyway. I've spoken to my lawyer about going back to court, but he says it is difficult to change an agreement unless I use something like custody to threaten her. I'm afraid to do this—God, what would I do if I won!

(38-year-old man, 3 years divorced)

While money may be the root of much conflict between couples before and after divorce, over 60% of the respondents cited disputes over visitation as a major postdivorce problem.

DISPUTES OVER VISITATION

Visitation is the legal provision for guaranteeing the noncustodial parent *and* the child the right to maintain their relationship even though they no longer reside in the same household. Unless it can be proven that the non-custodial parent's exercise of this right is detrimental to the well-being of the child, visitation cannot be revoked for any reason, including nonpayment of child support. Some couples agree to a relatively open-ended visitation arrangement, which comes close to resembling shared custody. In general, however, separation and divorce agreements specify where and when the visits will take place and the children will spend each holiday. The variety of arrangements that are legally approved of as constituting "reasonable" visitation defies the imagination. In contrast, a custody award designates which parent is to have legal guardianship of the children.

By order of the court or by private agreement, divorce encloses the parent-child dyad in a legal framework. If the divorced couple has a good relationship, the legal stipulations may be largely superfluous.

I felt like I lost my children and my marriage in one swift blow. Suddenly I was no longer a father but a friend and entertainer. "What are we doing today, Daddy?" was the greeting each weekend. I didn't realize that 'Allison' was unhappy with the arrangement until I nearly exploded one day. She wanted to be able to share the kids and the problems with someone, and also the responsibilities. We worked out a new arrangement, which meant that I had to move closer, but it has been worth it. My marriage may be finished, but I'm still a real father.

(41-year-old man, 3 years divorced)

I'm ashamed to say that the kids became a burden. I could never go out without a babysitter, and Saturday was the only day I had to myself, because they went off with their father. I had so many errands that even Saturday was a drag. We spoke to our lawyers and worked out a more flexible agreement. 'Michael' picks them up from school two days a week and they sleep over. They continue to see him on Saturdays unless he or I arrange earlier to change the schedule. It gives me more time to be by myself, and the kids love the change of routine.

(43-year-old woman, 2 years divorced)

The sentiments expressed by mothers and fathers in these quotations are supported in the divorce research. Noncustodial fathers are frequently beset by feelings of having lost their children; they feel anxious, confused, and alone (Hetherington et al., 1977; LeMasters et al., 1968). Custodial mothers complain about too many responsibilities; they feel overburdened and tied down (Brandwein et al., 1974; Weiss, 1975). While these problems can lead to violations of visitation rights, custody battles, and even child kidnapping, they can also be an incentive for structuring new arrangements that are advantageous to both children and parents. Sometimes considerable personal and professional sacrifices are required.

I was planning on remarrying last year. He was a wonderful man. The kids liked him and he liked them. The catch was that he had an important job in Chicago and it meant moving. My "ex" was beside himself. He worried that their stepfather would become the real father and he an occasional visitor. Maybe I had my own doubts, or maybe I just felt it was an unfair thing to do to my ex-husband. At any rate, I didn't get married. I'm not sure it was the right decision, but it seemed a fair one.

(32-year-old woman, 2 years divorced)

I was offered the job I had dreamed about all my life last month. It meant more prestige, money, everything. But it also meant living three hours away from the children. I refused it. I wasn't ready to give up being a part of their lives. If they were older, things would have been different, but right now I want to be around and watch them grow.

(41-year-old man, 1 year divorced)

Less than a decade ago court orders usually prohibited a custodial parent from moving to another state unless the other parent agreed to the move (Foote et al., 1966). Although some agreements still contain such clauses and many judges are reluctant to permit moves that will interfere with the visitation rights of the noncustodial parent and the court's oversight of the decree, the hardships imposed by such intractable regulations are being increasingly recognized (Hoffman, 1973). As a result, the custodial parent is generally free to relocate unless it can be proven that the move would be detrimental to the welfare of the child.

Yet the moving of a parent, particularly when it is out of state, can present a serious problem for maintaining the children's relationship with both parents.

Everything seemed so amicable. We lived near each other and the children saw more of 'Jim' after the divorce than before. Then Jim was transferred to Washington, D.C. We were all upset, but vowed that as long as the trains and planes ran, we would work it out. Well, the trains and the planes run, but Jim is always too busy. He calls less and less and the kids ask about him less and less. I don't know whether they've accepted his absence or just can't talk about it.

(40-year-old woman, 2 years divorced)

'Mary' felt that her opportunities for a job were limited in _____. When she heard of a job in California, she applied and got the offer. I asked her to stay and offered more money as an inducement. But it really was a marvelous chance for her, and her family lived in California, which was an extra bonus.

The kids stay with me in the summer and during Christmas and April vacations, but it is hard not to see them more often.

(37-year-old man, 3 years divorced)

Besides the relocation of one parent, the remarriage of one or both parents and the changing needs and demands of children can jeopardize even "ideal" postdivorce relationships.

'Bob' and I had worked out a visitation arrangement satisfactory to both of us and the children. Everything was fine until he remarried. The children began to complain that they never saw their father alone and they didn't like his wife. We tried a variety of different things to better the situation, but nothing seemed to help. Bob sees the children less often now, and most of the time without his wife.

(39-year-old woman, 3 years divorced)

Before the kids were in school they did not mind and in fact enjoyed dividing their week in 'Rich's' house and mine. I had custody, but we had decided that liberal visitation should really be liberal. Anyway, once they went to school they began to complain that it was confusing to tell their friends that they could only play on some days and not on others. We finally agreed that they should spend every weekend and two nights a week with Rich but be home during the afternoon all week. So far this is working out okay.

(32-year-old woman, 2 years divorced)

Whereas the stories quoted above are by and large examples of individuals who managed to adapt to changing circumstances and needs, there are others who for one reason or another found the problems insurmountable.

I dread the days 'Rob' picks up the kids. He honks the horn and they meet him outside. When they come home they always have long stories to tell about what he said about me: "Daddy says you take our money and spend it on yourself."

And there are phone calls in which he threatens me with going to court and calls me an unfit mother for working. Even though we never see each other, it is like he is always there, disturbing my life.

(34-year-old woman, 11 months separated)

The kids are never ready when I come to pick them up. Once I came to get them for Christmas vacation, my time by court order, and she said they were at her mother's. I told her we had arranged it all two months before, but all she kept saying was they weren't home.

(37-year-old man, 3 years divorced)

He is Santa Claus to the kids. All he does every Saturday is buy them things. Whatever they want, they get. Wherever they want to go, he takes them. How can I compete with him? I'm the one who has to make them do their homework, clean their rooms, brush their teeth, take their medicine. He is just the nice daddy.

(40-year-old woman, 8 months separated)

For those unable to resolve conflicts such as these, lawyers and courts become the principal agents used for redress. The courts can reverse visitation agreements and/or order the parties to comply with its terms,[11] but it cannot compel them to be cooperative or civil to each other. Recourse to the courts may not only be a costly remedial action, but it may also be an ineffectual approach for solving problems of this nature.

I wanted to have his visitation rights taken away unless he stopped bringing the girls to his 17-year-old girlfriend's apartment. The judge refused to deny visitation, but he did tell him to see the children alone sometimes and not in his girlfriend's apartment; now she is always at his apartment. There's no point in going back to court. It costs too much and doesn't solve anything anyway.

(33-year-old woman, 9 months separated)

In all fairness, reprobation cannot be directed solely to the law. A litigious society depends on the users of the system as well as on its providers. If we continue to turn to the courts to solve pre- and postdivorce problems that may not be legally resolvable, then we should not be surprised when the solution is inadequate or inappropriate (Sheffner and Suarez, 1975).

POSTDIVORCE LITIGATION

If most analysts of domestic policies and practices express concern over the upswing in postdivorce litigation, the issues involved in redressing the problem are exceedingly complex. On the one side, there is the issue of the constitutional right of appeal. In principle this supports any citizen's right to appeal a verdict, regardless of personal motivation. Thus, while it is recognized that the courts can be and are used to threaten or harass ex-spouses, the denial of access to these tribunals is considered an infringement on the legal entitlements of the citizenry. On the other side, there is the issue, particularly in custody suits, of providing children with continuity of care and the security of finality. It is argued that reopening such cases are against the best interest of the children unless extraordinary evidence can be presented in its favor (e.g., child abuse).

Apart from the ethical and psychological dimensions of the debate, we must also acknowledge that court-decreed support and alimony orders are often not obeyed,[12] and neither are visitation agreements upheld. Consequently, because the issuance of a court order does not ensure compliance, it becomes even more difficult to block avenues for relitigation. If the legal morass is obvious, the solution is not. What we do know is that the courts have become a repository for a host of postdivorce conflicts, many of which they are helpless to resolve.

CONCLUSION

There are those who believe that divorce laws and practices have been completely revolutionized in recent years. The "me" generation, they say, has spawned an era of easy divorce, available upon the demand of either party. No-fault statutes have not only escalated the divorce rate, but, by simplifying legal technicalities and formalities, they have also opened the courthouse door to citizen counsels. Do-it-yourself divorces and, to a lesser extent, shared-lawyer divorces suggest to some that legal representation may now be an unnecessary luxury. And this is not all that has been said or implied. The media's interest in joint custody has created the impression that this trend is taking the country by storm. Publicity on father custody, pushed further into the limelight by the Academy Award winning *Kramer vs. Kramer*, has caused many to think that male guardianship is available for the asking. The Supreme Court decision that state laws without alimony provisions for both parties are unconstitutional has disconcerted women and delighted men. While few would deny that there have been important changes in legal policies and practices, the pendulum has by no means swung as far as some think, or as far as others wish.

Decidedly, the law's control over and management of the divorce process are under challenge. Extralegal approaches (e.g., mediation, arbitration, divorce counseling) as well as do-it-yourself and shared-lawyer divorces are being accorded new credence. Still, contested divorce suits have not become legal anomalies, nor has the need for legal counsel been eliminated. If anything, the practices of domestic lawyers have grown along with the divorce rate, regardless of no-fault statutes.

The law has also responded to shifts in social climate and norms. Egalitarian notions are gradually becoming more discernible in the legislative design of new statutes, the resolution of custody and finance suits, and in separation agreements negotiated prior to court hearing. Ideas on child support, property division, and alimony are undergoing revision; but since alimony has never been a prevalent practice and noncompliance with child support awards (and alimony awards) has long been a serious problem, it is unlikely that many wives need to worry about supporting their ex-husbands. Alternatively, shared child support, equal division of all property held in common, and rehabilitative alimony are noticeably rising in appeal. To date they have been incorporated into law in some jurisdictions and translated into practice in others. The judiciary has demonstrated its increased willingness to sanction joint custody when parents present the courts with a detailed plan for the management of such an arrangement.[13] The father's chances for securing custody have similarly improved, although the mother remains the favored contender (see footnote 6).[14] This may, however, signify that more fathers are requesting custody and more mothers are agreeing to relinquish their claims rather than that the law is embracing a new precedent of impartiality.

Most assuredly, we have witnessed the onset of an assault against values that were regarded a little over a decade ago as sacrosanct. If equality of the sexes becomes a reality, these ideas will increase in value. Nevertheless, by any standard of measurement of divorce reform, change proceeds slowly and in a piecemeal fashion (Halem, 1980); the advent of no-fault, if anything, shows that reform has not resulted in a dramatic upheaval. It would therefore be unrealistic to conclude that today's divorce system is radically different from yesterday's or that it will be radically different tomorrow. In all likelihood the prospective divorce petitioner will for some time to come proceed through the legal system much like his or her predecessor: A lawyer will be retained by each spouse, dispositions of cases will be swayed by the abilities and biases of individual lawyers and judges, and rulings will be reversed or at times ignored. Neither new laws nor new trends in judicial decision making will in themselves eliminate the dilemmas of divorce adjudication. Because the decision is often considered unsatisfactory by at least one party, because judicial enforcement, to say the least, is inadequate, and because a legal ruling may do little to resolve interpersonal problems between spouses, the initial judgment may be challenged again and again in court on the basis of "new evidence," "changed circumstances," or failure to comply with court orders. Lawyers and social scientists have yet to devise a foolproof plan for eliminating the problems engendered by the divorce process.

NOTES

1. One cannot attribute the observed differences between men and women to variables such as who initiated the divorce action or whose idea it was. Curiously, there was almost an even split between men and women when asked whose idea the divorce was.

2. Neither Joan nor Marion (see pp. 27, 29) is representative of my sample of 50 women. Because both women worked full-time and earned salaries equivalent to their husbands', not only did they not request alimony, but they also agreed to shared child support. Had their husbands wanted child custody, in all probability their wives' careers would have become a significant issue in their suits.

3. The data compiled by Spanier and Anderson (1979) from 205 interviews with separated and divorced individuals in Centre County, Pennsylvania, corroborate the findings of this study, suggesting that the legal problems reported by the women (and men) of Westside are not unique to this sample or community.

4. The survey conducted by the Permanent Commission on the Status of Women in Connecticut and summarized in their November 1979 report, "Marital Dissolution: The Economic Impact on Connecticut Men and Women," presents similar findings.

5. Some psychiatrists (Derdeyn, 1975, 1976; Sardoff, 1975) have recommended that psychiatrists be court appointed so that they function as consultants rather than as advocates for one party. In contrast, others suggest that both parties and the judge partake in the selection of an expert or a panel of experts lest judges appoint witnesses who share their prejudices (Lewis, 1974).

6. Researchers on custody adjudication have consistently maintained that the mother is preferred by the courts as guardian of the children in nine out of ten suits (Kaufman, 1979; "Mother's Day in Court," 1980). Notably, however, the Hennepin County Department of Court Services in Minneapolis reported that mothers were awarded custody in 55% of the contested suits and the father in 45% from January 1, 1968 to December 31, 1969 (Foote et al., 1976). Whether this signifies a new trend cannot be determined until data from more jurisdictions are compiled.

7. For those interested in a more detailed discussion of custody and finances in divorce adjudication, the following readings are recommended: Addeo and Burger, 1975; Bodenheimer, 1975; Brandwein et al., 1974; Dullea, 1980b; Fisher, 1974; Foster, 1974; Fox, 1973; Freed and Foster, 1974; Gettleman and Markowitz, 1974; Grunwald, 1976; Kanowitz, 1969, 1973; Kay, 1972; Lake, 1976; McManus, 1977; Ross and Sawhill, 1975; Rule, 1978; Wallerstein and Kelly, 1980; Watson, 1970; Weitzman, 1974; Westman and Cline, 1971; Wheeler, 1980b; Wilkerson, 1973.

8. A similar finding has been noted by other researchers. See references cited in footnotes 4 and 12 for these comparative statistics.

9. When the U.S. Supreme Court ruled on March 5, 1979 that state laws providing alimony for wives and not husbands were unconstitutional, more than a few commentators pronounced this verdict a dramatic reversal of precedent. Yet only seven states were affected by the ruling.

10. Would it then follow that alimony awards to men should also require chastity on the part of the receiver?

11. A domestic relations commissioner in California ordered a divorced father to

pay his ex-wife the federal minimum wage of $2.90 an hour whenever he was late or did not arrive to pick up his children for scheduled visits ("Divorced Father Is Told to Keep Dates or Pay," 1979).

12. For more information on the problem of noncompliance with child support and alimony awards the reader is referred to the following sources: Cassetty, 1978; Chambers and Adams, 1979; Eckhardt, 1968; Foote et al., 1976; Nagel and Weitzman, 1971; Winston, 1971.

13. While the experts continue to disagree over the merits of joint custody in any one of its many configurations (Dullea, 1980b; Goldstein et al., 1973), the idea has widespread popular support. Assemblyman Howard Lasher of New York State has, for example, proposed a measure that would establish joint custody as a legal precedent. His bill, which passed by a wide margin in the New York Assembly in April 1980, would, in effect, allow judges to *impose* joint custody on parents who did not want it. Up until now joint custody has been considered workable only if both parents are in agreement and can prove to the court that such an arrangement is in the best interest of the child ("Mother's Day in Court," 1980).

14. In 1979, 17% of families with children were headed by mothers and 2% by fathers, as compared to 10% and 1%, respectively, in 1970 (U.S. Bureau of the Census, 1980, p. 3).

CHAPTER 2

SHEILA
AND THE LAW

In 1979 a Westside newspaper printed a letter which the editors entitled
"Pain of Divorce." The author, one of eight children of a woman divorced
at 55 after 27 years of marriage, wrote about her mother's legal experience
—an account of a long and unsuccessful ordeal involving numerous lawyers
and judges, protracted judicial proceedings, legal associations (State Bar
Association and State Board of Overseers), and state congressmen and
senators. Despite years of effort and much expense, and despite the fact
that all petitions for appeal had been denied, neither mother nor daughter
considered the case closed, having recently submitted a request to the state
for a judicial review.

This letter cannot be used to illustrate the injustices of the state's divorce
system; it presents one side of the many personal and institutional sides of
every divorce. Nor can it serve as an example of a typical case. The majority
of divorce suits do not drag on for years in the courts, and the majority of
petitioners do not work their way up the legal and governmental ladders,
appealing for assistance and redress. If, however, we look beyond the
particulars of the case, there is, I believe, an important message in this
daughter's story. She also tells us about the ways in which divorce petitioners learn about the law and the legal system—a learning process which
is frequently time consuming, frustrating, and costly. Step by step, they
must proceed through the divorce system. From the acquisition of basic
information about their legal rights, the selection of legal representation,
and divorce proceedings to the issuance of a dissolution decree, the learning
process continues. And sometimes, as in this woman's case, it may continue years after the decree has been finalized.

It was precisely this educational process in which Sheila Ash was most
interested. Her assignment was to investigate Westside's public and private
legal resources, compiling information on the number and nature of these
services. In addition, two specific roleplaying tasks were planned. Follow-

ing the route of over 50% of the interviewed women (see pp. 24-26), Sheila was first to obtain information on the legal process, her own entitlements, and legal fees without *hiring* a lawyer. Second, she was to initiate a search for legal counsel. The word "initiate" is crucial. Sheila could neither retain a lawyer nor enter into negotiations. As such, the simulation of the learning process was limited to the preliminary stages of the divorce process. To supplement this venture interviews with lawyers who were informed about the research project and its goals were conducted.

SEARCHING FOR LEGAL INFORMATION

A newspaper article entitled "How to... retain a lawyer" (Zack, 1975) contained an interesting statement from the Director of the State Bar Association's Legal Referral Service. The agency, according to its spokes-man, supplied information about the justice system, explained legal rights, and often counseled prospective clients *not* to seek legal representation. In support of his claim, the Director presented statistics: From over 13,000 calls received the preceding year, the agency had referred only 3,239 to lawyers (ibid., p. 12).

Perhaps, I thought, the women I had interviewed had not known about this agency or they had not been aware that a referral service would answer legal questions. Believing that I had unearthed a real find, I telephoned the service. In response to my request for information on the legal aspects of the divorce process, I was immediately told that I needed to consult a lawyer. I protested, pointing out that the article I had read specified that the agency answered inquiries about the legal system. There was a pause. Then, speaking to me as one might to a foreigner who had little command of the English language, the agency employee responded:

"Madam, if we took the time to give detailed information every time someone called, we would be unable to help as many people as we do every year. The legal system is a most complex one and cannot be summarized in a few sentences."

"Could you instead explain my rights in contesting the divorce?" I asked.

Again he spoke of the difficulty of condensing information. I might, after all, be misled or misinterpret him and thereby jeopardize my case. He would not want that to happen. It would therefore be in my best in-terests if I consulted a lawyer who would have the time to discuss my problem in depth. The agency would, of course, be happy to furnish the name of a matrimonial attorney. I made one last effort, asking him to tell me the average fees charged by divorce lawyers. Obviously, this too was a complicated question. The only response I received was that they varied, depending upon the case and the client's ability to pay. To end the conversation I told him that I'd call back when I needed the name of a lawyer. He urged me not to wait too long, since divorce was a "serious affair." (Was this a pun of sorts?)

Since it was conceivable that the individual to whom I had spoken did not want to or even could not answer my questions, I tried three more times. Each telephone call to the agency was a replay of the first, although I spoke to a different person every time.

I looked elsewhere—to the County Bar Association, to the City Bar Association ("City" refers to the nearby metropolitan center, not to Westside), and lastly, to the service sponsored by the National Organization for Women (NOW). NOW proved to be the most responsive. Not only did I speak to an attorney, which was in itself a unique feature of this facility, but she explained the state's divorce law (its fault and no-fault grounds and the procedural and technical differences between them), supplied information on the range of lawyers' fees and court costs, and recommended pamphlets and paperbacks on the state's divorce law and procedures. She also encouraged me to call back if I had any additional questions.

I was impressed. I had not been rebuffed or put down. Still, a woman seeking a divorce needs a higher education—one that cannot be obtained from a telephone conversation. I began to check the sources recommended by NOW's adviser. One of the readings, written expressly for women by a female attorney, was surprisingly comprehensive. Presented in an easy-to-read format, this 60-page, three-dollar booklet described the different steps in the divorce process, defined legal terminology, reviewed the state's divorce statute and procedures, as well as the ancillary issues of custody, child support, alimony, property division, and visitation. Moreover, it discussed other legal issues relevant to divorced women (e.g., name change, social security entitlements, and state laws on credit, property, and inheritance). And there was more—listings of the state's courts and judges, legal aid offices, women's centers, suggested readings, and sample divorce forms (with explanations).

A source such as this one can be invaluable. For those who choose to be their own counsel, it can help to penetrate the morass of legal terminology, technicalities, and formalities. For those who choose to retain a lawyer, it can help to be more knowledgeable and participatory consumers. Was this, then, the answer to all those who complained that they were unable to find responses to their legal questions? Interview data suggested that it was not. The majority of the respondents indicated that they had not looked to the literature on divorce for information until after divorce. Further, many had shied away from the very groups in which they might be introduced to booklets of this nature. Thus, until some method is devised to increase the dissemination of such information, it is likely that only a small minority of separated and divorced women would use this or any booklet. And even this may be an overly optimistic assumption. It appears that the search for information is linked to the need for personal contact. If this is true, publicizing books, guidelines, or any form of written material, no matter how good, will not solve the problem. While, admittedly, I had pondered some rather wild schemes for advertising this booklet, I reluctantly banished all such ideas, looking for alternate ways to obtain legal information.

Another newspaper article, which stated that the city, county, and state referral services arranged for low-cost consultations with lawyers, led me back to these associations. The conversations started much as before. I asked for information; they, after inquiring where I lived, gave me the name of an attorney. I asked about fees; they replied that they varied according to my income, the nature of the case, and the law firm. Only when I specifically referred to the article and its special fees for initial consultations did the agencies inform me about this service and its cost. All first sessions were price fixed, with fees from $5 per half-hour at the City Bar Association, to $10 at the County Bar Association, to $15 at the State Bar Association. (Curiously, the cost rises as one climbs the governmental ladder.) After on up. "Up to what?" I asked. "Oh, that is hard to say; you might hire F. All inquiries as to the meaning of "usual" were never satisfactorily answered. For example, one individual told me that it could range from $25 an hour on up. "Up to what" I asked. "Oh, that is hard to say; you might hire F. Lee Bailey." (I wondered if Bailey really did do consultations for the Bar.)

In addition, the County Bar Association offered a free weekly clinic at which one could speak privately to an attorney. Although this service was also cited in the newspaper article, here again no information was provided until I mentioned the clinic by name. In contrast, NOW, the only place where I had received answers to my questions and spoken to a lawyer, did not operate a low-cost consultation service; lawyers were recommended from a pool selected for their sensitivity to and interest in women's issues and problems, but it was the client's responsibility to obtain fees for consultation and follow-up work.[1]

Attracted by the low fees, I decided to sample the offerings of these referral agencies. My first half-hour consultation was with a Westside lawyer recommended by the State Bar Association.[2] His secretary took down the vital information—name, address, telephone number, income, and reason for visit. After a 35-minute wait, court delay I presumed, my consultation began. I explained that because my husband wanted a divorce, I had come to him to learn about my legal rights, the divorce process, and the cost of obtaining a divorce. I had not come, I continued, to hire a lawyer, at least not yet. (I was pleased with this addendum, thinking it would prevent him from writing me off as a possible client, while still getting the point across that I was looking for information more than representation.)

Instead of responding to my questions, he asked his own.[3] (I had found a legal Socrates!) "Did I have children?" "How many?" "How old?" "Did I own property?" "Any inheritance?" "Were my parents alive?" "Were they financially well-off?" "What did my husband do for a living?" "Were we on good terms?" "Was I in a rush to get a divorce?" (I hadn't even said I wanted one.) "Was there another woman?" "Had I seen other men before or since my husband mentioned a divorce?" "Did we own a house?" "Approximately how much was it worth?" "What was the mortgage on the house?" "Did we have stocks, bonds, additional property, money in savings accounts?" "How many cars did we have?" "What year and make?" "Did we own them outright or were they financed?"

Although I did try several times to interject a comment or draw him back to my original queries, his skills at interrogation were greater than mine. Before I knew it, the half-hour was almost up. He made his summation: "Mrs. Ash, this looks like a complicated divorce. You have two young children, no job, no property or money apart from your husband. You are, in short, dependent upon him, and we have no idea whether he is going to be cooperative. The next step is to make a detailed list of all your joint assets and those of your husband. I'll need to know how much he earns and owns. Then we'll plan our strategy." (The word "our" seemed out of place; up until this moment, it did not even appear as if I would be a party to the divorce action.)

"But," I objected, "I'm not sure I want a divorce. You haven't answered any of my questions. If I do proceed with a divorce, I don't know how long it will take or how much you will charge me."

"I understand," he said. "This is a difficult time in your life; but there are no straight answers to your questions. Go home and give the whole thing some more thought. If you decide to seek a divorce, come back and we'll talk some more."

"What is your fee?" I asked again.

The answer—$50 an hour with a minimum of a $700 retainer. He was not sure about the latter because he did not have all the facts on my case yet. He rose, shook my hand, and escorted me to the door.

By the time I had completed my five- and ten-dollar consultations, I felt as if I were rehearsing for a play, so similar were the scripts. Still, I made one last telephone call—this time to the lawyer recommended by NOW. She was willing to discuss fees over the telephone—$20 for an hour consultation, $40 an hour for her time outside of court, $50 an hour for in-court time, and a $500 retainer. I questioned the retainer fee, telling her that this was a very simple case, since my husband and I had already agreed on the terms of the settlement. "If this is true," she replied, "I might be able to lower it to a $400 retainer.⁴ But don't forget," she cautioned, "there are so many variables involved that often what seems simple is not."⁵ Not being a bargainer by nature, I did not haggle over price any further and thanked her for her time—calculated to be approximately four dollars' worth.⁶

I did not make an appointment with NOW's attorney, a decision that was unrelated to anything she had said. Rather, I realized that these consultations had led me away from my search for information on the legal system and process, more closely approximating the second task of lawyer selection. Moreover, "lawyer hopping" had proved to be an inefficient and costly method, even at these "special" prices, of learning about divorce law and practices. The only tangible information I had collected pertained to fees, and here too, without any ceilings (e.g., a maximum cost of $600), it was impossible to calculate the cost of the divorce. One hardly needed a vivid imagination to conjure up visions of an exorbitant final tab.

At this stage of my research I had learned something about the different grounds for divorce in the state (from NOW) and had a rough estimate of hourly legal fees and retainers (from attorneys). Still, Sheila remained relatively uninformed about the legal procedures and processes involved in a divorce action, as well as her own rights under the law.⁷ Positing that such information might be secured from the courts instead of individual providers, I, as Sheila Ash, contacted the Probate Court of Westside. By all indications I was the first to make such inquiries at the courthouse. After speaking to four individuals it became obvious that the court did not provide any counseling, legal assistance, or information for those involved in a divorce action. I was, however, referred to the 'City College' Legal Assistance Bureau, which serves residents of Westside and two adjacent communities.

This proved to be another dead end, since eligibility was contingent upon proof of indigence. When I asked for the income levels classified as indigent, I was informed that the City College Bureau followed federal guidelines, but that the figures were confidential.

"I don't understand," I retorted. "You said you followed federal guidelines; these can scarcely be regarded as confidential."

"Yes," she replied, "we do follow the federal standards, but there are variations which we cannot reveal."

I tried another approach. "I'm unemployed, but my husband earns over $20,000 a year. Would I qualify as indigent if I sued him for divorce?"

"In divorce suits," she explained, "we have to consider your husband's income. You would only be eligible for our service if you could bring us letters from two private attorneys who had refused to take your case *and* refused to petition the court for your husband to assume responsibility for your legal fees. Once you do this, we will schedule you for an appointment, but we are not taking any more domestic suits until the middle of January." (The date of the telephone call was November 6.)

"Would it be possible, either by telephone or in person, to obtain some basic information about the divorce process in the state before January?"

"We are really too busy," she responded, "but you could come in and get a copy of our pamphlet on divorce."

My encounter with the 'Metropolitan' Legal Aid Society yielded similar results. The only difference was that they would give priority to my case if I could attest to the fact that either I or my children were physically at risk if the divorce action were delayed. And, since even under these circumstances I would not be taken right away, so long was their waiting list, I was advised to find a private attorney who would take my case and petition the court for my husband to assume legal costs.

I had inadvertently stumbled across a problem not unknown to middle-class separated women. Since they are not single persons, their economic status is determined by their joint income with their husband. This can pose a special dilemma for the unemployed or part-time employed woman whose husband's income disqualifies her from consideration by legal aid providers, even though she would be classified as indigent on the basis of her *own* ability to pay.[8] The separated middle-class woman without personal funds or a job must therefore rely upon the good will of her husband or on a court order to pay her legal fees. Nor is her husband's position an enviable one. He might be compelled to pay his own legal costs and hers, often not an inconsequential sum. (Unless, of course, the property or financial settlement is substantial enough for the wife to use these funds to settle her account.)

This is not simply an economic problem. The recognition that in separation, as in marriage, the woman is dependent upon her husband is far from an ego booster. It can impede the search for an identity apart from her spouse, reinforcing any existing feelings of helplessness and dependence. One woman described this feeling to me.

How can I explain what it is like to know that you cannot even pay for a lawyer by yourself? The thought that I was poor was a revelation. I became angry, but that didn't chase the fear away. In the same breath I told my lawyer I didn't want alimony and I had no money to live on. It seemed so unjust. I could never climb a professional ladder to the top at the age of 41. I felt finished without ever having remembered starting. Who was to blame? Society? My husband? My parents? Myself? Even if I knew the answer, it wouldn't help. It wouldn't make my problems vanish or make up for all the years gone by.

Another woman put it this way.

There was no way that I was going to get a second-class lawyer while he hired _____, the most notorious divorce lawyer in town. But when I realized that he had to pay for my tab, I felt like a child. It was more than that. I felt that he controlled my case with his money. I wondered if the lawyer would be a fair representative for me knowing that the payment of his bill depended upon my husband. I became paranoid, not trusting my husband, my lawyer, or anyone. Yet I wouldn't go to Legal Aid even if I qualified. It would be a declaration that I was worth nothing, that I had to beg for help.

Like these women, I had never thought of Sheila as indigent nor planned for her to seek free legal assistance under the guise of poverty. Telephone calls to City College and Metropolitan Legal Assistance were intended to uncover facts on the law, not to retain a lawyer. But because these facilities serve only those who are unable to hire private attorneys, they remain closed to all who cannot prove financial need. As a result, my conversations with their personnel centered on the issue of economics, rather than on the divorce process. Thus it was necessary to consider alternate resources for compiling facts on the legal system. A decision was made to redirect the investigation away from the legal system to advocacy and support groups for separated and divorced individuals. But because many sample participants had purposively avoided joining these groups, Sheila's plan was to gain information without feigning an interest in becoming a group member. In short, these groups were to be approached as educational resources. (In a later chapter I will consider these groups from different perspectives, e.g., as self-help groups, social groups, and consciousness-raising groups.)

Inquiries at three local groups revealed that they did not dispense legal information. While each of the groups periodically invited lawyers to their meetings and one had a legal adviser on their board, their organizational goals were primarily of a social nature.[9] They did, however, suggest that group membership would give me an opportunity to speak to others who, on the basis of their own personal experience, might be able to answer some of my questions. Although I knew from sample respondents that this was one way to learn more about divorce law and procedures, I had resolved never to roleplay in order to gain entrance to groups for single parents or the separated and divorced. Sheila did speak with group representatives, but her contact was limited to telephone conversations.

The remaining two names on my list can be best categorized as advocacy groups, albeit they also acted as support groups. One was specifically targeted for women, the other for men; both were located in Westside. I approached the women's group first. Involved with numerous projects besides their work with women in marital transition, this cooperative proved to be a valuable resource. Upon inquiring whether the group disseminated legal information, I was told that they were not lawyers, but in an informal way, be it through referrals, discussions, or contacts, they endeavored to "demystify the law" for women unfamiliar with divorce law and procedures. Moreover, they recommended the same booklet as NOW, selling it to members and others like myself who called for legal information. At this point the conversation took an unexpected turn. As I was about to thank her and hang up, she began to talk about the state's divorce law. For over a half-hour we continued to converse, discussing alimony, child support, children, tax considerations in divorce, and lawyers.

Responding to a fictitious person's request for help with sensitivity and interest, in 30 minutes this woman provided more information, insight, and guidance than practically all the other conversations and interviews put together. Still, I wished I had never made the telephone call. In truth, I felt guilty for having deceived someone, who, to be trite, deserved better. If, by chance, the reader recognizes herself as this person and remembers speaking to an individual named Sheila, now you know my true identity and the nature of my "crime." Please accept my apology and if it is any consolation, you should know that after this conversation I never again roleplayed Sheila, even on the telephone, to individuals who were members of groups for the separated, divorced, or single parents.

Consequently, my next telephone call to a group for separated and divorced fathers was made without the benefit of roleplaying. Not only does this organization conduct advisory sessions in which some members relate their legal experiences and offer feedback to others in the group, but it also helps members to obtain legal representation. Concerned with securing equality for divorced men, particularly with respect to custody, distribution of property and finances, alimony, and child support, the group requires that all lawyers who are referred to or who recommend themselves to them submit to an examination session before their names can be furnished to prospective clients. In addition, the group functions in an advocacy capacity, sponsoring new laws and the adaptation of existing legal practices and policies (Kaufman, 1979). Members are also committed to research in the area of divorce and single parenthood, having participated in various projects, including one that monitored courtroom decision-making practices and another that focused on compiling interview data from single parents.

Until recently, women have maintained a low profile as advocates for the revision of divorce laws and the delivery of special services. NOW has indicated its interest in single-parent families and has been instrumental in calling the public's attention to the special needs of female-headed households. Other groups have acted more informally, providing services to a limited membership and/or conducting local campaigns directed toward channeling monies and services to separated and divorced women residents. Still, overall, women have been less successful advocates for their own special interests than have men, their efforts being more sporadic and erratic.[10]

Women's groups, such as the one in Westside, the ones in Seattle and Philadelphia (see footnotes 9 and 10), and other sister organizations foreshadow a change, suggesting that women may at long last emerge as strong, even powerful, advocates of their own causes. In 1975 when I began this research, there were few groups for the separated and divorced and even less specifically for women. The ones which I did contact in and around Westside had frequently disbanded between the time that I learned about them and the time of contact. Most letters were returned as "not forwardable," but in some instances I received responses explaining why the group had disbanded.

These letters bespoke the problems facing women who were overburdened by trying to do too much, in too little time, and with too little outside help or finances; they wrote of the difficulties of working and raising small children and of legal problems with husbands who reneged on their support obligations and/or for all intents and purposes forgot that they were still fathers. It was for these reasons that they had tried to publicize the problems of divorced mothers and obtain public support (particularly for economic subsidy programs and stringent enforcement of court-ordered child support and alimony awards), but it was also for these reasons that the existence of many groups was short-lived. Organizing and running group activities became one concern too many. And so ventures begun with high hopes and visions of changing divorce laws and procedures and the delivery of social services collapsed as one women's group after another closed their doors.

While women's groups and, in fact, groups in general have a tenuous life span, the outlook has improved. As divorce rates have climbed and the population of separated and divorced men and women has become more visible, there has been a growing recognition of the need for services. While more community, state, and federal agencies have supplied public and private funding for the creation of groups and services for single parents, there are still too few of these groups and insufficient monies to respond satisfactorily to the demand.[11]

Even in Westside, where a group does exist, many of the women with whom I spoke avoided even minimal contact with this organization. Some considered membership a sign of personal failure, an inability to make it on their own; others viewed it as a radical feminist operation, and still others simply refused to join groups of any nature. Nonetheless, of all the resources surveyed by Sheila in an attempt to obtain information on divorce laws and procedures, this group was by far the most helpful. Membership is not a prerequisite for utilizing services or participating in support groups. The group offers one-to-one contacts with other individuals, as well as answers to questions and referrals to lawyers. If nothing else, its value as an educational resource cannot be gainsaid.

Westside, like many other cities and communities, does not have any public facility to assume the responsibility for educating residents on the law and/or dispensing routine legal information to nonindigent consumers. By default, small, local groups have tried to fill this void. But while the women's and men's group in Westside presented residents with the most accessible resources for learning about the law and the legal system, these groups cannot, in themselves, solve the target population's need for increased information. Clearly they lack the staff and funding to function as major disseminators of legal information.

Of late, local colleges and community organizations have begun to offer seminars and short-term courses for *women* on the law. Some sessions cover a wide range of legal issues, and others are directed specifically to single parents or to the separated, divorced, or widowed. Whereas five years ago such courses were a rarity, today they are becoming almost commonplace. Decidedly, this is not a solution, and certainly not one for those who are seeking immediate answers to their legal questions. Yet this development reveals that the community is becoming aware that separated and divorced individuals, particularly women, need increased access to legal information apart from the law's delivery system. It remains for the community to find an effective and efficient method for creating and delivering such services.[12]

SELECTING A LAWYER

In creating Sheila, I conceptualized her as a woman unfamiliar with the state's laws and legal system. Conceivably, she had been present during legal negotiations for the purchase of her home. Besides the fact that legal representation was probably provided by *her husband's* lawyer, the experience could scarcely be counted as a legal education. Thus, because Sheila, like most of the women with whom I spoke, was an uneducated consumer, the hiring of legal counsel constituted another task that required a personal investment of time, effort, and money.

The local telephone directory seemed a logical first step. But even with my fingers "doing the walking," I soon tired. The list of lawyers in the Westside area directory was imposing; the list in the metropolitan directory was overwhelming. Since lawyers are not categorized by specialty, there is no simple way to expedite the selection process. You might begin by identifying those lawyers located in or nearby Westside, but even this list is substantial. Alternatively, you might be more creative by selecting names which appeal to you or begin with a favorite letter of the alphabet or include business *and* home telephone numbers (a sign, perhaps, of personal commitment to clients). Dissatisfied with these ideas, I scanned the pages again. This time I noticed three rather prominent advertisements for the bar referral services. (Prominent, that is, in comparison to the blinding list of single-spaced names appearing on page after page of the directory.) At least, I reasoned, this was a way to obtain names of local lawyers specializing in domestic law.

And names I did receive—three, to be exact (one per referral service). For clients who are dissatisfied with the referral, another name is furnished. (I am, however, unsure of whether there is a limit to the number of permissible "dissatisfactions," since there was neither the time nor the money for scheduling multiple consultations.) Lawyers who are retained through referral pay the association 10% of fees over $100, with a maximum payment of $500.

Sheila scheduled the first appointment. The purpose was ostensibly simple: Her husband had requested a divorce, and she needed legal representation. She told this to 'John Blacker,' along with the fact that she had two children, ages 2½ and 5½. Predictably, he took over, proceeding through the by now familiar set of questions (see p. 57).

"Excuse me," I interrupted. "I realize that these questions are necessary, but before my time is up, I'd appreciate it if you could answer some questions for me."

"Shoot," he said.

"I want to know which divorce ground you would recommend, since neither my husband nor I has committed a fault offense."

"That is hard to say. It would really be your choice. No-fault takes more time and depends very much on how close you and your husband are to reaching a mutually satisfactory agreement. In general, I recommend the ground of 'cruel and abusive treatment.' It does not require actual proof of bodily harm and is broad enough to cover many instances of marital conflict."

"Then we would have to lie in court."

"Lie? I suppose you might. But everyone does to some extent.[13] And if you and your husband agree to this ground, you can also agree on what will be said. It is really just a way to expedite the case. But if it is repugnant to you, then 'irretrievable breakdown' or what is known as 'no-fault' might be a better choice."

With time running short, I aimed a bit higher. "How do you feel about a joint custody agreement?"

"How do you feel about it?" he responded.

"Well, it seems a good choice. We would share responsibility for the children, and they would have a chance to remain close to both of us."

"That sounds great, but it rarely is. If you're lucky, initially you'll be able to agree on the mechanics of the arrangement. Then as time progresses, things will change: He'll remarry; you'll remarry; he'll want to move; the children will grow older and want to be with their friends more often. Also you'll get less child support this way, and maybe still have more than your share of the custody burden. Or, he may decide that as long as he has joint custody, he might as well go all the way and get total custody. And back to court you go. With young children your chances of getting custody *now* are very high, but as time goes on things might be different."

Changing the topic, I asked, "How much alimony can I expect?"

"You certainly ask hard questions," he quipped. "I really don't know. You don't have a job, although you have a good education and presumably could get one. With *custody* of the children, we'd argue that their young ages require you to stay at home and request child support and alimony at least for the next ten years, maybe until they are 18. But I still don't know enough about your husband's finances to answer this."

"Would I get child support with joint custody?"

"Mrs. Ash, I wish we had more time. I understand that you have a lot of questions, but there are no definite answers. I could promise you the moon and you could end up with nothing. It's a wait-and-see game. We should schedule another, longer appointment in which we can talk about this at greater length."

"Oh, I forgot to ask what your fees are."

"Fifty dollars an hour and a retainer fee of about $1,000."

"Oh," I repeated. (I was moving up in the world! Did the fee have anything to do with what I said?)

John Blacker had seemed nice enough; he had responded to my questions without any visible signs of annoyance. His answers, although not always to my liking, had been reasonable and plausible. I could accept his support of a system that encouraged perjury under the guise of expediency, especially since he was not inflexible on the selection of grounds. It was on the joint custody issue that he and I seemed to be on opposing sides. While I did not dispute his reasons for believing joint custody to be risky, I was unsure whether he would be an effective advocate if I pursued this course of action. Would his personal ideas and biases intervene, interfering with his ability to argue persuasively and forcibly? Or would his recognition of the potential difficulties cause him to be more thorough in working out the details of the arrangement? Perhaps answers to these questions hinged on my husband's feelings on custody. I caught myself. I had begun to believe I was Sheila—a revelation which was both surprising and frightening.

For my next referral (this time from a different agency) I requested a woman attorney. A woman, I thought, would be more aware of another woman's feelings of vulnerability, more understanding of the uniqueness of the female situation. In truth, I did not know if John Blacker had such an awareness or not; I had, albeit unconsciously, or maybe self-consciously, avoided any discussion of feelings. I had played the part of Sheila the researcher so totally that I had forgotten about Sheila the woman. Although a change in approach would invalidate comparisons of interview data, I rationalized that a woman (or a man) might very likely vary her (or his) presentation of herself and her case depending upon the person to whom she was talking. With this in mind, I prepared myself for a consultation with 'Joan Harrington.'

Our exchange began with the same questions, the same responses. But this time, when I interrupted the questioning, I presented a different front.

"Excuse me, but I have some questions I'd like to ask you and some things I'd like to say before our time is up."

"Of course," she replied.

"I am more than a little scared over the whole idea of a divorce. I have two small children, no job, no recent employment experience, and no money or property of my own. I've never been alone before and it is scary. I don't want an ugly divorce, but I don't want to be left with all the responsibility. That is one reason why I am thinking about joint custody. I also don't want to remain dependent upon my husband's money forever. Can you advise me how I should proceed? I guess I'm asking what I should do."

"I can't really tell you what to do, personally or even at all times legally," she replied. "You have all the problems you mentioned, and probably others as well. Divorce is a difficult time, but it need not be totally bleak. Joint custody is a possibility, but it may bring on more problems than it solves. I don't know enough about you and your husband and your plans to answer this. Right now I would advise you to sit tight and especially not to get a job. Dating is also out of the question until we have a written agreement.''

"I don't want to date," I interrupted angrily. "That is the last thing on my mind! I want to know what is going to happen to me and my children.'' (Again, I had thought I *was* Sheila!)

"Mrs. Ash, I honestly don't know. I will do my best to obtain a good settlement for you, one that will not leave you destitute or totally dependent upon your husband. But much of the success or failure of the settlement will depend upon you and your husband. It is therefore very important that the two of you cooperate. Look at yourselves as parents first, if that changes the perspective and helps you both to plan intelligently. Think over what we've talked about, and if you want me to represent you, let me know.''

"By the way," I asked before leaving, "what are your fees?''

"Fifty dollars an hour with a retainer of anywhere between $500 and $700.''

"Whom would I hire?" I asked myself as I typed my interview notes. So many of the women and men with whom I had spoken stressed the importance of matching client and lawyer with respect to personality, beliefs, and objectives. The difficulty of achieving this goal was becoming increasingly apparent. One consultation, even two, was barely enough time to provide the background information requested by the lawyer, let alone to engage in a discussion which would reveal the lawyer's personality and position on issues important to the client. Further, many clients, particularly women, do not initially approach a lawyer with a specific goal in mind (e.g., a joint custody award). In the beginning, unless the husband and wife have already pretty much worked out an agreement, there is so much uncertainty and confusion that the interviews are likely to be unfocused. (This may be one reason why clients report changing lawyers in midstream; once their goals are clearer and their needs more defined, they can be more explicit and directive in their interviews, demanding definitive answers to their questions.) How, then, under these circumstances and within a limited period of time, can individuals decide which attorney would best represent their case? The answer, I believe, is that they cannot. Sheila's interviews were more structured than most recounted by sample members, and yet she, knowing full well that she did not have to make a choice, had trouble weighing pros and cons. Moreover, prejudices that I thought I had buried long ago surfaced. I wondered if a woman could be as forceful an advocate as a man; I wondered if the "famous few"—lawyers known for their combative ability—were the advocates of choice, regardless of their exorbitant fees.

Perhaps in the final analysis there are no scientific guidelines to be used in selecting a legal representative. Indeed, the client's efforts to match his needs and personality with those of an attorney may depend more on luck than on specific techniques or tactics. This is not to suggest that individuals should not be discriminating in choosing an attorney. What it does suggest is that serial, random consultations as a selective method might not yield the desired results. With over 18,000 lawyers in the state (even though all do not practice matrimonial law), it can be economically inefficient and scientifically inaccurate. Interviewing as a selective device works best when the client has clear-cut objectives in mind and especially when she or he has a specialized type of suit (e.g., contested custody). It is then that Molinoff's advice to cross-examine attorneys becomes plausible. For these cases it is also easier to obtain referrals. NOW or most women's cooperatives can steer women to lawyers who are particularly interested in issues relating to women. Groups for separated and divorced fathers perform similar services for men.

For relatively simple divorces, bar association referral services offer a slight advantage over the Yellow Pages. Referrals are based on the location and area of specialization. While a recommendation to a participating lawyer by the state, county, or city bar associations is not limited to lawyers engaged solely in the practice of matrimonial law, it does mean that the lawyer or firm handles domestic cases. Probably the Martindale-Hubbell Law Directory would be just as helpful. It lists the lawyer's age, education, date of birth, and year of admittance to the bar, as well as the areas of specialization of law firms and individual practitioners. Some firms are also rated. Friends, relatives, and colleagues are another way to secure the name(s) of a lawyer and, of course, selection can be narrowed down, if you are willing to pay the "price," by hiring the "best," the "most ruthless," or the most "famous" of the matrimonial lawyers.

INTERVIEWING LAWYERS

Sheila's assignment had been completed. The remaining task was to obtain appointments with lawyers who would be first apprised of the nature and goals of my research. I had no difficulty convincing five attorneys to grant me a personal interview and three others to be interviewed on the telephone. While these interviews essentially support the conclusions drawn from roleplaying, they help to elucidate some of the major issues and dilemmas of divorce suits and the attorney's role in handling these cases. Nonetheless, these statements cannot be taken completely at face value. We cannot ignore the basic underlying need for self-protection and the justification of personal and professional positions and actions.

In substance, I concentrated on five questions. The following quotations are representative of the interview group of lawyers.

Why do lawyers frequently depict divorce suits as among the most complex of legal cases?

Divorce suits *are* by far the most difficult cases, not because of the legal work involved but because of the personal problems that occur so often. What happens has little to do with what judge you get or who the other lawyer is. Mostly it depends on what happens between the couple during the divorcing process. If one of the children begins to act up or the roof of the house springs a leak, the whole case can change overnight. It is this instability, this constant chance for chaos that makes it impossible to judge the complexity of the case in advance and makes us all suspicious that every case will be a difficult one. It also makes it impossible to be unequivocal in suggesting legal strategies. Who knows what will work or if it works today whether it will work tomorrow?

Why are there such wide discrepancies among lawyers' fees and retainers?

Fees among lawyers vary greatly, maybe more than among other professionals. Most of us have set hourly rates which we can lower at times if a client cannot afford this much. But retainers are a different issue. We try or should try to base the retainer on an estimate of what the cost of the divorce is likely to be, or, in other words, the number of hours involved times the hourly fee. Some lawyers use the highest possible figure to avoid complaints later; others undercut the price to get the case and then bill the client for additional work.

Since the Supreme Court decision on advertising clients are questioning our fees more and more. They see all the ads for $150, $200, or $250. What they don't realize is that it is possible to obtain a divorce for this price, but unlikely. These ads pertain to couples without children, money, or property.

There are other factors also. If a client calls you repeatedly, you might have to bill him or her, because no one can afford to run a practice for one client. Or for clients who you already represent, you may handle their divorce as a matter of courtesy. I don't mean for free, but for less.

The lawyer who practices by himself or in a small firm tends to charge the least and work the hardest on a divorce case. He might, in fact, end up losing money. Then you take a lawyer like _____; he can charge $100 an hour or more and demand a retainer of $5,000 or more. For some of his richer clients, I bet it's even higher.

Why do lawyers frequently evade questions on issues such as custody, alimony, and property division?

How can you answer these questions? Often they are asked before we even know much about the clients or their circumstances. What is true or good or reasonable for one is not for another. The answers are not standard. And even if it is a fair solution, it may fail. For example, take a woman of 60 who has all her life been a homemaker. Her husband wants a divorce and is well able to pay her alimony. Should she get it? Sure. But will she get it? I don't know. And even if she does, we cannot guarantee that he will pay it, despite all the power of the courts. He might leave the state or force her to keep dragging him back to court until the aggravation and the expense become too much for her.

The divorce process is unwieldy and often unjust. But we have to work within the system and with people. This is another problem. People differ in their needs, wants, and ability to carry out their own plans. More and more couples are talking about joint custody, but few realize how difficult it is to make it work. It often means that the couple's relationship has to be more open and flexible after divorce than it was before. And then again, as in most things relating to divorce, there is no consistency. Situations change with adults and with children. Maybe this is the third problem. I mean that divorce does not end a marriage in a personal sense. If there are children, visitation and support continue and so does the relationship. But the couple changes and so do their lives. He no longer wants to pay alimony; he wants a reduction in child support. Or she wants his visitation curtailed or eliminated. I could go on forever.

It really boils down to the fact that most of the decisions should come from the couple. We can offer guidance, but we can't make the agreement work. Yet if you tell this to a client, they get upset. They want to know why they need a lawyer if they are doing all the work. To be honest, they need a lawyer as a professional adviser; they need one to tell them things they have forgotten to consider—taxes, education, health care, and so on.[14]

They also get angry if you tell them about the pitfalls in a possible arrangement. They think this means you are rejecting their ideas. If I tell them about the problems, I risk losing them as clients at the beginning; if I don't tell them, I'll probably lose them later if things do not work out the way they planned.

Where a lawyer is really needed is in the few all-out legal fights like you read about in custody suits.

What is the lawyer's role in a divorce suit?

I know they want you to be their parent and shrink as well as their attorney. But this is not realistic. We do not have the time to be a friend or a parent. This doesn't mean the lawyer should be cold or inaccessible. But it does mean that his role is a limited one, limited by his expertise and time. There are better people and places to go to than an attorney for this kind of help. That is why we often make referrals to therapists or counseling services. It is not a way to get the client off your back, although this is sometimes necessary, but a way to get help for them that we cannot provide.

What tactics and/or questions would help prospective clients to retain a lawyer whose personality and goals are compatible with theirs?

Choosing a lawyer is no different than choosing any professional. You need to select someone you can trust, have confidence in, and can talk to. For relatively straight-forward legal business your personal feelings about an attorney are not that important. It's like going to a medical specialist for one or two visits. For a divorce it's different. A divorce usually is an emotional as well as a legal experience. Also, it may take a year or more to obtain, and even afterward you might need a lawyer. Because of the time and the personal nature of the case, it is very important that you select a lawyer carefully. How you do this, I'm not sure. Probably a recommendation followed by a consultation is the best you can do. If you're lucky, you already have or know a lawyer that you like. But it is possible that a lawyer who is terrific at handling your business is a lousy matrimonial attorney. If he is ethical, he will refer you to someone else; that is, if he knows matrimonial law is not his thing.

CONCLUSION

Neither Sheila's research nor my interviews with lawyers produced any revelations. In essence, the investigation of legal services in Westside and its environs verified many of the criticisms voiced by sample participants. First of all, Sheila too had learned that obtaining a divorce is a costly procedure. (In 1975, the median hourly rate was quoted at $50.[15]) Second, for those who have legal questions pertaining to separation or divorce but who are technically nonindigent, there are, to my knowledge, no public facilities in Westside where an individual can obtain free legal information or counsel. Outside of a limited number of support groups for men and women and written material, individuals must contact a lawyer for answers to even routine legal inquiries. Third, the process of matching client and lawyer is a difficult procedure, the lawyer-client relationship being too intangible and complex to be guided by any precise methods of selection. Yet the high rate of dissatisfaction with lawyers reported by both men and women respondents[16] suggests that most currently used methods are either inadequate or irrelevant. Perhaps dissatisfaction can, at least in part, be attributed to some kind of displacement process in which anger, guilt, anxiety, or other feelings related to the divorce are projected onto the attorney. Alternatively, it is hard to dismiss the avalanche of charges that have been building up against matrimonial lawyers, which, in fact, have been coming from within as well as outside the legal system.[17] Fourth, it is practically impossible to initiate even a no-fault divorce suit without obtaining legal assistance on issues pertaining to property division, child custody, child support, and alimony.

There have, however, been some changes noticeable in the years 1975 through 1980, and there are more in the offing. When this research began in 1975, lawyers were not permitted to advertise their services or fees. Since the U.S. Supreme Court ruling of June 1977, this is no longer true. While, as of yet, advertising does not seem to have lowered the cost of legal counsel, it does seem that clients have become more aware and wary consumers. Overall, this has affected sole practitioners and small firms rather than the corporate giants. (Most large corporations shy away from matrimonial law anyway.) Legal clinics, nonexistent in this metropolitan area in 1975, are also exerting pressure on providers, challenging their high fees for divorce as well as for other kinds of litigation. If the marketplace is far from a competitive arena and the cost of a divorce is, by any standard, high, especially for those who retain the most well-known matrimonial counsels, public pressure is building up. Increasingly, divorce seekers are realizing that spending $1,000, or $5,000, or $10,000 for a divorce is an economic drain on husband and wife—an outlay which might not reap benefits worthy of the cost and which most cannot afford.

Still, divorce petitioners remain very much the captive audience of a relatively closed system. To gain entrance most need a guide trained in the terminology and technology of maneuvering the procedural hurdles. Even the state's enactment of a no-fault divorce ground (the 46th state to do so) has done little to redress this problem. Not only is no-fault one of eight different grounds for divorce, but the original bill required couples to wait ten months in uncontested suits, and 24 months in contested suits, with an additional six-month period for decree finalization. The infrequent use of this ground (estimates ranged from 7 to 10% of the divorces granted in the state) led to legislative amendment, shortening the waiting period to six and 12 months, respectively, with the same six-month finalization period. Since most petitioners continue to favor grounds that offer a more expeditious route to dissolution, there has neither been an appreciable increase in no-fault suits nor has the reform reduced the need for legal representation.

If independent providers and legislators have failed to make the system more responsive to consumer needs, the courts have been no better. The Domestic Relations Division of the Hennepin County Department of Court Services in Minneapolis, Minnesota, provides a striking contrast to the county court serving Westside residents. In Hennepin County a three-part program is offered at no charge, covering the legal process of divorce, the divorce experience, and children and divorce. Although this court and its ancillary services have been nationally publicized and even spotlighted on an NBC special, "Children of Divorce" (January 19, 1976), along with other demonstration programs provided by various state, county, and city governments and agencies, the county court for Westside residents remains seemingly unaware, or at least unaffected, by the changes manifest in different jurisdictions.

The state's judicial system continues to be governed by and for the legal profession. The need for special facilities where individuals can obtain preliminary legal counseling and information prior to instituting suit has been virtually ignored by the profession. Its members appear to have neither questioned nor explored alternative methods of delivering legal services as part of law practices or as extensions of the court system; they retain control of the process and the information.

The one dent in this barricade can be largely credited to nonprofit groups and centers for the separated and divorced, which often function as legal referral agencies and educational resources on the law. Moreover, as the call for change continues to grow louder, extralegal services and procedures are increasingly being viewed by divorce petitioners, as well as legal reformers, in a more favorable light. Several interviewees reported that their divorce agreement contained a clause stipulating that future disputes between the parties would be settled by arbitration. In some cases an arbitrator or a panel of arbitrators was to be chosen by the couple, and in others the American Arbitration Association was used. This latter organization now operates a Family Dispute Service near Westside which provides arbitrators for resolving postdivorce disagreements, referees for helping couples draw up separation agreements, and conciliators for reconciliation counseling. While recourse to the courts is still possible, the arbitration process is based on the premise that extralegal settlement is less contentious and less costly. It is, of course, possible that couples who choose this route are those most likely to engage in productive legal negotiations outside the courts.

Although a strong case can be presented for reforming divorce policies and proceedings, the chances for achieving major changes in the near future are small. More plausibly, change will continue to come slowly and from outside the formal legal system. Many more groups may have to be formed and many more advocacy campaigns launched before the legal profession demonstrates a greater degree of public accountability. This applies equally to local, state, and federal governments; they have not done their part either in providing citizens and residents with the facilities and services they seem to need and want. In the meantime, existing groups and services might be persuaded to make minor adaptations. Community pressure might be exerted, for example, to encourage a facility like the City College Legal Aid Bureau to disseminate routine legal information to an expanded clientele, particularly if they received support from the city government; or they might collaborate with local groups for the separated and divorced in the formation of a legal packet of information and the sponsorship of special sessions for the public on the divorce system and process in the state.

NOTES

1. Nevertheless, not only was the consultation fee of the NOW attorney equivalent to the "special" price advertised by the County Bar Association, but the

lawyers from both agencies quoted the same hourly rate of $40 and retainers of $500.

2. It is important to remember that, unlike Sheila, in the early stages of separation many interviewees did not go to lawyers for legal information. In contrast, they sought advice from family and friends.

3. While I was unable to tape-record interviews conducted during roleplaying, I did take notes during most sessions, under the pretense that I was writing down the different questions for which I needed to find out more information. I also wrote detailed notes immediately after each interview.

4. Since the U.S. Supreme Court ruled in June 1977 that lawyers were permitted to advertise their fees, the newspapers carry daily advertisements for low-cost, uncontested divorces. Yet I know of no lawyer who has ever matched the $150 charge I have seen in the classified sections of various newspapers and magazines. Indeed, according to the lawyers I spoke to, it appeared that the only way to dissolve a marriage for less than $1,000 (remember that there are two attorneys to be hired and while it is always possible that part of the retainer will not be used, I have never heard of this happening) was to write out an agreement in advance, have no children or property, be best friends with your prospective ex-spouse, and have an income roughly equivalent to his. In a case like this it hardly seems necessary to have a lawyer, let alone two of them.

5. This argument has some merit. Because Sheila had no job, property, or income of her own, and because she and her husband had children, there was sufficient reason to presuppose that even a prearranged agreement would need to be revised before decree approval. While some respondents had blamed their attorneys for the breakdown in communication, others had charged their spouses with changing their minds about the settlement, and still others had admitted that they had altered their own position during negotiations.

6. While I had learned that the amount of a legal retainer is not, after all, cast in stone, I remain unsure as to why I deviated from my standard scenario during this conversation. Perhaps my bravery was inspired by the telephone's guarantee of anonymity.

7. Because I doubted that many women would actually study the kind of semi-technical literature recommended by NOW, particularly in the early stages of separation, the information garnered from these readings has not been included as part of Sheila's accumulated knowledge base. Moreover, as we will note later in the chapter, I was soon to learn that my information on legal fees and retainers was far from adequate.

8. In general, when this research was conducted, individuals with a net income not exceeding $3,713, or $4,913 for a family of two, were classified as "needy" (Miller, 1978). Income levels rose according to the number of additional dependents and proof of other financial liabilities and obligations.

9. Lay persons who dispense legal information risk being charged with practicing law without a license. Although nonprofit groups can perhaps better justify their efforts as educational than can profit groups, nonprofit status does not exempt a group from being investigated or sued. For example, the Women's Divorce Cooperative in Seattle, Washington, assembled a packet of legal information which attempted, among other things, to translate legal jargon, list papers required for a

simple, uncontested divorce, and review legal procedures. Subsequently, the local bar association requested copies of this packet and notified the group of their intent to investigate them for practicing law without a license. Although the story had a happy ending, since the bar did not institute suit, even though they were refused a copy of the material, this experience again illustrates the tenuous position of any individual or group attempting to dispense legal information without the blessing of a license.

10. Women in Transition, located in Philadelphia, is one example of a women's advocacy group that has reportedly been successful in mobilizing public support for their platform and in providing survival skills and assistance to women experiencing separation, divorce, and/or single parenthood. Published in 1975, their extensive handbook (538 pages) is a compilation of information and recommendations for facilitating the adjustment of this target population.

11. The woman from the Westside group told me that she regularly received telephone calls from women living at considerable distances from Westside because their communities did not have similar groups.

12. The Permanent Commission on the Status of Women in Connecticut noted the same need among individuals surveyed in their study. Accordingly, they recommended the creation of both written informational guides and an Info-Line for state residents (1979, p. 35).

13. Of their sample of 205 separated and divorced individuals, Spanier and Anderson (1979) report that 37% had exaggerated their marital difficulties and 27% had lied or presented fabricated stories during negotiations or court appearances (p. 609).

14. Note that this lawyer's response also pertains to the next question on the role of an attorney in a divorce suit.

15. Legal clinics offer potential for middle-income individuals to secure legal services at a more modest rate. Use of paralegal aides, sharing office space, and concentration on more routine cases reportedly lower operating costs and pass the savings on to the consumer (Downey, 1975). At the time of this writing there are two clinics within a half-hour's drive from Sheila's home in Westside.

16. See the report of the Permanent Commission on the Status of Women (1979) in Connecticut and Spanier and Anderson's (1979) study in Pennsylvania for supporting statistics.

17. Indeed, the law, in general, and lawyers, in particular, have been the object of an all-out media blitzkrieg aimed at exposing the injustices of the legal system and the ethics of the profession. For example, the cover of *Time* magazine reads: "Those #*X*!!! Lawyers!" (April 10, 1978); *Boston* magazine features an article entitled "First Thing We Do, Let's Kill All the Lawyers" (Hartman, 1978); and the *New York Sunday Times Magazine* talks of "Legal Pollution" (Ehrlich, 1976).

CHAPTER 3

THE ECONOMIC PROBLEMS
AND CONCERNS
FACED BY SEPARATED
AND DIVORCED WOMEN

In 1977 five out of six single-parent households were headed by women (U.S. Bureau of the Census, 1978, p. 4). In 1978 there were 8.2 million female-headed households, as compared to 4.5 million in 1960. Of these families, 63% included children under 18 years of age (an increase of 13% from 1960); 34% of these families were maintained by divorced women (an increase of 19% from 1960);[1] and an additional 22% were maintained by married women whose husbands were not present, the majority of them having separated because of marital discord (U.S. Bureau of the Census, 1979, p. 4).

Stating that, "Families in which no husband is present are often among the most impoverished," the 1979 Census Report identified the economic problems of female-headed families as a major social policy issue (ibid.). The Bureau of the Census is not alone in reaching this conclusion. The disadvantaged status of female-headed households and the economic consequences of divorce for women have been well documented in the social science literature (Bane, 1976a, 1976b; Bradbury et al., 1979; Brandwein et al., 1974; Espenshade, 1979; Kriesberg, 1970). Of particular significance to this study of middle-class women is the pattern of downward economic mobility, or slippage, following separation and divorce. As economists Ross and Sawhill (1975) have noted, "Whatever their prior income status (and many were middle class), women and children who form their own families run a high risk of poverty. Almost half of them are poor and a similar proportion spend some time on welfare" (p. 3). And in a study of a group of middle- and upper-middle-class families with a mean income of $24,000 prior to divorce, psychologist Dorothy Burlage found that one year after divorce the total per annum income of the female-headed families from all sources averaged $8,000 (McLaughlin, 1978, p. 21).

The economic difficulties of female-headed households are undeniably a primary reason, if not the predominant one, why the majority of unemployed separated and divorced mothers enter the labor force, others seeking higher-paying jobs and/or returning to school for advanced degrees and employment training. Nevertheless, the reduced financial status of these families cannot be viewed solely from the perspective of its impact on employment trends. Employment-related areas pertaining to child care, household responsibilities, and maintenance not only affect a woman's performance as an employee but may also narrow her job choices and significantly reduce her "real" income. Moreover, housing and credit emerge as additional issues that influence the financial stability of these families. Therefore any discussion of problems and concerns categorized as economic in nature would be incomplete and misleading if it did not include, along with employment, issues relating to child care, household management, housing, and credit.

In this chapter and Chapter 4 we will consider each of these areas separately, focusing first upon the different experiences of the interviewees (and questionnaire respondents) and secondly upon Sheila's investigation of community resources. It should, however, be noted that economic issues (like legal issues) have a personal as well as a practical dimension. Not infrequently, individuals saw their inability to negotiate in the marketplace, to provide financial security for themselves and their children, and to be independent of their ex-husbands as proof of their incompetence. Failures were like depressants; successes like invigorating tonics. Because their reactions rebounded upon their capacity to cope with and adjust to the marital dissolution, they had implications not only for the individual's well-being but also for their relationships with children, family, friends, and ex-spouses.

THE WORLD OF WORK AND ACADEME

A demographic study on the number of working women has projected that only 25% of married women with children will be full-time housewives and mothers in 1990 (Smith, 1979). While the study received headline billing in newspapers and magazines, creating the impression that a startling new development bode ill tidings for marriage and family, the researchers made no such proclamations. Indeed, they noted that slightly less than one-third of married mothers are currently full-time homemakers, whereas over 50% of married mothers with children between the ages of six and 17 and 38% with children under six are employed (See also Gordon and Kammeyer, 1980). In addition, they maintained that no existing studies on child care have uncovered evidence that the children of working mothers are adversely affected.

Regardless of how marital moralists look upon these data, separated and divorced women may be the unintentional beneficiaries of the "exodus" from hearth to workplace. As a group they have long mirrored the employment rates of men with respect to their participation in the labor force. According to Grossman (1978), 77% of this population was employed in 1977 as compared to 73% in 1974 (Kreps and Clark, 1975), and a study of 449 separated and divorced women by Mott and Moore (1978) revealed a similar movement of women into the labor force after divorce. Of all the women unemployed in 1967, 63% of white women and 53.7% of nonwhite women had jobs in 1973. While separated and divorced mothers may continue to have more financial problems and outside responsibilities than do married mothers, at least there may be less stigma and guilt associated with their employment.

Still, the employment outlook for women, in general, and separated and divorced women, in particular, is far from heartening. Despite the substantial number of women presently employed,[2] the projection that 11 million more women will be entering the labor market by 1990, and the 1963 passage of the Equal Pay Act, the discrepancy between the salaries of women and men has increased during the last 20 years. In 1978 full-time employed female college graduates earned salaries 60% of that of similarly educated males (Cerra, 1980b, p. 46). While the lower earning capacity of women is somewhat offset in households where husband and wife are both wage earners, separated and divorced women have no such advantage. The majority have to support not only themselves but also their children on wages lower than those of their ex-husbands. Insufficient or nonexistent child support and alimony awards do little to boost their financial status, leaving them consistently worse off than their former husbands (Espenshade, 1979). Moreover, the special problems of displaced homemakers are well known to many separated and divorced women.

The Displaced Homemaker Movement began in 1974 when a group of unemployed, older women petitioned the California state legislature for job-training programs. Since then, the needs of women 40 years and older who are forced to enter the workplace after years of unpaid service in the home and often without prior experience or training have received much publicity and some attention.[3] Although the skills cultivated by homemakers are innumerable, they are often inestimable. All too frequently employers are interested solely in the nature and scope of an individual's "paid" experience, and all too frequently job applicants haven't the vaguest idea of how to translate their experience into the lingo of the workplace or where to sell their talents; indeed, they might not even be aware that they have any to peddle. Ironically, they are the very women who prior to the death, divorce, separation, or desertion of their husbands symbolized the American ideal of full-time nurturer and housewife, the traditional homemakers who, many fear, will constitute the 25% minority of married women by 1990.

The stress and anxiety described by separated and divorced women who had difficulty entering the job market portray the plight of the displaced homemaker. In this study I have included women under 40 years of age if they had been married for at least ten years and had either never worked or had been unemployed for at least five years prior to the initial separation. The former group comprised 8% and the latter 40%.

I've been trying to get a job for a year now, but nobody seems to need an ex-English major who can't type fast or take steno. This experience is not helping my self-image. It seems as if I'll have to go back to school in order to get a job, but that takes money and I don't have any to spare.

(40-year-old woman, 2 years divorced)

It took me a long time to be able to ask what I could and could not do. I came up with more could nots than coulds, but it was a step in the right direction. I began to apply for jobs, listing all my academic honors in college and my one year of work experience. Rejection after rejection came back. Many said they'd keep my résumé on file for future openings. For a while I believed this expressed interest, but I soon learned it was only a polite refusal. After a year and a half I got a job. The pay was lousy, but it was a chance to prove my skills. I have received three raises in five months and things are looking up.

(47-year-old woman, 2½ years divorced)

I never worked. I had been brought up to believe that women went to work only if their husbands couldn't support them. My husband shared this belief until our separation. Then he became a feminist overnight. "The world has changed," he said, and I could no longer expect him to cradle me like a child. This might have sounded different if we were still married. But I took it as a slap in the face. It was bad enough he wanted a divorce, but to expect to get off scot-free was more than I could bear. I fought back, had my lawyer request a higher sum of alimony and child support, but I didn't get what I wanted. In truth, as a divorced couple money was a problem.

I was constantly depressed and tired. When I realized that I couldn't go on like that and neither could the kids, I began to look for a job. A friend told me about an opening in a day-care center. I applied and got the job as a teacher's aide. I don't earn much, but I'm going back to school for my teaching certificate. I'd love to be a head teacher.

(41-year-old woman, 3 years divorced)

Many respondents criticized the rigidity of employment practices—inflexible work schedules, reliance on traditional credentials, and standardized work tasks—and the prejudices toward women and, in particular, women with children (Stocker, 1980b). In addition, they expressed, often poignantly, the need for community resources and support services.

Somehow, at some time, some enlightened community may suddenly realize that it can help its residents. I can't understand why employment information cannot be centralized. They can also help people learn the skills of marketing themselves and make available listings of jobs. It would ease the tension of being alone out there in a work world that doesn't know you exist.[4]

(42-year-old woman, 11 months separated)

People who are separated need information, emotional support, financial support, and counseling on jobs. Employers need information too. How can you convince someone that you have the skills they want when you never get a chance to talk to them? My résumé must be in 40 wastepaper baskets!

(35-year-old woman, 5 months separated)

There are two components to these stories. The first pertains to the trials and tribulations of the homemaker's search for employment. Decidedly, these women face biases and obstacles unknown to their employed sisters (Caldwell, 1980; Ferris, 1971; Laws, 1979; Waldman and Grover, 1972). The second pertains specifically to separated and divorced mothers. At a time when these women are feeling most vulnerable and in need of support, they are forced to deal with the realities of the marketplace.[5] Simultaneously, they have the responsibilities of single parenthood. Whereas before they shared the obligations of caretaker with their husbands, now they are essentially sole custodians. Even if the husband had played a minor role in the operation of the home and care of the children, his absence from the house leaves a void, real or perceived. It is not surprising, then, that feelings of rejection and resentment toward their ex-spouses for "having done this to them" underlie many of their recounts, irrespective of who initiated the divorce. Nor is it surprising that many view themselves as alone, their energies drained and their ingenuity taxed. Nonetheless, their immobilization seemed to be predominantly short lived. Perhaps my sample was unique—all the women had postsecondary education and were under the age of 50—but even among women who had not yet secured employment, none had given up.

The divorced woman who has been employed prior to separation is in a less precarious position (financially and emotionally) than those who can be classified as homemakers. Of my sample of women (interview and questionnaire), 52% belonged in this category: 25% had part-time jobs and 27% were employed full-time. Yet many of these women also embarked on job searches. Of the part-timers, 65% were seeking or had obtained full-time employment, and 12% of those with full-time positions were looking for or had found different jobs. The reasons for change were not only primarily economic but also related directly to the divorce: These women now needed to earn more money.

I worked part-time until my separation. I was able to keep my profession and still be home when the girls returned from school. But after my husband left I could not afford this luxury. Luckily they had a full-time opening where I was working, and my mother lives close enough to help out when the girls are sick.

(42-year-old woman, 3 years divorced)

I've been working 25 hours a week for seven years, but now I am looking for full-time employment. My job is all right, but it doesn't pay enough now that I am divorced. I'm certainly not starving, but I'm also not eating caviar.

(32-year-old woman, 10 months separated)

I never stopped working when I got married. The children were born over summer vacations and I returned to teaching in the fall. I always liked to work. I think it has also made the separation easier. I know other women who sit home and dwell on their broken marriages. Sometimes the nights are long and frightening, but I don't allow myself to get too depressed. Yet money is a problem, more than it ever was before. I'm taking courses at night for a master's degree so I can get a pay raise or a job in another district that pays more. When you're separated, money suddenly seems so much more important.

(35-year-old woman, 8 months separated)

I was working as a nurse in a local hospital for two years before the separation. Now I am working in the city on the night shift. The pay is better and I don't have to put 'Jenny' into a day-care center. The money saved from child care plus the higher salary has made life easier.

(30-year-old woman, 1 year divorced)

It sounds calculating, but I found a job because I knew we would get a divorce. I wanted a chance to prove I could do it and also a chance to meet new people.

(33-year-old woman, ½ year divorced)

While the woman in the last quotation was concerned that her remark would be interpreted as "calculating," the decision to seek employment prior to separation is generally regarded by "experts" to be a wise one. Betty Berry and Elaine Livingston, creators of a pilot YMCA program, "You and Your Divorce," advise women to "prepare" themselves for divorce by getting a job (cited in Grunwald, 1976, p. 25). Others contend that financial independence is a necessity for all women. Data on the economic impact of divorce on women with custody of children and inequities in the salaries and employment opportunities available to women, especially if they have little or no work experience, support this argument.[6] But those who recommend employment both before and after divorce also offer other reasons unrelated to economics. Working is presented as a way to form new friendships and contacts, to view oneself in roles other than that of mother and wife, and even as an escape from the claustrophobic world of the home (Weiss, 1975). Or, as columnist Ellen Goodman (1978) explains, employment is "a hedge against the risks of life. Even at its worst, work seems to be an immense addition to the arsenal of self-protection. It offers a shielf of paychecks and friends and identity" (p. 15). And, in the words of two interviewees:

Working is a social experience. I am looking for new friends, people to date, and people to meet other people with. My kids are great, but they are not my friends. Working has helped me to enter the adult world.

(31-year-old woman, 1 year divorced)

I thought that all my problems were because I was divorced. I blamed my loneliness and my depression on the divorce. But I think I was really lonely way before the divorce. Since I've been working everything has lit up. There is a whole world out there that I missed for years. How can I explain the importance of doing something that not only has its own satisfaction but that pays me for it?

(45-year-old woman, 3 years divorced)

Clearly a job is not like a bottle of Fantastic. It doesn't erase all the remnants of a marriage; and for some it is a burden.

I tried working two times, but it was too much for me. I had to arrange for day care and worry about what would happen if the kids got sick. I had to get up early and never got to bed until late. The kids complained that they never saw me, and I had no time to date. So I quit. I keep myself busy doing volunteer work. There I have met new friends who are also divorced. I don't regret not working; I just miss the extra money.

(40-year-old woman, 3 years divorced)

I wish I could describe my job differently, but I hate it. It isn't challenging and it isn't lucrative. Sometimes I get angry at my ex-husband and blame him for my not going to graduate school. Maybe if I meet a rich man I can save myself and the kids from all this anxiety.

(29-year-old woman, 1½ years divorced)

It's not so much the job that is the problem but all the other jobs. I am chief cook, bottle washer, and mechanic. I am mother, worker, and a bit of a slave. It is too much for anyone to handle. My husband complains that he's lost his children, but so have I. Who has the time to be with them anymore?

(39-year-old woman, 1 year divorced)

As to the psychological and social benefits which some find in the workplace, others find them elsewhere. Volunteer work, as one woman mentioned, provided an entrée to a new network of friends. For this woman the absence of salary, pension, and fringe benefits were minor deprivations compared to the gain in personal freedom. (But this "freedom" comes only to those who can afford it.) For others schooling presents multiple advantages. Of the women who had returned to school or who were contemplating it, 56% regarded education as a means to improve their employment options, 27% stated that it was a way to meet new people, and 8% saw it as a productive diversion. Not unexpectedly, some considered it a bit of all three.

Going back to school has helped me in all sorts of ways. I am meeting people, training for a new career, and, most importantly, I'm beginning to feel less sorry for myself.

(35-year-old woman, 6 months separated)

I never had the opportunity to go to graduate school and never really had the confidence that I could do it. My husband believed that it was a waste of time and money. After we separated I decided to take a course. Well, I liked it and, more than that, I found that I did well. I applied for a degree program and got accepted on a scholarship. This was the greatest moment in my life! Now I have something to look forward to and have met new people to share ideas and have fun with.

(37-year-old woman, 2 years divorced)

The increased sense of personal worth and independence described by many of these women did not hinge on any one solution. The common denominator was to be found in their optimistic outlook. Alternatively, those who resented the additional responsibilities and changes in their lives caused by the separation or divorce were more likely to dwell on the past. In general, this group was among those who were most recently separated and who had not been the instigators of the divorce action. Indeed, a significant number claimed to have been shocked at their husbands' request for a divorce.

Much of the literature on divorce focuses on the economic impact of the dissolution, zeroing in on the number of female-headed households who live at or below the poverty level. But what of the divorced who are not so disadvantaged? Curiously, the financial status of the respondents did not seem to be the critical factor affecting their ability to adjust to separation. Rather, differences in their relationship with ex-spouses, family, and friends, the circumstances surrounding the separation, whether they were employed and/or had interests outside the house, their own resiliency, and even the passage of time appeared to be the key determinants of a successful adaptation to single parenthood. Moreover, the realities of the economic position of the separated and divorced were often unrelated to individuals' perceptions of their situations. In my sample women who had been accustomed to living on $50,000 a year and now had to make do on $20,000 expressed reactions not dissimilar from those whose income shifted from $20,000 to $10,000.

We used to have a big colonial house and now the children and I live in an apartment. Separation has meant the end to summer camps and expensive vacations. I've got the kids and the struggle, and he's got the money and the freedom.

(33-year-old woman, 9 months separated)

This woman was not by any standard roughing it. Her apartment was in a luxury complex; she did not have to work (although she did); and she could still afford an expensive car and clothing. Yet there was no denying the existence of a problem. To her (and others), financial security offered scant reason for applause. She could not identify with those who suddenly found themselves in the untenable position of being poor, but she could identify with and condemn her husband's comfort and freedom. Her real income was discounted as the necessity of adjusting to a reduced standard of living overshadowed her life.

Others who had merely anticipated a luxurious existence were similarly angry at their husbands, believing that they had used them to achieve their goals and then discarded them.

I worked to put 'Peter' through medical school and his internship. No sooner then he finished his residency, he wanted a divorce. I invested in a losing proposition. He has the credentials to earn a fabulous living, and I'm left with the pieces of a lost dream.

(37-year-old woman, 1 year divorced)

These women are not of concern to policy makers. They do not require income maintenance plans and do not qualify for welfare. Yet, at least for the time being, they are experiencing difficulty in accepting the financial constraints caused by the dissolution of their marriages. In a psychological sense they have something in common with the divorced living at or below the poverty level. These findings suggest that a woman's perception of her financial status, as well as the reality of her situation, can produce emotional reactions that impede the restructuring process. This pertains to men as well as women.

I live in a small apartment and she and the children live in our house. Divorce has made me poor, even though I earn $35,000 a year. That may sound like a lot of money, but try and see how far it goes with two families to support.

(40-year-old man, 1 year divorced)

The data also suggest that economic security no more guarantees a successful adjustment to divorce than does financial insecurity necessarily result in an inability to cope.

THE WORLD OF HOME AND KIN

All of us who have been awed by a juggler's adroitness in balancing several objects simultaneously can observe a like performance without attending a circus. So commonplace is the phenomenon that few ever recognize the magnitude of the feat. I am speaking of the working mother, married or divorced, who day after day is faced with juggling the priorities and responsibilities of home, family, and work.[7] If she is successful, few stop to applaud her achievement, so effortless do her accomplishments appear. Unfortunately, it is when she is unable to perform her feats that attention is drawn to her failure, that the complaints can be endless. If married, her husband may help or the children may be assigned tasks. If there is enough money, a housekeeper may be hired, laundry sent out, or dinners eaten in restaurants. For the separated and divorced mother, these problems may be compounded and the remedies may be less affordable. In most instances there are insufficient finances to support a housekeeper or other luxurious "necessities." Moreover, unless her relationship with her ex-spouse is an exceptional one, or there is a joint custody arrangement, the possibility of the father sharing some of the child-care duties is remote. As a result, single-parent women commonly express feelings of being flooded and unable to cope. Paradoxically, their anxiety may have less to do with the care of children and housekeeping (albeit these duties are not to be minimized) than with having to assume responsibility for tasks formerly performed by their husbands—paying bills, repairing and servicing the car, cleaning gutters, gardening and lawn maintenance, repairing broken appliances, etc. Often not only do women not partake in such endeavors, but many never even consider them.

HOUSEHOLD MAINTENANCE

With separation comes the awakening, immediate at times and delayed at others. The car may break down or a letter may arrive from a collection agency before they realize that there are more things in heaven and earth than children, cooking, cleaning, and even working. It is not a question of capacity, but of rearing and conditioning. Too many women, whose minds have been cultivated and cultured by the finest schooling, have not been educated in areas relegated by tradition and society to men. When circumstances alter the order of nature (or man), these women do find a way to cope.

Some have to master new skills and assume new responsibilities.

I didn't know one end of the car from the other or when it had to be serviced, inspected, or anything. One day it wouldn't start. I had it towed to the nearest station, and the owner must have seen ignorance written all over me. Six hours later I had a bill for $150 for repairs that I couldn't fathom and was too ashamed to ask about. I enrolled in a course in automobile repair. I don't fix my car, but I have a fairly good understanding of what goes wrong and what it is worth to repair it.

(40-year-old woman, 2 years divorced)

I never paid a bill in my life and never balanced a checkbook. When we separated the bills piled up. But then the statements began to arrive with interest charges and I got scared. I went to the bank and the manager showed me how to write a check and do the statements. I felt like an idiot! Four years at Vassar and I needed to be taught how to write a check. But it worked. I pay the bills every month on a certain day—no more late charges and no bounced checks.

(30-year-old woman, 10 months separated)

I thought everything was fine until it came to the tax season. I hadn't the slightest idea how to file a return. A girlfriend helped me sort out the checks, and I went to a local accountant. The trouble was that I had never considered that I had to pay taxes on the alimony. My family lent me the money last year, but it won't happen again.

(38-year-old woman, 1 year divorced)

And others who have managed ingeniously to integrate home, children, and career commitments are stunned to find themselves unnerved by incidentals.

I thought I had it all together. I always paid the bills, argued with servicemen, and arranged for things to be done, so that I never thought I depended on 'Alex.' It took a broken door lock to shock me out of my senses. The door wouldn't open and it wouldn't close right and I sat down and cried. I never cried when we argued about custody or support payments or dividing up our possessions, but I was hysterical over the door lock.

(39-year-old woman, 1 year divorced)

"Who needs him," I thought when he asked for a divorce. He's never around much, and when he is, it is not much different than when he isn't. I have a job, money in the bank, credit cards, a car, and the children. But it didn't work out exactly as I planned. The basement flooded because I forgot about cleaning the gutters, and my heating bill escalated because I didn't have the burner serviced. The unimportant little things took over my life.

(42-year-old woman, 5 months separated)

In contrast, single-parent men may find their temporary undoing to be the laundry, arrangements for child care, cooking, cleaning, or combing their daughter's hair. Certainly work overload is a large part of the problem: Whereas two people once shared the management of a house and a life, each performing different tasks and assuming different responsibilities, now it is one. This requires not only adjustment to being single, but also the cultivation of new skills and the assumption of new duties. But this has a positive side too.

There may be, for example, less pressure to perform at home.

I don't hear my husband nagging anymore. Somehow he was always finding something that I had left undone or had no time to do. This, I must admit, is a benefit of divorce. I can deal with the kids complaining, but a nagging husband is unbearable.

(37-year-old woman, 2 years divorced)

It's not that I believed the Marabel Morgan garbage, but a similar kind of pressure was always there, even if not said aloud. The pressure to look beautiful, regardless of how tired you are, is always an issue: a little bit of whore and a little bit of mother and housekeeper, not always in the same order. Well, now I can choose the order without the guilt. I can look lousy without fearing I'm going to lose my husband; after all, I've already lost him. I can also look great because I want to, not because I have to. For the first time I feel in control, and that is an achievement nobody can minimize.

(40-year-old woman, 2 years divorced)

Marriage must have been invented by men. Oh, I've heard all those stories about the poor, hardworking man who has to support his family without any help from his wife. But I don't think there are many of these marriages around anymore. Women's lib has done more for men than women. Now over 50% of women work, and they still do all the things they did before. Few men really share the household responsibilities, although I'm sure many really believe they do. At least when you're divorced you know you have to do everything and there isn't any pretending. You also get all the credit, even if much isn't given out. Being alone is not a picnic, but it is also not a pretense.

(41-year-old woman, 1 year divorced)

CHILD CARE

Of the women who were first entering the labor force or changing jobs, 42% stated that child care limited their employment options.[8] For some, inadequate community child-care resources was cited as the major reason for working part-time.

I would work full-time if there was a good day-care facility in the community. As it is, the best centers are nursery schools which operate from 8:45 to 12:00. I was lucky enough to find a job as a teacher's aide in a public kindergarten. The nursery school lets me drop my child off earlier, and I get home about the same time she does.

(30-year-old woman, 10 months separated)

My children are both in public school, but they get out early two days a week. I found a job as a copy editor where I can work in the office 18 hours a week and bring my work home on the children's short days.

(34-year-old woman, 1 year divorced)

Others worked part-time because of the high cost of child-care services.

If I worked full-time, the extra money would be eaten up by day care. The costs of good day care are so high that you have to be on welfare or relatively well-to-do to afford it. By working part-time I don't have the extra expense, although my chances for advancement may cancel out my savings.

(39-year-old woman, 2 years divorced)

Obviously there are trade-offs in any employment choice. While the women quoted above decided to risk losing the possible long-range benefits of full-time employment, others did not.

Getting a good part-time job is close to impossible. There aren't many around and those that are are hard to get and are usually dead ends to nowhere. I made the choice to work full-time, even though most of my salary goes to pay for child care.

(29-year-old woman, 10 months separated)

At present it appears that part-time jobs are rare commodities, and good ones are even rarer (Permanent Commission on the Status of Women, 1979, p. 45; Stocker, 1980b). Those that do exist often do not provide pension and fringe benefits, nor are they integrated into the standard career advancement ladder. At least with respect to promotions within the company, they can indeed be dead ends. Federal and state bills for expanding part-time positions may ultimately improve the employment outlook, but unless there is a concurrent upgrading and restructuring of part-time work, it will continue to be less than a satisfactory alternative for most women (and men) (see Keniston, 1977, pp. 126-127).

For women who worked full-time, reconciling child-care responsibilities with careers led some to settle for jobs that were convenient, if not promising, some to relinquish a goodly part of their salaries for child-care expenses, and others to opt for less suitable coverage or none at all.[9]

My children call me to say they are home and what they are doing, but I'm always worrying about them. I keep telling myself that a ten- and nine-year-old can watch themselves, but I don't really believe it.

(40-year-old woman, 9 months separated)

Of the women with preschool and young school-age children, 57% employed babysitters in their homes at costs ranging from $1.75 to $4.00 an hour.[10] In part, the prevalent use of babysitters in lieu of institutional settings can be explained by the lack of day-care options and by the relatively poor quality of services. Yet these explanations may conceal more fundamental underlying motivations, specifically those relating to role conflict and additudinal and cultural norms. "The distinction between 'day care' and 'nursery schools' has lived on in people's minds" (Woolsey, 1977, p.

130), especially middle-class people who frequently view day-care providers as the keepers of poor people's children. In contrast to institutional care-takers, babysitters, another long-time preserve of the middle classes, are regarded as mother substitutes, thereby presenting those who require the full-time coverage not offered by nursery schools (and who can afford it) with an alternative.

You cannot imagine what a center for infants looks like. You see lines of cribs and always hear the noise of crying babies. It looks like an orphanage. First I brought him to someone's house, but I was never sure if he would be allowed to go hungry or to cry too long. Finally I decided to hire someone to do nothing but watch the baby. She is a lovely grandmother type. It makes it easier for me to go to work without feeling I'm deserting him.

(34-year-old woman, 1 year divorced)

I keep telling myself that I have a life to lead also. And then there is my daughter. She was in a day-care center, but she said it was horrible. I felt all tangled up and guilt ridden. I solved my problem by hiring a young woman who couldn't find a teaching job. My daughter seems much happier, although she still complains about my working. Sometimes I think she does it just to upset me.

(33-year-old woman, 11 months separated)

While child care can be a major problem for working mothers, it is not solely an employment-related issue. Interviewees frequently spoke, albeit sometimes hesitantly or apologetically, of the need to be by themselves or with adults, to have a respite from the daily chores and concerns of child care. Particularly early in the divorcing process, many alluded to the difficulty of "getting their heads together and their lives in order" while maintaining a façade of composure in front of their children. It is at times like this that the availability of child-care resources might prove beneficial, offering a temporary relief from the routines and responsibilities of mothering (Heclo et al., 1973).

I used to live in a community that had a drop-off day-care center. There should be a facility like that in Westside. It would give me a chance to think without being interrupted and help me to start pulling the pieces together.

(30-year-old woman, 6 months separated)

Being a mother is a 24-hour job, with or without a husband. But without one, at times, the responsibility can be terrifying. You look at these children you love and are not quite sure you will be able to do all you should, especially when you are without supports and confidence. Sometimes you simply want to run, and sometimes you want only to hold them and protect them. If there was only some service to use so we could get away without really leaving, it would help to relieve the guilt and help us to continue coping.

(42-year-old woman, 10 months separated)

Public policy on day care has been shaped by opinions and values on the role of women. Because policy makers have tended to view women primarily as homemakers and mothers, little attention has been focused on the public provision of child-care services.[11] Although various efforts to measure present and future demands for day care have not demonstrated any conclusive evidence of the need for institutional services (Rowe, 1972; Unco, 1975; Westinghouse-Westat, 1971), projections on the increasing number of mothers with young children entering the labor force have raised new concern and interest on the future direction of day-care public policy (Hofferth, 1979; Kamerman and Kahn, 1979; Masnick and Bane, 1980; "Who's Minding the Kids?", 1980).

TO MOVE OR NOT TO MOVE

Among the many changes caused by marital dissolution, relocation is one of the most common. Of the women interviewed, 46% changed their place of residence either during or after divorce.

Of this group, 26 % moved to establish a new life for themselves.

I just couldn't stay in the same house after 'Richard' and I separated. It was not just the memories; it was also the neighbors. There were too many questions, both asked and unasked. I thought people were looking at me strangely even if they weren't.

(46-year-old woman, 6 months separated)

Twenty-five % moved because the house was sold as part of the property settlement.

'John' and I agreed to sell the house and divide the money. Neither of us wanted the headache and expense of maintaining a 13-room house.

(40-year-old woman, 2 years divorced)

Twenty % moved because they could not afford to keep up the payments on their homes.

Without alimony and a job paying only $200 a week, there was no way I could pay the mortgage and taxes on the house. Although I received the house as part of the settlement, I had no choice but to sell it.[12]

(32-year-old woman, 3 years divorced)

Sixteen % moved because they felt an apartment would be easier to manage than a house.

I stayed in the house for a year, but it was too much for me to handle. I had to shovel snow in the winter, mow the lawn in the summer, and rake the leaves in the fall. Now the landlord does all that. It's like having the conveniences of a husband without the problems.

(35-year-old woman, 1½ years divorced)

Eight % moved to be nearer relatives.

My mother convinced me to move nearer to them. The arrangement is fine for now: She babysits and we frequently eat over. But she also treats me like an adolescent. I'm considering moving again, but right now it's easier to let someone pamper you.

(33-year-old woman, 4 months divorced)

Five % moved for child-related issues (e.g., to be closer to their ex-husbands, for day care, for better schools).

I wanted the children to be able to see 'Jay' whenever they wanted to, but he could not get an apartment near our house. So we both moved. It's great for the children, but I'm not sure it is good for me. Married or divorced, I can't seem to escape him.

(41-year-old woman, 8 months divorced)

When I heard about the after-school program at _____ Elementary School, I decided it would make my life easier. It was also cheaper than a babysitter.

(33-year-old woman, 5 months separated)

Of the men in the comparison group, all had to move either because their wives and children remained in the house or because the houses were sold.[13] Often it was not easy.

As I put my things in the car, I felt my life had ended. I drove around the corner and cried as I hadn't cried since I was a kid. I guess my fears and pains were for the family I had lost, for myself, and what I would become. But somehow I saw it as the house. I thought of the chair I read in, the side of the bed I slept in, and even the water stain on the dining room ceiling. Funny, I didn't think of the kids or my wife, only the house. Every time I return to the house the pain is still there.

(42-year-old man, 1 year divorced)

I asked for the divorce, but the house, ripping apart the house, was too much to bear. I became frightened like I was being torn apart. A part of me died, the part of husband, father of a family, owner of a house. I felt disoriented and uprooted. There was no place to call home anymore. I was alone.

(38-year-old man, 3 years divorced)

How do you split a lifetime down the middle? Yet that's what we do when we get divorced. The lawyers tell you what is practical. Practical, that is funny! We were told that 'Fay' and the kids should stay in the house, but that I should retain half the ownership. The division upon sale of the house was all figured out, allowing for inflation and upkeep and other incidentals. But I lost that house the day I moved out, no matter what it said on paper. I don't think anyone should stay in a house after a divorce. It's too painful for everyone. It's a farce, a mockery of what was and can't be anymore.

(46-year-old man, 8 months separated)

She got custody of the kids and the house, and I got a divorce I didn't want.

(40-year-old man, 10 months divorced)

While men focused on the emotional impact of leaving their homes, women spoke primarily of the difficulty of finding apartments they could afford and of the discriminatory practices operating within the housing market. With respect to financial constraints, the scarcity of multifamily dwellings in Westside, combined with an increase in the number of single-parent families and single people in the community, has kept the demand for apartments higher than the supply and contributed to an inflation in rental charges.[14]

I had to move to the worst part of town because it was the only area in Westside in which I could afford to live.[15]

(42-year-old woman, 1 year divorced)

It was, however, the discrimination of landlords against female-headed families which most aroused the ire of the respondents.

I was very naive. I told landlords immediately that I was divorced. I never understood why so many apartments had long waiting lists of interested tenants until I put two and two together. When I stopped volunteering information, the waiting lists shrunk.

(36-year-old woman, 2 years divorced)

One landlord asked me whether I liked giving parties and how many friends I had. Another wanted to know if I had tenure at the school where I was teaching. All these remarks were made as side comments, but the meaning was very clear. For a while I thought I needed my parents to countersign my lease. That would have been the final kick in the head!

(33-year-old woman, 11 months separated)

The prospect of wild parties and inability to pay rent were not the only reasons why single-parent women believed themselves to be low on landlords' lists of desirable tenants. Children seemed to be their greatest liability.

The questions were endless. Did the children run around a lot? Did they break things? Did they go to bed late? I'm ashamed to say I answered the questions, telling them how quiet and well mannered they were. Now I spend half the time telling them to be quiet. Next time I will find an apartment where the landlord does not live in the same house.

(39-year-old woman, 1 year divorced)

I lost two apartments because I had children. It seemed as if only the dumps or the apartments priced far more than they were worth permitted young children. It's almost as if they have a surtax on their heads.

(30-year-old woman, 9 months separated)

Oh God, I have to admit I resent my kids now! I can't live where I want or do what I want because I have children. How would you feel after six landlords told you straight out that they did not want young children in their houses? It gets to the point where you want to hide them or, worse, make them go away.

(36-year-old woman, 8 months separated)

Buying a house can be even harder for the single-parent woman.

After selling our home, I had $20,000 in the bank, a car worth $4,000, and $8,000 worth of jewelry. I thought this was quite a lot of money, especially since the house I wanted to buy was only $48,000. I practically had enough money to buy it outright. But would you believe that six banks refused to give me a mortgage because I didn't have a job? If it wasn't for my father who advised me to threaten discrimination charges, I'd probably still be in an apartment today.

(35-year-old woman, 4 years divorced)

My ex-husband and I earn similar salaries. Yet when I went to buy this house, I had trouble getting the mortgage departments to listen to me, let alone finance the mortgage. It is easy for me to see the sexual biases, because both 'Mike' and I bought houses. He had no trouble locating a bank. When I did find one, the amount of information I had to supply compared to him was outrageous.

(36-year-old woman, 3 years divorced)

Other data indicate that these stories are not aberrant incidences. In a study conducted in five cities by the National Council of Negro Women, Inc., and funded by the Department of Housing and Urban Development (HUD), the investigators concluded that sexual discrimination toward women (single, divorced, separated, and widowed) in buying and renting housing was "a national problem" (Washburn, 1976, p. 22). Even the so-called "victorious," those who overcame the barriers imposed by landlords, real estate brokers, and bankers, often did so at a price. Some found their privacy invaded and their credibility and creditworthiness subjected to scrutinization far more than their male counterparts (Christensen, 1976; Dietz, 1976; "Housing Bias Not Eliminated—Rights Panel," 1979, p. 8).

Ironically the state has an Anti-Discrimination Statute (Appendix C) which, in theory, prohibits such practices. Still, sexual biases persist, particularly toward divorced and separated women with young children, suggesting a contradiction between the law as it is written and as it is practiced (Hutson, 1978, p. 14).

With respect to the consumer the sophisticated subtlety of the discrimination may catch some off guard; others may be unfamiliar with their entitlements or with the mechanisms for redress; others may simply choose not to pursue the matter for personal or practical reasons.

I never realized that an apartment-house owner could not refuse to rent an apartment to somebody with children. So many of them said it so often that I assumed it was their prerogative.

> (29-year-old woman, 6 months separated)

I'm in a way ashamed that I let him get away with something I knew to be illegal. But, on the other hand, I still needed an apartment and I would never live there after what happened. It was just easier to expend my energy and use my time looking for another place to live than to wage a vendetta.

> (48-year-old woman, 2 years divorced)

And there were some who had ideas for alleviating the problem.

It seems to me that there should be a central information bureau in Westside to disseminate information on the availability of apartments and to act as an agent connecting landlord or seller with prospective renters or buyers.

> (30-year-old woman, 1 year divorced)

The city has the clout not only to publish more information on the laws pertaining to renting and buying a house, but also to see that they are obeyed.

> (39-year-old woman, 7 months separated)

The efficacy of such suggestions remains to be tested. Meanwhile the law continues to be violated whether the business community does so clandestinely or overtly, and many women continue to be victimized (Johnson, 1980).[16]

BORROWERS VS LENDERS

Credit, more than money, is what makes the world go around. And perhaps at no time is this so apparent as upon the divorce or death of a husband. It is then that a woman learns that the automatic retort, "Charge it," might have depended upon the beneficence of her husband. It was his credit rating that permitted her to use cards instead of cash for life's necessities and amenities. She may have worked, earned as much money as he, and still the credit record was by tradition and law kept in his name.

I earned my own living and contributed as much to the financial management of the house as my husband. But foolishly I accepted being Mrs. _____. When we got divorced I discovered that, according to the banks, the department stores, and even to the gas company, I was nothing. I had given up my identity to get married. It has taken more than a few fights to establish my own name as a person entitled to credit.

(34-year-old woman, 2 years divorced)

If a divorced woman has the slightest feeling that she is a castoff, all she needs to do to confirm this is to apply for credit. After a few experiences she realizes just how little she counts for. A woman who does not have her own independence in marriage is a very vulnerable person. And by independence, I do not mean just having a job. I mean having her own credit cards, paying for her own loans, and having separate checking and savings accounts. If this sounds as if she is plotting a divorce before she says I do, my answer would be, "So what? It is necessary. It's not feministic propaganda; it's not antimarriage propaganda. It is commonsense." The message needs to be spread, but the only ones who know it, feel it, are those too downcast to scream.

(39-year-old woman, 10 months divorced)

Women have to stop being romantics and God-damned fools! If their marriage is forever, then they have lost nothing by having their own credit history. If it is not, they have gained more than they will ever know.

(35-year-old woman, 1 year divorced)

The absence of a credit history is one major reason why women have difficulty in buying or renting housing. Another reason pertains to discrimination by lenders and creditors on the basis of gender or marital status. All this was to be altered (or at least alleviated) by the passage of the Federal Equal Credit Opportunity Act of 1974, prohibiting discrimination in granting credit on the grounds of sex or marital status. What's more, creditors were to inform all consumers of their right to have their accounts listed in the names of both spouses. The response to mailings of over 310 million notices was shockingly low, with only 9% of married women filing the joint-listing forms (Dewan, 1978). Surveys conducted in conjunction with this venture revealed that many married women saw little reason, be it complacency or lack of information, for having their own credit ratings (ibid.; McCormack, 1978). One woman explained the problem differently.

How could I send in the form to receive credit in my own name? I never saw it. My ex-husband paid the bills and he never said anything about a new law or form to fill out. I don't think I'm the only woman who had this problem. Most of my friends' husbands pay the bills.

(35-year-old woman, 10 months separated)

Regrettably, too many women wake up to reality when the problem is hardest to combat. Upon the divorce (or death) of a spouse the middle-income woman suddenly finds herself without access to the credit she long took for granted. While most succeed in establishing their own credit, over 75% of the respondents described their experiences as traumatic and/or humiliating.

As I went from one car agency to another trying to convince them that I was a good credit risk, I began to pity myself more and more. "Who was I?" I kept asking myself. "Why did one prying sales agent after another keep reminding me that I was worth so little?" I tried to shrug it off, to discount these men as meddlesome fools, but all the while I wondered if I was the fool. "Face it, 'Ann'," I told myself, "until you get a job, you have nothing, no future."

Strange how working helped me. The money, some say, is secondary, but it is not. It is a testimony to your worth. It says I work here, I earn this much, and I want to buy this with my money and from my own labors. I am independent.

(37-year-old woman, 4 years divorced)

I applied to the store for a credit card and although nobody said the alimony would not be counted as income, they kept questioning the inadequacy of my part-time salary. It wasn't until I read that alimony and child support are considered a source of income that I was able to confront the store and get my credit card.

(43-year-old woman, 2 years divorced)

Reapplying for credit was a harrowing experience. It wasn't so much getting together all the information, even bringing in my divorce agreement, as having to deal with all the questions and prying at a time when my life was in turmoil. I began to feel paranoid, as if everyone in town was testing and checking up on me.

(32-year-old woman, 1 year divorced)

Furthermore, over 30% of the respondents who established their own credit ratings before or after divorce complained of excessive interest charges, but did not understand how these rates were computed.[17]

The small print on the back of the charge bill is difficult to understand. I'm not a computer expert, but it seems as if the late charges on my bills are astonishingly high. Last year alone I paid over $200 in late charges.

(45-year-old woman, 1 year divorced)

Thus, while recent federal and state credit regulations have been heralded by many as a major advance for women, they have been largely ignored by married women. Even worse, they appear to be ignored by lenders who, according to government statistics, continue to practice sexual (and racial) discrimination (Ross, 1980). (For example, in 1979, 89% of banks were found to be in violation of the equal credit law [Quinn, 1979, p. 39].)

Moreover, the impoverished status of many female-headed families severely limits their ability to attain credit, irrespective of enforcement of "equal" opportunity laws and practices.

CONCLUSION

At one time divorce was a remedy only for the well-to-do, desertion being the poor man's alternative. Times changed: Restrictions on divorce were eased, and legal resources became accessible to more of the citizenry. Divorce invaded the ranks of the lower classes, convincing some that poverty was the primary causation of social and personal pathology (Halem, 1980). If divorce still occurs more frequently among the poor, data on the rising divorce rate among the middle classes and the economic problems of female-headed families present evidence that poverty, or at least downward economic mobility, may be as much a consequence of divorce as it is a cause.

The problem is one of major proportion. If divorce produces poverty or near poverty among members of the middle classes, federal resources in the form of welfare and public assistance must either be divided among a larger percentage of the populace or increased public revenues will be required to meet the demand. Numerous solutions have been proposed to redress this problem. The more sweeping recommendations pertain to income maintenance programs and substantial changes in employment practices and salary scales for women. Reforms on a lesser scale include revised standards for child support awards in which custodial and non-custodial parents *share* the economic responsibilities and deprivations of child rearing,[18] enforced compliance with court-ordered alimony and child support, equal distribution of marital property between both parties,[19] pensions, life insurance, and social security benefits [20,21] to be counted as assets to be divided by the couple, and continuation of health insurance coverage by the husband after divorce.[22] Whatever the ultimate direction of public policy, the economic pressures on female-parent households cannot be denied or ignored.

NOTES

1. While there has been a 65% increase in the number of one-parent families headed by fathers between 1970 and 1979, the number of one-parent families headed by mothers rose 81% during the same period. Further, the proportion of one-parent families maintained by divorced women also increased to 38% (U.S. Bureau of the Census, 1980, p. 3).

2. According to a report issued by the U.S. Department of Labor, the proportion of women working at more than one job is also on the rise, increasing from

16% in 1969 to 30% in 1979, while the percentages for men remained stable (Brozan, 1980b, p. B6).

3. NOW's task force on older women has sponsored bills to provide homemakers with jobs, health coverage, and pensions (Corbett, 1975). Diane DuBoff, a New York lawyer and founder of National Organization to Insure Support Enforcement (NOISE), views divorce insurance as a means to guarantee individuals that a marital dissolution will not leave either spouse bankrupt. Others have sponsored bills to ensure that financial settlements in divorce cases take into consideration the duration of the marriage, the woman's earning capacity, her age and health, and her contributions as a homemaker. Of course the court may conclude that a wife's contribution has been a significant one and that her age and skills do not adequately prepare her for employment; but unless there is enough money and property to support both partners, there may be nothing the court can do to provide financial security for this woman.

4. Since 1975 several job-training centers have been created with state and federal monies to help women enter or reenter the labor market. In addition, various local universities have inaugurated programs with internships for similar purposes. CETA programs offer another possibility for the displaced homemaker.

5. Noting that 73% of the women in their survey who had been married over 12 years had only intermittent work experience and 39% of the women had difficulty finding a job after divorce, the Permanent Commission on the Status of Women in Connecticut (1979) recommended that the state create one position to increase employment opportunities for women and another to direct and coordinate services for displaced homemakers (p. 6).

6. In 1975 the median yearly income for divorced women in the United States was $7,922 and $12,231 for divorced men (U.S. Bureau of the Census, 1978b, p. 60). Similarly, in the Connecticut survey (see footnote 5), 62% of divorced women and 24% of divorced men earned under $10,000 yearly (1979, p. 45).

7. According to historian Carl Degler (1980) in his book *At Odds: Women and the Family in America from the Revolution to the Present*, married women today have the same domestic dilemmas as their sisters of yesteryear. Even those who work full-time assume the major responsibility for children and household tasks. Moreover, most men continue to believe that they are doing their wives a favor if they help with the children and domestic chores (See also Kirchheimer, 1980).

8. In the Connecticut survey (see footnote 5), 34% of the divorced women with custody ascribed their difficulties in finding employment to the absence of child-care services (1979, p. 44).

9. In a survey on child care conducted by *Family Circle Magazine* (February 1979), the data, based on the responses of 10,000 working mothers, revealed that nearly 30% of children ages six through 13 were left home alone after school or with siblings (Kirchheimer, 1979a, p. B1).

10. The 1975 Child Care Consumer Study conducted by the Office of Child Development also reveals that middle-class families favor the use of babysitters over institutional care (Unco, 1975, V2, pp. 5-12).

11. Federal subsidy of day-care services has focused on low-income families, either relating to the employment of welfare mothers or efforts to eliminate child development deficiencies purportedly caused by inadequate family environments.

12. In the Connecticut survey (see footnote 5), financial difficulties caused 15% of the women who were awarded the family home subsequently to sell their residences (1979, p. 19).

13. The only area in which property division appears to favor women is in the awarding of family residences. This seems to be related directly to the fact that the majority of women are awarded child custody.

14. Indeed, the trend shows no sign of abating. Apartments renting in 1975 for $350 are $475-$550 in 1980.

15. Noting that female-headed families frequently lived in less desirable areas of town than did two-parent families, Roncek, Bell, and Choldin called for more research to determine whether this pattern was a product of insufficient economic resources or discriminatory practices (1980, p. 168).

16. Homosexuals, unmarried couples, and even single men reportedly suffer from similar injustices (Christensen, 1976).

17. This figure is significantly lower than the percentage reported by the Commercial Credit Corporation. Their tabulations revealed that one out of two respondents did not comprehend the computation of credit interest rates (McCormack, 1978).

18. Some have put forth an alternative recommendation, suggesting that paternal custody be given preference by the courts in light of the higher economic status of male-headed families. This is by no means a novel idea. Prior to the late 19th century fathers had almost exclusive rights to custody on the basis of their economic superiority.

19. "Equal" distribution is not to be confused with "equitable" distribution. Opponents of the latter (e.g., NOW) argue that in states in which this concept has been enacted into law, the woman's share of the marital assets has been no higher than 33% and at times as low as 10 to 20% (Herman, 1980, p. B2). Moreover, these states generally fail to take into account the increased financial needs of custodial mothers.

20. The question of whether the Employee Retirement Income Security Act (ERISA) of 1974 prohibits assignability of pensions is in dispute. The solution to some is to compensate for the wife's (or husband's) pension assets through the allocation of other assets. Nonetheless, most state courts seem to agree that pensions can be garnished to enforce payment of support obligations (Van Gelder, 1979).

21. In the Connecticut survey (see footnote 5), 59% of the women lost life insurance coverage, 36% lost pension rights, and 23% lost social security benefits after divorce (1979), p. 5; see also Lipson, 1980).

22. In the Connecticut survey 63% of the women not only lost health insurance after divorce, but the majority had to pay higher rates for less extensive individual policy coverage (1979, p. 41; see also Lipson, 1980). Some women's groups have suggested that state insurance commissions investigate ways in which divorced wives may continue to be covered on their husband's group health insurance policy.

SHEILA ATTEMPTS
TO BEGIN ANEW:
AN ECONOMIC PROFILE

Sheila Ash—age 33, mother of two children, marital status separated, employment status homemaker—was charged with the tasks of looking for a job, locating child-care services, exploring new places to live, and evaluating as far as possible her chances for establishing credit. The purpose of this assignment was *not* to ascertain whether separated and divorced women could achieve these goals; I already knew they could and did. Yet, I also knew that most had encountered difficulties and obstacles along the way. On paper Sheila had many of the same problems and liabilities related by respondents. The crucial distinction was that Sheila, unlike those whose experiences she was to simulate, did not have to cope with the emotional and even practical aspects of a marital dissolution. Given this advantage, the key question was whether it would be easier for Sheila to achieve these objectives. It was thus the differences and similarities between Sheila's systematically planned exploration and those of respondents that I sought to compare. Following the format of Chapter 3, each of these investigations will be reviewed separately.

SHEILA LOOKS FOR A JOB

To an employer there were both positive and negative sides to Sheila's educational and professional history (see Appendix D for her résumé). In her favor was a B.A. degree with honors from a prestigious university, excellent references from employers, evidence of administrative experience in volunteer organizations (e.g., project coordination and supervisory responsibility), and demonstrated artistic ability. But there were also minuses: Sheila had two young children, she had not held a full-time paid position in seven years,[1] and her work experience was primarily in the field of education,[2] a profession in which the supply of applicants far outnumbered the demand. What's more, the employment outlook was dismal —declining birth rates and rising taxes had contributed to the consolidation of schools and layoffs of personnel. While there had been some increase in the number of day-care and after-school centers in response to the rising percentage of mothers entering the work force, the growth in this area had not appreciably improved the employment opportunities in the field.[3] Lastly, the decision to seek part-time employment might have been an additional barrier not encountered by others with a similar educational and employment profile.[4] Although halfway through the job search, without any possibility of employment in sight, Sheila did apply for full-time positions, we cannot dismiss the possibility that her initial interest in part-time work influenced the negative outcome of her employment search.

Sheila applied by mail for 35 jobs, sending her résumé and a cover letter to firms advertising in the classified section of newspapers, as well as to educational publishing companies, research firms, nursery schools, and day-care centers (see Appendix E for sample letter). All the letters stated that Sheila was seeking to resume her professional career and that she had special skills and abilities to meet that prospective employer's requirements; none mentioned her marital status. Of the 35 letters, nine letters of rejection were received. To the other 26, no responses were made. Not one employer asked for an interview. Most responses were standard rejection letters indicating nothing more positive than putting the letter on file for future reference (see Appendix F). The most helpful letter Sheila received was from a publishing company whose personnel director provided suggestions for redirecting her job search (see Appendix G). In addition to solicited and unsolicited letters of inquiry, Sheila contacted special counseling and placement services for women, public and private employment agencies and training centers, and personnel offices of major companies.

Sheila spoke to only two employers; both were telephone conversations in which she had responded to newspaper advertisements inviting applicants to telephone for information. The first position was for a director of adult programs for a community organization advertised by the 'Women's Educational and Business Center.' The conversation proceeded as follows:

"My name is Sheila Ash, and I am calling about the position for a director of adult programs."

"Tell me something about your background, Mrs. Ash."

"I have a B.A. in education and English literature from the University of Michigan. I have taught in both public and nursery schools. I have extensive experience as a project coordinator and staff supervisor for volunteer organizations. I have also tutored children with learning disabilities and helped plan a center for school dropouts."

"Have you ever held a position as a salaried administrator?"

"Well, no," I hedged, "but I have directed projects with substantial operating budgets."

"We are looking for an individual with a background in *paid* administrative positions."

"I can supply references verifying my administrative abilities."

"We recognize the possibility of your having the potential for this community project, but more credence could be given to your application if you had been paid for your previous work."

"Can you tell me something about the organization for which you need a director?" I asked, trying to redirect the conversation.

"It is a charity organization with a large budget. They need someone with *proven* ability to manage the staff of volunteers and to organize and direct a new project on adult education."

"This is exactly what I have done! I'm sure it would be mutually beneficial if we could talk about this position further in person."

"Mrs. Ash, or is it Miss?"

"Mrs."

"Mrs. Ash, do you have any children?"

"Two, but—"

"How old are they?" interrupted the interviewer.

"Two-and-a-half, and five-and-a-half, but. . . ."

"Mrs. Ash, the job pays around $10,000 a year; it is full-time, plus some evenings and Saturdays. You will also need a car, since it is in the _____ area. [None of this information had been in the advertisement.] Maybe since you have children and are a past teacher, you will find the salary too low and the trip too long."

"I would still appreciate the chance to talk to you in person."

"Leave me your name and telephone number and send me your résumé. [After all the "Mrs. Ashes," it seemed as if she should know my name.] I'll call you if we think an interview would be helpful. Thank you for your interest."

Postscript number one—Sheila never heard from the woman, although she did send a résumé along with a letter requesting an interview. Obviously she had been rejected as a prospective candidate as soon as the woman learned that Sheila's administrative experience was limited to volunteer work. In all probability, the rest of the questions and comments (on marital status, children, length of trip, and low salary) was used primarily to discourage Sheila and terminate the interview. But the very fact that such a conversation could have taken place and particularly with a representative from *this* women's center was disturbing. Although the Women's Educational and Business Center is a fictitious name, the real organization has a reputation for being a forceful and innovative advocate for women. They have long directed attention to the employment needs of working mothers, recommending, before it was fashionable, job sharing, flexible work hours, and more part-time positions. In addition, the center has publicly supported the accreditation of volunteer work as employment experience.

Perhaps we should not be too hasty in rendering judgment. The interviewer was only one person, not the entire staff and not the center. And it can be argued that if she had been more abrupt, asking only for a name, telephone number, and a résumé, this critique would never have appeared in print. Also, there may have been other applicants more qualified than Sheila. While both of these arguments have merit, they neither excuse nor explain the tenor and content of the conversation. One cannot help but wonder how other employers would react to an applicant like Sheila if a women's advocacy center provided this kind of reception.

Sheila's second telephone "interview" was with the director of a non-sectarian nursery school housed in a Westside synagogue. Their advertisement for a part-time teacher had appeared in the Sunday classifieds. The following conversation took place on a Monday morning.

"My name is Sheila Ash. I am calling about the position for a nursery school teacher."

"I'm 'Marian Douglas,' the director. We are looking for an experienced teacher to be a member of a two-person team, each of whom would have equal responsibility for the educational and recreational program of 22 children, ages three through five. Is it Miss or Mrs. Ash?"

"Mrs." (This seemed to be a standard question.)

"How many years have you been teaching, Mrs. Ash?"

"I taught second grade for one year and at 'Les Enfants' Nursery School for three years."

"Are you still teaching at Les Enfants?"

"No, but I have worked with children as a learning disabilities tutor and in preschool play groups, as well as in special community projects. I am also an amateur artist and have many ideas for arts and crafts activities."

"How long has it been since you left Les Enfants?"

"Seven years, but since then. . . ."

"Did you stop work to raise a family?" she interrupted.

"I don't think I ever thought I had stopped working. I was paid for tutoring and always viewed my volunteer jobs as work."

"How old are your children?" (I hadn't said I had children. Was this another standard question?)

"Two-and-a-half and five-and-a-half."

"You will understand, I'm sure, that we would prefer someone who has not interrupted her career to raise a family."

"No, I do not understand, Miss, or is it Mrs., Douglas?" (I was becoming a bit testy.)

"Miss Douglas," she replied, ignoring the first part of my response. "The job, Mrs. Ash, pays $4,000 a year for five mornings a week from nine to 12."

"It sounds interesting. I enjoy team teaching, and the hours and salary pose no problems." [I was trying to recoup any losses caused by my previous display of sarcasm.] When can I come in for an interview?'' (the positive, semiaggressive approach)

''Mrs. Ash, we will consider your application if the 20 scheduled interviewees do not meet our requirements.''

''Twenty interviewees! It is 9:30 in the morning; the ad *first* appeared in yesterday's paper, and yesterday was a Sunday.''

''The job market is a tight one. Send me your résumé, and we'll see what we can do.'' (It seemed as if ''I's'' became ''we's'' whenever the response was negative. Was this another trick of the trade?)

Postscript number two—Sheila was never interviewed nor was the receipt of her résumé acknowledged either by Miss Douglas or the elusive ''we's.''

Here was a job for which Sheila appeared qualified. Her recent experience with learning-disabled children and preschoolers as well as her artistic abilities were clearly relevant to the position. Even being a mother of two small children might be regarded as a plus. Still, the seven-year lapse of employment seemed to be an obstacle she could not talk away. Or, were there other reasons, hinted at but never mentioned, which disqualified her candidacy? Why, for instance, was she questioned on her marital status, on whether she had children, and on their ages? While a man, married or single, is a ''Mr.,'' a woman, irrespective of the trendy ''Ms.,'' still has to contend with the titles of Miss or Mrs. And children? Would any employer refuse to hire a man because he was a father? Unlikely! The idea of more men becoming single parents elicited revengeful thoughts. Would employers then worry that these fathers would miss days of work due to runny noses and temperatures? Or, better yet, would they then think that their responsibility (indeed, their place) was to be home with their kids, nurturing and caring for them? It was doubtful that even George Orwell would have resorted to such far-out forecasts. Yet, comforting as it may be, fantasizing does not produce jobs. And so Sheila decided to investigate agencies specializing in job counseling and placement for women.

One agency, 'Greater Opportunities for Women,' reviewed Sheila's résumé and advised her to personalize each cover letter, highlighting experiences which pertained most directly to the job for which she was applying. (Something she had been doing all along.) They could not, however, find a job for her or even arrange an interview. Next Sheila went to the Governor's Office on the 'Status of Women,' where she was informed that the current job freeze had limited extension of affirmative action policies. Finally, Sheila contacted the 'Jewish Vocational Service' for their free screening, counseling, and placement services. Alas, none of the three agencies helped Sheila to secure a job! She had been screened and counseled but not ''placed.''

All the stories Sheila had read and heard suggested that her situation was far from unique. Still she was not comforted. She had done more and known more than the typical job seeker. None of the interviewees had approached these "special" employment services, the ones that the media had touted as a major triumph for women. Forty-seven percent had utilized friends for job information, and 22% had relied upon classified advertisements. Maybe instead of trying to chart a new course, she too should rely on the obvious; in short, ask friends for advice. From these inquiries she received four leads, followed by four rejections—so much for the "old girl" network!

Employment agencies were another resource to be checked. They were scarcely encouraging. An economic recession, Sheila's teaching background, and her interest in part-time employment were, as they explained, all part of her problem.

There are not many jobs around. Those in your field we do not even handle, and, as you probably know, for every teaching, social work, or librarian position, there are as many as 200 applicants, maybe more. There are secretarial positions, but the better paying ones require stenography and excellent typing skills, not to mention previous experience. There are also some receptionist jobs you might get, as you are attractive and young. But I worry, and so will they, that because you are overqualified, you'll quit as soon as you find something better. Management training programs are another possibility, although your education and experience are not really what they look for. But you might be lucky. Try some of the insurance companies, banks, and utilities. But remember, these are full-time jobs.

Sheila followed the woman's advice. In one company after another, sitting in chairs in the far corners of personnel offices, she filled out long application forms. Politeness abounded. She was thanked countless times for her interest in the company, but as for any interviews or offers, there was none.

Under the advisement of another employment office, Sheila visited the Westside CETA office. CETA is a federally sponsored program for the unemployed who meet their eligibility criteria. To applicants who are handicapped, minority group members, Vietnam veterans, welfare recipients, people over 45 or under 22, school dropouts, persons with limited English speaking skills, previous manpower trainees, female heads of households, or workers displaced by technological advances, they offer training programs followed by employment in cosponsoring companies with salaries ranging in 1975 from $3.00 to $3.75 an hour.

Two of the eligibility requirements seemed to fit Sheila's position. She was a female head of a household, although she had no proof of being either separated or divorced, and she was unemployed. In addition, it could be argued, she thought, that the employment problems in the educational sector classified her as a technologically displaced worker.[5] But the only job which Sheila would even remotely consider out of the 38 listings was a position for an office clerk. The other jobs (e.g., offset pressman, electronic assembler, spray painter, carpet layer) were plainly unsuitable and definitely unappealing to her, despite any latent feministic or Thespian leanings.

Of the experiences Sheila had had in looking for a job, this was the most discouraging. Not only had she been reduced to a classification (e.g., female head of household, unemployed), but all her training and education seemed useless. Education, long the dream of the aspiring, no longer held the promise of upward mobility. Instead it disqualified her from jobs for which she was considered overtrained and failed to gain her access to others for which there were already too many like her waiting in line. Was it a woman's problem? She had read that 96% of all jobs paying $15,000 or more were held by white men. The rest of the population had to fight over the remaining 4% (Janney, 1975). But what about $10,000 positions? There didn't seem to be many of these either, at least not for Sheila, at least not yet.

Refusing to give up, Sheila telephoned each of the so-called "executive search" agencies which specialize in the recruitment and placement of professionals. While Sheila knew that these companies did not place teachers, she hoped that they might have contacts with educational consulting and research firms. To these agencies, however, Sheila was not a "professional." They were polite, but the responses were monotonously the same: "Try a different kind of agency, one that specializes in entry-level management positions, read the newspapers, and apply at industrial personnel offices."

Too qualified for programs like CETA and unqualified for professional placement services, Sheila aimed for a middle ground, visiting the state division of employment in Westside. According to their advertisements, these agencies offered employment testing, counseling, training, and referral services. To Sheila they offered nothing except another apology. Four hundred thousand people in the state were unemployed, they explained, far more than the number of openings in their job bank, far more than their personnel could process, let alone help. Regardless of the state's Job Opportunity Rights Act of 1975, a statutory enactment recognizing the right of every unemployed individual to a job befitting his or her educational and physical ability and development, the state was ill equipped to carry out this mandate. It had neither the monetary nor manpower resources to provide adequate services for the unemployed, to generate new public jobs, or to convince private industry to partake in this venture. As a result the state's record for reducing unemployment and in particular the credibility of its employment division have been attacked by state legislators. While well-meaning officials debate the state's problem in special committees and organize special commissions, Sheila and other residents are forced to go it alone.

The city of Westside's manpower division was the last of the employment resources on Sheila's list. Informal questioning of Westside officials had revealed two interesting facts about the city's employment policies: The city sponsored job banks for adolescents and the elderly and supported, at least in theory, preferential hiring policies for residents. In addition, much attention had been recently drawn to affirmative action hiring as residents and local officials took the city to task for failing to recruit and employ more women and minorities. Sheila resolved to give the city an opportunity to further this goal. The problem, however, was that there was no opening for which to be a candidate, affirmative action or otherwise. Perhaps at a later date, she was told, the city government would be able to create and/or advocate for new employment opportunities for single-parent women or women in general within the community social system. Meanwhile, despite positive indicators of the city's sensitivity to the needs of specific resident groups (e.g., youth, elderly), without additional revenues the city relied on the local CETA program[6] as its major offering to the increasing population of unemployed, female heads of households.

In summary, Sheila's survey of employment services and her job search revealed the paucity of resources available to unemployed women as well as the special problems of displaced homemakers. While she continued to scrutinize advertisements for employment and submit letters of application for part- and full-time positions, her success rate did not improve. Telephone calls to employers who had not answered her inquiries produced only excuses. "There were so many applicants that we were unable to respond to every one." Or, "We never received your letter, please send us another one." Or, "We have no record of your application, but the job has already been filled; we are sorry." If one could package and sell apologies, Sheila would be rich, but as for obtaining an interview, not to mention a job offer, Sheila had no luck. She remained unemployed.

SHEILA INVESTIGATES CHILD-CARE SERVICES

Because of the respondents' poor rating of Westside's child-care resources, Sheila was to canvass the community, identifying and investigating child-care options. From the outset the diffuseness of Westside's child-care delivery system impeded the exploration.

In 1975 there were two full-time day-care centers and three after-school centers. Of the five, three provided transportation, but only for "special cases." Indeed, the word "exceptional" would be a term more apt than "special," considering that the "cases" cited by the directors pertained exclusively to handicapped children.

There were also 32 part-time nursery schools with morning and/or afternoon sessions. While tuitions for full-time registration (three hours per day, Monday through Friday, September through June) ranged from a low of $350 to a high of $1,250, predictably, the quality of the programs did not always correlate positively with the fees. (Alternatively, in 1975 full-time day care averaged $40 a week.) Unable to inspect all 32 schools, Sheila, at times accompanied by 'Laurie,' selected 12, choosing representatives from each price category. The first visit was to a school housed in the basement of a local church. Laurie and I were greeted warmly by 'Mrs. Downey,' the teacher of the three-year-old group. (The four-year-olds and their teacher were in an adjacent room.)

"Mrs. Ash, I'm so glad you could come with Laurie. Feel free to participate or walk around. Laurie, I'm sure, will want to play a game with us." (Laurie did.)

After the game Mrs. Downey left an assistant teacher in charge of the children and came over to talk to me.

"Laurie is a delight," she said enthusiastically. "She is very mature and certainly adjusts easily to a new place and new people. I think she would be very happy here and a real asset to our program."

"Mrs. Downey, Laurie is two and a half. Although I was told on the telephone that you only accept three- and four-year-olds, I thought that if you met my daughter you might reconsider, since she is, as you have observed, a mature and well-adjusted child."

"Oh, Mrs. Ash, I wish you had told me this before. I would have been more careful about pushing Laurie into a new group. You know there is a world of difference between being two and a half and three. She will tire more easily and will need and want to be with her mother more than the others."

"But you have already observed her and commented favorably on her interaction with the other children and, in fact, on her maturity. Now, you tell me that she is too young!"

"You see, Mrs. Ash, you are here. If you left, things would change radically."

"Shall I leave for a while so that we can see what happens?"

"Please don't! We simply cannot accept a two-and-a-half-year-old. Try us next year."

It seemed incomprehensible to me that a child who had been regarded as a mature three-year-old suddenly became immature when it was revealed that she was two and a half. If anything, her maturity quotient should have risen. Perhaps, I thought, other schools would be more flexible. But my optimism faded as the same scenario was replayed at four more nursery schools. Admittedly, in one of these schools, my daughter's candidacy became questionable when she did not respond to the alias of Laurie. The director reported the incident in the following way:

"Laurie confuses me," she confided. "For the entire activity she played beautifully, but during the cleanup, when I called her name, she did not respond until I went over and told her what to do. Maybe she was just engrossed in the game, or maybe it is just that this is her first time here.''

It was obvious to me, having witnessed Laurie's behavior, that my daughter had forgotten her pseudonym and as a result failed to heed the woman's instructions. But the director did not know this, nor could I explain it to her. One hour later, with no additional mishaps, I did inform her of Laurie's age. She promptly rejected Laurie's application. The reason, of course, was her immaturity.

"Mrs. Ash, as you noticed, Laurie had difficulty following directions. Children of this age cannot be pushed to compete with three-year-olds, even if they are bright and capable. Let her mature naturally.'' The authority in her voice and the seriousness of her demeanor suggested that her decision was not to be countered.

Not only was Laurie rejected by five nursery schools, but in three of the five the attendance for even the three-year-olds was limited to three-day weekly sessions. In two other nursery schools I managed to convince the directors to admit Laurie on a provisional basis, a maturity trial of sorts. Such victories have a hollow ring. Besides the fact that placing a child on probation has negative connotations, too much might hinge on the outcome. If a parent is dependent upon the school for coverage during working hours, a dismissal might result in the loss of days at work, even the loss of employment. Nor can we dismiss the guilt syndrome which might arise out of this situation. Even if you are relatively confident that your child is mature enough to handle the curriculum, or even if you believe that the rules are capricious and outdated, there may still be, deep down, the nagging sensation that you have cast your child away at too tender an age.

Of the remaining five schools, only two provided coverage for two-and-a-half-year-olds. I considered neither school acceptable. I believe my evaluation was based on objective criteria—pupil-teacher ratio, the nature of the physical plant, equipment, and materials, and the quality of the program. But it is remotely possible that I viewed these schools with a jaundiced eye. After ten directors had told me that my child was too young to be "sent away" to school, were not those who accepted her of a lesser ilk?

Nevertheless, these were not the only child-care resources in Westside. There were also family day-care providers who offered child-care coverage in their homes. In 1975 there were an estimated 50 unlicensed family day-care providers, as compared to 15 state-licensed providers in Westside. (My estimate of the former would be much higher.)[7] One unlicensed home was well known to me. While I have never been inside the house and therefore have no knowledge of the facilities, I have observed some blatant examples of laxness. On one occasion, a child, who had been instructed to stay in the playground until the woman returned, appeared at my door for help. Tearfully, she explained that she could not find her babysitter. I brought her over to 'Mrs. Leslie' (a good guess, since the child knew neither her name nor address).

"Kids," she pronounced, "just don't listen anymore. I told her to wait for me!"

"I guess she just got tired of the playground," I responded.

"Why? She's only been there an hour and a half," she replied indignantly.

There was no point in informing her that one and a half hours can seem like a very long time to a child or that she was being paid to take care of the child, not to send her off. And so I left. But on another occasion, a child, who was supposed to be under her supervision, played all afternoon with my son without informing Mrs. Leslie of his whereabouts. When I suggested that he call Mrs. Leslie, he responded that she never worries. He was right! Upon walking him back three hours later, she remarked that she had wondered where he was, but added quickly that he was an independent child. This independent child was five years old!

I have heard stories about other unlicensed day-care providers in the neighborhood—tales of children being left in the care of an elementary-school child while the "provider" did errands; of children who "ran away" without being missed, only to be found by the parent(s), waiting in the dark in front of their own homes; and of children whose injuries appeared to have been related to negligent care. Although these stories are merely hearsay, articles in the local papers on unlicensed providers who take in as many as 20 children a day (the state permits a maximum of six, including the providers' children) and "watch them watch TV" suggest that Mrs. Leslie and her compatriots are far from atypical (Auerback, 1975, pp. 1, 10).

Babysitters, another alternative form of day care, offer advantages not provided by many child-care facilities. Separate arrangements do not have to be made for those with preschool and school-age children; work schedules do not have to follow the school calendar or hours, thereby eliminating the problem of coverage during school vacations, snow days, and before and after school, particularly for children attending the half-day sessions (and even the three-day week) of many nursery schools; transportation is no longer a consideration (albeit the parent may have to transport the sitter); and work does not have to be missed when a child is sick. Further, some babysitters will perform household chores, take children to lessons and doctors' appointments, and, in general, serve as a surrogate parent.

Nevertheless, babysitters are not necessarily a panacea for all child-care concerns. Unreliable sitters can lead to frequent absenteeism at work, not to mention the effect on job performance and morale; competency may be difficult to assess, especially for infants who are unable to communicate any information to the parent; and hourly fees are likely to be higher than that of child-care centers, although for families with more than one child a savings may be appreciated.[8] In addition, babysitters are not easy to find, particularly if the parent is selective. Any perusal of the metropolitan Sunday classifieds, as well as Westside weekly papers, demonstrates that the demand for these services far exceeds the supply. (Recent projections forewarn of a decreasing supply of in-home caretakers along with a spiraling increase in the fees charged [Hofferth, 1979].) Consequently, placement agencies for child care and/or household help provide a valuable service. Yet, unless the parent is interested in and can afford live-in help, there are few such agencies. (And even in the case of live-in help, there are not enough agencies to meet local needs.) To be specific, in 1975 Sheila found two sitting services for the Westside area: One specialized in infant care and charged $7 an hour; the second charged $2.35 an hour with a four-hour minimum requirement; additional costs were assessed for carfare and for more than two children. (Moreover, sitters were not allowed to dispense medication to children even under a doctor's orders.) While the woman that Sheila spoke to at the less expensive agency assured her that a long-term arrangement was a possibility, she made no guarantees.

"I am reasonably confident that we can provide a sitter every day once we know your working hours. But many of our sitters go to school or work elsewhere and do not want full-time jobs."

"Does this mean that I would have a different sitter every day?"

"Perhaps not every day, but there would probably be several serving you."

"That would be confusing for me and for the children."

"Not really. We might be able to get one person for three days a week and another for two days. This would cut down on the confusion considerably," replied the woman.

"If this becomes a long-term arrangement, is the hourly fee reduced?"

"After six months, you and the sitters can work out your own arrangement."

"On a daily basis, how much notice do you need in order to find a sitter for me?" (I was thinking of respondents interested primarily in short-term child care.)

"Twenty-four hours, sometimes less and sometimes more."

Because these referral services have to contend with a fluctuating supply and demand ratio, they often operate on a day-to-day basis, unable to make firm commitments either to their employees or clients. Obviously, the working parent in need of a long-term commitment cannot depend upon probabilities or possibilities. Consequently, they most frequently use these services for supplementary child care when regular babysitters are absent and for temporary coverage while they are looking for more permanent arrangements. In contrast, for those who employ sitters on a sporadic basis, such agencies can be an important and time-saving resource. They screen employees, conducting interviews and checking references; at times they even match sitters to clients (e.g., as to age preferences [a young, agile sitter or a grandmotherly type], compatibility of interests of sitter and children, experience with children of different ages).

In summarizing Sheila's research on Westside's child-care resources, we can conclude that the most salient feature of the "system" is the predominance of part-time nursery schools. This is hardly a startling phenomenon, considering that the middle classes (and Westside is decidedly a middle-class community) are the principal users of nursery schools (Woolsey, 1977). Alternatively, full-time day care is provided to a minority of the population in a few centers sponsored by community service organizations and in unlicensed and licensed family day-care homes; the majority who use full-time day care depend upon babysitters in their own homes and, where available, after-school centers.

The above description, however, was based on data collected in 1975, the year of Sheila's initial survey of Westside's child-care system. A follow-up survey in 1978-1979 revealed evidence of some shift in the direction recommended by respondents. There was one additional day-care center for preschoolers, as well as a new facility for full-time infant/toddler care (three months to two and a half years). Moreover, it appeared that the nursery schools were gradually becoming more responsive to parental needs for longer hours. The change has been far from dramatic, with but one school offering coverage from 8:00 to 6:00 and five others extending their hours to anywhere from 1:00 to 4:00 for daily or thrice-weekly sessions. Another improvement has been in the area of transportation, with 13 nursery schools now either including transportation in their tuition or arranging private contracts for parents. Similarly, day-care centers have lowered their transportation prerequisites, no longer mandating that children qualify as "special cases."

By far the most promising change has been for school-age children: Two private child-care centers offer after-school coverage, and 11 of the 20 elementary schools provide free space to parent groups for after-school programs. Unfortunately, not all of the public schools have space for these programs, and in schools where they are housed, waiting lists are the norm. Further, parent groups have to plan, implement, and oversee these programs, a collaborative venture that requires expertise as well as time, effort, and money. While some assistance on the procedural and operational technicalities of setting up after-school centers is available to Westside parents through the city's Office for Children, the real credit for the advancement in after-school care must be attributed to independent parent groups, not to public or private organizations. Even the school system's willingness to furnish space for these programs has, in part, a self-serving motive. By increasing the utilization of classrooms, schools with declining enrollment can better ward off pressure to close their schools. Concurrently, schools that house such programs have increased their enrollment as working parents selectively buy or rent housing near these facilities. Without cost to the system, building utilization increases and community pressure to close schools and increase the number of school hours decreases.

Meanwhile, formalized day care for preschoolers, the population evidencing the highest increase in working mothers, remains almost unchanged in Westside during this four-year period. While 37% of preschool children (or 6.4 million children) had working mothers in 1977 (Grossman, 1977), Hofferth (1979) projects that the percentage will climb to 45% (or 10.4 million children) by 1990 (pp. 650-651). Moreover, the figures for female-headed households, a population noticeably increasing in Westside, are even higher (see pp. 77-78). The addition of one center for toddlers and infants and expanded service in a small percentage of the city's nursery schools can scarcely be considered a satisfactory response to the employment statistics reported by demographic studies.

In the 1977 publication of the Population Reference Bureau, Glick and Norton hypothesized that many very young children might be cared for by grandmothers, but in Westside this is an uncommon practice. (Indeed, the high mobility of the American population suggests that this theory may be a specious one for the country in general.) While there is evidence of an increased use of family day care in Westside, in 1978-1979 babysitters continued to be the preferred caretakers for preschool children of working mothers.[9] Yet there was only one more referral agency in 1979 than there was in 1975. Without any funding, this new agency, operating out of a private residence, is dependent upon volunteer help.[10] Personal contacts and advertising thus remain the principal means for locating sitters. In Sheila's investigation, services and agencies for the elderly were contacted as possible resources for sitters. The director of one agency offered little encouragement.

It is possible to find a woman who would like to work a few days a week to supplement her social security. But it is almost impossible to find one who wants a full-time job. Even those who will work, say, two days a week rarely want to commit themselves to an 8:30 to 5:30 day. We can best help those whose working hours are flexible. For example, we were able to help one woman who wanted someone to care for her infant two days a week while she worked at home.

Since Westside has no drop-off sitting service, perhaps employment of the elderly might best help those who need a few hours a week of time off from child-care responsibilities. But even for these mothers the probability of finding an elderly caretaker is not high.

Furthermore, many respondents were not even aware of the child-care options that existed in Westside. Between 1975 and 1979 some improvement in the dissemination of such information was discernible. The Office for Children issued an updated guide to child care in Westside; a local newspaper, which first published a special section on child care in 1974, continued to revise and print this section annually until 1979, when it closed its operation; and in 1978 the city printed a resource guide, the first extensive compilation of information on Westside since 1974, when the Chamber of Commerce sold a modest pamphlet for $1.50. (The new guide costs residents $1.00).[11] In addition, the new referral agency provides information on institutional as well as noninstitutional child-care services.

Nevertheless, consumer use of these sources is limited by inadequate publicity. Residents have to know about, call, and pick up the Office for Children's booklet and the city's guide. With respect to the latter, I tried to obtain a copy by requesting that the city office mail one to me upon receipt of a check and a self-addressed, stamped envelope. I was told that since they did not know the postal costs, the only way to obtain a copy was to pick one up between 9:00 and 5:00 on weekdays. There has been no effort to distribute booklets either to City Hall or local libraries, two locations which would increase the visibility and accessibility of the publication. (Yet, the *New York Times Book Review* is sold in all public libraries.)

Although Westside considers itself a progressive community, sensitive to the needs of its residents, its child-care delivery system has not kept pace with evolving social norms and practices, particularly with respect to infant care; neither, for that matter, has the public school system, whose elementary schools still operate with a two-day release time of 1:00. What we find is a diffuse and fragmented child-care system, befitting an era when preschool and after-school education was primarily for enrichment and care for infants was provided by mothers or relatives (Beck, 1973; Rothman, 1973; Woolsey, 1977). Why the outcry from the residents has not been greater can be understood by those familiar with the mores of suburban living. People complain to each other, but maintain the attitude that "you can't fight city hall." With respect to day care, a different dynamic is also at play. Parents are reticent to speak out publicly about their need for child care, viewing it almost as a proclamation that they have abdicated their responsibility as caretakers. It is much easier, emotionally and socially, to create one's own solutions—to form a parent-run after-school center, to hire a babysitter, or even to leave children at home by themselves.

It does appear, though, that change will occur in Westside, albeit it may be gradual and may proceed along established pathways. Increased efforts to generate information on community child-care resources are already underway. If effective methods for disseminating these publications have not yet been devised, at least community agencies have demonstrated their awareness of the need for such information. Even if one agency does eventually assume the responsibility for compiling and disseminating child-care data, the centralization of information would not necessarily increase the use of child-care facilities. What it does address are problems caused by inadequate or inaccurate consumer knowledge bases; increased resource visibility helps individuals make informed decisions based on a realistic appraisal of existing options. In no way does this affect the provision of child-care services in the community. Therefore it does not appreciably impact on the working mother's need for child coverage, nor does it provide "crisis" services to alleviate some of the responsibilities and burdens of single parents.[12]

Ironically, salvation for working parents may come from the most troublesome problem confronting the Westside School System—declining enrollment. In the superintendent's opening of the 1978-1979 year address, he alluded to the possibility of a major change, that of lowering the school eligibility age to four years old. Although four elementary schools, both high schools, and one junior high school house nursery schools, a lower admission age for school attendance is a much more significant and different approach. While one can question whether nursery schools and day-care providers will react by concomitantly expanding the number and kinds of services they offer or by launching a campaign against the proposal, irrespective of the response, it is likely that the city will move in the direction of providing educational services to new resident populations. The preschool and adult populations (for the latter group some kind of reaction from the city's postsecondary institutions can be expected) present the most obvious sources for increasing school enrollment. The facts are simple: The City can no longer defend the operation of 20 elementary schools, five junior high schools, and two high schools in the face of declining birth rates and citizen demands for lower taxes. (In 1980-1981 two more elementary schools were closed, and in 1981-1982 a junior high school and at least one elementary school are scheduled to be closed.) One strategy, as noted by the superintendent, is to redefine educational goals and programs in order to service more of the citizenry; another is to use existing plants for public and private projects, one of which could be the provision of full-time day care. It is not beyond possibility that the school system will move in both directions simultaneously, endeavoring, as part of its reorganization, to meet the child-care needs of residents. Certainly the incentive for innovation is present; the direction and nature of the change effort, if there is to be one, remain to be seen.

SHEILA CONSIDERS MOVING

If in 1979 there were 1.2 million divorces in the United States (U.S. National Center for Health Statistics, November 13, 1980d, p. 9), then there were at least 1.2 million people who had to relocate. If we add to this number those among the separated who moved and divorced families in which both spouses moved, the figures on relocation become overwhelming. Despite these high percentages, there is hardly mention in the literature on separation and divorce of the dilemmas associated with moving. Yet over and over women respondents stressed the difficulties of finding suitable places to live, citing financial constraints and discrimination in the housing market as major obstacles.[13] And over and over men emphasized the emotional aspects of leaving their homes. Perhaps this was because the men had less choice. Irrespective of the reasons, the majority of the women in this study who moved said they wanted to, while the reverse was true for the majority of the men, who claimed that they had no alternative. Thus to Sheila, too, befell the task of seeking a different residence. Since the most common relocation pattern reported by women participants was the move from ownership of a single-family house to residency in a two-family or multifamily unit, Sheila concentrated on rental properties. Only cursory attention was directed toward buying a house, and then only as it related to the issue of women's creditworthiness.

Sheila began by telephoning three realty agencies who purported not only to "specialize" in rentals but also to "guarantee" the client a satisfactory apartment within a specified price range and locale. The price of the guaranteed service ranged from $20 to $30 in 1975. The following conversation is recorded from Sheila's first encounter with one of these agencies.

"I'm calling in reference to your advertisement for a three-bedroom luxury apartment in Westside for $250 a month."

"The apartment has been rented, but we have many others."

"Are they similar to the one you advertised?"

"That one was a steal, but we have many to choose from."

"Could you describe the ones you have in that price range?"

"Not over the telephone. We charge a $25 fee, payable in full before we can open our listings. But for this token fee we guarantee that a reasonably priced apartment will be found in the area where you want to live," explained the agent.

"What does reasonable mean?"

"After you pay the fee we can discuss that."

"Before I waste your time and mine, it seems logical that we both agree on what is a reasonable rent. I may not be able to afford your listings."

"Listen lady, I don't have time to play games," he replied angrily.

"I said we would guarantee that you find an apartment. What more could you ask for?"

I could think of a lot more—old-fashioned courtesy or straightforward answers—but instead I just thanked him for his time. He had not questioned me about my marital status, number of children, or even my name. The next agency, a $30 variety, did.

"I'm calling about your advertisement for multiple listings of two- and three-bedroom apartments in Westside."

"Your name, please," asked the agent.

"Sheila Ash."

"Mrs. Ash, when do you and your husband need this apartment?"

"There is no husband," I responded, wondering if this was an artful attempt to determine Sheila's marital status. "As for the occupancy date, I can be fairly flexible."

"Do you have children and pets?"

"I have two children and a dog."

"How old are the children?"

"They are two and a half and five and a half; but why are you asking these questions? [Naturally I was well aware of his reasons.] Shouldn't you be asking me what kind of apartment I want and how much I can afford?"

"I'll ask that too, but if there are old people in the building, the landlord won't rent to anyone with young children. Others have different reasons for objecting. Landlords can be funny people. I'm not a landlord; I'm only an agent."

"Do you have any nice two- or three-bedroom apartments in Westside for a family like mine for around $300 a month?"[14]

"I'm sure we'll find one. First I'll pick you up and take you to our office. After you pay our fee we can begin to set up appointments for you."

"Is my $30 refunded if I don't find something I like?"

"The fee is nonrefundable, but we *guarantee* satisfaction. When can I pick you up?"

"That won't be necessary. I'll come in myself."

"Fine. When?" (Assuming that he wanted to see where I lived, I had expected him to be more insistent.)

The next day, upon payment of the fee, the agent pulled out, with some fanfare, a pile of listings from his desk. Each had a sad story. Many were rented (very recently); some were too dangerous for children; some had elderly tenants; others were too expensive, too small, or not in Westside. After a half-hour of woeful tales, the pile dwindled to five listings, all of which had to be checked to see if the landlords would agree to rent to a two-children, one-dog family. However, I was not to worry. My $30 was good for a "whole year, in which time something nice was bound to turn up." Over five years later I am still waiting. (He did call twice during that year, but the apartments I was shown, those owned by landlords who permitted kids and pets, were not satisfactory to this handler of the kids and pet.)

Already $30 down, I was grateful that the last agency charged $20. 'Mrs. Bain,' the agent, told me that they had 100 Westside apartments listed in the $250-$300 price bracket. When I tried to question her about the apartments, she refused to answer. In fact, she hung up. I called back and was told that she was in the "process of having a nervous breakdown." That should have been sufficient warning, a sign that this agency was even less reputable than the others. But intent on checking all three agencies servicing Westside, I answered their inquiries on my marital status and children and made an appointment, again refusing the offer for a ride.

After paying the $20 fee, the listing of 100 apartments proved to be a myth. Once more I partook in the charade of seemingly endless card flipping, only to learn that each apartment was rented or unsuitable. This time I reacted with anger.

"I want to see the listings," I demanded. "How do I know whether your cards are blanks or on apartments in other towns or ones rented months, even years, ago?"

"These listings are confidential," retorted 'Mr. Sands,' waving a card in front of my face, presumably to show that it was not blank. "Why are you so upset? You have our word that we will find you an apartment."

"Because I don't believe you ever had 100 listings of Westside apartments. If you did, there would surely be one that met my needs."

"Mrs. Ash, you have already done much harm here, upsetting Mrs. Bain until she ended up puking in the bathroom. Now you are questioning our integrity. I suggest that you go home; when we have an apartment, we'll call *you*."

"I want my money back," I demanded, attempting to be heard above his shouting.

"The fee is nonrefundable. Please leave."

Leave I did. Hear from them again, I did not.

All real estate agencies handling apartment rentals charge a fee—some to the landlord, some to the tenant, and some to both landlord and tenant. (In the latter case, a percentage of one month's rent is customarily divided between the lessor and the lessee.) This is not unreasonable. An agent might show a client numerous apartments without renting any of them and therefore not receive any payment for his time. When he does rent an apartment, his commission is significantly lower than when he sells a house. For these reasons many real estate agencies do not even list apartments, and those which specialize in rentals are at a premium. Thus a $20 or $30 fee would indeed be a bargain, if such agencies did provide the services they advertise. Probably no agency could operate for long by promising so much for so little. With no way of knowing beforehand whether a client's needs (or dreams) can be satisfied, a year of obligation is a hefty commitment. What's more, discussion of rents and apartments is contingent upon receipt of the service fee—a taboo which virtually guarantees the ignorance of both contractual parties. Perhaps this is the best indicator of the reputability of an agency—a mandatory, nonrefundable payment prior to reviewing client requirements or showing apartments should be viewed with suspicion, particularly if the agency makes grandiose promises (e.g., guaranteed satisfaction, one year of service, 100 listings in one community).

Precisely because real estate agencies receive a commission only if they rent an apartment, Sheila did not approach any of these agencies.[15] Classified advertisements in the local and metropolitan newspapers became her major source of information on available rentals. Although Sheila made 50 telephone inquiries and inspected 25 apartments, I have chosen only to relate those experiences I regard as representative. Some additional anecdotes depict the hazards of roleplaying and the more comical side of this project.

Three major conclusions were drawn from Sheila's investigation: Discrimination toward families with children is the norm; landlords do not look favorably upon women without husbands as tenants; and high rents further limit the number of apartments available to single-parent women.

First and foremost, landlords do not like kids! Or to use more temperate phraseology, landlords prefer to rent apartments to families without children. Preferences are, of course, easier to understand than biases. Who could blame the owner of a well-maintained apartment for "preferring" a childless couple as tenants over a family with children, especially young children? Kids can be noisy, even destructive "creatures." In short, they are a gamble, one which owners of desirable dwellings usually do not have to chance. As the demand for apartments has increased at a rate greater than the supply, landlords are in a position of authority. Caught in the push and pull of such capitalistic forces, the state's antichild discrimination statute has been reduced to a paper tiger. Few file complaints, and the state's investigatory agency tends to view those that are filed as less than top priority (Hutson, 1978). Thus, while the law prohibits the refusal to rent to persons with children except in dwellings of two units or less[16] and in dwellings of three units or less in which one unit is occupied by an elderly or infirm person (see Appendix C, subsection 11), landlords continue to exercise their independence, acting almost as if a ban on children had the blessing of the state and federal authorities. If perchance this assessment seems unjust, I offer in evidence the following stories, along with an invitation for the reader to examine the media's exposés of discriminatory housing practices (e.g., "Housing Bias Not Eliminated—Rights Panel," 1979; Hutson, 1978; Washburn, 1976).

mod., 3 bdrm., frpl., ww, d&d, $375.

"How old are your children?" asked the landlord after showing Sheila the apartment. (She had mentioned neither her marital status nor her children.)

"My children are two and a half and five and a half, 'Mr. Stone.' "

"I was worried about that. You see, I am the second owner of the house. It is somewhere between 25 and 30 years old. [The title search required for purchasing a dwelling specifies the year in which the house was built.] If the house contains lead paint, it cannot be rented to anybody with children under seven."

"But the apartment seems to have been painted recently."

"It was painted a year ago, but there may be lead paint under the new paint. I've asked the city to check the house, but who knows when they will get around to it."

"If somebody without young children wants to rent the apartment before the city inspects it, will you give preference to those who have seen it first?"

"I wish I could. You seem like a nice lady. But if the city finds lead paint, you won't be able to have the apartment anyway, and in the meantime I'll have lost other tenants."

"Perhaps I can call the city and hasten the inspection process."

"Don't waste your time. The city moves at its own pace [a smile and a pat on the arm accompanied this statement]. I'll do my best to hurry them along and call you as soon as the paint is checked."

"Would you also call me if you rent the apartment before then?"

"Certainly."

He kept his promise. Two days later Mr. Stone's wife called to say that the apartment had been rented. When I asked whether the tenants had children, she said she knew nothing about them; her husband handled the business in the family. Yet, since Mrs. Stone also lived in the house, one would presume that she would have at least inquired about the people who were moving into *her* house.

mod. 6 rms., avail. July 1, 3 bdrms., eat-in kit., dinrm., $345.

"This is a lovely apartment, 'Mrs. Kelley.' "

"Yes, that is why we only rent to families. Single people are so wild!

You're not single, are you?'' she asked, scanning my left hand in vain for a wedding band.

"No, I have a family—a son, five and a half, and a daughter, two and a half.'' (I stifled any inclination to defend single individuals— clearly another group subjected to discrimination.)

"Mrs. Ash, to be honest, I am getting on in age. Young children are too noisy for me, although I'm sure you have very nice children'' (emphasis on nice).

"Yes, they are *nice*, and I'm sure they would not bother you.'' (Mrs. Kelley was either remarkably well preserved or at most 50 years old. According to the state's antidiscrimination law, "elderly'' was defined as a person at least 65 years of age.)

"Let me think it over and call you if I change my mind,'' she said.

After two weeks, I called her. Much to her regret, or so she said, the apartment had been rented to a lovely (emphasis on lovely) couple, both of whom worked all day. She was confident that I understood, her age and all, that this was preferable to young children running around, although she did love (emphasis on love) children. Indeed, she loved them so much that she would "hate to be responsible for cooping them up.'' (As time passed, my "understanding,'' which so many seemed to think was inexhaustible, began to ebb away—another example of the principle of supply and demand.

6 rms., 3 bdrms., cab. kit., $300.

"Do you like the apartment?''

"Yes, it is very nice. When it is available?''

"Next month. Is that convenient for you?''

"Yes.''

"You don't have any children do you?'' asked 'Mr. Howard.'

"Yes, I do—a daughter, two and a half, and a son, five and a half,'' I responded, having learned that it was a waste of time to try to hedge or evade such questions.

"How lovely! Why don't you think about the apartment and call me when you decide.''

"I'll call you tomorrow, if that is all right with you.''

"Fine.''

At last, I thought, I had met an unbiased landlord. But that evening he telephoned to apologize for a "small oversight.'' He had forgotten to mention a family who had seen the apartment yesterday. To his surprise they had decided to rent it, and he, because of the "first come, first serve'' maxim, had to comply.

Was this fact or fiction? Unable to resist the temptation of checking, I had a friend inquire about the apartment. Mr. Howard was only too happy to show it to her. She canceled the appointment, and I added Mr. Howard to my list of child discriminators.

I soon grew accustomed to being told (often after the fact) that someone else, who had seen the apartment previously, was to be the new tenant. If I had to rank excuses, this was the most common. The lead paint story was among the more original, but there were others. For example, the house with the dangerous stairs (this sounded like a Nancy Drew mystery) presented, according to the owner, an insurance problem. In truth the stairs were rather ordinary, easily negotiated by an average one-and-a-half year-old. There was also the landlord who averred that his dog bit young children, even after the animal and Laurie played in the yard for over 30 minutes. Then there was the landlady who could not afford to replace her newly seeded lawn after "my" kids dug it up. (Now my children had become moles in disguise.) And there were others who defended their refusals, vividly describing previous experiences with tenants who had children. Some, however, offered no pretenses, merely stating that they did not rent to families with young children. (Had we indeed raised a generation of bad seeds? After listening to many recollections of children who wantonly and brazenly destroyed all but the foundation of residences, not to mention their raucous behavior by day and by night, one had cause to worry about the nation's future!)

Children, it appeared, were albatrosses, their very existence creating a Berlin wall between the apartment seeker and a choice residence. Of the 25 apartments visited by Sheila, 15 landlords either refused outright to lease an apartment to a family with young children or in some way revealed a reluctance to have children on their premises. At other times Sheila was dismissed summarily on the telephone; in eight of these instances the owners stated that they did not rent to families with children or with young children. While not all landlords discriminated against families with children, the number who did was disproportionately high; and for obvious reasons, they were typically the ones with the nicest rentals.

The second conclusion of Sheila's investigation was that landlords do not consider single women as desirable tenants. Admittedly, it is difficult to discern whether a landlord is biased toward single women, divorced and separated women, single-parent women, or single parents. Still, it appears that single-parent women have two strikes against them—children and no husband. The following examples illustrate discrimination, be it overt or covert, toward single-parent women (or divorced and separated women). Again it should be noted that the state's antidiscrimination statute prohibits landlords from refusing to "rent or lease" accommodations because of "sex, age, ancestry, or marital status" (see Appendix C, subsection 6).

6 mod. rms, near transp., avail. July 1 or Aug. 1, $360.

"Mrs. Ash, does your husband work nearby?"

"He works in _____, 'Mrs. Ross.' " (Prior to a judicial decree of separation Sheila was, in fact, still a married woman.)

"My, he has a long trip!"

"Yes. Do you prefer a July 1 or an August 1 occupancy?"

"The people living here will know next week when they will be leaving. By the way, how many cars do you have?"

"One."

"So, you make do without a car?"

"No, I have a car," I responded, realizing that the reckoning was dangerously near.

"How does your husband get to work?"

"He drives. We are separated." (There seemed no point in delaying the inevitable.)

"Do you work, (pause) Ms. Ash?"

"No, but I'm looking for a job."

"Would you mind if I asked how you are planning to pay $360 a month plus utilities?"

I did mind, but supplied an answer anyway: "My husband supports us, and after the divorce he will still contribute to my income. Also, as I told you, I plan to work."

"Wouldn't it be wiser to look for a cheaper apartment?"

"Mrs. Ross, finding a place to live, not money, is my problem. I will be happy to give you a month's deposit and sign a one-year lease as you requested."

"This is a most awkward situation for me, Ms. Ash. I'm sure you'll find a job, but from my position it is risky. I would not have the heart to ask you to leave if you couldn't pay, and I can't afford to keep up the house without the rent money. I'm sure you understand."

This was a novel twist: Because of the landlady's kindness, a woman with too big a heart to cast out a lone woman and two children, Sheila was turned down.

6 rms., frpl., immed. occ., $350.

The place was not only a wreck, but the landlord wanted a security deposit and a two-year lease. Considering the condition of the apartment and the rather high rent (see footnote 14), I was confident that the landlord would regard Sheila as a choice tenant. Wrong again!

"Mrs. Ash, I apologize for the mess; I made the mistake of renting to two single men. You can see the result. You're not single, are you?"

"I'm separated," I replied.

"Do you give many parties for your friends?" asked 'Mr. Blake.'

"No, and when I do, they are quiet gatherings, not wild bashes."

"You look like a nice woman, but I promised the wife that I would only rent to married couples. It's too expensive to keep fixing the place up."

"How are you going to renovate the apartment for immediate occupancy?" I asked.

"I mean to clean it up and fix a few things."

"But, the place needs a lot of work. Surely cleaning the apartment is not a big investment, and I would consider repainting it myself." (Perhaps, I thought, he needed an incentive to change his mind.)

"I'm sorry, but I promised my wife. I'm sure you'll find an apartment."

While Sheila, if there was a real Sheila, would not have rented this apartment, regardless of the landlord's receptivity, discrimination under any guise continued to be painful.

6 rm. single family house, near schls., $330.

The reference to schools suggested that children might not be a liability. Further, the house was tiny with closetlike rooms, no basement or garage, and only crawl space in the attic for storage. A family of more than three members would be cramped. Another point in Sheila's favor, I reasoned.

"What do you think of my house?" inquired 'Mr. Jackson.'

"It's very nice, and the yard is lovely."

"I'm glad you like it; you are the first to see it. My wife and I have lived here since it was built. We have just moved to an apartment. Would you like to come back this evening with your husband and children?"

"My husband and I are separated, and I know that my children will like the house, especially the yard."

"Why don't you think it over then and call me in a week or so."

"If I wait that long, in the interim you might find other tenants."

"Take your time. Renting a house is a big decision for a woman without a husband."

Taking time proved to be a mistake; a week later the house was rented. There had been clues which I should have heeded: "Call me in a week or so," he had said; and "renting a house is a big decision for a woman without a husband." Although wary, I had chosen to believe in his sincerity. Perhaps at the time he was being honest; perhaps Sheila was rejected for reasons unrelated to her marital status; perhaps Mr. Jackson had found the tenants that landlords dream about—a childless couple past the age of childbearing.

Discrimination had many façades. Sometimes it was stated bluntly, at other times only intimated; sometimes it was directed toward children, at other times toward single parents or the separated and divorced. Still, even I, who was merely roleplaying, never became immune. Each of these experiences aroused anger, distrust, and pain. They were the hardest to understand, the ones which kept me awake at night. There were others, though, which added a touch of levity to the research. For instance, there was the time when I visited an apartment advertised as follows.

7 rms., 4 bdrms., gar., $450, Aug. 1.

The landlady welcomed me graciously. She appeared so unconcerned about my children and marital status that I ventured to tell her that I had a dog, an 85-pound boxer to be exact.[17] This didn't bother her either: She loved kids, dogs, everything. Her benevolence was not, however, motivated by humanitarianism. One bedroom in the apartment was off limits. (She used it to store her belongings and kept it locked.) The kitchen had no cabinets (only a few shelves), a stove on which two of the four burners were permanently clogged, and a refrigerator which appeared to predate the advent of electricity. And there was more: The paint was peeling off the walls and ceilings; the garage door was fixed in one position—up; and the yard, what there was of it, was used by the other tenant for parking his car and for storage of garbage containers. This owner could scarcely afford to refuse occupancy to anyone who was willing to part with $450 a month, lest they were known escapees from a leper colony, penitentiary, or mental institution, and perhaps not even then.

2 fam., 2½ bdrms., ww crpt., dinrm., frpl. livrm., mod. kit., d&d, mod. bath, gar., $385.

After seeing the apartment, the landlady and I continued our conversation over a cup of coffee. All the standard questions were asked and answered until she knew as much as I did about Laurie, Peter, and Sheila. In turn, she volunteered her life story: She had three children, worked at a job she did not like, and was divorced for three years; her ex-husband paid child support regularly and was remarried; their relationship was "as good as could be expected." Then came the unanticipated blow.

"I wish I could rent the apartment to you; you'd be great company. But every house needs a man in it."

"I don't understand what you mean." I was not feigning; I really did not follow her reasoning.

"Things break down in a house so often, and a man, well, a man is better at fixing things."

"You can't be saying that you'd only rent this apartment to a man or a married couple? *You* are divorced," I stated incredulously.

"The hardest adjustment after my divorce was getting used to doing 'man things.' I learned that a man tenant makes my life easier. I mean nothing more than that; please understand," she implored.

I nodded and left.

Only in retrospect did this experience seem humorous. At the time I was angry and hurt. Despite the landlady's understanding of Sheila's situation, her empathy, if you will, she too chose to discriminate against a single-parent woman. Her stereotypical view of men and women is not as important as her inability to comprehend the injustice of her actions, the irony of her words. She was prejudiced against women no different from herself. Herein, of course, is the irony: Tomorrow the same thing could happen to her.

Nonetheless, there were some encounters in which the comical element was unmistakable.

3 bdrm. apt., kit. w. d&d, frpl. livrm., dinrm., ww, gar., $420.

Imagine for the moment the following scene: Here was Sheila greeted at the door by a woman whose child was in 'Peter's' class. If I had not recognized her name on the telephone, in person there was no doubt about whom she was. Nor was there any doubt that she knew me. The expression on her face dispelled any thoughts of concealing my identity. Before she could say anything, I spoke:

"Hi, 'Mrs. Gilman'; my sister called you yesterday about seeing your house. Unfortunately she had to go to New York today, and I volunteered to come for her. I hope you don't mind." (I do not have a sister, but as necessity is the mother of invention, at this moment I needed and created one. I hoped that any remembrance of my "sister's voice" would be considered a filial similarity.)

The visit was brief and pleasant. She asked enough questions to lead me to believe that my story had been a convincing one. Not wanting her to think much more about our meeting, I telephoned the next day, explaining that my sister had decided to rent a house in another town. I think she believed me, but after this encounter the risks of roleplaying seemed greater, and Westside smaller than I had ever pictured it. Consequently, I resolved never to inspect an apartment in the vicinity of my home, thereby depriving "Sheila's sister" of a starring role. Yet there was no way to prepare for situations such as the next one, where I failed to recognize either the name or face of an individual.

6 rm. apt., 3 bdrms., 1½ baths, formica kit., disposal, dishwasher, cent. a.c., full bsmt., $450.

The apartment was at the other end of town. Although not many miles away, in Westside you generally do not have to travel far to secure anonymity. In this instance, however, generalizations did not apply. Allow me to explain in more detail. Laurie was with me, having been told that we were playing a pretend game in which we looked for apartments and used different names, a secret game unknown to everybody except her and me. She was splendid, a regular Shirley Temple spinoff. Yet halfway through our tour of the apartment, the landlady suddenly stopped, and with a puzzled expression on her face, asked:

"Isn't your daughter in a play group with 'Blair Lawrence'?"

(I was stunned. Laurie was in a play group with Blair. If I denied it, Laurie might disclose the truth. If I admitted it, the woman might question the discrepancy in names or check up on us afterward, even spreading the story to Blair's mother. I imagined the worst—a rumor that I was plotting a divorce unbeknownst to my husband, thus accounting for the phony names. [The real plot behind my ruse, I did not think anyone would guess.] I would have to telephone all five mothers of children in the play group, describe my research, and ask for their cooperation, particularly their secrecy. Moreover, the story, in whatever version it assumed, might be conveyed over the suburban hotline before I contacted everyone. Alternatively, if I lied, there was a possibility, even if Laurie said nothing, that I would not be believed. And then, too, I would have to withdraw Laurie from the group, an act which was not only unfair to her, but one that could conceivably have negative consequences, giving rise to more rumors instead of squelching them.) These thoughts whizzed through my mind as I tried to collect myself sufficiently to reply.

"Not that I know of," I finally responded. "She is in a play group, but I do not recall a child by that name."

"Amazing, she looks so much like the child in my niece's group. Maybe it is just that they both have long braids. It was a silly question anyway, as the other child's name is Samantha. I only saw her once when I was visiting my sister-in-law on the other side of town."

Surprisingly Laurie became my savior. Her restlessness turned into whining, providing me with a needed excuse for leaving. Still, I worried that there would be repercussions. Had the landlady's curiosity been aroused? Would she speak to her sister-in-law about the incident? Would she reappear at the play group? I didn't know the answers and not knowing did nothing except change Laurie's hair style for all subsequent play group sessions. I do not think the episode had any carry-over, unless there is a rumor around town that has been concealed from me. When the play group disbanded a month later, I must confess that I welcomed its demise. Laurie felt differently.

And there were other occurrences that had a humorous side. One landlord refused to consider Sheila as a tenant, not because of her children or her marital status, but because she had a car. "From November to March the city prohibits parking on the streets, and I hate a crowded driveway," he explained. "If," he added, "you can find a place to leave your car for five months or sell it, the problem will be solved." Then there was the landlord who did not rent his apartment to anyone who planned to hang pictures on the walls. All hooks, nails, tape, and possibly fingerprints were forbidden. In another case, a couple claimed that they only rented to families with children the same ages as their own. Apparently, their kids could not find any neighborhood playmates unless they imported them. Sounds unbelievable? Consider the landlord who would only rent to families with a teenage daughter who could babysit for his children. Perhaps the babysitter as well as her parent(s) had to sign a contract.

Ostensibly these experiences had little to do with social prejudices; yet a refusal to rent, even for an absurd reason, can be exasperating. Apartment hunting is often time consuming and frustrating, but when individuals encounter biases over which they have little or no control, it is understandable that they consider themselves victims and the search for housing a desperate hunt in which they must continuously defend themselves.

Looking for an apartment was the most debasing experience of my life. Here I was, an attractive woman with two adolescent children and a good job being treated like a criminal. At first you argue, then you beg, and the last step in the whole degrading experience is when you give up. A year later a friend of mine had a vacancy in a house she owned and I moved in. If not for her, I probably would have kept my house until they carried me out.

(45-year-old woman, 3 years divorced)

While this woman stayed in her home because at the time she believed she had no alternative, others remained for different reasons, one of which was financial.

I cannot afford to sell my house. It's cheaper than a rental. Even run-down places here are expensive. There is no rent control and not enough apartments, so landlords charge whatever they want, knowing that sooner or later someone will pay it. Many do not even advertise. They just pass the word along. These are usually the best places. And there's no guarantee that a $400 rent one year won't be $450 the next.

(43-year-old woman, 2 years divorced)

Sheila too found the high cost of rentals to be another problem for single-parent women looking for apartments within Westside. This constituted the third conclusion of her housing investigation.

Using Sheila's hypothetical situation as an example, let us assume that Sheila *did* have the option of staying in her home. On the basis of 1975 figures, it would have cost her between $510 and $520 a month to maintain the house and the tax advantage of ownership, exclusive of upkeep costs. Alternatively, suitable apartments ranged in rent from $300 to $500 a month. (The norm was $380, exclusive of utility costs.) Further, because there are relatively few apartment complexes in Westside, the vast majority of rentals are in single-family and two-family houses in which utility charges are assumed by the tenant. (These dwellings are also not covered by the state's antidiscrimination law.) After the cost of utilities is calculated into the rent, Sheila would save approximately $94 a month by moving to a $350 apartment. Thus, given a choice, it appears that for persons in a situation similar to Sheila's there is not sufficient financial incentive to move unless money from the sale of their homes can be used more advantageously or if the cost of upkeep becomes an economic liability.

The scarcity of apartments in Westside and the inflated cost of rentals also pose a problem for separated and divorced men who want to reside near their children. The higher the rent, the less money is available for one or both parents and their children.

We thought it best for the children that we be both around and available. This meant that we both had to live in Westside or move to another community. Because the kids had friends here, we decided to stay. But it is an expensive town and running two houses costs more than running one. We just can't live like we used to anymore.

(40-year-old man, 3 years divorced)

While economic considerations affect decisions on whether and where to relocate, they are among the most tangible of the housing problems faced by single-parent women (and men). Far more subtle and uncontrollable are the discriminatory policies of landlords. Pervasive biases against children and single-parent women (see footnote 13) limit the options available to these families; among the least desirable of tenants, their bargaining powers are reduced; in fact, they are often nonexistent.

Truly landlords do not like to rent to women with children. It is a combination of factors that operate against these women. Landlords see her as a financial risk. They worry about her leaving children unattended while she works or dates. They are concerned about property damage and noise. Put all this together and you have a client with many liabilities, even if she earns an adequate salary.

(Westside real estate broker)

And they are not the only victimized group: students and groups of unrelated singles constitute an even lower order of species to landlords and real estate agents.

I don't know any landlord in Westside that wants to rent to students. Those who have to are the ones with apartments nobody in his or her right mind would rent. And they charge them plenty. Since the rent is divided by a group of students, they can afford what a family or an individual cannot. Also, landlords don't like singles who live together, particularly men. This is why more single men and women, who can afford it, are buying their own homes.[18] Then at least they don't have to deal with these kinds of prejudices.[19]

Perhaps misery loves company, but it is unlikely that victims of housing discrimination find solace in such elusive associations for long.

Essentially this represents a legal issue—the disparity between antidiscriminatory laws and actual practice. Yet few victims of housing discrimination avail themselves of legal redress. In part, individual tolerance of discriminatory practices can be attributed to inadequate enforcement of existing laws, time-consuming bureaucratic regulations, and the legal immunity granted to owners of single-family and two-family dwellings, residences which in Westside constitute a majority of the rental properties. Perhaps the state needs to enact more stringent laws and enforcement procedures; and perhaps community backing for compliance with anti-discrimination regulations can be, in the long run, instrumental in influencing the attitudes and practices of local realty firms and landlords. This kind of community venture also applies to the issue of credit; we now turn to this topic.

SHEILA ASH: A WOMAN IN NEED OF CREDIT

The state law was amended in 1973 to make persons "furnishing credit or services" liable in an action of contract if they "deny or terminate such credit or services or...adversely affect an individual's credit standing because of such individual's sex or marital status" (see Appendix C, subsection 14). In 1975 the State Commission Against Discrimination went a step further, prohibiting on credit applications questions pertaining to an individual's sex, marital status, or spouse's name and occupation. An individual's income was to be the *sole* criterion for granting credit, irrespective of whether the source was alimony and/or child support or employment. Although state laws and the Federal Equal Credit Opportunity Act of 1974 have constituted a step forward, the step has been a small one. According to a survey conducted by the Commercial Credit Corporation, "overt and covert discrimination" against women has not been eradicated; "nearly all women continue to experience large or small problems in establishing credit" (McCormack, 1978, p. 35). And from the stories recounted by participants in this study, women did indeed appear to have credit problems in spite of the law's mandate.

Sheila's ability to assess the extent and/or kinds of credit problems encountered by single-parent women was limited. Not only was Sheila a woman without a job or property, but because her history was fabricated, she, armed only with identification cards, had no tangible evidence to support her creditworthiness. Consequently, it was recognized from the outset that only a cursory exploration could be conducted.

Sheila's assignment was to approach different businesses (e.g., department stores, banks, automobile dealers) to obtain credit applications and discuss informally her chances for securing credit. Sheila did not take part in the second phase of this investigation. Instead I arranged interviews with selected credit officers in which I described Sheila's background and circumstances and attempted to obtain information on her creditworthiness. (Naturally, anonymity of both the institution and the individual was guaranteed.) For each of these tasks hypothetical figures for alimony and child support were used.

Beginning with department stores, Sheila obtained her first application. Since the form was not to be submitted for processing, a bogus savings account number and social security number were filled in; Ms. was selected for the title code; and the sections on marital status and spouse's name, occupation, and employment data were left blank along with questions pertaining to the applicant's recent employment. In reviewing the form, some of the omissions seemed to be justifiable by law, while others clearly cast doubt on Sheila's candidacy for credit. Nevertheless, I handed the application to the credit officer, requesting that he review it with me. Screening the form quickly, he remarked:

"Ms. Ash, perhaps I can help you with the questions you have left out. For one, are you married, single, widowed, divorced, or legally separated?"

"I chose to leave that blank because I thought the question was not supposed to be on credit applications. What I mean is that it is illegal, is it not?"

"Illegal? Not unless the information is used against you."

Not wanting to antagonize him by quoting the State Commission Against

Discrimination, I answered the question as well as those pertaining to spouse's employment. (Sheila was, after all, neither divorced nor legally separated.)

"What about credit cards listed in your husband's name and in both your names?"

"This card is for me, not my husband."[20]

"Ms. Ash, are you employed?"

"No. I am looking for a job."

"Do you have property in your own name or receive income from a source other than employment?"

"According to my separation agreement, I will be receiving $10,000 a year for alimony and child support for three years. After that, I will receive $6,000 for child support."

"What if your husband doesn't pay you as he has promised?"

"In that unlikely event I suppose you could close my account."

"You know credit cards can be dangerous. People forget how much they have charged, and when they get the bill they can't pay it. The interest piles up, and they are in debt. I'd advise you to wait until you find a job. When you have your own income, it will be safer and easier for you," he stated paternally.

"Are you saying that I will be turned down?"

"No, I'd have to process this and review it more thoroughly, checking your references, savings bank, and so on."

"What is the 'so on'?" I queried.

"Your husband might be called to verify the alimony and child support and things like that."

"If he verifies the amount, would I then receive credit?"

"I already told you there is a review process."

"Don't you extend credit to families or individuals who earn $10,000 a year?"

"I don't have these figures at hand, and anyway they are confidential."

"I think I'll wait. I don't know if I really want an account here."

"You are a wise woman," he responded seemingly oblivious to the annoyance in my voice.

This scenario was repeated in three other department stores, with minor variations in approach and format. All four application forms contained questions relating to marital status and husband's name, occupation, place and duration of employment, and income. Only one did not pressure Sheila for this information when she defended the omission with reference to the state law. This store was also the only one to offer her a temporary purchasing voucher prior to processing the application. Since neither the acceptance of credit nor the submission of applications for processing was permissible in this study, Sheila refused the voucher.

However, questioning banks on Sheila's prospects for securing a mortgage loan was not off limits. While studies since the passage of antidiscrimination legislation (Dietz, 1976; Washburn, 1976) indicate that women buyers continue to be discriminated against by banks and real estate brokers, Sheila did not have adequate credentials to test the policies of local bankers.[21] At best, she could present credit officials with a prefabricated financial picture and record their stated impressions of her creditworthiness.

In substance, Sheila told each of the four bank officials with whom she spoke the following story.

My husband and I are separated. When the negotiated settlement is approved, I will receive one-half ownership of our home assessed at $44,900. We have decided to sell the house, which according to three real estate brokers has a market value of $65,000,[22] and to divide the money remaining after the $27,000 mortgage is paid off. I plan to use part of my share as a downpayment for a smaller, less expensive house in Westside. My income will include $10,000 in alimony and child support. After three years the alimony will stop, although I will continue to receive $6,000 a year for the support of my two children. In addition, my husband will pay for their health insurance and summer camps. Besides the money from the sale of the house, my assets will include an additional $8,000 in cash from the divorce settlement and a car valued at $2,500.

I realize that it is somewhat premature to discuss mortgages before I have sold my house or looked for another one, but on the basis of the assets and liabilities I have described to you, if I were to purchase a house in the price vicinity of, say, $40,000 to $45,000, would I be able to obtain a mortgage loan from your bank?

In substance, this was their response.

Unless you are employed, your chances for securing a mortgage are not good. The mortgage payment will continue after the alimony stops, reducing your income to $6,000 a year. That is barely sufficient to support one person, let alone a family of three and a house. Even if your monthly mortgage payment including taxes is less than you would pay for rent, this is not viewed by the bank as a bargaining point. If, on the other hand, you had a job paying about $15,000 a year and were willing to put up bonds or some other collateral, you would be regarded as a more reliable candidate.

All four banks stressed the importance, indeed, the necessity, for Sheila to be employed. And at all four banks, Sheila questioned the salary figures which varied from $12,000 to $15,000 among the banks.

"You do not seem to be considering the $10,000 in alimony and child support payments. Even if I earned $8,000 a year, I'd still have an income of $18,000, of which $6,000 would not be taxable." (Her husband would pay taxes on the child support and she on the alimony.)

"But," replied one bank official, "after three years this would be reduced to $14,000."

"That seems sufficient for owning an inexpensive home, especially since $6,000 isn't taxable, and in addition, you would be holding securities as collateral."[23]

"*If* you did earn $8,000 a year, your husband might not pay you or he might be erratic in sending the money. Then you would have nothing *but* $8,000 a year."

"You are assessing possibilities, not facts. A man earning $50,000 today could go broke tomorrow." (Of course, the $8,000 was also only a possibility.)

"In this business risk assessment is very important. Some men earning $50,000 are poor risks. And so is dependency on alimony and child support a poor risk."[24]

Out of the $19,000 Sheila would receive from the sale of her house, approximately $10,000 would be needed as a downpayment for a $45,000 house, leaving her $9,000, less any capital gain taxes. Despite an additional $8,000 from the divorce settlement, she appears to be in a poor bargaining position. Possibly permanent alimony or higher alimony and/or child support payments might strengthen her case. Nonetheless, since these sources of income are generally not accorded the same accreditation as are wages and property, it seems as if a woman like Sheila, without a job, would have a difficult time securing financial backing for the purchase of a house.[25] Only one bank official out of the four did not mention the problems of considering alimony and child support as income. Yet he too held out little hope for obtaining a mortgage unless Sheila was employed.

Similar experiences were related by unemployed respondents who wanted to purchase a house.

I was shocked when I couldn't get any bank to give me a mortgage because I didn't have a job. I thought anyone with enough money for a downpayment and with money in the bank, not to mention child support and alimony, could not be called a bad risk. Funny, it costs me more a month to stay in this house than the one I wanted to buy, and I have met my payments for two years without one late charge.

(41-year-old woman, 2 years divorced)

Because buying a house (by any standard) entails a substantial investment and a long-term commitment to a lender, Sheila approached car dealers to ascertain her creditability on a smaller scale. After speaking at length to one salesman about the features of different models, the discussion of the financial terms for purchasing a $4,200 economy car began.

"I would like to trade my car in and obtain financing for the balance," I explained.

"If you sell your car yourself, you would probably get about $2,500. I can only offer you around $1,800 or $1,900."

"That is low! What about the financing?"

"When you come back with your husband, we can fill in all the information and calculate the monthly payments."

"My husband and I are separated."

"Where do you work, Mrs. Ash?"

"I don't work, but after my divorce I will have sufficient money in the bank to buy the car outright if I choose to do so."

"Is this your money or is it in a joint account?"

"A joint account. What's the difference? It is my money as much as my husband's."

"Sure, but he could withdraw it before you paid up the loan."

"So could I."

"Mrs. Ash, wouldn't it be wiser to buy the car after your divorce, or if you really want it now, have your husband countersign the loan? If all you say is true, I'm sure he wouldn't mind."

"Are you saying that without a job or my husband countersigning the note, I would not get financing even though I have my own car and money in the bank?"

"No, I am not. I am saying that I'm not sure if you'd get a loan. You could buy it outright instead, since you do have the money. Right?"

"Wrong! I don't want to buy it outright."

"Fill in this form, and we'll see what happens. You could also go to your own bank for a loan. Since they know you, they'd probably be more receptive."

"I'll think about it. Meanwhile I'd like to look at other cars. Thank you for your time."

Conceivably the salesman's efforts to dissuade Sheila from taking out a loan were sincerely intended. Certainly he did not fit the stereotypical picture of the aggressive, pushy car salesman. If anything, he was, by his own advice, jeopardizing his chances for making a sale. These thoughts occur to me in retrospect. At the time I felt angry and mistreated, my privacy violated and my independence denied. If, as with the department stores and banks, Sheila's encounters with other car dealers were analogous to this one, I would have dwelt no more on this experience. It would have been just another shred of evidence, suggesting that for a separated (or divorced) woman starting anew can be an external as well as an internal struggle—

a struggle waged on many fronts. But the others *were* different and so I wondered.

In visits to two other car dealers Sheila was assured that buying and financing a car would not present any problems. She was never questioned on her marital status or savings. Even her unemployment did not seem to disturb them. (Maybe they assumed the presence of a husband or a co-signer; or maybe it did not matter.) After trading in her car, the remaining $2,200 would be financed by a chattel mortgage. In other words, they explained, the creditor would hold the title papers to the car until the loan was paid. If Sheila defaulted on the payments, the car would be repossessed. Obviously the loan was small enough and the new car worth enough to ensure that the creditor's risk would be minimal at the worst. Still, these were only preliminary inquiries; no papers were filled out or processed. And, as such, any conclusions are speculative.

What if, I mused, Sheila did not have a car to trade in? Would this change the outcome? Predictably the answer was affirmative. Without a car to use in partial payment, the amount of the chattel mortgage rose from $2,200 to $4,200. So too rose the risk to the creditor. Since as soon as a car leaves the showroom it is no longer worth its sticker price, repossession does not solve the creditor's problem; it means a loss. For Sheila, it meant that her creditworthiness had to be scrutinized. First one, then two, and then three car dealers proceeded to question Sheila in depth (at the time it seemed as if they performed this ritual with relish), asking about her marital status, employment, credit record, bank accounts, her husband's occupation and income, and on and on.

In summary, these men presented Sheila with the same options, albeit disguised as advice. A recapitulation of one performance will thus cover all three.

"Mrs. Ash, you should consider waiting until your divorce is finalized before you buy a car."

"Why?"

"Right now you have no money, property, or income of your own. If you are correct, after the divorce you will have cash in the bank and part ownership of a house to support your application for a car loan."

"But I receive alimony and child support now as part of my separation agreement."

"That is not the same as having *your* own property and money, is it?"

"It is! The checks are payable to me, and I receive them regularly. They are, in fact, considered income."

"You could also have your husband countersign the loan," he suggested, ignoring Sheila's statement. "Since he knows how much he pays you, he will also *know* that you will honor the loan."

"I can't do that. We are separated."

"Do as you like. I'm only advising you as I would a friend."

"A friend? Would you turn down a friend's application without even checking on the accuracy of the information?"

"I would if I thought *she* was acting imprudently."

"Imprudently! 'Mr. Bell,' I am looking for a job. Not having a car is a handicap that I can't afford."

"Having a car may be a handicap that you *can't* afford. [He was smarter than I had thought.] You'll have to pay insurance and taxes, and buy gasoline. It is an expensive luxury."

"Fifteen minutes ago you told me how cheap the car was to own and run. 'A bargain,' you called it. Now you call it 'an expensive luxury.' "

"It is a bargain, if you have the money. And you do not." [Another clever parry.]

In essence, these sessions (either this is a poor choice of words or it reveals how much I viewed these conversations as interrogations) were no different than Sheila's first experience described earlier (see pp. 134-135). This confused me; ambivalence resurfaced. Were these three men also well intentioned? Had I misinterpreted honest opinions as acts of duplicity? It was true that Sheila's only source of revenue was $10,000 in temporary alimony and child support. It was true that insurance, taxes, gasoline, and servicing a car were additional expenditures. Was it then also true that Sheila was a poor credit risk? If so, this meant that a woman dependent upon her ex-husband for $10,000 of income was poorer than one with an equivalent salary, despite the fact that in the first situation $6,000 of the money was nontaxable. Even more unsettling was the realization that an unemployed separated or divorced woman would not only be forced to justify her financial worth, but also to defend the reliability of a husband to whom she was no longer married. Over and over she would have to admit her dependency and beg for consideration.

While state and federal laws stipulate that consistent alimony and child support payments are to be regarded as income, in practice it does not always turn out this way. And even if the loan is eventually approved, too frequently the excessive number of questions which must be answered and of defenses which must be furnished casts suspicion on the worth of the triumph. I understood now more than before why women respondents had considered their experiences in the marketplace as trials. Far more than symbolic acts, they came to be viewed as proof of their personal, not financial, worth. Indeed, it was hard to consider them otherwise.

The conclusions drawn from roleplaying were substantiated by *my own* interviews with credit officials. If there were no inquisitions, no attempts to put me on the defensive, the bottom line in most cases still read "rejected." As an unemployed person without a credit history, Sheila, I was told, had two strikes against her. And in this game there was rarely a third chance at bat. While no one denied that alimony and child support would be considered income (how could they, when I cited state and federal laws?), most stressed the unreliability of such monies. In the main, department stores responded more positively to my hypothetical example than they had to Sheila's inquiries. Bank officials were the most conservative, invariably pointing out the burdensome responsibility for an unemployed person to meet mortgage and tax payments. Money in the bank or negotiable bonds was little security to them unless they were held in escrow against default. For a $35,000 mortgage they calculated that approximately $10,000 would have to be held by the bank for a set (but never specified) period of time or until the financial outlook of the mortgagee improved sufficiently to warrant reassessment. This, they explained, was pure conjecture, as hypothetical as my example. In actuality, they would be extremely wary of underwriting a mortgage for any such person unless she was employed. On the other hand, one credit officer posited the following:

"If this woman of yours bought a house for $25,000, instead of $45,000, and put down $10,000, that would change the picture considerably."

"Would she also need to put up collateral?"

"Maybe only $5,000," he responded.

"For a $15,000 mortgage you are requiring $5,000 in collateral against a possible default of $10,000, a sum which would be paid over a period of, say, 20 to 30 years."

"Yes."

"That doesn't seem like much of a risk," I remarked.

"No bank wants to lose even $10,000. If her alimony and child support stop, we would have a problem."

"How? You'd still have the property which in all likelihood would have increased in value, perhaps even significantly."

"Nobody wants to auction off a house; there's no telling what will happen."

"By the way, do you think there are houses in Westside for $25,000?"

"I doubt it."

"Then this is not a viable alternative for my hypothetical woman, is it?"

"Not in Westside, but there are other places to live."

Not surprisingly, the reactions of Westside real estate brokers mirrored those of bank officials.

A bank is not a charitable institution. When an unemployed woman says she wants to buy a house and has nothing but a downpayment and a promise of alimony and child support, how can they help her? They know how taxes and the cost of utilities keep rising in this town. They are doing her a favor by discouraging her. A house should never be a burden, and that's what it would be for the woman you are describing.

Another real estate broker put it this way:

A woman without a job cannot afford a house unless she owns it, her ex-husband pays the mortgage, or she gets a very high divorce settlement. Even a woman who works has a rough time. The banks do not consider her income as being as stable as a man's unless she has a very important position. They worry about all kinds of things, even that she will get pregnant. Until things change women have to recognize that they will have a harder time getting a bank to take them as seriously as a man who earns the exact same income.

In my interviews with car dealers a curious phenomenon occurred; my fictionalized woman became two people: one so real that she might at any moment materialize, sign on the dotted line, and drive a car out of their lots; the other so abstract that she required no explanations, no consideration. Perhaps I read too much into what they said or projected my own ambivalence onto these men. After all, I too became confused, at times actually believing that Sheila existed, even that I was she. Nonetheless, they were remarkably uniform in their assessments of Sheila's credit status. Without a credit history, property, or employment, her chances for obtaining financing were slim. If she had a car to offer as a trade-in or money for a substantial downpayment, they foresaw no major obstacles.

"Would a man earning $10,000 be able to obtain a loan without owning any property?" I asked.

"He is employed. *Your* lady is not."

"But, as I explained, she receives $10,000 in alimony and child support, which is more than a $10,000 salary, since $6,000 is non-taxable." (I was getting tired of saying this.)

"That is not the same as being employed." (And I was tired of hearing this.)

"According to the Equal Credit Opportunity Act it is!"

"Lady, with taxes, insurance, and all the other costs, a car can be really expensive. The purchase price is only a small part of owning a car. It's not worth it if you have to worry about extra costs."

"We're not talking about worrying; we're talking about obtaining credit. The worries would not be yours. All you have to discern is whether her income is comparable to that of other applicants to whom you extend credit."

"The worry would be ours if she defaulted."

"That would apply to anyone to whom you extended credit. The question is the same: Would other applicants with incomes of $10,000 a year qualify for a loan?"

"I don't know. It depends on their assets, liabilities, size of their family, credit record, and so on."

Infrequently was I able to redirect or channel these debates. Around and around in meaningless circles we would argue, without any evidence of a victory or defeat on either side. They never said that a woman who did not have a car to trade in or money for a substantial downpayment would be turned down, but neither did they say she would be accepted. She would be considered; that was all.

One car agent did, however, tell me that I should have my friend come in and apply: "Who knows, she might get the loan." Another asked me if I was the fictitious woman. "You can confide in me," he urged gently. "You don't have to pretend you are a researcher." Apparently my suspicions were not entirely figments of my imagination: Two out of six car dealers believed my story was true. Maybe they needed a customer, even if she was a credit risk.

Clearly, credit is another area in which separated and divorced women experience difficulty. But the issues involved are not limited to this population or even to women as a group. They must be viewed in a larger framework, as pertaining directly to legal and human entitlements. The law prohibits discrimination in credit and housing, but still discriminatory practices persist. Undoubtedly, more women are aware of their rights today than a decade ago, but the number of them who seek legal redress is low and the number who have problems is high (Dewan, 1978; McCormack, 1978). As long as some women accept being victimized and as long as others do not even know that they are being victimized, such discrimination cannot be eradicated. In recognition of this, the U.S. Department of Housing and Urban Development (HUD) has initiated a program in 23 cities to educate women on the subject of credit. According to HUD officials, more women would be homeowners if mortgage lenders knew more about their credit-worthiness and if women knew more about their credit rights ("Women and Credit: What Does the Law Provide?" 1980, p. D1). The most puzzling part of HUD's conclusion has to do with creditors, not borrowers. Why, we should ask, are mortgage lenders among the uninformed? Moreover, if they are, why is HUD's program directed toward women?

Indeed, even the idea of women's banks has not yet fully come of age. While some have managed to raise sufficient capital to finance their enterprise, others have not. In the state of which I write four women announced at a press conference in February 1976 their plans to have in operation a full-service commercial bank for women (and men) by the fall. Not long afterward the project was dropped; to date, no venturesome successors have come along. Had these women pioneers aimed too high? Were their plans to help women understand and negotiate in the marketplace too lofty, too unrealistic, or too threatening?

CONCLUSION

The findings from Sheila's search for employment, child care, housing, and credit are easily summarized: Sheila did not obtain a job; Sheila found Westside's child-care system to be confusing, inflexible, and inadequate, especially for those in need of full-time day care; Sheila was rejected as a tenant by far more landlords than she was accepted by; and lastly, Sheila's ability to secure credit proved to be minimal, despite laws which supported her candidacy.

My personal reactions are more difficult to summarize. Perhaps it is because the experiences which I have labeled as ''economic'' and recorded in this chapter were in many ways the hardest for me to understand and accept. So much of the literature on divorce and separation spoke of the need to establish an independent identity, to restructure one's life as a single person. But here was Sheila Ash, a woman who attempted to do precisely this and found her path blocked by barriers that were not of her making. And also, many writers on divorce discuss the psychic aftermath of a marital dissolution, the feelings of guilt, anxiety, fear, anger, and isolation that hinder, even prevent, an individual from moving ahead. The separated and divorced must, according to these experts, come to grips with these emotions in order to make a new life for themselves. But here we have seen problems of a different origin. Sheila was not defeated or thwarted by inner conflicts. Her searches for a job, child care, housing, and, to a lesser extent, credit were systematically planned ventures. That she failed does not, of course, mean that if she continued her searches, she would be eternally defeated. However, it does illustrate the very real dilemmas encountered in the marketplace. It does illustrate the discrimination of many, be it overt or covert, toward single-parent women, divorced and separated women, or even women in general. It does illustrate the difficulty of gaining entry to the labor market after years of unemployment. It does illustrate how child-care services and even public schools are structured for the family in which the mother is the homemaker and the father the ''breadwinner.'' It does illustrate that many married women substitute, knowingly or not, their husband's identity for their own, thereby denying themselves ready access to credit upon the divorce or death of their spouses. And most poignantly, it does illustrate that a woman's efforts to restructure her life might be as traumatic and difficult as the dissolution of her marriage. Over and over, any feelings of doubt, insecurity, and fear are reinforced by evasions, biases, and slammed doors. A woman has to be strong and stubborn at a time when it may be easier to be self-indulgent and placid.

I take comfort in the fact that many with whom I spoke succeeded in spite of the obstacles they encountered. But this does not excuse those who make it necessary for women—separated, divorced, married, or single—to fight battles that they should have won long ago, that in fact they never should have had to fight at all. I make no pretense at originality—all this has been said before. But still, the Sheila that I was and the woman that I am find it hard to understand and even harder to accept. For ourselves and others it needs to be said again and again and again.

NOTES

1. While Sheila's age and educational background gave her an edge over home-makers in their 40s and 50s who were attempting to enter (or reenter) the labor market, Sheila was still, like 48% of the interviewees, a displaced homemaker. It should also be noted that since the time period of this part of the study extended from 1975 to 1979, Sheila's years of unemployment ranged from seven to 11 years even though the employment search was conducted primarily between 1975 and 1976.

2. This choice of employment credentials was selected because over 50% of the respondents had been education majors in college, and my own experience in the field suggested that some overlap between my background and Sheila's would be advantageous in handling job interviews, particularly for education and education-related positions.

3. I had tried to compensate for the employment problems in the educational sector by incorporating into Sheila's résumé references to nonteaching experiences, extending her job search outside the education field, and including in all letters to prospective employers suggestions on how her teaching skills were transferable to other types of employment. In retrospect, however, it is conceivable that the es-pecially high rate of unemployment among teachers served to skew the results of this part of the research.

4. Part-time employment had seemed a logical choice for Sheila. One child (Laurie, age two and a half) did not meet the minimum age prerequisities for most local nursery schools; the second child (Peter, age five and a half) was in kinder-garten with a dismisal time of 11:45. The cost and difficulty of attaining full-time child-care coverage for two children appeared to outweigh the advantages to be gained from additional income. Further, working part-time was viewed as a way to ease the transition from home to labor market, an acclimation period for mother and children. With this in mind, Sheila's letters of inquiry specifically stated her interest in becoming a full-time employee the following year.

5. While other states had special programs and centers for retraining unemployed teachers, particularly for jobs in industry (Cerra, 1980a), to my knowledge no such opportunities existed in the state in which Sheila lived in 1975-1976. In 1980, however, a $79,000 federal grant was used to provide a 23-week high-technology course for 36 unemployed teachers (Pave, 1980a).

6. By 1979 it was unclear whether the on-again, off-again debate on CETA funding would result in cutbacks or the termination of these projects.

7. In 1979 the state licensing director estimated that the 2,600 licensed family day-care providers constituted one-third of those operating in the state (Kirchheimer, 1979a, p. B1).

8. Babysitters who work for a family more than 20 hours a week are now covered by minimum wage laws.

9. Of late some employers have gone into the day-care business, opening centers at places of work. As yet the number of such offerings are too limited to increase day-care options for any but a small minority of Westside parents (Morris, 1980a, 1980b; Osgood, 1978).

10. Although still dependent upon volunteer help, in 1980 the agency received free office space in a public junior high school.

11. Whereas the Office for Children lists each program's prices, philosophy, hours of service and length of school year, eligibility ages, and scholarship and transportation availability, the city's directory is much less detailed. Moreover, because services are alphabetically listed, there is no one section on child care, forcing the reader to keep referring back to the index.

12. Perhaps community resources oriented toward servicing individuals during family crises (e.g., by the provision of child-care and homemaking services) can become support facilities for separated and divorced single parents. Presently their utility is restricted by their reliance on conventional definitions of the family unit and family crises. Any adaptation or extension of their services would be predicated upon the organizational reorientation of existing values and goals.

13. Undoubtedly these problems were exacerbated by the presence of children. Since none of the men in this study had child custody, we cannot compare the differences in obtaining housing between male and female single-parent households. Thus we have no way of knowing if the reported discrimination was being directed to single parents, to female-headed households, or to women.

14. This was a relatively high rental fee in 1975.

15. To supplement and verify information compiled from roleplaying on rental housing and mortgage loans, I did conduct interviews with several real estate brokers.

16. This exemption can itself be discriminatory in a community like Westside, in which the vast majority of dwellings are one- and two-family units.

17. This was the first landlord I told about my dog, having learned that life was complicated enough for a single-parent woman without adding a pet. The picture on glossy tabloids of a family posing with "man's" best friend was not a landlord's delight, particularly if there was no man.

18. Between 1970 and 1976 the U.S. Department of Housing and Urban Development (HUD) noted an increase of 141% in the number of single women owning

homes (Gatto, 1979a). In a survey conducted by Esmark, Inc., in Chicago, a similar trend was observable for single parents. While their sample excluded low-income, single-parent families, Esmark reported that single parents were investing their money in housing, insurance, and securities at a higher level than two-parent households (Mills, 1976).

19. While two unrelated persons may have relatively little difficulty buying a house in Westside, larger groups do. Fearful of the devaluation of their property, neighborhood associations have sought to limit the sale and occupancy of large, single-family homes to a maximum of two unrelated persons. Interestingly, in 1975 the City Planning Department released data indicating that 39% of households of unrelated adults were elderly people, and the average number of unrelated people in one household was 2.5 persons, as compared to 3.7 in "traditional" units (Kowal, 1975).

20. Prior to the Federal Credit Opportunity Act of 1974, checking a divorced or legally separated woman's ex-husband's credit history was common practice. If the husband had a poor rating, this information might in turn be used against the former wife (Chesler and Goodman, 1976). Studies on women's credit following the passage of the Federal Act suggest that this practice still continues (Dietz, 1976; Washburn, 1976).

21. For the reasons cited on pp. 118-119, Sheila's assignment did not include an investigation of real estate brokers (see also footnote 15).

22. Three brokers did assess the market value of the house.

23. One guideline for purchasing a house is that the cost of the house should not exceed two-and-a-half times the purchaser's income. This helps to explain the $12,000 to $15,000 salaries suggested by bank officials. At $12,000 plus $6,000 child support, the two-and-a-half rule of thumb justifies the purchase of a $45,000 home. From the conservative perspective (and banks can hardly be considered anything but conservative) the high of $15,000 would be insufficient without additional income. This suggests that the child support, at least in part, was calculated by these officials along with a proposed salary. By Sheila's own admission alimony was to cease in three years, perhaps explaining the creditors' hesitancy to consider it as income.

24. The credit official is not entirely incorrect in considering such payments to be a form of risk-taking. While Michigan, for example, requires fathers to pay support monies directly to the courts, this is not the case in this state or most others. Consequently, women are frequently forced to take their husbands to court for enforcement of support (and alimony) awards. The cost of such actions is high and the record of success is low (Farrell, 1976; Winfrey, 1979).

25. Even women with jobs reported difficulty in obtaining mortgages (see pp. 93-94).

CHAPTER 5

SEPARATED AND DIVORCED WOMEN SPEAK OF THEIR SOCIAL NEEDS AND CONCERNS

If you were to guess what subject elicits the most responses from readers of a newspaper columnist who conducts interviews on a variety of topical issues, would your answer be: International peace? The state of the economy? The decline of the cities? Or something closer to home, like parenting, property taxes, or getting rich without any effort?

All of the above are incorrect. The answer, according to Darrell Sifford (1978a), is "how" the divorced can get back into "social circulation" after ten or 15 years of being married (p. 19).

Sifford's data may never be cited in scholarly journals or publications of the U.S. Bureau of the Census; they may not be deserving of a headline in *Newsweek* or *Time*. For all we know, his measurements are statistically insignificant, calculated on the basis of a handful of letters versus two fingers' full. But the boldly entitled article, "Bouncing Back from a Divorce: Words of Caution about the Sea of Matrimony," replete with a depiction of a *woman* in a rowboat drifting between a closed and an open door, is a graphic portrayal of a *woman's* frantic search for a mate. (Why else would she venture out in this unseaworthy vessel, standing, no less, and clothed in a dress, to look behind doors? Surely she knows that she has no oars, that the boat can capsize unless she sits down, and that a dress is inappropriate boating attire. How dimwitted can she be? Or how desperate?)

Clearly the article is written for women. With the assistance of psychologist Edward B. Fish, Sifford provides his audience with what is supposed to be a helpful, sympathetic guide for reentering the social scene. Suggestions are numbered to lead the hunter to "the right places at the right times" (p. 21). While the choices are "endless," we are told, those listed include: singles' organizations, dating services, newspaper advertisements, church groups, and places to work where there are higher quotas of eligible men. And this is only the first installment. The second article, appearing the very next day (who could wait longer?), is entitled "On the Rebound?

How to Act at a Singles Bar.'' Now we get down to basics. We learn whether to go alone or with a friend, how to dress, the best time to arrive, to befriend the bartender, not to bar hop, what drinks to order, and how to find out if a man is married or single (or should it read, ''Naughty or Nice?''). Alas, after all this instruction the lesson ends with a downbeat moral: Most men who frequent dating bars are looking to bed down for the night, and most women, who are, of course, looking for a relationship, possibly even a new spouse, give up the ''bar scene'' (Sifford, 1978b, p. 21).

Sadly enough, these articles typify the garden variety kind of printed advice for the divorced (particularly divorced women) that appears repeatedly in newspapers, magazines, and books. While I do not dispute the fact that meeting new people is of major concern to many separated and divorced people nor the possibility that some find these articles helpful (and others are indeed avid followers of their advice), I view these commentaries as stunning examples of tragicomedy, fare for the theatre of the absurd. Their ''heroines'' are tragic because they are doomed to defeat. They are comic because without the character or nobility to be undone, even by hubris, they do not fall from great heights; they stumble. And thus their misfortunes give rise to laughter, not tears. If ''Mary Hartman, Mary Hartman'' was still on the air, these poor souls would be perfect casting choices. Where else would we find women who purposively order Beefeater gin and tonic instead of simply gin and tonic because the good doctor tells them that this projects an image of sophistication (ibid.)?

And I also object to the fact that these articles are written predominantly about and for women, not infrequently by men. Oh, there are some pieces on the hippy, divorced man who lets his hair grow long, dons a vest, well-washed jeans, boots, and jewelry in the pursuit of youth and a chick, and there are a few others which offer tips on how (and where) to expedite this quest (e.g., Hinds, 1980). I regard these as equally demeaning and objectionable. My anger is fueled not by an alliance to women or an interest in protecting my image and that of my sisters; more fundamentally, it arises from the observation that women have been the principal target and main characters of this genre of self-help literature.

As if this were not enough, divorced women, better known as divorcees, have also been described in prose and envisioned in the minds of ''men'' in a quite different fashion. Unlike the bereaved widow, the divorcee, according to folklore, has nothing to mourn and hence nothing to restrict her freedom. Divorce becomes her ticket to ecstasy, her license for immorality. Thanks to the illogicality and versatility of the pen and mind, the word ''divorcee'' has been translated not only into a judgmental ''statement about morals,'' as columnist Richard Cohen (1980) points out, but one whose negative connotation applies ''only to women'' (p. 14). Although I have met women who were physically personifications of Lolita, grown up and divorced, none conceived of divorce as an erotic trip or a carefree journey.

Divorce is plainly too complex an act to be portrayed as uniformly pleasurable or painful. For each individual it has its ups and downs, its moments of triumph and depression. Nor do the social needs and concerns of the divorced revolve only or even primarily around dating and mating. While the formation of alliances with members of the opposite sex is not to be gainsaid, neither are ties to family, friends, neighbors, and even ex-spouses. All of these relationships are of social as well as psychological importance, influencing the way in which an individual adjusts to a marital dissolution. Moreover, social acclimation, like any adaptation, imposes new demands on people and requires the cultivation of new skills, the learning of new behavior, and the acceptance of new responsibilities.

THE FIRST CIRCLE: FAMILY

Fear of desertion or condemnation by one's family appears to be largely unfounded. Few exhibit the jubilance evident in the following announcement.

> Mr. and Mrs. Solomon Scher
> have the honor of announcing
> the divorce of their daughter
> Mary Jane
> from
> Sidney Gerbil
> in the Year of our Lord Nineteen Hundred Seventy-two
> Supreme Court, New York, New York
>
> (Kahn and Kahn, 1972, pp. xi-xii)

But neither do most go into mourning or retire in seclusion, apprehensive that leakage of the news will dishonor their family. Nor, generally, do they denounce (or disown) the divorcee on moral or ethical grounds. As the divorce rate has escalated along with changes in social norms and attitudes, the stigma associated with divorce has diminished. Naturally, there are families who, for religious or personal reasons, react with shame and indignation, but their number has sharply declined. Further, when such behaviors are manifested, in the main they are of short duration.

My mother is a storybook Catholic who believes implicitly in the teachings of the Church. To her the only way out of a marriage is death. When I finally got up the courage to tell her about my decision to divorce 'Jerry,' she ranted and raved about a family, the children, and every so often snuck in a word about the Church. But we also talked. I told her we were unhappy, that we tried to make it work, but couldn't; it was unhealthy for us and the children. She never liked the idea, but she accepted it. Every once in a while she moans about it, but in general she's been great, encouraging me to get a job and even to date.

(33-year-old woman, 1 year divorced)

Almost unanimously respondents expressed gratitude to their families, especially parents and siblings, for their help and support.[1] Some parents offered financial assistance.[2]

If it were not for the financial help that I receive from my parents, I would be unable to manage. Housing was a benefit of my husband's job, and so when we separated I had to move. It costs me $278 a month plus heating and utilities now; and that's a lot of money for me to handle with a part-time job.

(31-year-old woman, 4½ months separated)

Others sought to shelter and protect their child, treating her almost like an adolescent who had broken up with a boyfriend.

My parents flew 2,000 miles to cuddle me. My mother patted my hair and hugged me, and my father told me how he wasn't the first and he wouldn't be the last. [He meant boyfriend, as 'Ira' certainly was my first husband.] I think they enjoyed the opportunity to play mom and dad again in the way they knew best. I too enjoyed it, but it didn't help me to face the world as an adult. When they returned home, I missed them and I also grew up.

(35-year-old woman, 10 months separated)

Others provided companionship and friendship.

'Tom' had never gotten along with my parents, and as a result we had drifted apart. The separation helped to rebuild our friendship. Two years later my parents remain two of my best friends.

(41-year-old woman, 1½ years divorced)

And still others helped with child care and household responsibilities.[3]

If my mother did not babysit for the kids while I found a job and got myself together, I don't know how I would have managed. She did so many things, including cleaning the house and cooking meals. It is no longer necessary for her to do all this, but I know she is there if I need her. I'll always be grateful for her support.

(29-year-old woman, 1 year divorced)

Still, many parents seemed to be more concerned about a daughter's divorce than that of a son.

When my brother was divorced, my parents hardly said anything. Their major concern was whether they would still see his children. Once that was settled, they removed themselves from the situation. Yet when I got a divorce, they worried about how I would manage alone, what I would do for money, and how I'd meet another man. To them I was not self-reliant enough to be on my own. Ironically, my brother remarried after six months, and I, three years later, am still single. I enjoy being alone. I have proven that I am capable of supporting and taking care of myself and the kids.

(40-year-old woman, 3 years divorced)

Closer in age and interest, siblings, particularly if they lived nearby, at times proved better able to help the separated and divorced make the transition from married life to single parenthood.

I worried constantly that my sons would become homosexuals, even though they saw their father twice a week. My brother's visits helped to ease my fears, but he did more. His companionship with me and the boys helped me to see my own strengths and realize how ridiculous some of my fears were.

(38-year-old woman, 1 year divorced)

My kid sister became my confidante and best friend. She listened to my problems and convinced me to join the world again. She even got me dates the way I had for her when I was in college.

(37-year-old woman, 1 year divorced)

I depended too much on my brother's help, having him repair things, balance my checkbook, fix the car, and advise me about financial matters. It wasn't until his wife complained that I realized what a burden I had become. We are still good friends, and I know I can count on him, but not as a replacement for a husband.

(30-year-old woman, 2 years divorced)

Not all families rush to the aid of the separated and divorced. Some live too far away, some do not know what to do, and some remain too hurt, guilt ridden, or estranged to be of much use. Others are unintentionally destructive or overly protective and intrusive.

My father watched me like a hawk, questioning everything I did. He even began to take over with the children. It took many fights before he calmed down enough for me to take his behavior in stride.

(46-year-old woman, 4 years divorced)

Moreover, while many of the divorced spoke of their dependency upon parents and/or siblings, this reliance on kin was confined principally to the early stages of the dissolution. As if they had been transported backward in time to a premarital state, the newly separated looked to relatives for the comfort and support they had formerly sought from spouses. But the regression, when it did take place, was temporary. The need to break away again, to reassert themselves as independent, generally led the divorced away from the passive security of kin.

CONCENTRIC CIRCLES: FRIENDS

Among the separated and divorced, some turn to both family and friends, finding in each a fulfillment for different needs, a help at different times. Others depend exclusively (or primarily) on one or the other; the pattern varies from individual to individual. But sooner or later most seek companionship outside the family circle in existing and new friendships.

FRIENDSHIPS OF OLD

Women who had divorced or single friends were socially in the most advantageous position, at least initially.

Because I worked, I had several friends who were unmarried. After my divorce, and before too, these friends were lifesavers. They helped me to reorganize my life and to function as a single woman; and they got me out of the house. I had friends to go out with, not to meet men, but to do things.

(44-year-old woman, 2 years divorced)

'Jan' and I have been friends since college, but we never saw much of each other until I separated from 'Harold.' One day I was feeling alone and I called her. It turned out that she had been divorced for over a year. It is unbelievable how much she taught me. She also showed me that divorce was not the end of life but the beginning of another.

(31-year-old woman, 10 months separated)

Indeed, having friends, married or single, who are not part of the husband and wife's social circuit is helpful. This does not preclude the continuance of relationships in which the husband (or wife) was involved, but it does imply that the transition from marriage to life as a single person may be easier for those who start anew (McConnell, 1979). As psychiatrist Arthur A. Miller (1970) explains, if the divorced person "remains in this group, he is exposed to the currents of his friends' attempts to cope with their own emotional conflicts. He becomes the object of pity, comforting concern, control, envy, or suspicion. An unattached person may be seen as being a threat to the continuing marriages. Such emotional complications may make it necessary for the divorcee to withdraw and find new friends" (pp. 85-86). For some there is no choice.

We were three couples, all friends for over eight years. Then 'Mark' left and our friendship disintegrated. Oh, not at once, but slowly. If I asked one of their husbands to fix something or advise me on something, I began to get funny looks. I thought it was my imagination, but when they stopped calling or coming over, I realized they were worried that I was out to get their husbands.

(36-year-old woman, 1 year divorced)

Our friends became 'John's' friends after our divorce. They had him over for dinner and got him dates. But me they virtually ignored. They would stop and chat if we met, but no more than that. It would have been nice if they had not withdrawn so suddenly.

(39-year-old woman, 6 months separated)

In the questionnaire and interview sample, 63% of the women and 42% of the men stated that meeting new people of the same or opposite sex was one of the more difficult problems of separation.

Your married friends desert you when you separate. You feel socially isolated and lonely. Finding new friends is difficult, especially when your life is filled with crises that leave you unable to search for new friends.

(Parents Without Partners social chairperson)

In one way or another separation is a period in which friendships are dissolved and new ones are formed. How these alliances are made becomes an important question.

NEW ALLIANCES: FEMALE COMRADERY

It is not uncommon for separated and divorced women to look for female companionship in groups whose membership consists of those in a like situation.

Here I was with a large circle of friends and not one girlfriend who was single. Somehow the divorce boom escaped my friends. I tried adult education classes, political groups, and even some volunteering. But the only women I met were married. Out of desperation I joined a group for the divorced. I really did not get much out of the talk about legal battles, fights with ex-spouses, and children. I had been divorced over a year and much of that was behind me. But I did meet 'Carol,' and our friendship has helped both of us to keep doing new things and experimenting.

(36-year-old woman, 3 years divorced)

After divorce you feel especially lonely and isolated. Knowing people is a tremendous help, even if it is only someone to share a cup of coffee with or go to a movie with. I joined a women's support group to meet new friends, although the group was designed to help you cope with divorce, and my shrink was there for the coping part. It is amazing how quickly you form relationships in short-term groups. People admit that they are there for a purpose and are more receptive to overtures of friendship.

Some of these relationships last and others do not, but the group provides a safe and relatively convenient way to meet people.

(40-year-old woman, 1 year divorced)

Some found alternative groups better suited to their tastes and needs.

I joined a small CR [consciousness-raising] group. These groups provide an environment that is helping and that allows you to meet people with similar problems and interests.

(34-year-old woman, 4 months separated)

Of the women respondents who joined support, social, or educational groups for the separated and divorced, only one remained a member for more than a year. These groups served a purpose, but only temporarily.

I joined a group for the formerly married. It gave me a place to go once a week, a chance to meet new people who understood my problems. I don't belong anymore. It gave me the boost I needed, but now I'm more comfortable with one or two friends than in a large group.

(39-year-old woman, 2 years divorced)

I felt that only people who had gone through the same experience would truly understand how I felt. I had read about PWP [Parents Without Partners] and decided to give it a try. The people were friendly and helpful. It was like an AA [Alcoholics Anonymous] group for the single parent. But it never really met my needs. I had to get on with my life as a single woman and not as a leftover wife.

(31-year-old woman, 1½ years divorced)

While practically all respondents advocated the creation of groups and felt there was a void of such resources in Westside, paradoxically, even women who did join groups soon pulled away, and a significant number avoided groups of any kind. They met people through work, friends, and community activities.

People who are separated need a respite from divorce, not a room full of fellow sufferers. The way to meet friends is by joining community organizations and through work and other people.

(41-year-old woman, 10 months separated)

NEW ALLIANCES: DATING, MATING, AND LIVING TOGETHER

Men, by dint of training and custom, appear to be the first to venture out in search of companionship with the opposite sex. Whether they are inspired by their fantasies of the "new" sex, their visions of swinging singles, or their need for friendship or a relationship, onward they march. And not infrequently single bars or vacations advertised as havens for the jet set become their first stops. That they walk away disappointed, even lonelier than before, was the story presented by many of the men with whom I spoke.

After 'Kathy' and I separated, I began to frequent singles bars. At first it was like a dream come true, a chance to relive my youth at a time when morals were looser and women were not playing the dating game. But I began to feel old and tired. I didn't have the energy to be witty every night after working all day. What I really wanted was a relationship, not a string of one-night stands.

(38-year-old man, 9 months separated)

My married friends envied me; they thought it was great to be free and a swinger. But it really isn't. Dating bars are all right, but most nights you end up with a woman who you would never ask for a date if you had met her anywhere else.

(30-year-old man, 1 year separated)

Some shrugged it off, considering it a bit of adventure and a bit of comic relief, something one should try for the experience, but with the recognition that it is only an experience. Others were bitter and angry that it failed to fulfill their dreams or dispel their solitude.

Women were generally not as adventurous as men. Less accustomed to going out alone, when they did frequent bars, attend socials, or go on trips, it was typically with a female companion. Yet alone or with company, they too were often disenchanted.

Dating bars seem more sophisticated than frat mixers because everyone tries to be casual and uninterested, but in truth it is the same old game. It is like being an adolescent, subject to the up-and-down glances, the smiles, and the turning aways.

(34-year-old woman, 9 months separated)

Certainly not all expressed such negative reactions, and none was so damning as Judith Rossner in *Looking for Mr. Goodbar*, the book and movie which shocked many and enraged others. But significantly or coincidentally, dating bars were repeatedly described as a "setup for a letdown." Similarly, social gatherings sponsored by clubs and organizations for singles or the divorced and separated were viewed by the majority of women and men respondents as disillusioning, even humiliating, experiences.

Every time I attended a dance or a social for singles, I would spend hours deciding what to wear and how to arrange my hair until my bedroom looked like it had been hit by a hurricane. Even worse, I would fantasize the evening, conjuring up images of men who were attractive and intelligent. But I never did, at these places, meet anyone. Maybe I was so nervous that it showed, or maybe it was just that I got lost in a crowd in which the women outnumbered the men five to one. Whatever the reason, I would come home feeling more lonely than before I went. Fantasies are easier to take than rejection.

(40-year-old woman, 3 years divorced)

In light of these observations, one cannot help but wonder how so many of the divorced manage to date, and so frequently.[4] Is it that they settle for less—date just to go out? Or is it that ultimately most come to terms with their fears and insecurities, learning in the process to play the game in whatever way is best for them? According to those with whom I spoke, it was the latter.

I was afraid to date for almost a year, and then I decided, what the hell! Anything is better than four walls and a TV screen. So I went to a few mixers and even tried a computerized dating service. It was depressing, but I also learned that I could reject others too and that some people still found me attractive. Most of all I learned that I didn't need these crutches to get dates.

(35-year-old woman, 2 years divorced)

After my separation I became everyone's best bet for a dinner partner for the lonely men of Westside. Most of the time it was downright awful! But occasionally I have met men who are worthwhile. They make up for the rest.

(30-year-old woman, 10 months separated)

Getting dates is easy. The trick is to find the interesting ones. I joined political groups and tennis and swimming clubs, where I knew there would be men with interests similar to mine. You also have to learn to be more open, aggressive almost. It is hard for women who think that men must always approach them to change their behavior, but after the first awkward steps it gets smoother.

(36-year-old woman, 10 months separated)

Still, suburban living is not geared toward single people. Westside, like other middle-class suburbs, is a community for families. There are few apartment complexes; multifamily dwellings (predominantly two-family houses) present the principal alternative to single-family homes, and they are in the minority. The recreational, cultural, and religious life of the city is characteristically family oriented. And despite the census definition of a family as "a group of two persons or more related by birth, marriage, or adoption and residing together" (U.S. Bureau of the Census, 1979, p. 152) and the rising number of single-parent households, in Westside a family refers to the traditional constellation of two adults and their dependent children.[5] As such, places for singles are relatively scarce, either for residency or entertainment. Yet, while many separated and divorced men leave

Westside, moving to towns and cities catering to singles, in contrast their ex-wives often remain behind. Their reasons are mainly child oriented: better schools, open space, and organized recreational activities. More importantly, they argue that the continuity of their children's social and educational life is maintained by staying in the same community. But whatever the rationale, suburbia is decidedly not conducive to life as a single person. While most manage to overcome the disadvantages of suburban living, the penalties exacted for retaining the house, for good schools, and for open space, they do so in spite of the community rather than with its help. Perhaps this what anthropologist Paul Bohannan (1970) was referring to when he suggested "amending and improving the community life" of the divorced (p. 297). And perhaps this is why employed women adjust more easily to single life; work, besides its economic and psychological advantages, offers an entrée to another world, a world in which there are more opportunities for making new acquaintances—male and female.[6]

If you work you don't have to look for companionship. When you're married it's as if your senses are tuned down. When you are free again, everything wakes up too. You begin to react to flirtations you brushed aside before.

(41-year-old woman, 2 years divorced)

When I got divorced I thought dating would not be a problem. All those men who flirted with me before would now be there to ask me out. They flirted all right, and some asked me to go to bed with them, but that was it. So I had to start from the beginning. It meant changing my job and establishing friendships with other single women. Once you have new contacts, in comparison the rest is easy.

(31-year-old woman, 1 year divorced)

Few men reported difficulty in meeting women. The problem, as they described it, was not the scarcity of companionship but the suitability. It is Ms. Right, be it for a night or for life, that is hard to find (Kirchheimer, 1979b). Women confront the same problem in addition to having more trouble reentering the dating scene. But these problems are ofttimes misunderstood, particularly by well-intentioned advisers to the divorced. The cadre of individuals who write all those manuals for "creative" and "productive" divorce typically presume that the divorced woman's (and to a lesser extent, man's) need for companionship is synonymous with the need for a new spouse. And because they see remarriage as the solution for social and physical isolation, their goal is to enhance the marriageability rating of the divorced. To this end they advise women to move to the city, to put ads in the paper discreetly publicizing their availability, to join male-dominated organizations, and to change jobs. Others are more subtle in their approach. For example, the National Association for Divorced Women (NADW) advertises under the heading of "Social Opportunities" that NADW membership offers women social bonuses that include "ideas about jobs" which provide opportunities to meet community members, professionals, and other interesting individuals, "hobbies and services" which increase contacts with individuals of like interests, and "sports, travel and other ideas to help you make new friends—easily" (p. 10). Moreover, they furnish information on "diets," "trim-down exercises," "cosmetics," and "fashion." Surely the purpose of this helpful guidance is not solely to improve the physical health and social outlook of divorced women. Trimming down, dolling up, and getting out are quite clearly preparatory training for a manhunt. And since the search for an eligible man is regarded by some as worthy of great sacrifice, one male divorce counselor recommends that women consider a relocation to Alaska because of the abundance of unattached men (Tubbs, 1973).

If these writers and organizations were not so serious, we might be able to enjoy the vaudevillian flavor of their suggestions. But the majority do believe that remarriage is the panacea for all that ails the divorced; and unfortunately their viewpoint is shared by a goodly number of the divorced population. Perhaps too readily they accept society's verdict, so ably reinforced in these "helpful" manuals, that the single-parent family is an abnormality, that remarriage is the ticket to a promising tomorrow. Still, despite the continuance of high remarriage rates,[7] there appears to be an increasing number among the divorced who are renouncing this solution, who are in fact choosing to remain single. This may be related to the rise in the rate of women who never marry or who marry later, thereby legitimizing the status of single women[8] and/or it may reflect women's educational and economic advances. For women there is a negative correlation between remarriage and the level of educational attainment: The more educated the woman, the lower is the probability that she will remarry (U.S. National Center for Health Statistics, February 14, 1980a). In addition, while the rate of remarriage among men correlates positively with income,[9] the reverse is true for women (Bahr, 1979; Carter and Glick, 1976). Because the pressure on women to remarry is economic as well as social, women in higher economic brackets can afford *not* to remarry.[10]

I earn a good salary, nothing remarkable, but I do nicely. It would be lovely to have more money and maybe some day I will. But it is also lovely to be independent. I can afford to stay single even if it means less clothes, older cars, and less luxurious vacations.

(41-year-old woman, 2 years divorced)

Perhaps the relative economic advantages of women respondents and the fact that all had postsecondary education are two reasons why none had remarried at the time of this writing, although many of their husbands had. Some stated frankly that they would like to remarry, and some that they expected to in the near future. Others were more reluctant, as yet unwilling to relinquish their freedom.

For the first time in 17 years, I am doing what I want. It may sound selfish, and I suppose it is. But I have not abrogated my responsibilities to my children in the process. All I have done is cultivate a new career and pursue it with vigor. It is something I should have done years ago, and the sheer enjoyment of it and the discovery of my own talents have made me decide that this is not the time for considering remarriage. Maybe tomorrow I will feel differently; maybe I have not yet met anyone exciting enough. But at least for now I don't have to worry about running, because I'm happy where I am.

(40-year-old woman, 3 years divorced)

Furthermore, a declining remarriage (or marriage) rate[11] may also be attributed to an increase in the number of people who choose to live together either as a temporary or permanent substitute for marriage. That divorced men constitute the largest proportion of unmarried adults living with an unrelated woman (Glick and Norton, 1977, p. 34) indicates the appeal of informal unions, at least to men. Yet the 117% increase in the number of unmarried couples from 1970 to 1978 suggests not only that cohabitation is more than a passing fad, but that high divorce rates and the growing social acceptance of such unions may in the near future make cohabitation an ever more attractive option for the divorced—women as well as men (Glick and Spanier, 1980; Hyatt, 1978; Newcomb, 1979; "Unmarried Couples Rate Up," 1979).

Maybe I should marry 'Al,' but right now living together seems a wiser decision. It is a chance to test our relationship and see how it is affected by the children. For all of us it is a trial period and a pleasant one.

(45-year-old woman, 2 years divorced)

THE FORMER CIRCLE: EX-SPOUSES

These women were not among the deserted—women abandoned by men for destinations unknown. On the basis of national statistics, they would be classified as an advantaged group. For example, 70% received child support payments regularly, a figure significantly higher than national estimates (see Chapter 1). There were no women living below or even at the poverty level, albeit economic slippage was considerably more evident among women than men. All but four children had maintained contact with their fathers, although relationships varied in nature and frequency of contact. Yet these observations reveal little about the postdivorce life of mothers, fathers, and children, and even less about interpersonal interactions. Nevertheless, I will present no models of behavior by which to categorize families or individuals. Relationships are not static. At times attentive fathers became less available after divorce and at times relationships improved. Similarly, some women and men reported a betterment in their relationship with ex-spouses over time, and others a deterioration. The variables that affect such relationships are too numerous and the factors too inconsistent to be translated into specific patterns or predictive mechanisms. Indeed, this should not be surprising. There is no reason to presume that there would be uniformity in divorce any more than in marriage.

Yet the literature on divorce, in its never-ending search to be scientific, frequently concentrates on the identification of "patterns" of postdivorce behavior. (e.g., "Most of the divorced fathers saw their children and their ex-wives less and less as time passed." [Hetherington, Cox, and Cox, 1977, p. 145; see also Wallerstein and Kelly, 1980]). At present the sameples used in studies of this nature make it impossible to assess the accuracy of their conclusions. (e.g., the above statement is based on a comparison of 48 divorced families with 48 intact ones.) But even if such forecasts are eventually corroborated by researchers, they are still only generalizations. And generalizations, although informative, can also be harmful, causing some to anticipate problems and others to exacerbate them.

I read Grollman's book and believed that 'Steve's' good relationship with the children was bound to be short lived. And this wasn't all. So many had told me that once men remarry their new wife and new kids interfere with whatever contact they had had with their children from the first marriage. I have been waiting for this to happen for three years. Every time Steve has a business trip or something comes up, I'm sure that it is the beginning of the downfall. But maybe I'm wrong. He's always around when they [the children] need him, and even though he has remarried, it has not interfered with his being with the kids.

(37-year-old woman, 3 years divorced)

When will he stop paying child support? When will he stop visiting them so often? Will he pay for their college as he says? These are questions that I keep asking myself and him.

(30-year-old woman, 2 years divorced)

Respondents maintained that arguments with their ex-husbands most frequently focused on child-related issues. Even in monetary disagreements, number two on their list, the conflict seemed in some way to be associated with their children. This is understandable: For many, children constitute the primary bond between the divorced parties, at times forcing them to continue a relationship which one or both might prefer to terminate. Yet there is also the attachment which brought them together and for various reasons kept them together long enough to have a child or children; this is not easily cast aside. Good and bad memories linger and habits die slowly. There are a whole series of dependencies, often unnoticed during marriage, which upon separation can leave a void that is both painful and anxiety producing.

I wanted the divorce. And although I do not regret it, I miss 'Eleanor.' She had a way of ordering my life that made things easier. I never thought about it; in fact, I took it for granted. But now I'm disoriented, can't quite remember all the things I have to do. I don't know if this is love or just dependency. All I do know is life is better in some ways now but much harder.

(34-year-old man, 1½ years divorced)

I kept calling 'Bob' to fix things around the house, to take care of the kids, to talk to. But it tapered off. I made new friends, and the need to hang on abated.

(36-year-old woman, 2 years divorced)

Some remain dependent upon former spouses longer than others.

'Mary' still does my laundry, and I service her car. My friends tell me it is childish, but I'm not sure. Right now it serves a purpose for both of us and eases the adjustment.

(42-year-old man, 10 months separated)

To seduce or not to seduce was long the game I played with 'John.' Somehow I thought if I got him to have sex with me, he'd see all he was missing. And we did go to bed several times. But somehow we both knew we couldn't go back together. And this game was affecting the kids, getting their hopes up. We stopped it, but a part of me will always long for him. Perhaps that's okay.

(39-year-old woman, 1 year divorced)

We still go to open school night together and visit the kids at camp. I guess it is strange, but we are, after all, in this together.

(42-year-old man, 1½ years divorced)

For the most part the individuals quoted above are among those who have achieved what has been labeled the "friendly" or "compatible" divorce. For others, relationships with ex-spouses are anything but amicable.

Sometimes I think he has my line tapped. Every time I have a date he knows about it and has at times appeared in places where I go with a date. He doesn't make a scene, but his presence is unnerving. I begin to feel guilty for no reason and end up having a horrible time.

(41-year-old woman, 9 months separated)

She tells the kids how rotten I am, and I tell them about her. We both know this is harmful, but we don't seem to be able to stop it. The anger is too deep and too recent.

(40-year-old man, 7 months separated)

After he remarried he began to complain about everything. The kids are not being raised properly; they don't see his parents enough; the house is too sloppy. It is one constant feud without a beginning or end. It's worse than before the divorce, and now there seems no way out. I can't divorce him again. All I can do is harass him through his lawyer.

(45-year-old woman, 2 years divorced)

For better or worse, together or apart, a relationship between two individuals is not easily severed. Sometimes its remnants are most noticeable in their positive aspects—concern, friendship, shared interests—and sometimes in negative aspects—anger, revenge, pain, guilt, distrust (Hunt and Hunt, 1977). A couple may maintain civility for "the sake of the children"; they may continue to function as a unit out of habit, loneliness, or even affection; or they may be patently destructive, believing that their *raison d'être* hinges on the ruination of the other. Not always, but more often than not, the intensity of the emotional attachment diminishes with the passage of time.

I hated him. Yet I couldn't ignore him. I could see his face in my son's eyes; I saw him in the house, remembering the rooms he painted. For a while I tried to suppress every nice remembrance. This hurt more than it helped. It was only after I went back to school and stopped pitying myself that I could face the good memories and accept what was.

(47-year-old woman, 2¼ years divorced)

As individuals learn to separate their identity from that of former spouses, there is less of a need to hold on either through clinging dependency or aggressive retaliation. The ability to look outside of and beyond old relationships does not depend upon remarriage or the formation of alliances with members of the opposite sex, although many theorists do their utmost to argue this point (Hetherington, Cox, and Cox, 1978; Raschke, 1977; Spanier and Casto, 1979). Nor is synchronization of growth always possible or likely. For some it comes before separation, for others at the time of the decree, for some months or years afterward, and for a few it never comes. Extreme cases, however, reveal nothing except that aberrant behavior can occur in any situation. The divorcee who dreams of a reunion ten years after the final decree has been issued is no more typical than the widow who keeps preparing supper for her husband ten years after his death.

The point to be made is that the bonds between spouses do subsist after divorce and cannot be construed as uniformly deleterious. Indeed, divorced couples who retain ties, be they the product of affection, friendship, or shared responsibilities, in general have less difficulty structuring a workable postdivorce relationship; it is easier for them and for their children.

I thought there was something wrong with me because I cared about 'Ann.' First I thought it was guilt for having initiated the divorce, then guilt over the children, and then just a habit. But the more I thought about it, the more I realized that Ann will always be a part of me. This doesn't mean I wish we were still married. I'm happier apart from her, although there are things I miss. I can't say it's better for the kids, but I don't think it's worse either.

(40-year-old man, 2 years divorced)

'Al' always took the kids for their lessons, to the doctor, and bought their clothes. He still does after four years of divorce. It's as if we made a pact—a postmarital contract to divvy up responsibilities. We don't perform services for each other much anymore, but for the kids we continue much as before.

(46-year-old woman, 4 years divorced)

How can you take 11 years and toss them away? Two people share so much; even when they disagree, there is a togetherness. It is natural and it is important. For the kids, yes, but for me too. I don't want to negate 11 years of my life with bitterness.

(34-year-old woman, 1½ years divorced)

THE INNER CIRCLE: CHILDREN

CUSTODIAL MOTHERS AND THEIR CHILDREN

Divorced women with custody of their children see their responsibility as a mixed blessing: Children provide comfort, love, and companionship, but they also require constant care, attention, and supervision.

Whenever I feel really down, I look at the kids and realize, corny as it sounds, that he has lost more than I have. I have the kids, and he, well, he has his freedom.

(37-year-old woman, 10 months separated)

My daughter talked me into going back to work. She helped me compose a letter of inquiry and a résumé, picked out an outfit for the interview, and made supper to celebrate my getting the job. And she was only 12 at the time. I try not to treat her as a friend, in the sense of an adult. But it is hard; her maturity can be deceptive.

(46-year-old woman, 3 years divorced)

My kids are young enough to want to go out with me. We make the rounds of museums, theaters, and such. I've learned to see it through their eyes and enjoy it as they do. Just knowing that they are there and that they care was indispensable in the beginning, although as time passes I am becoming less dependent on them for activity and affection.

(34-year-old woman, 6 months separated)

Undeniably, children, in and of themselves, provide a social outlet for the divorced, offering them friendship, affection, and at times companionship. Still, they are a 24-hour-a-day responsibility with little time off for good behavior. Not only do children add to the problems involved in managing and supporting a family and a household, but their very presence limits the freedom of the custodial parent to socialize and to form new relationships.

My children are responsible for helping me to go on after the divorce. They justified my existence and provided the affection that I needed. They also complicated my life. I hesitated to date, believing that they would not accept my relationship with any man other than their father. It wasn't until my 12-year-old daughter asked me why I never had any men friends that I realized that I had been responsible for my own stagnation.

(40-year-old woman, 2 years divorced)

Every time I dated my children wanted to know when I was getting married. Sometimes they asked my friends if they were "going to marry Mommy." I can't count the number of embarrassments, but after a while you begin to laugh and it eases the tension.

(35-year-old woman, 11 months separated)

Although in retrospect such embarrassments seem humorous, at the time they can be disconcerting. One woman related how her ten-year-old son and six-year-old daughter would hide her shoes, bag, and coat while she was dressing to go out. When her date arrived she was forced to scurry around the house, searching for the missing articles. This happened on three different occasions before she had enough presence of mind to forewarn her children that such behavior was not permissible. When asked why they did this, they very innocently replied that they did not want her to leave them. In another instance an eight-year-old girl made several attempts at bolting the doors, both in an effort to keep the intruder out and her mother in. One nine-year-old boy politely asked his mother's date if he could hang up his coat. Unhesitatingly the man handed over his coat only to discover when he got into his car that his keys had been lifted.

Fear of losing the custodial parent is not uncommon after a divorce. As psychiatrist E. James Anthony (1974) explains, the child's "insecurity may be intensified by the thought that if one parent can leave him, there is nothing to stop the second from doing the same" (p. 472). Not all children experience the same fear, and among those who do, their behavior can be strikingly dissimilar: Some refuse to converse with any of their parent's dates, others hide, and still others openly exhibit their hostility. For example, one 12-year-old boy was particularly persistent in his plots to rid the house of interlopers. Besides "minor" irritants such as exploding cherry bombs a foot away from the unsuspecting visitor, he feigned suicidal exploits using anything from kitchen knives to pill bottles.

Some children adopt a dramatically different posture, doing everything short of performing the marital rites.

After two dates my daughter told one man about a great place for our wedding and who she wanted to invite to the affair. He never asked me out again.

(33-year-old woman, 2 years divorced)

When 'Sam' told my children what a wonderful mother they had, my 16-year-old son replied, "If she's so terrific, why don't you marry her instead of just sleeping with her?" That night I got a proposal.

(42-year-old woman, 5 years divorced)

Others appear friendly and even excessively demonstrative.

'Alice' would snuggle up to any man who entered the house. I was never sure if she was flirting with them or just needed affection. She was, however, so demonstrative that one man asked me why I couldn't be as affectionate as my daughter.

(38-year-old woman, 1 year divorced)

'Tom' greeted each of my dates with an invitation to see his room, followed by asking them to play with him. There were times when the game lasted long enough to prevent us from going out. It was hard to balance my anger with my attempt to understand the meaning behind Tom's behavior. Thank God, this did not last! I began to delay being ready long enough for them to have some time together, and I could still have an evening out.

(36-year-old woman, 1½ years divorced)

Like the woman quoted above, Eve Baguedor writes poignantly in *Separation: Journal of a Marriage* (1972) of the dilemma of balancing her needs with those of her children.

I *do* find myself, consciously separating my interests from that of the girls—for the first time. "They're young," I rationalize, "with all their lives ahead of them, while I am vulnerable to physical threat, to financial insecurity." By good fortune, it never comes to a drastic choice. But living with the knowledge that my interests can be separate—even competitive—with my children's is a humiliating, unenjoyable discovery. One of the uglier lessons of separation (p. 129).

Many individuals are not as perceptive as Baguedor. Unaware or unable to acknowledge that their interests may not only differ from those of their children but conflict with them, they approach dating as if it were a family affair. Some even exchange places with their children, allowing their offspring to assume dominant, often domineering, roles in the family constellation.

Now I can see that 'Marcy' had become my mother and I, her child. I would ask her what she thought about each of my dates. None of them quite naturally measured up to her father, and she was clever enough never to make comparisons. But she did always find some flaw. One was too heavy. One was too loud. One was too silly. Stupid me listened. Yet, when I finally met someone I did like, I was able to place her comments in the proper perspective—they were, in fact, childish. Only at this time could I counter her without going into details that were in truth things one did not discuss with a 14-year-old daughter.

(38-year-old woman, 1½ years divorced)

Depending upon the age and sometimes the sex of the child, this practice varied. But even young children were often pulled into the question-and-answer quiz on mommy's friends.

In part, such behavior appeared to be motivated by personal anxiety and insecurity, and, in part, by an almost obsessive concern for their children's well-being.

I watched the children wtih each man that entered the house. Would he be nice to them? Did he *really* like children? It was as if I was testing each one, not for me but for them. But I wasn't marrying these men. I didn't even want to. It is absurd to screen each friend as if you are picking a father for your children instead of a friend for yourself.

(42-year-old woman, 11 months separated)

Some went so far as to structure trial sessions for their dates. An evening at home, family picnics, and outings to the zoo or museum all posed hurdles for the suitor. Under the ever-observant eye of Mom, interaction between her companion and children was carefully scrutinized. At times this was a prelude to getting serious, be it going to bed with the man, living with him, or marrying him. At other times it was a ritualistic performance staged with every prospect who managed to last beyond the first few dates. Predictably more than a few dashed for the nearest exit once they caught drift of the plan.

I arranged evenings so that they were family events, leaving little time for a man to see me alone. I refused to allow myself the luxury of companionship with any man who did not qualify as an exemplary dad. I stopped only after I realized that even the few who passed my tests did not care to see *me* again. I must admit the kids found the whole process as tedious as did my dates.

(43-year-old woman, 2 years divorced)

Other women reacted quite differently. Indeed, some became self-indulgent, overly preoccupied with their own needs and fears. Rarely was such behavior confined to the sphere of social relations, and in all cases it appeared to be of short duration, usually occurring fairly soon after the separation or divorce.

I felt as if I had to build a new life for myself instantly. I got a job, enrolled in school, and started dating all within three months of my separation. When the school called me to tell me 'Jan' was withdrawing in class, I realized that I had forgotten that her life was also important.

(30-year-old woman, 1 year separated)

While none of the women with whom I spoke was either a true narcissist or martyr, at times their actions seemed to better approximate one of these extremes. Eventually, though, the vast majority approached dating with more nonchalance. For the most part women, even after four or five years of divorce, were still somewhat cautious about revealing to their children details of their relationships with men, intimate or otherwise. The few who were living with men expressed, as did many others, concerns about the effect of their alliances on their children.

I still worry that the kids will think less of me because I live with a man who isn't my husband. I tell myself and them that it is better than marrying someone before I'm ready.

(41-year-old woman, 3 years divorced)

NONCUSTODIAL FATHERS AND THEIR CHILDREN

In recounting the roles children play in their social lives, fathers[12] tended to minimize adult friendships and dating, focusing instead on the absence of their children. Many depicted themselves not only as lone wanderers cast adrift from hearth and kin[13] but as the victims of a society that enshrines motherhood.[14] Yet these men had not lost custody battles. To the contrary, most had accepted defeat from the outset. Some had flirted with the idea of suing for custody, but were dissuaded by their lawyers. Others were wary of the responsibility of guardianship, unsure of their ability to perform as homemaker and breadwinner.

I always considered myself a nurturing parent. I changed diapers, prepared bottles, cared for them when they were sick, and played an active part in their upbringing. But my lawyer cautioned me against a custody battle. "Mothers generally win," he said, "unless they are a mess, psychologically and socially." Well, 'Fran' wasn't a mess; so I bargained instead for very liberal visitation. I see them often and speak to them almost daily, but I'm not there and it hurts.

(39-year-old man, 2 years divorced)

I thought of petitioning for custody, but to be honest I was afraid. What would I do with three girls? I work long hours and the problems seemed insurmountable. Five years later I'm thinking of reopening the case, but the legal fees are frightening and my new wife is hesitant. I guess my bravery hinges on having a woman in the house.

(45-year-old man, 5 years divorced)

In bemoaning the loss of their children, one man after another told how he resented the role of the occasional visitor and missed the companionship of his children.

I want to be there when they cry and when they laugh. I want to be there to help them and have them help me. Their mother claims she has no time to herself and tells me about all my freedom. Freedom? No! It has another name; it's called loneliness. I wanted the divorce, but not from the kids, just from my wife.

(35-year-old man, 1½ years divorced)

I feel I deserted my kids. They keep asking me to come home and make up with Mommy. How do I explain that I haven't left them, that I'll always be their father? To them it's all or nothing; either I want them and I'll come home or I don't and I'll stay away.

(41-year-old man, 8 months separated)

I amuse them like a high-priced babysitter. I tell myself to relax, sit around the apartment, and talk. The one time we tried it, we were all bored. We felt we had to sit in the same room, but ran out of conversation. It's just not natural.

(37-year-old man, 3 years divorced)

Most of these men had never anticipated the problems that they were experiencing, never predicted the intensity of their reaction to being separated from their children. During the decision-making period preceding divorce, in effect, clients and lawyers alike are engaged in blind negotiations. Without any knowledge of how each family member will respond, it is impossible to provide for every contingency or foresee the ramifications of each decision. With respect to children, critical questions, such as who is to be awarded guardianship, whether joint or split custody is a viable alternative, and whether a visitation schedule should be narrowly defined or open-ended, are oftentimes either not considered or inadequately thought through. Decisions are, of course, not irrevocable. Ligitation is one way to alter agreements; informal or formal changes negotiated after divorce are another. Children can also be the instigators of change. In a variety of ways their reactions to the separation may cause parents to revise schedules or living arrangements, to remarry or not, or even to reconcile.

Depending upon the ages of their children, their relationships with their ex-wives, and their personal circumstances and situations, these men found different ways of coping with the role of noncustodial parent. Some chose to see their children more frequently; others chose to limit visitations; and still others found an answer somewhere in between these two ends of the continuum. At times the relationship and/or style of interaction between father and children had to be restructured.

It took two years before the kids and I worked out a relationship. We stopped the mad whirl of circuses, shows, and museums, and began to enjoy games at home, friends, and just being in the house together. We sometimes take trips, but we try to keep it as natural as possible, avoiding like the plague the Sunday-visitor syndrome. Now they drop in just to say hello without it being Sunday, and now I can change the day without the heavens caving in. I was lucky; my wife cooperated.

(47-year-old man, 3 years divorced)

At first I was too bitter to be anything but a nuisance to the kids. I ignored their problems and used them to get back at my wife. When I started dating again and found an apartment that was really nice, I saw that unless I changed my behavior I would be a father without children. It still isn't easy, but it can be nice. I don't have much of the hassle, and I do have a lot of the pleasure.

(39-year-old man, 1½ years divorced)

I don't see my kids often. I moved out of town because of an excellent job opportunity. They visit me on February school vacation and for a week in the summer, and sometimes I get a free weekend and fly down to see them. I hope when they are older, they will be able to come and visit more often. I feel guilty, but I've accepted it.

(30-year-old man, 2½ years divorced)

If these fathers talked primarily about their relationships with their children, there was a remarkable similarity in the anecdotes which they did tell about their children's influence on their social lives. One common problem pertained to the curtailment of weekend dating.

Here I was trying to reenter the dating scene without having any free weekends. The kids stayed with me, and this was the only time I saw them all week. To up and leave when they just came was beyond consideration. I didn't want to bring anyone to the house either, fearful of how the kids would react. So I had to explain to those who wanted to introduce me to someone and to women I met that weekends were out. This continued for a year and a half until I changed the visitation to every other weekend. It was the only way I knew to work it out before I started to resent them.

(38-year-old man, 3 years divorced)

When the kids came to visit me, I usually had 'Mary' there. My ex-wife went crazy. She said it was a lousy influence on the kids, even though we never did anything in front of them. Maybe it did upset them; they were very attached to their mother, and this might have been disturbing. At any rate, my ex-wife threatened to take me to court to stop the visitation. I never bothered to test her. Instead I pick the kids up Friday night and bring them home at 6:00 on Saturday. That gives me time for dating, and I still see the children every weekend.

(33-year-old man, 1 year divorced)

The dilemmas of a living-together alliance and remarriage were other issues raised by these men. In general, those who were living with women or planned to seemed more anxious about their children's (and at times their ex-wives') response than those who spoke of remarriage.

I don't know how to tell the children that 'Pat' will be moving into my apartment. She's more than a girlfriend and less than a stepmother. How do you explain that to children?

(34-year-old man, ½ year divorced)

Still, remarriage also surfaced concerns over how (and even when and where) to explain the decision to children. While few resorted to rigorous testing of the parenting capacity of prospective spouses,[15] the major concern expressed by men before as well as after remarriage related to the nature of the stepmother-stepchild relationship.

My children could not understand how I could remarry. They kept telling me that Mommy was not remarrying, so why should I. Moreover, they asked, with great sagacity, if I liked being married so much why didn't I stay with Mommy. I did not have any answers. I was so sure that they would like 'Nancy,' see all the wonderful things about her, that I never imagined any difficulty. But to them Nancy was an intruder. She cut into the time they had with me, and she brought back painful memories of the divorce. I don't know if they will ever fully accept her. They seem to view her as a friend, but avoid use of the word "stepmother" or "mother."

(47-year-old man, 2 years divorced)

I never tried to pick out a new mother for my children. They had a mother. Instead I worried about finding someone with whom I could be happy, believing that everything would then fall into place. For the most part it has. 'Marge' takes things in stride. She understands that the children resent her in ways and like her in others. She has never tried to be nor does she want to be their mother.

(39-year-old man, 3 years divorced)

The whole situation was very awkward, especially at the wedding. The kids looked like they were at a wake. For a while I thought the whole thing was a mistake. I was prepared for another divorce or to spend a fortune on a shrink. But slowly it has improved. 'Gina' will never be their mother, but she has come a long way toward being their friend.

(38-year-old man, 4 years divorced)

CONCLUSION

Reading or hearing about the social lives of the divorced can evoke various responses. Some stories have a titillating effect, and even arouse envy and desire for emulation. We hear of the newly unencumbered male who becomes the darling of the jet (or almost jet) set, today's most eligible bachelor. News of his availability becomes fodder for the fantasies of unattached females. He is handsome, witty, and successful. His life is a social whirl, his options unlimited. Then there is our heroine, the divorcee. Her experiences are strikingly different. Beautiful, charming, and intelligent as she may be, her following is a cadre of seemingly unhappily married men who offer her consolation and themselves a sexual adventure. Although she appears independent and strong, it is a façade, hiding her loneliness and fears. But she is destined for better. And better, of course, means that she meets our hero. They gravitate toward each other in a script that should, but doesn't, make fairy tales seem realistic. He is glad to be free of his too chic and not so smart admirers and she to find someone who, by comparison, makes her ex-spouse look like Alfred E. Newman and seem as insensitive as Richard M. Nixon. If they marry, the story follows the "they lived happily ever after" end. If they don't, it is because her "new" sense of self propels her onward to a life of independence, at least for the time being. And this is what it is like, the moral goes, to be beautiful (or handsome), wealthy, and divorced.

Then there is the depressant variety of tales. The endless sagas of one-night stands; the men who follow the "hip, Honda, and hirsute syndrome" (Hetherington, Cox, and Cox, 1977, p. 45), discovering too late that youth cannot be recaptured and meaningful relationships cannot be found in singles bars. And not to be forgotten are the women who after trying everything from singles groups to bars begin to consider even their former rejects attractive.[16] Now, however, these rejects no longer want them. It is hard to discern whether these stories are presented as a warning to those who think that divorce is blissful and exciting or as accurate portrayals of the lives of the formerly married.

Yet lest anyone think that the mass media have concentrated solely on the dating and mating exploits of the separated and divorced, giving short shrift to their social relationships with family, friends, and children, take another look at daily tabloids, popular magazines, and television and movie programming. Whether your preference is "Extended Families Offer Salvation" (Stocker, 1980a), "Old Friends Take on a New Look" (McConnell, 1979), "The Children of Divorce" (Francke et al., 1980), or "The Travails of a Part-Time Stepparent" (Cole, 1980), there is bound to be some current offering to satiate your needs or curiosity.

The problem is not insufficient coverage but overexposure, which is too frequently misleading and at times frightening. Perhaps the truth is to be found between the extremes that make for better headlines and advertising copy. Or perhaps there is no true story or stories. Decidedly, there are similarities in the social experiences of the separated and divorced. There are also differences, attributable to the many factors and influences which make each individual's life unique. In the preceding pages I have tried to present some of both, but here too we see only glimpses of people's lives and thoughts. A few may be distorted by the passage of time; a few may be colored by anxieties and angers that are not consciously understood or recognized; and a few may be embellished for my benefit.

NOTES

1. For a more detailed discussion of this topic see Robert Weiss's *Marital Separation* (1975).

2. Goode (1956) reported that families provided the primary source of financial support for 57% of the 425 divorced women in his sample.

3. While neighbors often pitched in during the early stages of separation, assisting with child care, shopping, and other household chores, their overtures of help became less frequent over time. Neighbors who were rated as major sources of support were in general also considered friends.

4. Hunt (1966) claimed that 75% of people date in the year following their separation and a whopping 90% in the second year (p. 110). In this study the percentage of respondents who dated within the first two years of separation was slightly lower but still compatible with Hunt's statistics.

5. Headlines in the local paper such as "A New Kind of Family Makes Waves in 'Westside' " (1975) and "What's in a Family?" (1975) tell of neighborhood objections to proposals for small communes consisting of two or more single-parent families.

6. The nature of a woman's job is another factor that influences her opportunities for meeting new people. Those who remain in female-dominated professions, like teaching, are less likely to meet men at work than those who are employed in the private sector.

7. Norton and Glick (1976) estimate that five-sixths of divorced men and three-fourths of divorced women remarry. Moreover, between 1971 and 1978 the percentage of remarriages among women increased from 24% to 32% as compared to 25% to 35% for men (U.S. National Center for Health Statistics, 1980c).

8. It is, however, worth noting that in its provisional statistics for the 12-month period ending with February 1980, the National Center for Health Statistics reported an increase in the marriage rate to 10.6 per 1,000 population, as compared to the May 1977 rate of 9.9 (1980b, p. 2).

9. That wealthier men can better afford remarriage even if it entails the maintenance of two households is one common explanation for this statistic.

10. Some claim that this pattern is attributable to women's reliance on alimony. Since in many instances remarriage terminates alimony, these awards are viewed as

a deterrence to marriage. The low percentage of alimony awards and high non-compliance figures appear to contradict the validity of this argument.

11. Between 1977 and 1978, the remarriage rates of divorced women and men aged 14-24 years declined by approximately 10% with more moderate declines for those aged 25-44 years. Further, in the same period, the first-marriage rate also evidenced a decline, ranging from 2% to 6% depending upon the age group being studied (U.S. National Center for Health Statistics, 1980c, p. 2).

12. In this study only noncustodial fathers were interviewed. While their experiences differed, often notably, from those reported by custodial mothers, it appears that the variances are related largely to the responsibilities of guardianship and not to differences between the sexes.

13. This was true for men who did and did not initiate the divorce action.

14. Similar findings were reported in the survey conducted by the Permanent Commission on the Status of Women in Connecticut (1979, pp. 62-63; see also Hetherington, Cox, and Cox, 1977, 1978).

15. This may be related to the fact that they were, in contrast to women respondents, noncustodial parents.

16. If this seems exaggerated, I refer the reader to an article in the *New York Times Magazine* of August 29, 1976 entitled "The Re-Mating Game" (Blum, pp. 10-21). Here, for example, when one "attractive" woman was asked why she was attending a function at a social participation club, she replied, "It is better than suicide. I've tried everything else" (ibid., p. 10).

CHAPTER 6

SHEILA AND
THE HIGH SOCIETY
OF THE GAY DIVORCEE

Again and again I was asked if I had roleplayed (or planned to) a separated woman at socials, clubs, or bars. Others put it another way: "You didn't go to bars and places like that, did you?" I cannot help suspecting that more than a few wished for an affirmative answer. Perhaps they wanted to know what it was really like to be single. Was *Looking for Mr. Goodbar* true? Or perhaps they wondered how far I dared to go. Would I, a married woman, spend evenings (and/or days) searching for male companionship? And, if or when I met someone, what happened then? Despite my denials, my assertion that Sheila did not socialize or try to socialize, did not attend any groups or places for single people unde the guise of being a separated woman, there were some, I suppose, who believed otherwise—maybe they still do. So be it! While I may have disappointed those who anticipated a more risqué narration or those who are disturbed by the methodological inconsistencies created by this omission, the disconcertion of some is preferable to the deception of others.

Nonetheless, in the course of this research there were two different kinds of experiences that related to the social needs and concerns of separated and divorced women (and men) and thus merit recounting: One kind was planned; one was not. In the planned category belongs activities conducted outside of roleplaying. I, *not* as Sheila Ash, attended group meetings of separated and divorced people and single parents in order to elicit their help in compiling data. At these sessions I learned more about each group's function and left with some sense of what it would be like to be a member. In addition, I spoke to individuals who belonged to or had organized alternative groups for the same population. They too supplied information which will be reviewed in this chapter.

In contrast, the experiences which were not planned most often, but not always, occurred during roleplaying. While they differed in format and even in intent, they were all variances on the dating-game theme. Some were sophisticated, rather subtle expressions of interest—what one might call in the vernacular a feeler, or, in more formal language, a test of receptivity to a possible advance. Others were more directive: Without any pretenses or innuendos, their overtures were purely and simply propositions. Unplanned as these encounters were, they were not completely unanticipated. Many female respondents had reported similar incidents. If their stories were at times more dramatic than mine and if some had a larger repertoire from which to draw, the experiences recorded on the following pages are also illustrative of social issues pertinent to separated and divorced women.

GROUPS FOR THE FORMERLY MARRIED

The investigation of these groups began with Parents Without Partners (PWP). Although there was no chapter in Westside, the PWP group in a nearby community open to Westside residents seemed an obvious first choice—a way to begin at the top. Started in New York City in 1957 with 25 people, PWP has mushroomed into an international organization with 1,000 chapters and over 186,000 members in the United States, Canada, and Australia (Brozan, 1980a, p. A20). By far the largest and most well-known group for single parents, PWP publishes, at its international headquarters in Washington, D.C., its own journal, *The Single Parent*, in addition to monthly bulletins which are issued by local chapters. Like any corporation, PWP has a formal organizational hierarchy. The branch that I contacted had a four-member professional advisory board, a zone administrator, and a district supervisor, as well as chapter officers (including five vice-presidents) and numerous committee chairpersons.

Consequently, requests to conduct research had to follow procedural guidelines and be processed through appropriate channels. For example, I was required to submit information on the purpose and nature of my study, my academic credentials and affiliations, and the names of individuals who could be contacted for verification. Upon approval of my application, I was scheduled to attend a meeting, allotted time at the end of the session during which to describe my research, and permitted to distribute questionnaires to volunteering members. Three of us went that night: a colleague of mine, Barbara Intrilligator, who participated in the first phase of the research, my husband, and myself. There was no pretense. Naturally everyone knew that I was married, but also that I planned to assume the identity of Sheila Ash upon completion of the questionnaire and interview stages of the research.[1]

Many were clearly intrigued by the fictional character of Sheila, asking numerous questions about the roleplaying exercise: How would I disguise my identity? What places would I contact? What people would I speak to? The majority, however, appeared more interested in having someone to whom they could relate their experiences. The three of us stayed long after the program had officially ended, long after we had collected the completed questionnaires. We stayed to chat, but mainly we listened. There were so many stories in the room,[2] so many who wanted to be heard. Only the dimming of the light stilled their voices and invited our exit.

Logically we should have been elated. In one evening we had received over 100 completed questionnaires and the promise of more to come. Further, a quick perusal of the forms revealed that there would be little difficulty in recruiting interview participants. (Only a few had not indicated on the questionnaire a willingness to be interviewed.) Still, as we left, burdened down with piles of stapled papers, we felt neither pleased nor gratified. For reasons we could not express or understand, we felt saddened, even despondent. Were we merely experiencing an anticlimactic aftereffect—that all too common letdown following weeks of work and the ebullience of launching a new project? If so, why was my husband, who had not been and would not be closely involved in the research, similarly affected? More plausibly, our reaction was linked to the evening's activity. But how? Why? Explanations did not come forth until late that night. The further in time and space we were from the group, the easier it became for us to talk. At first slowly and then with growing intensity, we began to discuss and mull over the evening's happenings. Recounting the anecdotes, concerns, and feelings people had expressed to us, we tried to connect our emotional reaction to what we had heard and seen. Even then, all that emerged were vague speculations.

Had we seen glimpses of a future which we had not planned for ourselves, sort of like Scrooge's visions of what was to be? For a brief time we had become a part of a community of strangers. A community we had not intended to join. Were we afraid that this would be our fate? Perhaps in a way we were, but I think only in a very superficial way. If we feared joining this community, a group united by a shared experience of which we knew little, it was not because they were separated, divorced, or widowed; of that I am sure. It could have been any group in which people encounter frustration and disappointment, in which they fail to fulfill their expectations.

They had come, or so they told us, for companionship, to meet others like themselves. While they had indeed met people who had gone down the same road as they, it appeared that many had not found the companionship they sought. It was an assemblage of dissimilar people and personalities. Their bond was essentially single parenthood, not complementary interests, ambitions, education, background, or religion. The women substantially outnumbered the men. In addition, they were generally better educated, younger, and accustomed to living on higher incomes.[3] Had this been a time before they had married and had children, it is doubtful that either the women or the men would have sought each other out, even congregated in the same room. And as such, more than a few were disillusioned.

Yet here they stayed, at least for the time being. Some told us that they did not know where else to go, others, that they kept returning in the hope that it would be different. A new meeting might mean a new member, someone interesting and interested. And for still others it was a shelter of a kind —a safe, friendly, and undemanding place in which to be. Temporarily this has its own reward, even if it is something more than comfort that the individual needs or wants.

Thus the specter we saw, the apprehension we felt, was the image of ourselves having nowhere to turn but to a group that held no answers for us. The thought was disquieting. At the time this was the only group we had visited, and since we had no other with which to compare it, its effect on us was particularly potent. Maybe we would have been less moved by this experience, or at least more detached, had it occurred a few months later. But it did not, and the memory of that night lingers. And so too does Paul Bohannan's (1970) remark that "there must be *something* besides Parents Without Partners to fill the gap between dating bars and solitude" (p. 297). Had he also sensed the same undercurrent of loneliness despite the presence of a crowd of people? Had he also concluded that this was indeed a lonely crowd?[4]

These, of course, are but impressions, feelings shared by three people who were guests of a group for one evening. I say this not as an excuse, for my recount is an honest one, in no way meant to disparage the group or its members. The number of people who belong to PWP suggests that it meets the needs of many individuals. I do not wish to minimize its value or to quibble with its organizational goals. As in any group, there are some who benefit from membership and some who do not. Perhaps it is because I cannot visualize myself as belonging to such a group that I question how many others would also be misfits. It is for these people that I speak; it is for these people that other places and other routes have to be found.

The remembrances of the night at PWP did not vanish and in all probability influenced subsequent encounters. Yet I continued to look to organized groups for the recruitment of sample participants.[5] Telephone calls to civic, social, and religious organizations in Westside revealed two additional groups for single parents and/or separated and divorced individuals, both of which were affiliated with a religious institution. One of the two was sponsored by a synagogue. It was Sheila who made the initial contact.[6] The conversation, I believe, bears retelling.

"My name is Sheila Ash, and I'm calling to find out if your temple has a group for separated and divorced people."

"Are you a member of the temple, Mrs. Ash?"

"No, I am not."

"Then you don't qualify for membership. It is for temple members *only*."

"If you could tell me more about the group, perhaps I might decide to join the temple." (No duplicity was intended; I considered this to be a reasonable request.)

"Are you Jewish, Mrs. Ash?"

"Yes."

"What *kind* of Jew are *you* to talk of joining a temple because of a social group?" (Although grammatically a question mark is the correct punctuation for the above sentence, the woman's intonation of utter disbelief, even disgust, merits an exclamation mark. My motivation had been interpreted as irreverent, my words as blasphemous.)

"I have *not* called to discuss my religious beliefs," I replied indignantly. "I *have* called for information. Since you seem unwilling to help me, I would like to speak to the person in charge of the group."

"You can't be serious. This is foolishness!"

"I am *very* serious." (I was not only sinful but doltish as well. In light of the great esteem which we Jews have for intelligence, it is debatable which of my flaws was worse.)

"Leave your telephone number, and I'll have him call you."

Although I did not expect to be contacted by anyone from the temple, I was wrong. A week later I received a telephone call in which it was explained again, albeit more dispassionately, that group participation was limited to congregation members. The caller, 'Mr. Pollack,' continued:

"Jewish men and women come to this group to meet others with similar interests, people like themselves. If we open the meetings to the public, then we lose this closeness."

"Are there individual or limited memberships?" I inquired.

"Except for our young-people memberships for students, there are only family memberships, which cost $600 a year."

"That is a lot of money to join a group."

"Precisely! That is what 'Mrs. Rosten' was trying to tell you last week." (He had obviously heard about the conversation.)

"Mrs. Rosten said and implied far more than that. She took it upon herself to question my values and motives. Her comments were uncalled for and downright offensive."

"I'm sorry you misunderstood her. She is a kind lady, a wonderful temple worker. She found it hard to believe that you would pay $600 for membership in a social group."

Conceivably my inquiry might have seemed ludicrous to someone who knew the high cost of membership. Still, I was troubled by Mrs. Rosten's remarks, particularly by the question, "What kind of Jew are you?" Further, the temple's policy discriminated against Jews who either could not afford their initiation fee or who were not interested in a religious experience, only in companionship. Some to whom I have relayed this story concurred with Mr. Pollack. While few denied that Mrs. Rosten had been tactless, they suggested that I had misconstrued her comments. (I do not think I did.) Others chided me for recounting this episode. "It encourages antisemitism," they warned.[7] (I do not think it does.)

It is not a religious story, even though the actors and their actions are related within the context of a religious setting. To my mind the story illustrates the insensitivity of some to the problems of separated and divorced individuals. Although Mrs. Rosten's abrasive and value-laden remarks lend themselves readily to denouncement, Mr. Pollack's position was no more accommodating. His behavior also revealed a callousness and disregard for another person's needs. Neither understood how the need for companionship or the demands of socialization could become sufficiently overriding to justify even the joining of a temple. Membership in a club, group, or organization is supposed to be based on real reasons; in a temple, since it is a religious center, the joiner is presumed to have a religious motive. Perhaps if Sheila had said that she wanted to meet a Jewish man, she would have been rejected with more cordiality. This need, at least, might have struck a sympathetic chord, if not an affirmative response.[8]

At a later date when *I* requested permission to attend a meeting and elicit this group's participation in my research, I was turned down. I attribute the rejection to the group leader's interest in protecting the members' privacy. This I can understand. Moreover, both episodes occurred in 1975. If this synagogue has not reversed its stance in the intervening six years, maintaining a policy of closed membership, there are now other options in Westside, as well as in neighboring communities. Numerous synagogues have formed groups for singles both with and without requirements of congregational exclusivity.

The second group in Westside for single parents (and for single adults) was loosely affiliated with a Unitarian church. Membership in either the church or the group was not a prerequisite for attendance. 'Solo's'[9] primary purpose, like that of the synagogue's group, was to provide a congenial atmosphere in which individuals could meet new people. Thus by design and function it was a social group; its monthly calendar consisted of activities such as potluck dinners, ballroom-dancing instruction, game nights, folk dancing, films, and weekly social mixers. (In contrast, PWP has more broad-based objectives. While they sponsor an astonishing array of social events for adults *and* their families, educational programs, as well as other structured activities, are standard fare. For example, on the night that I attended, two lawyers and a court official delivered lectures on the legal aspects of divorce.)

Sheila had ascertained this information on Solo, but it was I who had to approach 'Mr. Hamilton,' the group leader, asking permission to explain my research project at a meeting and distribute questionnaires. The authorization was granted immediately, and arrangements were made for a presentation at the group's next meeting.

Because of the informality of Solo's meetings, I was permitted to outline my research project and request the group's participation early in the evening. Again the creation of Sheila Ash was a high point of interest. But, I explained, as people gathered around the table on which I sat, some in chairs, some standing, and some sitting on the floor, Sheila's materialization hinged upon the successful execution of the questionnaire and interview phases of the research. Thus it would be they, and others like them, who would be the writers of Sheila's script.[10] It would be their identification of the problems and needs arising from a marital dissolution, their evaluation of community resources, and their ideas for additional services and programs which would determine Sheila's assignment. Without this information, Sheila had no *raison d'être*.

Whether it was my salesmanship (or showmanship), their belief in the merit of the research, their need to talk, or a bit of all three, there was scarcely a person in the room who did not fill out the questionnaire and volunteer to be interviewed. Once more a sympathetic and interested listener appeared to be a prized commodity. And once more, my husband, my colleague, and myself stayed much longer than we planned, much longer than was necessary to collect the questionnaires or answer questions about the project. While people stood around chatting, eating, and drinking, it was as if a line, albeit not a clearly delineated one, had formed in front of us, each person holding a number verifying his or her turn to be heard. Only after they had spoken to us did they partake in the scheduled program of dancing and singing activities, even though the instructor repeatedly invited people to join in.

Were her pleas ignored because it was a lackluster program? Was the opportunity to discuss their concerns and experiences of a higher order, a la Maslow, than the reason which had prompted them to attend the meeting in the first place? Or were we just a novelty, like a double feature attraction or a surprise performer? I do not know the answer. Perhaps neither did the members of Solo. I do know, however, that we left with impressions not unlike those we had had at PWP. There were, of course, some differences. Solo seemed to be a more cohesive group, its members more relaxed and less constrained in their behavior. But these distinctions may be directly traceable to programmatic design, not to group characteristics. (Remember that PWP had guest speakers on the night of our visit; as such, the chairs had been arranged in rows, and there was less time for socializing. Also there were twice as many people in attendance.)

Nonetheless, the similarities between the two groups were far more transparent than the differences. Again, not only did the women greatly outnumber the men,[11] but they also appeared to be younger, better educated, and from higher socioeconomic backgrounds (see footnote 3). And again, both women and men spoke of the difficulties of meeting attractive and compatible people at these gatherings. "I sound like a snob," one woman whispered, "but these men are not my type. Besides, we have nothing in common but our rejection." The group gave them a place to go and a reason for going; it was a night away from their kids, a chance to be with and talk to other adults. For some this in itself was sufficient. For others, it was like waiting for Godot. And, like the characters in Beckett's play, they too were willing to partake in the aimless conversations (the games people play), knowing all along that they might be waiting in vain. While some were not as hopeful as others, they were by no means without hope; their presence at the meeting attested to this.

If we emerged less depressed than before, the variation was one of degrees. The satisfaction and sense of accomplishment were still absent. We had been prepared this time for such a response and had indeed steeled ourselves for it. Were we perhaps then responsible for the fulfillment of our own prophecy? I ask this because it is important to consider the possibility that we misinterpreted what was said to us, that we underestimated the group's significance. Yet, as I write, I still believe that our observations were not tainted by preconceptions and personal biases and that, in fact, despite a more informal atmosphere, Solo failed, as did PWP, to fulfill the expectations of a substantial number of its members. And thus there will be those, like their compatriots at PWP, who will have to forsake the sanctuary of the group, to search for a different place or way to satisfy their needs.[12]

PWP and Solo are not the only places where people encounter disappointment and frustration. It is endemic to the dating game. It can't be avoided—not at 40, not at 20, not at 15. Yet as we grow older we often glorify the past, remembering with nostalgia the flowers for the prom, the starlit night at the beach. The rest—the rejections and disillusionments, the dreaded socials, standing endlessly in wait to be asked to dance, the nights by the telephone praying for it to ring—is easier to erase. Particularly for married women and men, the trials of dating are forgotten or at least cease to be important. But upon separation or divorce many once more return to that adolescent stage of insecurity in which they need to prove their appeal, their worthiness. If it is hard to avoid comparisons to adolescence, the difference between playing the game at 30, 40, or 50 and 18 or 20 is very real indeed. The responsibilities and burdens of adulthood are omnipresent. In point of fact, we can't go home again. Nor can we luxuriate in an eternal future; our mortality becomes increasingly real, and we are scared. The expectations and dreams are reminiscent of those in youth, but now they seem more elusive. And this time, as we begin again, the awareness of our vulnerability is more keenly felt, and so the stakes seem higher, the disappointments more painful.

We have to rediscover what we learned long ago—that finding companionship and forming relationships are not accomplished by the wave of a magic wand; that there may be too many rooms filled with people with whom we have little in common; that there may be too many losers and too few winners. In truth, some may not be losers; but because they fail to measure up to our "ideal" man or woman—the Robert Redford or Albert Einstein, the Cheryl Tiegs or Madame Curie, to us they are losers.

For some this age-old dilemma has served as the inspiration for money-making enterprises. If modern technology and/or ingenuity have not rendered the proverbial matchmaker a creature of obsolescence, they have helped to produce a more upbeat and sophisticated reproduction of this calling. Computerized dating services and dating-by-appointment agencies, in any of their numerous configurations, are the most well-known examples. Many even accept charge cards (Kirchheimer, 1979b). And in keeping with changing fashions, Martin Plotkin, a divorced father, opened a weekend afternoon discotheque for single parents and their children in New York City. For the five to 50 set, this family-style disco offers customers a chance to socialize, gyrate, drink, and be a parent, all for the admission fee of three dollars per child. Parents are admitted free, another stab at readdressing life's injustices (Dullea, 1978, p. 62). Then there are also advisers to the lovelorn who have discovered that the sale of "wise" counsel can be a most lucrative business. Eric Weber, for example, claims that his organization, Symphony Press, Inc., in Tenafly, New Jersey, has grossed five million dollars from peddling his tips for "picking up women" (Hinds, 1980; see also Dullea, 1980a).

Enough? No, there are plenty more, including brunch clubs, dinner clubs, tennis clubs, and travel agencies, all of which cater to singles and the formerly married. Not to be omitted are the social clubs which run the gamut from sleazy to sumptuous. Here people pay a registration fee plus a per function charge in order to meet others who supposedly have been selected according to specific requirements (e.g., age, education, marital status, occupation, religion). Recently I heard of two women whose clientele was limited to wealthy singles. Not only did they guarantee their members that there would be an equal number of women and men attending each party, but also that their socioeconomic status would be upper class. Another example is the Social Participation Club in New York City. Written up in the *New York Times Magazine* in 1976, this Big Apple offering assured its clientele that they would meet people like their ex-husbands or ex-wives. While this seems an odd inducement for those who are separated and divorced, what is really being sold once again is a pre-screening service which, by weeding out the misfits and losers, is expected to produce a group of like stereotypes. Unfortunately the rest of the article revealed not only the impossibility of fulfilling this pledge but the pain of those who believed it would be (see Chapter 5, footnote 16).

New groups continue to emerge as others disband; new ideas for alleviating the problems of meeting people continue to be formulated as others are discarded. This is evident in Westside as elsewhere. In 1975 single parents had few institutional choices in Westside outside of the two groups affiliated with religious organizations; to attend PWP they had to travel outside of the community. In 1980 their options had increased. While the inner city still hosts far more groups, places, and centers for singles than do the suburbs, undeniably the boom in the singles industry has not left the surrounding landscape barren.[13] And, of course, not all recent additions have grown out of pecuniary incentive. Many of these groups and clubs have been started by the growing number of separated and divorced individuals seeking a solution to their own problems.

However, even as the number of social settings for singles burgeons, individuals continue to maintain that these groups are at best of limited benefit. Yet at the same time that they voice this lament, they speak of the need for more groups, for more structured ways to meet new people (see Chapter 5). How do we explain the paradox? Is it the old line about hope springing eternally from the human breast? Or something like that? Obviously, there is always the chance that one night, one time, there will be a someone across a crowded room. But enchanted evenings belong in fairy tales, movies, or dreams. In real life it doesn't happen this way, at least not often. Maybe what we are missing is the potion that will transform toads into princes or princesses, or maybe it is just that too many have for too long bought that "happily ever after" line about marriage, even those who know that "it ain't necessarily so."

The divorced will cease to be lonely when they find a new mate; that is the message sold in bookstores, blasted across television screens and over the airways. Indeed, one of the first signs, according to many "experts," that a divorced woman (or man?) is recovering from the "crisis" of dissolution is reentry into society, particularly getting back into circulation. She is finally pronounced cured when the third finger of her left hand sports a new ring—a round, gold one, to be precise.

My cynicism should not be read as a rejection of marriage. (After all,

I am married.) Rather I distrust and, in fact, reject the "sagacity" of those who have not only overly romanticized marriage but who have proclaimed, in their preachments, albeit at times with rarefied subtlety, that marriage is a fundamental human need. According to their gospel, those who are not so enjoined are therefore somewhat less than whole. And because I reject this ideology, I do not bemoan the recent statistical projection that the remarriage rate will evidence a decline in the 1980s. Our world turns too much as it is on demographics. We measure, analyze, ponder every infinitesimal rise or fall in the marriage, divorce, and remarriage rate as if the nation's security rose and fell with these indices. A decreasing remarriage or marriage rate is not a cataclysmic event. I am not even convinced that it is especially important. It would be important if it signified that people were no longer equating remarriage and marriage with survival, that we, as a people, have become more tolerant and accepting of different lifestyles, including single parenthood.

Ironically, such an occurrence might lead to another jump in the remarriage rate. If we believe Dr. Edward Fish (Remember that helpful psychologist so full of wisdom for negotiating the singles' scene?), desperate people emit an odor like rotten fish (no pun intended), scaring off potential suitors. Thus logic tells us that once the desperation and panic subside, our chances for dating and mating will increase. I guess the victorious are not those who try the hardest.

Those who come to our group looking for a new husband do not stay long. It is the rare person who finds a spouse in this group, in any group. We offer people friendship and help. In a way we are a support group without a therapeutic structure or a group leader. I would advise any woman or man that they not join if marriage is their goal. Some of our members have married, but not people they met here. Once they stopped looking to remarry, stopped trying so hard, they succeeded.

(Member of a group for single parents)

The moral: Those who look to groups for a support network and a sense of community seem to fare better and stay longer than those who join for the purpose of finding a new spouse or dating companions.

Others have no interest in becoming a member of a new community. They join a group for a specific purpose, staying only as long as it takes to meet their needs or to discover that they have come to the wrong place. One objective, frequently mentioned by respondents, is that of making new friends. Another is to receive help in making the transition from marriage to single life. But this really belongs to another part of our story; support or short-term "crisis" groups have been classified in this study as a form of counseling and will therefore be discussed in Chapters 7 and 8, on psychological needs.

THE BAIT AND THE BAITING

In the introduction to this chapter I referred to two kinds of experiences —planned and unplanned—which pertained to the social needs and activities of separated and divorced women. Up to this point I have spoken only of the former. In a sense, because they were circumscribed and clear cut, occurring at a particular time and place, they are the easiest to record. The other experiences, as the word "unplanned" connotes, were not part of the research design. Each constituted a variation on the ancient art of courtship, flirtation, or, more generally, male-female social interaction. While they were not totally unpredictable or unexpected, each episode was always somewhat of a surprise. In the main, they took place during role-playing. As Sheila applied for jobs, looked for places to live, spoke to lawyers, and visited community agencies, revealment of her separation was frequently interpreted as an indication of her availability.[14] Yet Sheila was not the only object of interest. Curiously or not so curiously, depending upon your point of view, most people assumed that I too was either separated or divorced (unless I specifically told them otherwise).

The presumption that interest in a subject derives from first-hand experience is deeply ingrained in the minds of many. There is another presumption which relates to the first: This is the presupposition that only those who are separated or divorced have the knowledge and understanding to analyze this subject. Thus not only does intimacy breed interest, but it is also a prerequisite for scholarship. I do not deny that personal experience can be valuable; this, after all, was one reason behind the decision to create Sheila Ash. But it can also be constricting. Individual prejudices and biases can interfere with the objectivity of study, limiting the ability to see things apart from one's self. To an extent, even roleplaying had this effect. At times I identified too closely with the persona of Sheila, felt too intensely her problems, and reacted too personally to the words and actions of others.

One last explanatory note is in order. Lest readers set their sights too high, I must forewarn them that these experiences are no more suggestive of sensuality or sexuality than are G-rated movies or censored television programs. They are but anecdotes much like those which have already been related, differing only in subject matter. Enough words of caution; I had best get on with my story, leaving it up to you, the reader, to judge the value of the following material.

It was early in the investigation that I discovered that people would assume that I was divorced. I had telephoned the president of a group for single-parent fathers in order to learn more about his organization. Although I described the objectives of my research and the kinds of information I was hoping to obtain, I did not mention Sheila, primarily, I think, because it seemed unnecessary. The man with whom I spoke proved to be not only knowledgeable but willing to discuss his experiences in detail. "The telephone is not," he advised, "the best medium for an interview." "A better way," he professed, "would be for us to meet somewhere." I agreed with his recommendation; I disagreed with his suggestions on the time and place for this meeting. His idea was for an evening at his apartment, where we would be able to relax with a drink and converse in leisure. My idea was for an afternoon at my office where we would be able to talk over a cup of coffee or tea. For a while we kept up this series of repartees which revolved solely around where and when to rendezvous. He maintained that his apartment was the most convenient place; I continued to present alternatives: restaurants, coffee houses, even cocktail lounges.

We soon reached a stalemate; silence deadened our exchange. Annoyed at my inept behavior, but still unable to dispel my suspicions, I decided to take on a different tactic. I explained that meeting him in the evening was difficult because I had two small children. "Why don't you get a baby-sitter?" he responded without hesitation. I was beginning to feel childish and more than slightly ridiculous, but it was too late to reverse the course. I acknowledged that his apartment might be a pleasant place, conducive to interviewing, but, I told him, evenings were especially hectic for me: I had to cook dinner for my husband and children, and by the time I finished cleaning up it would be too late to begin an interview. (This was not true; my husband was fully capable of cooking dinner and doing the dishes.) Silence again, then an apology: "I'm sorry; I did not realize that you were married," he said. Feeling relieved and quite magnanimous, I assured him that no harm had been done; it was a natural mistake. (As it happened over and over, I soon understood just how "natural" a mistake it was.)

For instance, there was the car salesman who, after a long, hard look at me, averred that I was far too serious. Did I not have other interests besides women and credit, he queried. I confirmed that I did (resisting the temptation to tell him that my interests extended all the way to women and employment, housing, the law, and day care), but the purpose of this interview, I emphasized, was to learn more about women's creditworthiness. He remained undaunted.

"I have an idea," he proclaimed as if struck by a revelation. "Why don't we finish our talk over a drink?"

"That sounds very nice, but I have several appointments today. It would be best if we finished this interview now."

"You can bring your tape recorder with you." (What better carrot could one select to entice a researcher?)

"I do not drink during the day with or without my tape recorder." (To my credit, I knew this statement was a blunder, indeed, an inducement for another invitation.)

"Then let's make it this evening when neither of us will have to rush."

"Please 'Mr. Bracton,' I appreciate your invitation, but I have come *only* to discuss the issue of credit."

"You really are too serious! How about another night? Say Wednesday, Thursday, or Friday?"

"No!" (In truth I would have liked to pursue the conversation. Recalling Dr. Fish's warning that a man who is busy on Saturday night is married, I briefly entertained the idea of experimenting, checking him out, as the doctor advised. But common sense prevailed; I decided to stick with the "no.")

"Have it as you like," he answered casually. "I do hope you don't have many questions left. I'm really very busy."

I proceeded through the remainder of my questions (and then some), although admittedly the value of his responses became suspect. But then my motives were by no means benign. In repayment for his churlish behavior, I protracted the interview.

It was not long before I built up an emotional armor which protected me and those I met from such retaliatory urges. If occasionally I still experienced sensations of annoyance and exasperation, more often I viewed these encounters with impervious detachment. With immunity came not only self-control but power. The advantage had been theirs as long as I remained preoccupied with pondering each remark, adjudging each glance, as long as I adhered to an "eye for an eye" mentality. Immunity evened the odds. I became increasingly adroit at fending off their overtures, and in time I learned how to accomplish this feat' without estranging "prospective" suitors and, more importantly, without disrupting the interviewing process.

Since the circumstances varied as did the resourcefulness of these gentlemen, undoubtedly my performance was better on some occasions than on others. One lawyer, I recall, was a particularly facile operator, so skillful that even with my attuned sensibilities I had not detected a hint of a proposition. We had been discussing the intricacies of certain divorce cases, when our conversation was interrupted by the ringing of the telephone. His secretary had already left, and he answered the telephone in an adjoining room. After a brief exchange he returned. Regretfully the interview would have to be terminated, he apologized; there was a parcel which he had to pick up on the other side of town. As we left the office, he asked if I would mind giving him a ride. "It's on your way," he pointed out, "and it would save me from flagging down a cab." Naturally I had no problem with his request; the problem was yet to come.

When I stopped the car to drop him off, he invited me to come inside and meet his friend who coincidentally also specialized in domestic law. "He might be willing to be interviewed," he said encouragingly. Unhesitatingly I accompanied him inside. (What is that line about the innocent lamb?) His friend was cordial but in too much of a hurry to discuss my research. He gave him the parcel and departed, leaving us behind. 'Mr. Manus' skimmed the papers he had been handed and then, seemingly exhausted, sunk down on the couch. Not totally exhausted, however, for he suggested that we finish our talk. His friend would not mind, he added, and besides it was an ideal place replete with a bar and comfortable couches. Indeed, we could even ignore the telephone, since any incoming calls would not be for him. Realizing by now that I was the parcel, I declined the offer, mumbling something about husband, kids, and dinner. He was refreshingly unperturbed. While he had presumed that I was divorced, he informed me, it didn't really matter. (To put his remarks in the proper context, although not in his words, between consenting adults, married or unmarried, a lay is a lay.) My naiveté astounded me. Where was it ever written that only single and divorced women were appealing prospects? Certainly, I had known this before I had begun this project. How had I forgotten it so soon? Nevertheless, it will come as no surprise to the reader that I left. Had I stayed I would not be telling the story. Would I?

After this episode, I began to wear a wedding band whenever I wasn't roleplaying. This reduced, but did not eliminate, the number of propositions I received. It was as if there were now three of us—Sheila, divorced me, and married me. Each of us has her own tales to relate. While those of the married me may be the subject matter for another book, they are irrelevant to this story. Of the three of us, Sheila's experiences are the most germane. Moreover, she had far more "adventures" to recount than I did (in either my real or presumed status). Those that I have selected are representative of a variety of similar encounters that occurred during roleplaying. The more dramatic and atypical happenings might make more interesting reading; however, the selective criteria used in nonfiction cannot depend upon literary appeal. In the interests of science we must forego, albeit reluctantly, the spectacular and the extreme. With this caveat, let us turn to Sheila.

In seeking employment, Sheila spoke primarily to women. Specialized employment services for women, schools, personnel departments of companies, and employment agencies were generally staffed by women—at least these were the people Sheila met. Rarely did she encounter any men. Consequently, during this phase of the research there is little to report. There were, though, a few pertinent occurrences, one of which is presented here.

The setting was the personnel department of a large corporation, one of the companies Sheila approached in the hope that she might be considered for a management training program. After completing the application form, she was told by the receptionist that 'Mr. Clark' would see her shortly. For 45 minutes Sheila waited, her patience sustained by the expectation that she was going to be granted her first interview with a company official. But Mr. Clark was not a personnel manager; in fact his position, which was to review applications to ensure that all the necessary information had been included, was scarcely a rank above that of a receptionist. Nevertheless, while he had no authorization to hire or even to prescreen applicants, it is conceivable that in a minor way he could, if he so chose, support an individual's candidacy or at least expedite the interviewing process.

Mr. Clark scanned Sheila's responses, focusing first on her marital status.

"Ms. Ash, I see that you are separated and have two children. Wouldn't that make it impossible for you to work full-time?" (Sheila had checked "separated" in the space allocated for marital status. On previous occasions when she had omitted this information, a tedious cat and mouse game had ensued until the interviewer succeeded, as he or she invariably did, to ferret out the concealed "facts." It soon became apparent that there was nothing to be gained by this subterfuge.)

"No, Mr. Clark, it would not."

"Being a mother *and* a worker is not easy."

"No, it is not easy, but it is possible. Many women manage to be both good employees *and* good mothers. I do not think I am unique."

"To be honest we do not have openings in our management training programs. Moreover, we prefer people with a background in business."

"I have had experience in managing several large projects, including the overseeing of the budget and staff."

"I was referring to paid employment and educational training, Ms. Ash (pause)—Sheila."

"I know you were, Mr. Clark, but I wanted you to realize that I am not inexperienced or unqualified. My background and education may differ from that of your other trainees, but it is applicable to the program."

"Sheila, you seem like an intelligent and motivated woman. I cannot be encouraging about employment, but things change rapidly around here. One never knows what will turn up."

"I hope you will consider me for any opening that does become available," I responded, rising to leave.

"Sheila, wait a minute. I have a coffee break. Maybe you could tell me more about yourself over a cup of coffee?"

"Fine, Mr. Clark."

"My name is John."

If I was not entirely at ease with the first-name basis we now seemed to be on, I had long ago discovered that it was common practice for individuals at personnel offices and employment agencies to use first names. It was, however, unusual to be asked to address others in a like manner. The conversation which followed verified that Mr. Clark and Sheila had embarked on a path which did indeed deviate from the procedural guidelines presented in personnel management handbooks.

It was not, as it turned out, Sheila's educational and professional backgrounds which interested him. After all, that was already in the application. What he was interested in was her personal life. "How long have you been separated?" "Do you and your ex-husband get along?" "What do you do for fun?" These were only the openers. Sheila's matter-of-fact answers and efforts to direct the dialogue back to employment somehow seemed to encourage him to probe more deeply; it clearly did not discourage him. "Aren't you lonely with just your kids for company?" "Do you drink?" "Do you have a boyfriend?" Enough was enough!

"Thank you, *Mr. Clark*, for the interview, but I have to go now."

"John is my name. Remember?" he asked. Before I could reply, he continued, "Sheila, I have a suspicion that there might be an opening soon in one of our departments. I'd like to discuss it with you, but I'm running behind schedule. Why don't we have dinner tomorrow? We can talk about it then."

"That is good news! I can see you in your office whenever it is convenient for you. But as for dinner, I'm sorry; I'll have to say no."

"It's only a business dinner. If you prefer a drink, that is fine too."

"Mr. Clark, I seem to be having difficulty making myself understood. I came here to apply for a job, not to have a tête-à-tête about my personal life or to make an appointment to go out."

"You misunderstand me, but I can see you're a bit gun-shy. Here's my card; when you are ready, call me."

One doesn't have to be a psychologist or a psychiatrist to figure out the meaning of being ready. It certainly had nothing to do with employment. Perhaps if played out, this story could have been a reenactment on a more modest scale of the fairly recent exposés of the "affairs" of heart and state of certain congressional employees. More likely it would have been a fruitless venture, since Mr. Clark (or John) had neither the credentials nor the influence to make the effort worthwhile. Poor Sheila never met anybody high enough up on the corporate ladder to test whether her appeal could be used an an entrée to employment. Still, in other places and at other times the implication that it could be a help was there.

In fact, had she chosen this route—peddled her feminine wares in exchange for goods and services—her search for suitable housing *might* have been expedited. On five different occasions this appeared to be a distinct option. There was, for instance, the case of the friendly, ever-available landlord who owned several two-family houses in Westside (or so he said).

"My apartments are never vacant. My rents are fair, and I keep the houses in excellent condition. Whenever there are problems with heating, appliances, plumbing, or anything, I come right over. Women without husbands really appreciate this service."

"It is a lovely apartment, 'Mr. West,'" I noted, attempting to avoid any discussion of women without husbands.

"I know how hard it is for women with young children to manage." (Although I remained silent, I was tempted to ask him how, in fact, he did know. Was it that he had a struggling ex-wife somewhere or other? Or had he acquired this knowledge firsthand from his tenants? My taciturnity accomplished nothing; it did not even, as I had hoped, put an end to his treatise on women.)

"There you are," he continued theatrically, "all alone in five big rooms. [At most they were medium sized.] Every time the burner turns on or the wind hits against a window it sounds like a burglar is breaking in. I understand this, and you can feel free to call me any evening. Who knows, there may actually be a real burglar there."

"You are very considerate, Mr. West. But I do not frighten easily. I live in a house much bigger than this apartment and am accustomed to the noises one hears in the night."

"I bet you go out a lot at night."

"No, I don't."

"I'm sure we'll be good friends. I too prefer evenings at home to going out."

Again I chose to ignore his comments; this time he seemed nonplussed.

"Mrs. Ash, you are a very quiet person. You are not one of those divorced women who hate all men, are you?"

"I don't hate anyone, Mr. West."

"Good girl! There are a lot of those women around, and I wouldn't want to rent an apartment to one of them."

Once again I remained silent; this time, however, he tried a different approach.

"Mrs. Ash, your children pose something of a problem. I usually give preference to couples without children. It keeps the cost of repairs down."

"Mr. West, my children are not destructive or unduly noisy. I'm sure you will find us to be excellent tenants." (Being an obliging tenant was, of course, an entirely different matter.)

"Uh, huh...I'm sorry, I forgot your name."

"Mrs. Ash." (Was this a test? Would Sheila pass, if she gave her name as Sheila rather than Mrs. Ash? Would that constitute an auspicious sign, an offering of friendship?)

"Ah, yes, Mrs. Ash. I should tell you that a lot of people have come to see the apartment. I have to give everyone a fair chance. Don't I? (smile) Call me in a few days. Okay?"

"Certainly, Mr. West. Thank you for your time."

Surmising that Sheila had flunked the test, I was not surprised to learn upon calling Mr. West that the apartment had been rented. Was Sheila the only one to whom it was no longer available? Or had he found another tenant—perhaps a more accommodating one? I have no answers to these questions; I can but theorize. To my mind, Mr. West's preoccupation with the trials and tribulations of single women was not of paternalistic origin, his motives not those of a benevolent guardian of and advocate for single women. Rather, his offer of 24-hour, on-call service had a disingenuous ring.

While Mr. West intimated that the leasing of his apartment depended upon the tenant's agreement to contingencies not spelled out in any lease, there were others who left little to the imagination. 'Mr. Woodworth' was one such person.

"Mrs. Ash, I'm sure you will enjoy living here. I've been divorced for three years, and I know what it's like to be lonely and alone. You and I can be a comfort to each other."

"Mr. Woodworth, I'm looking for an apartment, not companionship."

"Oh, Mrs. Ash...Sheila, that is easy to say now, but later you'll see how long the nights can be."

"What is the rent, Mr. Woodworth?" (In retrospect this must have sounded as if I was calculating the costs of his proposal.)

"Sheila, I do not take advantage of women by charging ridiculous rents. What would you think of $275 a month?"

"The rent is certainly fair. [Actually it was downright cheap, particularly for such a large and well-maintained rental.] May I call you in a few days? There are some other apartments I also want to see."

"Sheila, I don't make it a practice of pushing myself on women. These things have to be mutual. If you are interested in seeing how we get along, fine. You have nothing to lose. If things don't work out, you have a nice apartment for very little money."

"I understand, Mr. Woodworth."

Understand I did. Mr. Woodworth and others like him use their rental abodes as a lure to attract women. Undoubtedly there are women similarly inclined. For example, the landlady who had to have an emergency handyman on the premises is not above suspicion (see pp. 125-126). Perhaps she was really interested in procuring an unmarried male tenant, rather than an in-house repair service. Viewed in this light, the rent for these accommodations seems excessively high. To Mr. Woodworth I would have to pay $275 a month in addition to providing him with what he labeled as "comfort." A "kept woman" has a better deal! Yet maybe I am being too sanctimonious. While the advantages to the landlord (or landlady) are obvious, the advantages to the tenant, though more opaque, are not necessarily negligible. For women who have been subjected repeatedly to prejudicial housing practices, it is conceivable that an overzealous landlord could be preferable to, and in fact more controllable than, the amorphous discrimination so prevalent in the marketplace.

I knew that he expected more than the rent, but I also needed an apartment. I decided to play the odds, leading him to believe that we had similar intentions. I got a two-year lease with a clause prohibiting raises in rent, and he got nothing. Once the lease was signed and we had moved in, I let him know, nicely, that I was unavailable. At first he was furious, but I remained pleasant and he has become a good landlord. Period! I don't feel guilty. I figure he was being unethical and that warranted what I did. But I don't think I would have chanced it if he lived in the same house.

(34-year-old woman, 1 year separated)

In all likelihood there will always be those who will milk the principle of supply and demand for all it is worth; and there will be others who will continue to operate in accordance with the ancient economic system of bartering, using apartments, jobs, themselves, or any tradable ware as commercial products. In the final analysis there can be no transaction unless someone accepts the deal, no matter how unethical or amoral. In this kind of exchange proposition or contractual agreement, the seller or buyer (depending upon how you view the circumstances) is presented with an offer, terms are negotiated, and the deal is either accepted or rejected. While theoretically this terminology is applicable to a variety of human encounters, my meaning is a very limited one. In short, I refer solely to situations in which it is explicitly or implicitly clear that the woman (or man) is obliged to deliver sexual favors in return for securing particular goods and/or services. If in a sense it is a form of paid prostitution, undeniably the terms may be mutually satisfying to both labor and management.

While Sheila received her share of so-called exchange propositions, more frequently in her encounters there was no obvious or discernible intent to base present or future relationships on an interchange of commodities. In various ways and on various occasions, an expression of interest was divulged. Through subtle nonverbal or verbal clues or straightforward declarations, the gentleman revealed his attraction to Sheila. Detailed explanations are hardly necessary; quite obviously these overtures are part and parcel of dating etiquette. They constitute the first advance or preliminary step in what has been euphemistically labeled in this book as the "dating game." As the majority of women, be they single, married, or divorced, have an inventory of experiences upon which to draw and some knowledge of the rules of this game, albeit some of their skills may require polishing and updating, generally such advances present the least difficulty to the recipient and in fact offer the most potential for establishing new relationships. And there are also benefits which are not dependent upon mutual attraction. For those who are feeling rejected and unattractive, these encounters provide an ego boost, if only momentarily. The woman (or man) receives an affirmation of her (or his) appeal. Sometimes this makes her feel more self-confident, encourages her to be more adventurous, even if in the process she risks disappointment. At the very least it is a learning experience, a confirmation that meeting people occurs outside as well as within institutional settings. It can happen in many places and at many different times. As one woman pointed out:

I had forgotten how many dates I had gotten as a young woman through chance occurrences in department stores, libraries, restaurants, and parks. After my separation I shunned all such possibilities as if they were pickups, something respectable women did not do. What I refused to admit was that a meeting at a dance was just as much a pickup. Once you accept that the only difference is in your mind, then you are free to experiment and experience.

(39-year-old woman, 1 year divorced)

Moreover the element of suprise and the spontaneous quality of chance meetings offer additional benefits too often overlooked or underrated by observers of the social scene. When people attend dances, frequent singles bars, or go to cocktail parties, the purpose of their attendance is obvious to themselves and to others. The anticipation of outcomes may vary among individuals, but few do not have some preconception of what would constitute a successful evening. Conversely, in unplanned encounters expectations have not been raised. Outwardly and inwardly, individuals do not have to prep themselves or issue that firm reminder that the evening (or afternoon or morning) might indeed be a failure. As such they are spared, at least initially, the disappointment which can result from a disillusioning experience.

I gave up on dances and socials for singles. Now I meet men in different ways and never by design. This way you don't have to be with someone you find unattractive. If the person is appealing, you flirt back; if not, you walk away. It helps you to feel desirable again, even if you are being propositioned by an all-time loser. Sometimes it is just fun to play the game, even if you know you are only playing. Maybe it is Montezuma's revenge, female style.

                                        (40-year-old woman, 3 years divorced)

Unlike this woman, Sheila had no basis upon which to formulate comparisons between planned and unplanned social encounters. Yet she also discovered that the opportunities for meeting new people, particularly men, were far greater than she would have predicted prior to roleplaying. A visit to a lawyer to discuss "her" divorce suit was followed by an invitation to dinner and the theater. Interestingly, this was after he had warned her not to date until a separation agreement was finalized. Perhaps he regarded the evening as a professional meeting, for him a deductible business expenditure and for her a justifiable excuse to venture outside the confines of her home and her role as the aggrieved plaintiff. There was also a man in an employment agency who was most pessimistic about Sheila's chances for obtaining a job but rather enthusiastic about her possibilities as a companion. He proposed a weekend at his summer house. (Without doubt, the presence of Laurie and Peter would not be requested.)

These were not isolated incidents. Landlords who refused unabashedly to consider Sheila as a tenant because of her marital status or children, or who concocted untenable stories to defend the unavailability of their flats, had little compunction about suggesting some kind of get-together. One landlord was blunt to the point of being farcical.

I would not consider renting my apartment to women who live alone with their children. They are unreliable tenants who often leave their children alone at night, free to wreak havoc on my premises. But you are charming, and I would very much like to see you socially.

Unconcerned or unaware of any incongruity between his action and his words, he issued this statement with considerable aplomb. Both his refusal and his invitation were simply declarations of fact: Sheila was an undesirable tenant but a desirable woman. As a businessman, it would not be judicious to allow a personal attraction to interfere with his responsibilities; but as a man, he had no such restrictions.

And so the stories piled up without any evidence of there being a predictable pattern. Those who were adamant in their dismissal of Sheila as an employee, tenant, or credit applicant were just as likely to present themselves as prospective suitors as were those who were encouraging and helpful. Admittedly, this was one of the more surprising conclusions of the research. I had anticipated that a separated woman would receive a fair number of unsolicited proposals, but not from those whom I had categorized as being in the enemy camp. Although at times I regarded these advances as pure *chutzpah*, at other times I found myself disarmed by the ironic humor of the situation. How I would have responded had I really been Sheila, I do not know. That, I guess, salves my conscience and maintains my integrity to the end.

CONCLUSION

This chapter has focused on only one aspect of the social lives of separated and divorced women—the search for new alliances. Unfortunately, this kind of narrow treatment has the effect of emphasizing too many of the negative dimensions attendant upon reentrance into the dating arena. We lose all sense of the important roles played by family, friends, neighbors, children, and even at times ex-spouses solely because they were not part of Sheila's investigation. Thus the resultant portrayal is incomplete, the sense of wholeness obscured as interrelationships between different facets and interactions between different people are omitted. Still, there is something to be learned from this phase of the research, something quite antithetical to the message delivered in most self-help and diagnostic manuals and articles on divorce.

First, in Westside, as elsewhere, there has been a dramatic rise in the number and kind of groups for single parents (and the divorced) in the period between 1975 and 1980. All current indicators suggest the continuance of this trend. I am, however, less enthused by the increase in quantity than by the prospect of more diversified alternatives. More PWP is not, I believe, a particularly worthy goal. I suspect that my sample is not unique in expressing its dissatisfaction, nor am I in noting its deficiencies. As divorce becomes more prevalent among the middle- and upper-middle classes, we will have to confront the needs and demands of this population as a whole and those of its members as individuals. Large-scale institutionalized responses of any type may prove not only to be inappropriate but unnecessary.

Paradoxically, the major benefit of these groups is also its greatest liability. By offering a community of brethren and a support network, it can confirm the most devastating of the fears of the divorced—that they are sufferers, even losers, who require special sustenance and aid in order to *survive*. This is the outcast myth, so strikingly illustrated by that foolish woman standing in a rowboat, searching desperately for a new mate (see p. 145). Undeniably, some do see themselves in this way, especially in the early stages of a marital dissolution. But many others have helped to nurture their fears and insecurities. Social scientists, clinicians, and the media, in their zeal to assuage the pain of the divorced, have animated a mythical caricature into a real-live being. Groups for single parents and the divorced are as responsible as are the experts and the media for peddling this dismal prophecy, albeit unwittingly. To be sure, they offer crowds of people, not an endless sea. But one can also be alone and lonely in a room full of people. And when this does occur, the blow can be particularly ravaging. To have tried and failed in a structured and sheltered environment may be interpreted as irrefutable proof of one's undesirability, of the insuperable odds of ever finding companionship. To love and be loved again may now seem to be a goal beyond reach. Furthermore, it is precisely the attainment of this goal which is equated with recovery.

Second, social norms and attitudes on the family, as we have noted previously, feed the illusion that divorced families are inchoate units which can become whole only through remarriage. The well-documented economic difficulties of female-headed families introduce a different but related problem. Financial struggles substantiate the necessity of the two-parent constellation. Consequently, emotional and economic stability become confused, as all paths seem to lead in only one direction—to the altar. To repudiate this "evidence," to veto this conclusion, one has to advance past the stage of seeking consolation in the knowledge that others have experienced the agonies of divorce; one has to realize that divorce is not death, not spiritually, emotionally, or even financially; that it is not an illness treatable by a miracle drug called remarriage. It is a time of change, and it does require major adjustments, but so too do marriage, bearing children, retirement, old age, and the like.

Yet why, the question keeps nagging, do so many continue not only to write about the outcast myth but, worse, to believe in it? In so stressing this tale of sorrow and woe, is it not possible that we are creating the very conditions which will give rise to a self-fulfilling prophecy? And why, the question keeps nagging, do so many continue not only to write about the two-parent family as an idyllic unit but, worse, to create the impression that it is only in these families that one can achieve happiness and normalcy? In so promulgating this image, is it not possible that we have convinced many that their very survival hinges on remarriage? Because separated and divorced people believe this and fear that their future and that of their children are at stake, they embark on a frenetic search for a new spouse. Ironically, if the soothsayers are correct, this is in itself a self-defeating act. Their desperation closes rather than opens the doors through which they pass in their pursuit of companionship. Thus have we, the question keeps nagging, in our eagerness to console and to help, actually boxed people in between Scylla and Charybdis?

NOTES

1. A synopsis of the preliminary research results was mailed to a PWP officer for circulation among interested members.

2. Although the meeting was held in a large function room of a church, there were few vacant seats.

3. At the time, we had arrived at this conclusion on the basis of general impressions and information imparted to us during conversations. Nonetheless, a significant variation between the socioeconomic status of the women and men was confirmed during analysis of the questionnaire data.

4. Admittedly, there is a specious quality to my conclusions. I have related people's frustrations, their conveyance to us (implied or stated) that membership in a group had failed to fulfill their expectations. But I have told little about these people—nothing about how long they had been separated or divorced, the reasons for the separation, the nature of the separation, the number and age of their children, who had custody, or their present financial status. All of this is important and can have a direct bearing on the ease or difficulty with which individuals form new alliances and adjust to different social situations. Had I been able to draw comparisons between the related concerns of individuals and the data compiled from the questionnaires, we might note relationships or factors more significant than my impressions. Later the questionnaires were tabulated and categorized, but since we did not know the names of many of the people with whom we had spoken, there was no way of matching information on forms to these conversations. This kind of analysis did not take place until the interviewing phase of the research.

5. Questionnaire and interview respondents were also recruited from noninstitutional support groups for the separated and divorced, as well as from personal contacts. In addition two lawyers participated in the recruitment, mailing questionnaires to members of their clientele (see Appendix A).

6. Although Sheila did not attend any of these group meetings, it was she who conducted the preliminary canvassing of the community. With the exception of PWP, whose membership was known in advance, she telephoned all the Westside organizations listed in the Yellow Pages, as well as those located in bordering communities, inquiring at each whether they had a group for single parents or separated and divorced individuals.

7. A paranoia seemed to distort the reactions of some, interfering with their ability to adjudge the encounter objectively. At first I thought that they were being shallow; instead of considering the problems of those, like Sheila, who were being denied admittance to a group, they worried only about how others would view the rejection. Yet this shows my narrowness also. Their objection to this narration, if anything, confirms that they too disapproved of the response and the temple's policy; otherwise why would they want it to be kept secret? Somehow I also believe that if I had had a comparable story to relate about a church, they would not have objected so strenuously. The score would have been even and as such the injustice could be exposed.

8. In 1974 the Federation of Jewish Philanthropies formed a task force expressly to deal with the "problem" of Jewish singles. For various reasons, in-

cluding the concern that single Jews might leave the religion if their institutions failed to recognize them as a population with special needs, this group began to search for ways to reach out to such individuals and provide alternative programs and services within religious settings. Interestingly, some representatives argued that Judaism could not ignore the needs of the so-called "peripheral Jew" whose principal reason for participating in synagogue activities is a social one. If Sheila must be labeled a peripheral Jew, at least the term does not obviate the legitimacy of her needs as a single person, albeit in religious circles its connotations may be less than flattering ("Jewish 'Singles' A New Problem After Years of Focus on Family," 1976, p. 60).

9. Numbers offer PWP a certain anonymity. With 1,000 chapters and several within the vicinity of Westside, it would be difficult, even if Westside's identity were detected, to pinpoint the specific chapter of which I write. However, because the church group is not a chapter of a larger organization, a fictitious name has been used to protect the anonymity of the group and its members.

10. A synopsis of the preliminary research results was also mailed to this group.

11. In one more recently formed group in Westside, men comprise 25% of the membership, even though one of its two founders was a man (Wise, 1978).

12. It will be recalled that of the 50 women who participated in this study, only one remained a member of a group for single parents or for the divorced for more than a year.

13. In 1969, according to the editor of a bimonthly magazine for singles, there were two singles clubs in the entire metropolitan area, whereas in 1979 he was able to enumerate 50 (Gatto, 1979b).

14. Conversely, lawyers typically caution separated women, at least prior to attaining a written separation agreement, not to date. A "noninterference" clause in a separation agreement is specifically inserted to protect either spouse from being censured by the other for behavior relating to their personal lives. Yet even such clauses do not guarantee that one party will not attempt to support his or her case for custody, divorce, or, say, alimony on evidence of the promiscuous behavior of the other. In fact, litigation *following* divorce often revolves around allegations of this nature.

CHAPTER 7

WOMEN WHO COPE:
THE HIGH ROAD
TO RECOVERY

In the year 1979 a major metropolitan newspaper allocated eight days of coverage—more time than it took God, according to the biblical description in *Genesis*, to create the heaven and earth—exclusively to the "struggle" of women "to recover" from losing a spouse through death or divorce.[1] To appreciate why this subject was deemed to be of such significant import or appeal to warrant an eight-part series, we have only to read the first article. Here we soon learn that "women alone" face grave dangers—emotionally and physically. The "loneliness and isolation" that characterize their lives "lead to emotional deterioration and then physical deterioration."[2] Indeed, according to the author, Shirley Smith, "widowed, divorced, and single people have far more heart disease, strokes, lung cancer, and cirrhosis of the liver than married people do" (1979, p. 19). With the presentation of this "evidence," attributed without documentation to psychosomatic medical specialities and health studies, the struggle to overcome assumes mammoth proportions, a struggle certainly formidable enough to justify what now seems to be but a paltry eight days of news exposure.

There is no tempering of the prognostication that "loneliness and isolation lead to" (not "may lead to" or "can lead to") "emotional" and "physical deterioration." Although we are told that "someday, the pain will pass," "someday" is a word of indeterminate meaning, and thus the promise of a better future is at best elusive. Far more threatening looms the present, for it is in the here and now that the ravages of psychological debilitation and the dreaded maladies of heart disease, lung cancer, and cirrhosis of the liver must be stayed.[3]

I do not mention Smith's series because a prestigious newspaper considered the subject sufficiently noteworthy to warrant an eight-day run of copy that occupied as much as a half page of newsprint on some days in accompaniment with pictorial sentimentality. I do not mention Smith's series because her account of the effects of divorce and death on women and her strategies for cóping with loss contribute to our understanding and knowledge of "women alone." The only reason I mention this series at all is because it is a prototype of lay and even scholarly expositions on the repercussions of divorce. Like Sifford's articles (see Chapter 5, pp. 145-146), they beguile the reader into believing that a subject of immeasurable complexity can be reduced to a few aphorisms; and in doing so their intent to inform and to help is rendered valueless, even preposterous.

My point is not to challenge all extant knowledge on divorce, for there is much to be learned from the research and statistics. The emotional aftermath of divorce is well documented, affecting in varying degrees all of those involved, whether they be the instigators of the separation or the passive (innocent?) recipients. Divorce can be a painful experience. The divorced may suffer loneliness, depression, anxiety, and a host of other symptoms commonly associated with the dissolution syndrome. There is no sanguine substitution for these data. This does not mean, however, that we possess either the psychic or scientific clairvoyance to predict how different people will react to and cope with divorce. At most we can supply generalizations. The danger, of course, is that these generalizations or educated surmises will be interpreted as facts—as definitive statements of a cause-and-effect relationship.

Indeed, if we analyze the reams of data and narratives on divorce, it becomes clear that even the theorists are not all in concurrence. Not only do they disagree on the nature of this "problem" called divorce and the remedies to offer the "afflicted," but, more significantly, they remain divided as to whether intervention in any form is or is not needed. But the real world moves on as the experts haggle and debate. Even if the divorced were privy to this controversy, it is unlikely that it would have much impact. Their own discomfort emits a signal often too disquieting to ignore. The search for answers and cures cannot wait for the experts to resolve their differences. Because their symptoms most closely resemble those of psychological malfunction, because the daily tabloids, the popular literature, and the communication media in general play up the emotional traumas of divorce, and because psychotherapy has been extolled as the treatment of choice for mental disturbances and disorders, it is not surprising that so many opt for this therapeutic remedy. The processional march from the house to the couch (or the chair) has come to be almost predictable. Somewhat like operant conditioning, a marital dissolution becomes the stimulus for the response to seek some form of psychiatric assistance.

This chapter is not a summarization or explanation of the psychological effects of marital dissolution, for so many others, beginning with Willard Waller in 1930, have pondered and analyzed the psyches of the divorced that another rendition hardly seems necessary. I was interested instead in learning how women respondents had coped or were coping with needs and concerns that they perceived to be of a psychological nature, and, in particular, what community resources they had utilized or would have used had they been available and/or accessible. Decidedly, much of the emotional texture of marital separation is explicitly and implicitly exposed in the following quotations. But it is important to understand that in this study it is only a backdrop.

TIME PASSES, NEEDS CHANGE

Most divorce theorists maintain that recovery from divorce is both painful and slow. Sociologist Robert Weiss (1975), for example, estimates that two to four years will elapse after separation before the individuals are "fully themselves again," with the average recovery time nearer to the four-year mark (p. 236).[4] Moreover, he postulates that there are two definitive phases in the course of recovery: transition and recovering. During the transition period of approximately eight to ten months, the individual has to contend with the "crisis of identity" and begin the process of reordering his or her life as a single person. The recovering phase is a far longer period that does not end, according to Weiss, until the individual has established "a stable and resilient new identity and pattern of life" (ibid.).[5]

While I question Weiss's calculation of the time required for recovery from separation and, in fact, would argue that any such estimation is presumptive until there are more longitudinal studies on postseparation adjustment, my observations support his theory of a two-phase recovery process.[6] The following recounts provide a capsulized view of the progression of three women from "transition" to "recovering."

I knew our marriage had problems, but refused to contemplate the possibility of a separation. It took me a few months to admit that I had to make it on my own. Then I began to make decisions; I changed my job and sold the house. Neither was easy to do and both entailed other, smaller changes. But it kept me busy and I began to realize there were so many things I couldn't do as a married woman that I could now do. Oh, I didn't become a swinger, but I did become independent.

(39-year-old woman, 1½ years divorced)

I don't care who initiates the divorce, how much you want it, or even if you have a new man waiting in the next house. Divorce requires getting use to. It is a whole series of adjustments in which you have to stop thinking of yourself as Mrs. So-and-So and start being yourself. For me it meant a lot of change. I resumed my career; I made new friends; I bought a house.[7]

(43-year-old woman, 1 year divorced)

Divorce is the death of a marriage, even if the death is a blessing. You need time to mourn its passing and to get used to the idea that it is over. You need time to plan the things that now have to be done because of the divorce and because you are a single woman again. But it need not be the tragic affair of a death. Once you realize that you have to go on and that going on may be pleasant, you're more than half way there. Then you need to take a good look at yourself, decide where you are going, and how to get there. You may need help to do this, but most of us needed help before we got married.

(37-year-old woman, 3 years divorced)

This help, as we have noted previously, may come from many sources (e.g., family, friends, neighbors, lawyers, clinicians). It may be of short or long duration. Furthermore, different kinds of assistance may be required at different stages in the divorce process. In general, the need for outside support appears to be greatest at two times. The first occurs at the onset of the transition period and, in particular, relates to the "crisis of identity."

I didn't know who I was anymore or what I was supposed to do. Overnight I had been replaced by a younger face and more lithe body. But the woman I was, had become over eight years of marriage, I couldn't find. It seemed as if the zip had gone out of my life, that my energy was drained, and I had failed. I had a friend who suggested in an off-hand way at first and then firmly that I see a psychiatrist. It was the best investment I could have made. I began to rediscover myself—good and bad. I don't know if I am different today than I was before, but I do know who I am.

(32-year-old woman, 10 months divorced)

The second outreach period may take place at the end of the transition phase or during the recovering stage, but irrespective of the precise timing it seems to be most closely associated with the effort to restructure one's life. And here again it is not unusual for individuals to adjudge their needs to be of a psychological nature and hence to require the services of mental health professionals.

Whether to go back to work after ten years as a housewife seemed to be an enormous decision. Would the kids suffer? Would I be too tired to make friends and enjoy myself? Would he use this as an excuse to stop alimony? I didn't have the answers, just a feeling that going to work would be a wise decision. I asked friends and relatives, but I got so much advice that I became confused. I began to go to a social worker. We discussed the pros and cons sensibly and at length. We also talked about the kind of job I could get and how to go about looking for one. When I finally did get a job, I couldn't believe that I had made such a big deal about it.

(36-year-old woman, 2 years divorced)

As one woman went to a psychiatric social worker to help her decide whether or not to return to work, another, who experienced a serious financial reversal after divorce, looked to a psychologist for help.

'Leo' had earned a good living, in fact, more than good. Yet after our divorce he refused to work more than two days a week. The child support payments rarely came; the house had a second mortgage; the car needed to be repaired. I began to close off rooms to cut down on heating. My lawyer tried to intervene, but the judge couldn't force Leo to work. I imagined myself cracking up. All I could think of was money. I borrowed from my parents to see a psychologist. But my problems didn't vanish. I quit after a month and sold the house and moved into an apartment. I paid off my debts and now we manage. I'm getting a raise next week and, who knows, I might become a department manager.

(35-year-old woman, 1 year divorced)

Two women, both of whose problems appeared to be of a pragmatic character, sought therapeutic intervention. For one, the experience seemed beneficial; for the other, it did not, and as such, at least her course of action should be questioned. To ask of her the obvious—why did you seek the assistance of a psychologist for what was fundamentally an economic problem?—is not to obscure the role that emotions play in all aspects of life. Neither should it obscure the inescapable logic that an accountant or a financial adviser would have been a more appropriate consultant. Yet to the separated and divorced the exigent demands posed by a marital dissolution and the requirements of daily living frequently do become camouflaged, assuming enigmatic shapes of psychological fears and disturbances. "I imagined myself cracking up," this woman said. While she soon resolved her difficulties, others, who persist in viewing reality-based dilemmas apart from their true context, may engage, at least for a while, in inappropriate problem-solving behavior. At times therapists are able to address this issue with patients, offering them both practical and emotional counseling.

Divorce is a time of personal anguish and disruption. It is also a time when a lot of decisions have to be made. Often the woman who lived comfortably and did not work is especially at a loss. She is not used to making decisions, as they have always been made for her. This kind of inactive behavior may necessitate counseling. But the counselor has to understand that her problems are more than psychological. He has to wear two hats. At times he acts as a therapist, and at times he has to be more directive. The patient also has to understand that her life will not change overnight. People come to us expecting a miracle. Sometimes when it doesn't happen they quit; sometimes they become their own miracle workers.

(Divorce counselor)

Because the number of the separated and divorced who receive some form of psychological counseling, for whatever reason or from whatever source, is incredibly high, it behooves us to examine more closely how respondents assessed these services and supports.

THE SEARCH FOR HELP

In the questionnaire and interview sample, 74% of the women and 43% of the men sought help from mental health professionals. (Psychologists and psychiatrists were seen by 52% of the women and 35% of the men; social workers by 15% of the women and 5% of the men; and divorce counselors by 7% of the women and 3% of the men.) If we add those who consulted family physicians (6% of the women and 3% of the men) and clergymen (5% of the women and 2% of the men) for what they perceived to be emotional problems, the percentages jump to 85% for women and 48% for men. The proportion of children who received individual or group counseling was substantially lower, tabulated at 35%.

For several reasons these data can be misleading. First, because the questionnaire did not list support groups as a mental health service, it is impossible to know whether these figures included at all the utilization of such groups by questionnaire respondents. Second, the fact that some individuals displayed drifting patterns of utilization, sampling a variety of services, means not only that some percentages may be inflated, but also that the extent to which each service was used is not revealed in the data. A one-time visit to a physician is recorded in the same way as a three-year commitment to psychotherapy. In actuality, all that the percentages show is which mental health providers were consulted more often by sample members, regardless of the assessed value of the care received or the duration of the commitment. Further, the data illustrate that women outnumbered men as consumers of mental health services.[8]

PHYSICIANS AS CARETAKERS

With few exceptions, interviewees who turned to their family physicians for emotional support found them unequipped or unwilling to help.

I have been using 'Michael' as a doctor for 20 years. After my divorce I began to get terrible headaches and decided that a checkup was in order. Michael found nothing wrong, but he did prescribe Valium to calm me down. I tried to talk about how I felt, but he seemed uncomfortable with the discussion. Finally he said if the 5 mg. were not enough he would raise the dosage to 10 mg. and I was dismissed! For Christ's sake, a casual acquaintance would have had more sensitivity!

(44-year-old woman, 10 months separated)

My family physician never bothered to examine me when I said I had been feeling run-down after the divorce. He suggested a hot bath, a good cry, and exercise. Furthermore, he added, it would be a shame to pay him for listening to me when a psychiatrist was trained to do just that. I somehow thought that he would turn off the fee meter, at least this time, and play at being a person.

(46-year-old woman, 1 year divorced)

Whatever happened to the family doctor who was your counselor and your healer? Mine can prescribe antibiotics and diagnose a viral infection, but he refuses to see that there are other factors involved in making the human machine run.

(30-year-old man, 1 year divorced)

In a paper delivered at a meeting of the American Medical Association, psychiatrist Peter Martin posed the very same question as the respondent quoted above. Arguing that "physicians have abdicated their centuries-old position as emotional...caretakers," Martin charged family practitioners with neglecting the mental health of their patients. As a result, treatment is delayed and patients become prey to a virtual "jungle" of unqualified experts who call themselves counselors (1978, p. 3; see also Chapter 8, pp. 225-226; 228-229).

CLERGYMEN AS CARETAKERS

From the comments of respondents it appeared that clergymen, like physicians, had largely "abdicated" their traditional role as "emotional caretakers."

Of the people I spoke to, my minister was the most inept at discussing my divorce. All he could say was, "Talk to your lovely wife, and I'm sure you can both work it out." He also added the line about "for the sake of the children." Probably it was "lovely children." I'm being sarcastic, but at the time I was stunned and more than a little hurt.

(40-year-old man, 2 years divorced)

Four years ago when I separated from my husband, it seemed as if there wasn't a rabbi in town who knew anyone who was divorced. "Jews have such a low divorce rate," my rabbi said, "because they value their family. If you get a divorce, it will be hard to find another nice Jewish man and, as you know, they make the best husbands." Too bad he didn't take his own advice, because a year later he got a divorce. I wonder if his wife found a nice Jewish man.

(37-year-old woman, 3 years divorced)

Unexpectedly, the only religious institution to receive accolades was the Paulist Center, an affiliate of the Roman Catholic Church. Through the efforts of one outspoken maverick priest, the Center has become a leader in a movement to bring separated and divorced Catholics back to the Church (Ryan, 1975). In light of the absolutism of Catholicism's stance on divorce, this was no small objective. Canon law, since its adoption in 1884 by the American bishops of the Roman Catholic Church, has stipulated automatic excommunication for divorced and remarried individuals. If relatively few were ever formally excommunicated, most believed that they had been (Franklin, 1977). For Catholics this meant not only living with the knowledge that they were sinners, but also that they were condemned to hell. The penalty therefore extended beyond one's life to the hereafter. Repudiating this policy, 'Father John' of the Paulist Center became a key figure behind the drive to liberalize Church policy on divorce and remarriage.[9] In November 1977 the Vatican lifted the excommunication ban, although remarriage was still considered a violation of Church law unless the first marriage had been annulled (Franklin, 1978). But the Paulist Center, under the direction of Father John, has done more than carry the banner for ideological reform. In particular, it offers courses and support groups for separated and divorced Catholics on topics ranging from the reconciliation of personal and religious dilemmas and the transition from marriage to divorce to single parenting and postdivorce life.

To say that for many Catholics the Paulist Center has, in effect, lifted an albatross from around their necks sounds like, but is not, a literary hyperbole. The following statements of two respondents read much like testimonials.

For me the decision to divorce was monumental. Not only was my family to be changed, not only was I faced with the sole responsibility of three children, but I had to reconcile myself to being a sinner. The choice was between a hell today or one in the future. I chose the latter, but with much regret and fear. Without exaggeration, Father John saved my sanity. He assured me that I wasn't an outcast and did not have to fear an afterlife in hell. I won't say this made divorce easy, but it certainly made it easier. Once my religious fears were erased I was able to put the other problems in their proper perspective. The Paulist Center helped here too. They provided information and an introduction to others with similar problems.

(48-year-old woman, 3 years divorced)

My family did not support my decision to end my marriage. If it wasn't for the Paulist Center group, I would have found it exceedingly difficult to reconcile my religious beliefs with separation. With their help I remained in good standing in my church and still could attend to my personal needs.

(45-year-old woman, 4 years divorced)

THERAPISTS AND THEIR THERAPIES

Still, there were few whose quest for solace, guidance, or asylum led them to the fold of any religious denomination. And among those who did turn to the men of cloth, fewer still found the help for which they came. Most looked elsewhere. Because they accepted their pain as psychological in origin, it took no great leap of faith to conclude that psychotherapy was the remedy to be sought and the psychotherapist the healer to minister the treatment. Yet this statement is deceptive in its simplicity, for the web becomes tangled as we discover that under the rubric of psychotherapy there is not one but many forms of therapy, some of which bear little resemblance to classical theory and methods. Consequently, there is no purism in the extant state of the "science," nor are its practitioners purists, either by training or inclination. That the meaning of a word has become murky and even distorted over time is not my point; rather, it is to inform the reader that respondents, using the same terms, often spoke of different kinds of therapy as practiced by different kinds of clinicians in different kinds of settings. It is to these therapists and their therapies that we now turn.

Conjoint Therapy: In Marriage and in Divorce

By no means do all proponents of conjoint therapy concur on either the purpose or the mode of such treatment. Some, who are adherents of an essentially traditionalistic school of thought, are committed to the goal of saving marriages. With this orientation they focus on the resolution of interpersonal problems, sometimes combining individual with conjoint therapy. Others view the objective and nature of the intervention quite differently. Emily Brown of Divorce Counseling Services in Washington, D.C., for example, contends that the clinician's role is to help the couple determine whether the marriage *should* be saved (Kiester, 1975). In a sense this therapeutic method is an amalgam of marriage and divorce counseling. If the decision to divorce is made, the therapist and the couple, in a manner of speaking, reverse gears and begin to concentrate on the issues related to divorcing. Thus the emphasis shifts as the sessions are now directed toward coping with and adjusting to the dissolution (Fisher, 1974).

When I told 'Rich' I wanted a divorce, he insisted that we go to a therapist first. Initially I refused, but my lawyer advised me that it would look better in court to cooperate. "If your husband attests to his willingness to save the marriage," he said, "and you don't do likewise, the judge may grant you a lower settlement or something else along this line." Reluctantly I consented, but the experience was a good one. The psychologist helped us to talk about our problems, something we had rarely done before. Although we still divorced, we each had a more tolerant view of the other. He also spent much time helping us to decide about the children— custody, support, visitation, predictable reactions, and so on. I think we are better parents because of this experience.

(33-year-old woman, 1½ years divorced)

While overall conjoint therapy received higher ratings from respondents than did individual psychotherapy, this evaluation needs to be qualified. That the "judges" were all eventually separated or divorced leaves us with a sample of individuals whose needs undoubtedly differed dramatically from those of reconciled couples. Moreover, conjoint therapy was valued primarily when the participants believed it served a utilitarian function.[10] In particular, they spoke of counseling geared toward decision making and establishing ground rules for the couple's relationship before and after divorce. In contrast to orthodox psychotherapy, techniques of behavior modification were markedly evident. Many therapists not only played down the past, but they often "forced" the couple to focus on the present by stressing the necessity of developing new and different patterns of behavior as a divorced couple. Not infrequently the emphasis was on the children. This appears to be a deliberate choice, as one therapist explained.

Commonly, the divorcing couple see their interests as divergent, even antagonistic. They see their spouse as the enemy, the person responsible for the chaos and confusion occurring in their lives. By forcing the couple to look away from their own personal feelings toward each other and concentrate on their children, it directs the therapeutic session away from their anger and provides a common ground of interest. It is necessary, especially at the time of or right after the divorce, to get both individuals to deal immediately with establishing priorities and making sure that they do not forget their children. They need to understand that they have to deal with each other as long as there are children around, and for the sake of the children and for themselves, it is best to eliminate as much of the contention from the situation as possible.

In many respects this kind of approach approximates the current fad of divorce counseling. Although there are variant themes on this idea, in general, divorce counselors[11] presuppose that there are good and bad divorces. Cooperation, communication, and intelligent decision making are the key ingredients to the "making" of a divorce in which all stand to be winners: Without the tensions of postdivorce conflict, parents are free to structure new and productive lives for themselves, and children continue to be nurtured by two caring parents. There were respondents who believed that counseling had yielded these benefits.

It is necessary to tie up those loose ends dangling after the end of a marriage before you can begin life as a single person. Counseling provided me with this help, and I know my ex-husband feels the same way. The therapist made us see the importance of providing stability for the children and for establishing a relationship with each other. We only saw him for a few months, but we still go back when a problem arises that we cannot solve. For us it is a better way to handle disagreements than calling lawyers. It costs less and is not as emotionally draining.

(36-year-old woman, 2½ years divorced)

After our divorce we argued more than before. In exasperation we sought professional help. The psychologist made us work out new guidelines for visitation,
helped us to understand the children's reactions, and, in general, was a super
strategist. He talked more than we did, but he also set out stipulations which we
had to adhere to. As we saw the children improve, we were encouraged to keep it
up. After a year we no longer needed his help; we were able to discuss our problems
more openly with each other and with the children.

(32-year-old woman, 2 years divorced)

Not all, however, who participated in this form of therapeutic venture
see its value. 'Marilyn's' account was scarcely complimentary.

Our therapist concentrated so heavily on the problems that would result from
divorce and especially the way the children would react that my husband and myself
were at a loss on how to function. And there was more; he kept telling us to be nice
to each other, loving and kind, and never to tell the children anything bad about the
other one. Well, if being loving and kind was so easy, there would be no need for a
divorce. I'm not saying that we should fight in front of the kids or ridicule each
other, but it's also not easy to be divorced and to act as lovers.

(37-year-old woman, 11 months divorced)

Unquestionably, to some extent Marilyn had a distorted perception of the
therapist's explication of the impact of divorce as well as of his recommendations. Yet her recollection raises two issues that cannot be blithely
dismissed. I refer first to the thorny question of how a therapist should
handle in the course of therapy an individual's or a couple's decision to
terminate their marriage. There are those who argue that unless the therapist adopts a conservative stance, conveying explicitly to the patient the
negative consequences of divorce, he is, by this very omission, deluding the
patient(s) into believing that his or her problems will vanish upon the
dissolution of the marriage (Kressel, 1980). Alternatively, others argue with
equal verve that the revealment of any ideological position is not only
contraindicated in a therapeutic relationship, but, in fact, interferes with
the patient's ability to think and act independently.

Nevertheless, both of these arguments sidestep critical considerations that
pertain directly to the manner and nature of the therapist's reaction to a
patient's decision to divorce. Consider, for example, the case of 'Grace'
and her husband.

I walked away from therapy with the fear that divorce was as bad as cancer. Even
under the best of circumstances the pain would be terrifying; the children would go
through many transitory disorders and possibly long-term ones; and my husband
and I would be caught in a deadly battle. The fright was so real that we stayed
together longer than we had planned, but eventually, a year later, divorced. Maybe

I should be thankful to this Machiavellian psychiatrist, because the problems we did have seemed minor compared to what we had anticipated.

(41-year-old woman, 2 years divorced)

And another example of this kind of therapeutic conduct can be garnered from psychiatrist R. V. Fitzgerald's published account (1973) of his statement to couples in treatment who decide to divorce.

Divorce is akin to death; in some ways it's even more difficult. You are experiencing a loss, and yet the person you are losing is within reach.... Even if it does not at the moment feel like the loss of a person, at the very least it is a loss of previously shared feelings, aspirations, hopes, and goals. A sense of profound failure and guilt may well plague you for a time. It's not to be gone through without some kind and degree of hurt (p. 96).

Furthermore, he forewarns the couple that "for their children the divorce represents a grave crisis" (ibid.). This prediction is somewhat cushioned by the addendum that the impact of divorce may be mollified through sensitive and thoughtful planning for the welfare of children and by leaving the door open for future therapeutic help either for the couple or their children. But the bottom line here, as in Smith's series (see pp. 198-99), remains unchanged: Divorce is a time of endangerment and anguish.

As I see it, the crux of the issue does not pivot on whether the therapist should or should not explain (or explore) the difficulties inherent in a marital dissolution, but rather whether in so doing he or she actually stages a miniature horror show. Grace's comparison of divorce to cancer and Fitzgerald's comparison of divorce to death and his use of the words "plague" and "grave crisis" are suggestive of the latter.

Moreover, there is still a second point in question that we have not addressed. To be specific, I am talking here about this entire notion of the "good" divorce. The reader will perhaps recall from Marilyn's narrative (p. 208) her characterization of the therapist's prescription for a friendly postdivorce relationship as anomalous in nature. Marilyn's criticism would be of little significance if she alone were challenging the logic of the "good" divorce. But she does not stand alone. Indeed, mental health clinicians have been lining up on both sides of the fence, some for, some against, and some simply fence-sitting, mulling, analyzing, but noncommittal. In the main, their concern is for the children of divorce, and as such, the debate boils down to the question of whether the good divorce may in effect be more detrimental to children than the bad divorce. As psychiatrist E. James Anthony (1974) explains:

This has been attributed to the fact that the child finds it more difficult to make sense out of the situation. In his own thinking, when people fight they part, and when they're friends they stay together. In the "good" divorce the child is confronted by two people who speak well of each other, relate well together, and apportion no blame, and it may be hard for the small child especially to understand this curious double communication. . . . It may be difficult for children to interpret this in terms other than hypocritical (pp. 468-469).

Yet the import of this argument is unclear. Certainly no one would suggest that a combative divorce is the model of choice. But what then are they suggesting? The most obvious conclusion is that divorce, good or bad, places children in a position of risk. While it is understandable that clinicians would demonstrate dogged persistence in surveying any and all causes that might result in pathological syndromes, where does this leave the divorced?[12] One respondent offered her opinion.

All you read and hear dwells on problems. It gets to the point where you can think of nothing else. No matter what you do, you're damned!
(35-year-old woman, 10 months separated)

In addition to this Orwellian prophecy of postdivorce dysfunction and conflict for children and adults, some individuals recoiled in anger at the prescriptive remedy.

She not only had us expecting every conceivable difficulty, but she strongly insinuated that unless we work through the problems which led to the breakup, we could not expect future happiness, single or remarried.
(39-year-old woman, 1 year divorced)

And Grace's recollection (see p. 208) was not dissimilar.

He kept saying that the underlying causes of our problems could not be ignored. To me he said, "You selected 'Robert' because he was weak, and you will go on selecting weak men only to reject them later unless you understand why you do this. Divorce will rid you of Robert but not of your neurosis."

The salespitch may be subtle, but the message delivered to these women and their husbands was not: Because divorce is symptomatic of untreated neurosis, the dissolution will not remedy the disorder and may even exacerbate it. Thus, without a commitment to psychotherapy, the prognosis for recovery is at best guarded. While there is obviously no way to know whether in the above cases the evaluations were accurate, like diagnoses are so frequently reported by individuals and so frequently appear in the divorce literature that its universality is striking. Gettleman and Markowitz (1974), two clinical social workers, also see the psychopathological diagnosis as a recurrent motif, a motif with ominous overtones:

The bias built into the psychological literature on divorce is that emotional pathology and personal tragedy are an inevitable component of the divorce experience. The language that clinicians use to describe divorce and the way in which they perceive their own role heighten the potentially traumatic impact of divorce on families (p. 66; see also Halem, 1980).

Alternatively, it is conceivable that during the divorce process and for a time afterward individuals may have a lower tolerance for psychiatric intervention and an even lower tolerance for psychiatric "truth." This appears particularly noticeable among couples who had conjoint therapy. More than a few revealed their aversion to having their psyches probed in the presence of their ex-spouse or soon-to-be ex.

I wanted him to tell 'Sal' that he had all the problems. It wasn't normal to be chasing after a woman ten years younger than himself, was it? But he seemed to feel that we were both to blame. I was shocked, hurt, and angry. I refused to continue with the counseling or go to anyone else. If I needed to hear about what was wrong with me, it was cheaper to stay married to Sal.

(40-year-old woman, 10 months separated)

Whether the therapist actually focused on blame or whether this was the patient's perception of what he said is not important. What is important is that at the time the individual may have other needs which can inhibit and even prohibit the development of a doctor-patient relationship. This can occur in conjoint therapy even if the therapist sees the spouses separately as well as together, and it can occur in individual therapy.

Individual Therapy: In Separation and in Divorce

With their physical and psychic energies drained, the separated and divorced may react with anger and denial to what they interpret as personal attacks. Their expectations have been shattered. They went to the therapist in search of reassurance and support, help in dealing with the transition from marriage to divorce,[13] and perhaps also exoneration. To be told instead about their problems may lead to an instantaneous retreat, as the therapist comes to be seen as another betrayer. Some therapeutic "dropouts" attributed their withdrawal to the therapist's insensitivity and others to poor timing.

I felt vulnerable and unwanted. The answer was logical—see a shrink. But he asked me to talk about my past in order that we could see how the problem came about. I was too consumed with the present and scared about the future to bother with the past. I didn't want to admit any problem and certainly not any share in it. I bolted. Two years later I did seek psychiatric help, but by then I was strong enough to face my problems.

(38-year-old woman, 3 years divorced)

For the most part, psychiatrists know little about divorce. They do not consider the real difficulties facing the divorced. The legal problems alone are worthy of attention, not to mention the economic ones. If they spent some time helping you deal with the immediate changes, they might find more people willing afterward to probe the causes of the divorce.

(37-year-old man, 1 year divorced)

Perhaps this explains why 20% of those who went for psychotherapy at the time of separation stopped treatment after a few sessions and then resumed it anywhere from six months to two-and-a-half years later. Two phenomena in particular appear to be at work: One is the pervasive belief that psychotherapy will palliate, even eliminate, the traumas of separation; the second phenomenon is tied to the readiness factor I spoke of earlier.[14]

Others who had unsatisfactory experiences changed therapists.

There was no way that I could establish any rapport with a doctor who was didactic, unsympathetic, and aloof. My second therapist was terrific. He did not hestitate to offer advice when it was needed and appropriate.

(39-year-old woman, 1 year divorced)

After two different psychiatrists I gave up on the profession. I found a psychiatric social worker who wasn't afraid to express opinions and carry on a conversation. We discussed the different decisions I had to make, including selling the house and arranging day care for 'Jennifer.' She was informed and supportive.

(32-year-old woman, 11 months divorced)

And still others may be considered, metaphorically speaking, members of the elect, the fortunate ones who did not experience any difficulty in finding a therapist and, more importantly, who were unequivocal in deeming their treatment a success.

I went to a social worker, a man, and he was excellent. He helped me adjust to seeing my kids less often. We talked about my ex-wife, about me, and about the women I dated. It only lasted a few months, but it was very structured and very helpful.

(42-year-old man, 1 year divorced)

Blue Shield coverage entitled me to $500 of psychiatric care. After I used up my $500 neither I nor my therapist saw any reason for my continuing. When I think back over the experience, and it was a good one, I realize that what I most needed was to stop feeling sorry for myself. The psychiatrist helped me to realize this.

(43-year-old woman, 2 years divorced)

I went to a woman who described herself as a divorce counselor. I don't know what kind of credentials she had, but she certainly knew a lot about divorce. She had been divorced herself and was very familiar with the problems that one experiences.

(35-year-old woman, 11 months divorced)

Once again the therapist's willingness to address the practical aspects of divorce seems to be critical. That the vast majority of respondents believed that the therapeutic experience should have both a clinical and an educational dimension is noteworthy.

The Group Experience: Support Groups in Separation and in Divorce

While some respondents attended short-term support groups for the separated and divorced, predictably, the reviews on this kind of counseling resource, as all others, were mixed.

I found a divorce self-help group the best and most inexpensive way to deal with separation. Here was a group with ten women all going through the same experience, led by a counselor who had been divorced and subsequently remarried. There were women in the group who had been to shrinks but found them unsatisfactory. We didn't need our heads examined; we needed practical advice and occasionally a shoulder to cry on.

(41-year-old woman, 3 years divorced)

If you like funerals, the group is your thing! Nothing else comes as close to the morbidity and oppressive climate created by ten or eight stricken individuals coming together in one sterile environment. I attended four of the eight sessions, and maybe it got better after I left, but four times was enough to set me back two months in adjusting to my separation.

(46-year-old woman, 1 year separated)

FOR THE CHILDREN

There was nary an individual who did not express concern about the effects of divorce on their children. Many became watchful and expectant, worrying as much about the children who did not evidence signs of disturbance as the ones who did. Whether children vocalized their feelings or were taciturn, whether they got into trouble or were models of decorum, their resiliency and ability to cope were devalued by their parents. In its place arose the image of their children as brittle and weak, a population at risk. And this is what they said.

Just because she seems cheerful does not mean she's okay. I know that under this exterior there is a troubled child.

She is too affectionate. I guess it is to be expected now that she feels abandoned.

He has started to answer me back when I tell him to do something. The divorce has produced a fresh nine-year-old.

Why doesn't he cry more about the divorce? He says he understands and it's okay. But it's not okay for a ten-year-old to adapt to divorce in a year's time.

She's reading too many books. It must be an escape for her. But whenever I ask her, she says she loves to read.

My daughter has become so grown-up. I think my wife is turning her into an adult at 14.

My son never used to go to kids' houses so much before; he did not even play with other kids much. Now he goes all the time. Maybe he hates being home since the divorce or he's ashamed.

That 35% of the children of questionnaire and interview respondents received some form of counseling is by no means startling, especially in light of the overwhelming number of parents who evinced anxiety over their children's "problems."

As each child showed signs of reacting, we sought psychiatric help for them. They didn't go long and it was geared toward helping them deal with the divorce. 'Bob' and I also had to go and it helped us too. By working on the children's problems, we settled some of our own.

(45-year-old woman, 1 year divorced)

'Sara' began to act out all the time, and I didn't know how to calm her down. Maybe I didn't try hard enough as I wasn't feeling all that marvelous myself. It was too much to cope with her and my problems at the same time. I talked to 'Jay' and he agreed to pay for Sara to see a psychiatrist. The doctor insisted that we all participate. Somehow it helped get us over that very difficult time at the beginning when you are sure your life has collapsed.

(34-year-old woman, 6 months divorced)

The school told me 'Jessica' needed to see a psychiatrist. I couldn't afford to take her privately, and I didn't qualify for public assistance. The school arranged for her to see their psychologist, and I saw her too from time to time. I would have preferred to do it on my own, but I really didn't have the money.

(38-year-old woman, 3 years divorced)

As these quotations illustrate, parents of children undergoing treatment are not infrequently required (or requested) to participate. Others, whose children were not in counseling, cited child-related issues as the reason for obtaining treatment for themselves. Indeed, 42% of those who listed themselves as consumers of mental health services belonged to this group.

'Allison' acted as if I had thrown her father out of the house. She kept asking me why I had been so mean to him, causing him to leave home. I tried in a hundred ways to explain that it wasn't meanness but differences between two people. She called me all kinds of names, suggested I dress like 'Barbara,' her father's girlfriend, and apologize to Dad. I began to think that 'Arthur' should have custody, since Allison and I did nothing but fight.

(39-year-old woman, 3 years divorced)

While it is not uncommon for children of separated and divorced parents to display aggression toward a parent, the difficulty of dealing with this and other kinds of "aberrant" behavior can be quite unnerving. For Allison's mother the solution was not to relinquish custody, as she first thought, but to obtain therapeutic help for herself.

If only a minority of parents, divorced or married, ever become truly inured to a child's anger or anguish, for the separated and divorced, especially if they view themselves as the injured party, the injustice of a child's hostility may seem intolerable.

He left me and I got blamed by everyone, even my children. It took a lot of therapy and stamina to make me go on, to help me realize that they had no one else but me to blame. I was there all day, every day. They saw him only once a week.

(45-year-old woman, 4 years divorced)

Whether it was because adults who utilized mental health services for child-related reasons could more easily accept going to, say, a psychiatrist or psychologist for the "sake of the children," as one woman put it, or because much of this therapy, too, had a practical orientation, most of these individuals reported satisfaction.

STILL SEARCHING

There were others who professed, often poignantly, the need for clinical guidance and support, but did not secure help for reasons which ranged from concern over fees to issues of availability, accessibility, and confusion over the goal and focus of such services.

Where does one go for psychological help if you are not very poor or rich? My ex-husband can't pay for it, and I can't afford $50 an hour. So I guess you just muddle through.

(33-year-old woman, 5 months separated)

I did not want to go to a psychiatrist, partly because of the expense and partly because I did not believe I was mentally ill. I asked around and looked in the papers, but could not find any group or service for the separated. The closest thing to it was a self-help group for widows. Oh, there was PWP, but that was a social club. I didn't want to meet men; I wanted help in making a new life for myself.[15]

(37-year-old woman, 1 year divorced)

There are many days when I feel the need for reassurance and guidance, but do not know what exists besides psychiatrists and pitiful groups.

(43-year-old woman, 1½ years divorced)

CONCLUSION

From the singular standpoint of utilization, the percentage of women and men who consulted mental health professionals for divorce or divorce-related (e.g., children) causes is staggering: 74% of all women and 43% of all men in the questionnaire and interview sample were at some time consumers in the mental health sector. The precise reason why men were less frequent users of mental health services than women is difficult to ascertain (see footnote 8). The notion that treatment would connote personal incapacitation and helplessness was stated by some. That men cannot break down, be "cry babies," or reveal weakness is inculcated in many from birth. Since they believe that they must maintain an image of invincibility, for these men shame and also fear impede their ability to express and comprehend emotional anxieties. Others balked at the fees. Comparing their incomes to the ones they projected for psychiatrists, they adjudged the rates to be excessive. One man alleged, "The fees of psychiatrists are outrageous. No way am I going to pay someone a yearly annuity just because he had an expensive education." Others were already too overburdened financially to afford treatment.

I am a walking testimonial to the divorce syndrome. I drink too much; my performance at work is getting progressively worse; I am depressed and angry. But I have to give my ex-wife child support and pay off a cash settlement. There is no money left for psychiatry.

(38-year-old man, 5 months separated)

And still others distrusted mental health professionals, averring that only the insane needed "head shrinkers."

Nonetheless, the statistics are imposing, even more so if we include those who went to family physicians and clergymen for emotional guidance and/or support. We can now state that 85% of the women and 48% of the men sought some form of professional help. Further, if we take into account all those who indicated an interest in and need for such services, we would very likely come close to 100% for the women and a lower, but still high, figure for the men.

The implications of this observation are, however, cryptic. Does it mean that divorce is a symptom or form of mental illness necessitating clinical remedies? Does it mean that we have come to value psychotherapeutic remedies in their own right, irrespective of the nature of the problem? Obviously there is truth in both assumptions. For, while some respondents ascribed the emotional repercussions of divorce to psychological maladjustment, others did not. They attested to and elaborated upon, often in minute detail, their loneliness, depression, and anxieties, but conceded to the normalcy of their feelings. Yet they, too, frequently followed the well-trodden pathway to the therapist.

A curious phenomenon seems to be at play in which there is almost a cause-and-effect relationship between separation and the utilization of mental health services. Increasingly the separated look upon psychotherapy as they do legal counsel, concluding that the dissolution of a marriage mandates both legal and clinical intervention. Some, in fact, recommended that legal and therapeutic services be combined.

A lawyer should work with a psychiatrist. One would provide the legal advice and the other would help you adjust to the emotional impact of the split.
(33-year-old woman, 9 months separated)

And there are lawyers who seem to agree. From those who advocate a therapeutic speciality of law (Konut, 1968; Mariano, 1958) to those who regularly refer clients to psychotherapists, the legal profession, either because of its inability or unwillingness to deal with the emotional aspects of divorce or because it also subscribes to the mental health mystique, is helping to draw law and psychiatry closer together.

Perhaps this has all come about because we have no tolerance for discomfort or change. Is that not the assertion of those who characterize us as a nation of pill poppers and alcoholics, a people in pursuit of pleasure, known for their excesses instead of their abstinences? Or perhaps this has all come about because we share the belief of psychoanalytic visionaries that psychiatry and psychology and its allied professions (e.g., social work, marriage counseling) possess the answers, hold the cure for erasing our suffering. Or perhaps this has all come about because we have been brainwashed by two antithetical messages. One says that individuals should be free to pursue their own pleasures, do their own thing. The other says that life's changes are times of crisis; even those who call it "transitions" or "passages" often hint at the insidious dangers lying in wait as we proceed from one stage or step to another. With these two communications in mind, for the moment envision those who have come to the realization that their spouses are stultifying their lives. Thus the termination of the marital contract or sentence (call it what you may) will grant them the freedom and happiness that message number one says are their just desserts. And this may happen, but not always immediately. Hence in comes message number two. It tells them that the anxiety they are feeling, the mood swings, and the anger are symptomatic of an identity crisis. They need to pull it all together before they can fulfill their dreams. But how long do they tarry? A day? A month? A year? No one says, for no one knows. Those who fear that they can wait no longer may turn to others, seeking to ease the transition, to make tomorrow come today.[16] Some may have little choice as they neither know where to go nor have the finances to pay their way.

And the majority do succeed, many of whom have received clinical assistance. There are numerous success stories in the annals of psychiatry as many respondents have corroborated. But if we view psychiatry or any of its offshoots *only* with respect to the role it plays in the lives of the separated and divorced and consider carefully the needs and concerns they express, we cannot help but notice the importance attributed to therapy that has a utilitarian component, if not focus. This suggests two conclusions: The separated and divorced may need practical information on how to restructure their lives as much as emotional support; *and* this may be accomplished in a variety of ways, only one of which is through psychotherapeutic modes of treatment.

NOTES

1. The theory that divorce and death are similar experiences was not invented by Shirley Smith. One therapist, Nora Ferdon, contends that the stages of recovery from divorce mirror those outlined by psychiatrist Elisabeth Kübler-Ross in *On Death and Dying* (Foreman, 1978b, p. B1). The literature on divorce is amply sprinkled with analogous references between these two occurrences. In Smith's series, however, there are few analogies. Instead, both kinds of losses are treated as like events leading to like outcomes. The failure to point out the dissimilarities between divorce and death should not be given short shrift. Not only are the acts themselves different, but so are the circumstances that surround the loss (before and after the occurrence), as are the effects. Indeed, the differences among individuals' reactions to divorce (and to death) are in themselves significant enough to warrant special treatment.

2. To illustrate just how few axioms there are to be found in the annals of social science, eight months after this series was printed, another major metropolitan newspaper reported Dr. Anke Ehrhardt's finding that married homemakers, not widowed, divorced, and single women, have the highest depression rate (Nemy, 1979, p. B10). While Ehrhardt's analysis bodes a stressful future for the traditional homemaker, it offers some consolation to those who have long been the frontrunners in studies on depression. The importance of Ehrhardt's research to us lies not so much in its findings, but in the fact that, by presenting evidence which

refuses prevailing "data" and beliefs, it demonstrates that there are no conclusive data, that the state of mental health research, like much other research, is replete with contradictions and confusions.

3. Articles such as this one are predominantly directed toward women. Men can rejoice, at least in this respect, that writers and researchers have manifested less interest in the problems that they encounter in coping with loss. Yet their respite appears to be short lived. Of late, theorists have begun to look more closely at the men of divorce, attempting to uncover similarities and differences in the ways in which men and women adjust to a marital dissolution (Bloom et al., 1978; Chiriboga and Cutler, 1977; Kressel, 1980). The question remains as to whether the remediation of this scientific void will in fact help the new population under study.

4. Without a specific definition of what recovery entails, other than feeling "comfortable with themselves" and being "as stable as their nature permits" (Weiss, 1975, p. 240), it is impossible to substantiate or invalidate this thesis. On the basis of my observations, however, the figure seems excessively high. Moreover, many of the separated and divorced make such dramatic changes in their lives (e.g., obtain employment, go back to school, relocate) that even if their marriages were still intact, an adjustment would be necessary. My point, simply put, is that the time factor for recovery cannot be accurately determined without attention to the many variables involved. In addition, I'm not sure that divorced individuals should strive to be "themselves again"; the divorce, even if unanticipated and unwanted, should hopefully serve as an incentive for growth and change.

5. There appears to be an inconsistency in Weiss's argument. On the one hand he discusses the search for and even attainment of a "new identity," while on the other hand he talks about being one's self again. Undeniably, personalities do not ordinarily undergo dramatic metamorphoses, but one would assume that a "new identity" would signify that some kind of major change has occurred.

6. If some have chosen to subdivide Weiss's categorizations, listing separately, for example, periods of denial, mourning, and anger (Kressel, 1980, pp. 236-237), there is no substantive difference between these classifications and those of Weiss.

7. According to Kressel (1980), women's "subordinate economic, educational, and vocational status" during marriage may ironically serve them in good stead after divorce. The number of major changes that women are forced to make after divorce come to be looked upon by them as accomplishments, evidence of their ability to cope. In comparison, men often have less need to initiate such changes and thus less evidence of tangible achievements (p. 237).

8. The literature on divorce presents contradictory conclusions as to whether a marital dissolution has a greater psychological impact on women or men. For example, Albrecht (1980) concludes that women experience significantly more trauma and stress than do men (p. 66; Campbell, Converse, and Rodgers, 1976). In contrast, Bloom, Asher, and White (1978) report a substantially higher admission rate to psychiatric hospitals for the men of divorce than for the women. And Kressel (1980) suggests that men may be more reticent to divulge (and even unaware of) their emotional problems and therefore *appear* to experience less stress.

9. To maintain the anonymity of the locale and individuals, the name of the priest under discussion has been coded.

10. Maintaining that too few counselors, even among so-called divorce therapists, are willing to help divorcing individuals deal with the practical issues and concerns of divorce, Kressel (1980) argues for an expanded conception of the therapeutic role. The number of major decisions that have to be made during divorce and the "impairment" of the individual's "decision-making ability" are, in Kressel's view, sufficiently compelling reasons for redefining therapeutic involvement (pp. 238-239).

11. Psychiatrists, psychologists, social workers, and marriage counselors may also function in the capacity of divorce counselors, and divorce counselors may employ classical modes of therapeutic treatment.

12. At first it appears as if we have come a long way. The centuries-old debate over whether divorce is better for children than living in a conflict-ridden, intact milieu has not yet been laid to rest, but has to some extent been upstaged by the "good versus bad" divorce question. Indeed, for a time it seemed to be a sign of definite progress that the adjective "good" was being used in descriptions of divorce. But there is no denying that this word has now taken on a negative connotation. And, even more so than the debates of yesteryear, the "good versus bad" controversy borders on the absurd. One can be against divorce, but can one be against "good" divorce or for "bad" divorce? Moreover, the questions this new controversy pose may well be irresolvable. Instead of adding to our scientific knowledge of divorce, it may not only unduly traumatize the divorced, but leave them nowhere to turn.

13. This may be one reason why therapy that has a utilitarian focus tends to be rated as more worthwhile by the separated and divorced.

14. There are other variables of no less importance that also affect the therapeutic relationship and experience. To mention only a small sample: the factors leading up to and following the separation, the timing of the treatment (e.g., before, during, or after divorce), the relationship with the ex-spouse, the relationship with the children (including custody, visitation, and the children's reaction to the divorce), the frequency of the treatment, the individual's life circumstances (e.g., financial status, living arrangements, work satisfaction), and the training and orientation of the therapist.

15. This interview took place in 1975. Since that time, more support groups and counseling services are available. More recent offerings will be discussed in Chapter 8.

16. Most assuredly, this group includes those who have long been interested in obtaining clinical assistance. For them divorce becomes an excuse or a legitimization for wish fulfillment. Others have been previous, even periodic, users of mental health services; for them, it is a natural response for dealing with problems. And still others have no inkling of the pending separation or are decidedly opposed to it. For this group, separation is particularly difficult, having little to do with the pursuit of pleasure or self-satisfaction; indeed it can constitute quite the opposite. Consequently, utilization rates provide incomplete evidence for drawing conclusions. Any inferences from the data must be regarded as inconclusive or merely suggestive.

SHEILA AND THE PSYCHE
OF THE DIVORCED:
A DISCOURSE ON
A COMMUNITY'S CARETAKERS
AND THEIR CARE

To speak to women about separation and divorce is to hear stories of legal battles, of economic struggles, of social junkets, of dolorous days and evenings. But it is also to hear more, for real-life stories differ from the exaggerated sentimentality of melodramas—they have ups and downs, moments of humor and moments of sadness, times of comedy and times of tragedy. Yet there was a recurrent theme throughout these recounts which appeared and reappeared with such habitual regularity that it sounded almost like a conversational refrain. Repeatedly women (and men) interrupted their discourses, pausing to interject some comment, some allusion to the insouciance of society, of their lawyers, of their physicians, and of their clergymen to their emotional needs. And because I asked and because I was interested, they also spoke of their community and, in particular, of the scarcity of resources specifically geared to their problems. They did not speak in despair or in desperation; but they did speak of psychological needs that were not being met by a community that pretended to care. Thus to Sheila befell the task of researching this community that said it cared. And because my interest in this phase of the study centered primarily on the psychological needs and problems of the separated and divorced, it was to public and private mental health resources and providers that Sheila turned her attention. Her assignment was to determine the kinds of services available in Westside and, by comparing these data to that of respondents, to ascertain discrepancies between alleged needs and the availability and accessibility of existing resources. In addition, *I* interviewed providers in the mental health sector to obtain their assessment of community services and their suggestions, if any, for change.

While both Sheila and I participated in the investigation, once again Sheila did the bulk of the leg work. It was she who went from agency to agency inquiring whether they had counseling programs or services for the separated and divorced and/or their families. It was she who spent hour after hour on the telephone contacting organizations and individuals in and around Westside, including every clergyman in the community. Sheila, of course, did not enter into therapy, receive guidance from clergymen, or join a support group. As in the exploration on the social needs and concerns of the divorced, there were limitations on her involvement, times when traditional modes of research had to be employed and when I had to assume the responsibility for their execution.

Three major areas were covered: individual and group counseling services for adults, family counseling services, and children's services. Although I have not invented these classifications, borrowing instead those in current use by public and private agencies and providers, a cautionary preamble is in order. In particular, the reader should note that these categories are not mutually exclusive. Not only are there interrelationships and overlaps between them, but each category can be subdivided into different groupings, each of which would have an independent integrity. In part this is because of the variety of offerings and in part because organizations and individuals have invented a seemingly endless number of labels and terms to describe and advertise a limited number of services. And thus, because the mental health delivery system in Westside, as elsewhere, appears much like an intricate maze, maneuvering through the system challenges one's ingenuity and tests one's endurance. That this can be especially trying for the separated and divorced is undeniable. At a time in their lives when they are already drawing on a depleted reservoir of strength, they must amass not only enough energy to actively explore community resources, but must also decipher bureaucratic lingo and contend with procedural obstructions. Even in noninstitutionalized settings, the procurement of accurate information can be a difficult and tiresome endeavor. That the diversity and complexity of the system pose problems for the researcher is also undeniable. Consequently, the presentation that follows is by no means to be considered an exhaustive portrayal of Westside's mental health delivery system.

INDIVIDUAL AND GROUP COUNSELING SERVICES FOR ADULTS

As respondents had spoken of problems related to the availability, access, and cost of counseling services for the separated and divorced, these issues became the foci of Sheila's investigation, an investigation that began with a search for any publications which might be used by this resident population as a guide for securing help. In 1975 there was but one—a four-page outline of public and nonprofit agencies compiled by the area office of the State Department of Mental Health.[1] (Copies could be obtained without charge at Westside's City Hall or at the local hospital.) Although this brochure did not include resources in the private sector, it provided Sheila with a starting point—the names of specific places to contact.

In total there were five listings under adult counseling, none of which had any individual or group programs for separated and divorced individuals. This Sheila learned when she queried spokespeople at all five agencies on the availability of "special" services for the divorced. They responded with bewilderment to her question.

We are a counseling facility, not a special interest group. We do have patients who are divorced, although this is not necessarily the reason why they need help. Public services cannot respond to every social problem which exists today, not if they want to stay in business.

What an absurd request! I don't mean to put you down, but why on earth would you want special counseling? There are many reasons for neurotic behavior. Divorce is not a reason; it is an act. You need to understand why you have chosen to solve your personal problems through divorce.[2]

Perhaps their bewilderment was justifiable, for their reasoning was far from illogical. I cannot refute the assertion of one that the capacity of any agency to respond to the myriad of social problems extant in society is limited. For if priorities are not established, is it not possible that service delivery will become so fractionalized that effectiveness in every area will be threatened? I cannot refute the assertion of the other that the divorced may not need "special" counseling. For if we do target or label a group, like the divorced, as a population at risk, is it not possible that we may unintentionally stigmatize people—set them apart from others as different?

And is there perhaps another element of "absurdity" inherent in Sheila's inquiry that they did not detect? I refer specifically to the needs and, more importantly, to the *wants* of a middle-class clientele. We cannot so easily overlook the possibility that respondents, irrespective of their avowals, might not avail themselves of *public* counseling services, be they targeted or open-ended. Their past record in using public resources suggests that their words belie their wants, that in actuality what they may *want* is access to private counselors at clinic fees or even at public expense.

This might explain why no respondent ever contemplated using any of the outpatient counseling services which *were* available at these agencies and institutions, often at considerably less cost than similar offerings in the private sector. Conceivably, these institutions were simply poor publicists, unable to mount effective campaigns for promoting their services. Yet this explication seems specious. I am more apt to conclude that the middle-class divorced did not reject these services because, in point of fact, they never considered them as options. To them public counseling agencies were established to tend the poor; utilization of these facilities would thus not only be personally inappropriate but demeaning.

I cannot deny that my husband has reduced me to being a charity case. But before I walk through the door of a place that caters to the poor, I'll commit myself. If things reach a point where therapy is truly imperative, I may have to swallow my pride and borrow from my parents to see a shrink.

(34-year-old woman, 4 months separated)

Because the anonymity and exclusiveness of private services are prized features, difficult to duplicate in public settings, it is highly questionable whether the creation of additional public services would yield a return worthy of the capital outlay. Perhaps expanded options in the public sector would languish from disuse, unless, of course, a concerted effort was made to "destigmatize" such offerings.

Indeed, institutionalized services in general may suffer from an image problem. For example, only a small minority of women and men sought help from the clergy, and among those who did most were extremely vocal in condemning the indifference of the clergymen to their needs and concerns. The singular exception, as noted previously, was the Paulist Center for Roman Catholics. Interestingly enough, Sheila's telephone calls to Westside clergymen in 1975 did not corroborate this charge of indifference. Over 50% of those contacted invited Sheila to see them privately in their offices. Whether they did so in the hope of saving her marriage (as she was separated, not divorced) or of redeeming her soul, I do not know. I do know that many expressed their willingness to offer pastoral guidance to an outsider. This was an unexpected development, especially since Sheila made no pretense of being in great emotional turmoil. Her approach could best be described as an informational inquiry: "Do you have any provisions for group or individual counseling for the separated and divorced?" she had asked. (Hardly an SOS!)

Nevertheless, because the majority of respondents had no close or formal affiliation with any religious denomination, we should resist the temptation to read into this observation. More telling is the Westside Public School System's aborted effort to create support groups for single parents in the 1975-1976 academic year.

There are schools in Westside which are approaching close to a 50% population of single parents. We know this is a major and growing problem, but have not been able to devise a way to reach these parents. When we organize groups for the parents of handicapped children, we get a terrific response. But with divorce, the reaction is apathy. Few are interested in dealing with their problems.

(Representative of pupil personnel services)

There is no evidence to support the allegation that single parents are apathetic. Nor is there any reason to suspect that individuals would view the schools as an agent of the poor. A more plausible deduction is that the schools, in not seeing the difference between the problems faced by single parents and parents of handicapped children, in some way displayed an insensitivity to the very individuals they sought to help—an insensitivity which did not go unnoticed.

Whether community utilization patterns could be altered by an increased sensitivity to the needs of the separated and divorced and by the provision of more specialized and individualized public counseling services still remained a question three years later. For in 1978, as evidenced by the listings in the newly created Westside resource directory and in the 1978 edition of the four-page brochure,[3] the status quo prevailed. While this did not indicate the absence of counseling resources in Westside, it did reveal the absence of public and institutional services targeted for the separated and divorced. In contrast, there was quite a bit more to-do in the private sector. If in 1975 it was hard to locate services specifically catering to the separated and divorced, in 1978 it was hard to escape them.

THE DIVORCE COUNSELING MOVEMENT

The rising divorce rate and cost of psychiatric therapy served as an inspiration for cashing in on the divorce trade. The result was a mushrooming of counseling centers, purporting to have special expertise in divorce. While stalls have still not been set up in supermarkets, or booths outside of courthouses, these commercial enterprises, some of whom surprisingly maintain a nonprofit status, seem destined to become the McDonalds of the counseling set. They profess to offer their clients privacy, low hourly fees, and short-term focused therapy; there are no eligibility standards other than the ability to pay and no lengthy waits.[4] Or, at least, so go the advertising claims. Although these entrepreneurial developers have not yet opened branch counseling shops in Westside proper, there are others who are offering similar wares on a smaller scale. Imitating the marketing pitch of the superstars, private practitioners with a wide assortment of credentials are increasingly advertising in Westside newspapers. Their invitations are simple: Come all ye separated, divorced, and unhappily married and sample our therapeutic services—confidentiality, convenience, and reasonable costs are guaranteed.[5]

Most assuredly, divorce therapy was not invented in these centers. Since the 1960s divorce counseling has had a substantial cadre of proponents. Even earlier in the century, theorists had extolled the benefits of directive therapy for the divorced. While it may seem that this new industry is a legitimate response to a need, filling a void in the provision of public and private mental health services, there are other sides to these ventures which make one hesitant to applaud. In particular, there is the troublesome issue of standards, troublesome because there aren't any. Neither state licensing nor professional training requirements exist to deter the ambitious and/or unscrupulous from capitalizing on the increased demand for therapeutic services. Because there is no regulation of this industry or of its practitioners, there is little to prevent anyone from going into the counseling business or from calling himself or herself a counselor (Karagianis, 1975; McLaughlin, 1976). Moreover, fees are not exactly in the rock-bottom category; indeed, some exceed the rates charged by public agencies. In general, $25 an hour is the norm (although some charge as much as $45 an hour), a cost which, incidentally, can also purchase the services of some psychologists and psychiatrists in the public sector and psychiatric social workers and even some psychologists in the private sector. This is not to say that all commercial centers are bogus, predatory enterprises or that all counselors with "unique" training are duping the public, but it does suggest that buyers should be wary. Further, it suggests that consumers should consider alternative modalities of treatment besides individual and group therapy. Here there are various options, the most popular of which are support groups. In fact, when respondents were asked to order their preferences, such groups ranked in second place.[6]

THE SUPPORT GROUP MOVEMENT

By the early 1970s support groups for the separated and divorced were scarcely unknown, having been rather well publicized as an effective approach for helping individuals adjust to marital dissolution. Nonetheless, in 1975 Westside provided residents with only a smattering of social clubs. Sheila's canvassing of the Westside community revealed the following data: Two religious institutions had groups for this population, but both described their objectives as primarily social in nature; three noninstitutionalized groups were identified, all of which held weekly social gatherings; one community center, of the four listed, tried to organize a support group for the separated and divorced, but abandoned the project when advertisements in the local newspapers failed to attract enough participants; and lastly, two advocacy groups, one exclusively for women and one for men, sponsored seminars and drop-in evenings for people in marital transition—in their goals and function, these latter groups were the closest of any to being a facsimile of a support group.

In truth, for those seeking support groups in the year 1975, the pickings outside as well as inside Westside can be most generously described as meager. While librarians in the eastern region of the state (which included Westside and its environs) had participated in the creation of a Single-Parent Program Packet replete with materials and suggestions for organizing support groups,[7] to judge by the responses from agencies and clinicians in and around Westside one would have thought that the packet was printed in Old English. There was no sign of a rush on the libraries; indeed, the most noticeable sign was the absence of interest by both public and private organizations and providers. Since most of the greater metropolitan area maintained its allegiance to traditional modes of delivering mental health services, cities and towns were reluctant to expend public funds on what they regarded as an unorthodox and/or untested ameliorative technique. Conceivably, some were even totally unaware of this treatment option. Insulated by design, tradition, or ignorance, the group as a therapeutic tool for divorce-related problems had not come into vogue.

But communities as well as people can be fickle. By 1978 it was obvious that the group approach was not only considered fashionable, but was well on its way to becoming a "hot" item. The number of short-term groups, often called seminar, discussion, or support groups, for the separated and divorced began to multiply. This development can be attributed to several interrelated factors. For one, the media had continued to hype the subject of divorce, presenting a seemingly interminable stream of programs and articles on the negative repercussions of marital dissolution. And not infrequently these presentations referred to the successes, real or proclaimed, of the small-group method for coping with the transition from married to single life. Then, too, endorsements were to be found under the covers of popular and professional books. In *Creative Divorce*, Mel Krantzler (1973) described for the lay public his role as a leader of "divorce adjustment seminars," and in *Marital Separation*, Robert Weiss (1975) offered a more scholarly version of his experience as director and leader of "Seminars for the Separated." In addition, there were handbooks with explicit directions for designing and implementing groups for the formerly married. Most notable among these was the feminist handbook, *Women in Transition*, published by the writers in 1972 and then picked up in 1975 for national publication by Charles Scribner's Sons. Other factors also enhanced the status of support groups, in the process adding fuel to what was fast becoming a movement for a "new" remedial approach to the problems of divorce. For instance, the recognition that groups with a limited number of participants and a limited life span were less expensive to sponsor and easier to administrate than long-term individual or group therapy provided an irresistible inducement for public and nonprofit agencies to carry the banner for support groups.

One agency after another jumped aboard the bandwagon. A trend was in the making, revealing not only that the group approach had come of age, but that it had received the blessing of those who held the public's purse strings. Town, city, and state social service agencies and departments became involved in the formation of divorce therapy groups. Court clinics and philanthropic religious organizations as well as other nonprofit lay and religious centers and institutions also joined the movement. Even the area's largest community health plan, servicing over 80,000 members, many of whom were from the middle and upper-middle classes, created groups for the separated and divorced. Indeed, the 'Health Plan' became the recipient of funds from the National Institute of Mental Health (NIMH) to conduct research on what they described in their membership newsletter (1977) as "a new approach to helping people undergo marital separation" (p. 2). Although from a historical perspective the claim of innovation was clearly disputable, for subscribers to the Health Plan it did constitute a new treatment option.

If the research on the effects of such programs has been far from adequate or conclusive,[8] and some participants with whom I spoke did not issue any commendations, group advocates remain undaunted. Scarcely a week passes without an announcement of a newly formed group.

By no means are the godfathers (or godmothers) of the support group confined to the public and nonprofit sector. Representatives from the private sector have also presided at its baptismal dedication. For these mental health providers there were other incentives, the most compelling of which came in the form of financial rewards to be drawn from the potentially large supply of clients. Not only could more people afford treatment (although it is rarely labeled as treatment), which lasted, say, from eight to ten weeks, but therapists could keep the hourly rate relatively low and still receive substantial remuneration for their services. Thus a mélange of counselors from all walks of life began to cash in on the private therapy trade; they, like others, found the group approach to be another lucrative avenue worthy of pursuit.

Unfortunately, the popularity of "new" ideas or solutions can be a mixed blessing. In response to the demand for increased therapeutic services, new options and opportunities for the separated and divorced have arisen. But so has this era of divorce therapy spawned a new aggregation of caretakers for the separated and divorced and a new industry "dedicated" to their treatment. That some of these caretakers are not reputable practitioners and that some parts of this industry are of rather dubious merit is perhaps the downward side of reform—the side which permits commercial ventures and vendors to flourish, unchecked by the regulatory standards which govern licensed institutions and professionals.[9]

You have only to look at California to see what can happen when anybody can proclaim himself a therapist. One storefront operation after another appears, each promising a cure-all for everything that ails. It is a frightening portrayal of man's search for meaning and identity. The search is not new. Nor is the existence of people who for profit or self-aggrandizement capitalize on the pain of others. Some actually believe they are saviors. Some of these people are in institutions; others are getting rich. Regulations, such as licensing, are important, but they are not the solution. People will continue to look for the quick and easy cure as long as they are suffering, as long as they feel alone and without supports from their society and their fellowman.

(Psychiatrist)

Hence it would be foolhardy to believe that this is a problem to be eliminated by posting warnings, cautioning consumers to be wary of glib advertisements and lofty promises, or even by enacting *and* enforcing stringent regulatory controls. At best these would be stopgap measures; at worst they would serve to push the problem underground, a problem that, by the way, exists in the public as well as the private sector. The people who run these operations and practice their own brand of therapy are of minor importance; in a sense they are only the front men. The etiology of the problem lies elsewhere; in particular, it is traceable to the very individuals who are their clients, some even their victims. They are not just the separated and divorced, for as a group they are in less danger, as the above quotation implies, than are others who expend so much of their time and energy in the search for self.

Undeniably, psychotherapeutic remedies from the traditional to the trendy will long be in fashion: New problems will surface even as we proclaim victory over others, and we will continue to brush off the dust from yesterday's reforms and peddle them as new creations. But the clinical legacy is not the only bequest from our past that deserves mention. Of late, other innovations, all purported to be of recent origin and to have some basis in psychiatric theory, have received a fair amount of publicity. It is to these innovations that we now turn.

HELP COMES FROM DIFFERENT QUARTERS

I cannot resist beginning with what I call "the rite of divorce." In substance, it represents a modern version of the ecclesiastical equivalent to the judicial divorce decree. The divorced couple participates in a religious ceremony to consummate the dissolution of their marriage. Publicly they exchange vows, forgiving each other for past transgressions and reaffirming their respect and esteem for each other as individuals. The fulfillment that they were unable to find in their lives together, they now wish for each other.

Ecclesiastical divorces, of course, predate civil divorces by thousands of years. For example, the Hebrew bill of divorce known as a "get" is still considered by conservative and orthodox Jews as the only recognized method for dissolving the marital bond. Moreover, the get is not simply a document but a mystical procedure deemed necessary for severing the spiritual ties between spouses.

In an anthropological sense the theory behind "the rite of divorce" is also of ancient vintage; it goes something like this: Life is a series of passages, each of which constitutes both an ending and a beginning. Although customs vary, all societies partake in ritualistic commemorations of life's passages. The best known are those which pertain to birth, the attainment of adulthood, marriage, and death. And so it would seem to follow that there should be a formalized rite or recognition of the termination of a marriage, a ceremony marking the end of one stage of life and the beginning of another. This, in short, is the intent behind Rabbi Earl Grollman's and Unitarian Minister Marjorie Sams' involvement in the performance of divorce ceremonies (Foreman, 1978a, p. B7). Through participation in a religious divorce the couple acknowledges not only the end of their union but also the beginning of a new period in their lives as individuals and as parents of children for which they are both responsible.

My problem with this idea is that I view it as somewhat naive, indeed flawed in its logic. Others have noted and even eloquently articulated (e.g., Marris, 1974) the need for a period of mourning in divorce as in death. Integral to ceremonial grieving is the inducement of emotional catharsis in which the widowed (and all mourners) begin the process of accepting their loss and the movement beyond what was, to what is and what will be. For the divorced there is no prescribed ritual—the only ceremony and closure is the issuance of the legal decree, and even here it is not uncommon for only one of the spouses to be present at the judicial "rite." Nonetheless, a ritualistic observance of a marital dissolution is an inchoate replica of mourning customs, for it offers the divorced neither the supports nor the rites accorded to the widowed. The mere performance of a ceremony does not and cannot either duplicate the period of mourning and the grieving accompanying death or substitute for the gathering of family and friends who succor the widowed during the time of bereavement.

Furthermore, from a psychological standpoint this approach is subject to other criticisms, not the least of which are oversimplification and faulty reasoning. It seems inconceivable that those who have not come to terms with their divorce will achieve emotional closure through the utterance of a few lines that profess forgiveness and promise benevolence. Surely it is not because witnesses are present. People do, after all, perjure themselves in courtrooms filled with witnesses, and people also vow to love and cherish each other until death do them part in a marriage ceremony and then file for divorce. Surely it is not because they fear holy retribution, at least not for the majority of people. Anger, conflict, and pain, to mention but a few of the psychological dimensions of divorce, are not that easily cast aside.[10]

In the final analysis this kind of solution or method for coping with divorce may work best for those who have already structured a new life for themselves and established a new relationship with their former spouses. To ask why these individuals would need to partake in such a ceremony is a logical question. Perhaps in a way it is like a graduation—a ceremonial acknowledgment that they have fulfilled all the requirements for the degree of a "compatible" or "friendly" divorce. A bit of memorabilia can now be added to the family album, to be passed on to the grandchildren.

If it is all too obvious that I will not be carrying any placards to promote religious divorce ceremonies, I do, however, view reforms such as these as symbolic of a more profound development that does indeed have my endorsement. Increasingly representatives of organized religion are coming to realize that divorce cannot be wished or preached away. As divorce rates have risen among clergymen[11] as well as parishioners (Hutchison and Hutchison, 1979; Longcope, 1976), the churches have had little alternative but to moderate their longstanding antidivorce posture. Practicality and humanity demanded that an unyielding, nonactivist position on divorce give way.[12] And to a significant extent the change has been a dramatic one. More and more churches have reached out to the separated and divorced, offering solace, guidance, and even practical help in rebuilding their lives. Nowhere has the transformation been as evident as in the Roman Catholic Church, the staunchest opponent of divorce. This is why the Paulist Center's creation of groups and programs for divorced Catholics deserves special tribute as a daring clerical initiative (see pp. 205-206). But the efforts of other religious groups ought not to be slighted simply because they had long ago bowed to public pressure to legitimate divorce. In 1975 Sheila had identified two religious institutions with groups for the divorced, but by 1980 the majority of churches and synagogues in Westside were sponsoring either formal or informal programs for this population (see p. 172; p. 196, footnote 8). In all religious denominations the proliferation of groups for the separated and divorced is a noteworthy development, if only because it signifies that religious organizations too move with changing currents of social climate and norms. While some social analysts maintain that there have been no major alterations in ecclesiastical practice and thought on divorce—only the nuance of reform—if we view these changes through a historical lens, the significance of the churches' present efforts in Westside and elsewhere cannot be gainsaid.

Perhaps to fully appreciate the import of the churches' contributions, we should not dwell on evolutionary progressions in attitudes and practices, for many have long ago grown weary of hearing about changes which have been centuries in the making. Instead, the perspective to be taken is a comparative one in which the churches' awakening recognition of the psychological needs of the divorced is adjudged within the context of the present, particularly in comparison to other local initiatives independent of those occurring within the mental health sector. Here one of the newest and most promising developments is the Family Dispute Service, created in 1977 by the nonprofit American Arbitration Association (AAA), an organization known for its work in conflict resolution and the negotiated settlements of disputes.[13] In its approach to divorce and family grievances, the AAA has pooled its resources and expertise with those of another nonprofit service, namely, a divorce counseling center (Fripp, 1977). Thus what they have designed is an intersystem program which considers divorce-related as well as marital disputes as both interpersonal and legal in nature. But while the conciliators, mediators, referees, and arbitrators provided by the AAA may assuage the tensions between parties, shorten the legal process of negotiation, and even appreciate a savings of time, money, and psychic energy, they do not replace lawyers. Because individuals who divorce still have to deal with the law and its representatives, the AAA program is only a partial response to sample members who recommended an integration of legal and psychiatric services.

Of all AAA offerings, its conciliation service comes closest to approaching a legal/psychiatric model. Marriage counseling techniques are employed to help couples understand their problems and to eliminate underlying sources of conflict. Similar to the approach used by the California Conciliation Courts since 1939 and the more recent programs of other court-connected agencies, the counseled couple confirms their intent to reconcile by entering into a contract that delineates their responsibilities to each other and the patterns of marital behavior necessary for regenerating their relationship.

Admittedly, I remain suspicious of any technique which purports to save marriages by translating relationships into contractual terms. To my mind human behavior and interactions do not lend themselves to prescriptive guidelines, regardless of who signs on the dotted line. Alternatively, I am more optimistic about the AAA's role in the extralegal handling of divorce and divorce-related conflicts (see p. 73). Arbitration appears to be a saner, more expeditious, and frequently less expensive route than litigation or even continued reliance upon lawyers for the negotiation of postdivorce disputes. And, burdened by the growing volume of divorce business, the courts are increasingly demonstrating their compliance through the acceptance of arbitration clauses in divorce agreements.

Although it requires a stretch of the imagination to classify the Family Dispute Service, irrespective of its association with a counseling center, as even a quasi-mental health resource, advocates of such programs do, in fact, defend extralegal arbitration and negotiation principally on the basis of its psychological advantages for the adults and children of divorce. Any method, they aver, which favors discussion and problem solving over court verdicts will act to reduce the psychic toll of divorce. The rising rate of postdivorce litigation among families with children has added fuel to this argument (Freed and Foster, 1974; Wheeler, 1980a, 1980b).

Again and again they return to the courts to solve their family disputes. The number of children involved in these ongoing feuds is cause for great concern. Caught in between their fighting parents, they are never given a chance to adjust to the divorce. If only for the children, we need to work out before divorce a more reasonable way to approach the disagreements that inevitably occur after divorce.

(Divorce counselor)

Still not all families agree to arbitration as a forum for handling disputes; nor would all families benefit from this approach to conflict resolution.

Unless the couple is committed to an equitable resolution of conflicts, they often continue to carry on their warfare after the judge has officially ended their union. Those who can afford it return to the courts or their lawyers, complaining, nagging, even suing for violation of their agreement or a change in terms. Some do so because they seek to engage in revengeful games. I would hope that arbitration would solve some of these problems, but for those who are obsessed with hurting their ex-spouses, it is unlikely that arbitration will work. They have to stop hating before they can talk and reason.

(Psychiatrist)

At times more deep-seated emotional problems or protracted inter-personal dissension call for different techniques and measures. While some maintain an unflagging allegiance to psychotherapy as the remedy of choice, dismissing all other ideas as superficial forms of palliation, others argue that the clinical method is equally meretricious. It is not psycho-therapeutic treatment per se which they deprecate, for they base their proposals on psychological concepts and suppositions; it is the tunnel vision of practitioners who fail to take into account the legal dimension of divorce to which they object—a dimension not infrequently viewed as a cause of family acrimony and upheaval. As such, they recommend, as reformers have in the past, the creation of more experimental variants based on the legal/psychiatric theme, some of which are dependent upon the active participation of the judiciary. One such venture, the Postdivorce Clinic, staffed by the Legal Psychiatry Section of the Department of Psychiatry at the University of California, Los Angeles, provides an interesting paradigm of this kind of interdisciplinary effort on the part of legal and mental health professionals. In a sense the clinic functioned as an arbitrator for a select population unable to resolve postdivorce disputes

without repeated recourse to the courts. Even more importantly, it functioned as an advocate for the children in these families, performing evaluations, making referrals for treatment, and suggesting court revision of
custodial awards and visitation agreements (Sheffner and Suarez, 1975).
The news in 1976 that the Clinic's precarious financial status had not only
resulted in a moratorium on plans to formally evaluate its program but had
also raised questions as to whether funding would be forthcoming to continue its work should have come as no surprise to those of us familiar
with the course of innovation. But it was a surprise and a disappointment
to those of us who welcomed this program, at least as a refreshing derivative
of the prosaic treatment afforded the divorced, especially when under the
auspices of the courts. Naturally we should have known better!

Perhaps such services are not needed in California or in Westside,
although this is hardly the message one extrapolates from the statistics
and literature on California. Nor is it the message of respondents in Westside.

The law fails to understand that divorce is an emotional as well as a legal situation.
Until the courts and the psychiatrists get together and take a new look at divorce law
and how the divorced are handled in the courts, they can expect agreements to keep
breaking down. They are only documents. The real issue is the people involved.

                                            (41-year-old woman, 6 months divorced)

Yet while this individual and others call for cooperation between legal
and mental health professionals, in the main their words go unheeded. In
1980 one heard no more talk in Westside of intersystem ventures than in
1975. Alliances between these two disciplines tend to be spasmodic and
superficial and more than a few seem content to keep it that way.

The courts can look at the couple dispassionately and render a decision based on the
good of all. If the agreement proves unworkable because of emotional problems,
then it is time enough to suggest counseling. To work with a psychiatrist from the
start is to ask for problems.

                                            (Divorce lawyer)

It is hard for me to imagine working with divorce lawyers. Those whom I have met
seem basically insensitive to the personal problems of their clients. When it comes
down to the nitty-gritty, all they are interested in is litigation.

                                            (Social worker)

This does not mean that Westside professionals view the present situation as
satisfactory. All I can tell you is that there has been no outcry for change, at
least not one loud enough to be heard by those supposedly in the know—the
media, the policymakers, the court officials. If professionals have been

plotting revolutionary strategies or planning a legal/psychiatric federation, the movement is very much underground. The nearest we have come in Westside to a legal/psychiatric service is the one offered by the American Arbitration Association in consort with a divorce counseling center. And even this service is not located in Westside.

Thus the court and mental health systems in Westside and its environs continue to operate as the separate entities which they are, performing their jobs in much the same way as they did five and six years ago, Routinely lawyers refer clients to psychiatrists; routinely the courts employ psychiatrists, psychologists, and social workers to conduct inquiries and make evaluations; and routinely psychiatrists and other mental health professionals point out the destructive effect of legal combat on divorce petitioners and their children. And, as my grandmother would have said, "So, what else is new?"

FAMILY COUNSELING SERVICES

Generally, when social scientists speak of family therapy, they refer to the model of treatment associated with the work of psychiatrist Nathan Ackerman. If others, such as John Bell and Clarence Oberndorf, can be more accurately considered the pioneers in this field (Alexander and Selesnick, 1966), Ackerman was its best publicist. And because he was also one of the family's most ardent supporters and more than a conscientious objector when it came to divorce, Ackerman was scarcely the person to use the therapeutic forum as a place in which to examine the stability of a marriage or to broach the subject of its dissolution. While many family therapists still adhere to Ackerman's parochial conception of family therapy, others march to the beat of a different drummer. Some believe in subjecting the marital relationship to clinical scrutiny in order to determine the vitality of the union, and others of a more iconoclastic ilk use family therapy techniques for treating divorcing and divorced couples (see pp. 206-207). It seemed plausible, then, to expect that these different schools of thought would be accorded separate representation, even if not equal representation, within Westside's mental health system.

A LOOK AT THE PUBLIC SECTOR

Again Sheila began her investigation with public and nonprofit agencies, looking first to Westside's three family counseling facilities. And again a presupposition of mine proved to be fallacious, for all three agencies focused solely on the provision of services to intact families. To be sure, marital problems were a primary area of attention, implying that those who were not divorced would qualify for counseling whether or not they were contemplating divorce or even committed to it. That they might also find themselves in the untenable position of having to justify the logic of a divorce to a therapist who operated on the premise that divorce was never or, at any rate, hardly ever a solution of choice is well within the realm of possibilities.

Before you slam down the cover of this book, averring that such a therapeutic stance is as outmoded as crewcuts or as rare as a bottle of Château Lafite Rothschild '29, I beseech you to withhhold judgment, to indulge me just a bit longer until you read the following conversation.

"Do you provide counseling services for separated families?" I inquired.

"Separated families? What does that mean?" asked the woman quizzically.

"I mean families who are filing for a divorce," I explained.

"Divorce? [Her habit of repeating my words was becoming irksome.] If you are getting a divorce, why do you want counseling?"

"Separation is a difficult time for any family; it is a time of adjustment and a time when many decisions have to be made. Family counseling might help all of us to adjust more easily. It might also help us to discuss our plans for the future more openly and rationally." (My words echoed in my ears, sounding more like advertising copy for a divorce counseling center than those of the "real" Sheila Ash.)

"I'm sure it is a difficult time, but we are not divorce lawyers. [To my surprise, she had "bought" my story!] Our agency offers marriage counseling and family therapy. But you are not asking for marriage counseling, and there would be little need for family therapy when the family is going to be broken by a divorce. I don't see how we can help you."

"But by your definition we are a family, and after the divorce we will still be a family. Our children will have a mother and a father even if they don't live together. Obviously, I'm not asking for marital counseling. [Dare I mention divorce counseling? I thought not.] But family counseling does not seem inappropriate."

"I'm sorry, but we don't provide the kind of counseling you are talking about. Maybe others do, but we don't." Pausing, she then added in a more conciliatory tone, "I wish you good luck."

"Thank you," I replied in a more conciliatory tone.

What inferences can be drawn from this exchange? For openers we can presume that the agency directs its services to traditional family units. And —this is somewhat more speculative—they do not consider any constellation other than the conjugal one as a family. I have arrived at this second presumption on the basis of the woman's use of the term "broken family," a term which for me has an almost involuntary rankling effect. The agency's refusal to counsel separated and divorced families lends additional support to this conclusion. Yet perhaps you remain unmoved? Where, you wonder, has it been stated or even intimated in the dialogue quoted above that the agency is philosophically and theoretically opposed to divorce? Your point is well taken. In truth, I have not proven my accusation that family counselors frequently harbor an antidivorce bias; and worse, I have weakened my case by revealing prejudices that in themselves give rise to skepticism. Your hesitancy is understandable. I can see that it is easy to be a nonbeliever when the libelant is an individual whose back instinctively arches at the use of words that may have pejorative overtones only to an overly sensitive (or sensitized) receiver. Before you issue a final verdict, allow me one more chance to present evidence to bolster my argument. For your consideration the following conversation has been recorded.

"I have come to find out about your family counseling programs. My husband and I are separated, but we are interested in family therapy for ourselves and our two children," I stated.

"You and your husband are to be commended. Far too few people come for help. Please fill out this form so that we can set up an evaluation appointment. Marriage counseling might be more suitable than family therapy, but that decision would be made after the diagnosis."

"Then your marriage counselors also do divorce therapy?" I asked.

"Of course not. Haven't you come to save your marriage?"

"Actually not. We have made the decision to divorce. But my husband and I believe that counseling will help to ease the trauma of divorce and also help us to work through our differences in order that we can plan intelligently and constructively for our future and our children's. [This time I spoke with the conviction of a true confidence man (or woman). So bold did I become, so sure that my ruse would go unchallenged, that I began to explore the different treatment options without waiting for his reply.] Maybe counseling for my husband and myself would be more productive than family therapy, or maybe we can enter into family therapy after conjoint therapy. But, as you pointed out, these decisions are made after the evaluation."

"I'm afraid you and I are on entirely different wavelengths. We are a *family* counseling service, not a divorce service! If we provided divorce therapy, as you call it, we would be encouraging families to break up. That is an *unthinkable* goal for any family service." (This was no ordinary retort; his words were uttered in the measured beat of a preacher delivering a sermon. Was it my imagination that he appeared to grow in stature as he spoke, that his voice became more sonorous, his statements more imbued with a sense of righteousness? I think not, for he saw his cause as a noble one. He stood for marriage and family and thus he spoke from the mount. And I, what was I? A misguided, foolish woman? Or worse, a self-centered destroyer of kin and hearth?)

"How would you be encouraging families to divorce?" I asked haughtily. "People have divorced before and will continue to divorce with or without your counseling!"

"You missed the point. We are a family counseling service. We do not support divorce. We know people divorce, but we also know we can help people save their marriages. That is our goal—saving marriages. We can help you, believe me! Give your marriage a chance; give your kids a chance. Kids from broken homes have a hard time. Think of your children," he implored.

"I am thinking of my children. How can they be happy if my husband and I are unhappy? Besides, I am requesting family therapy to help my children. A counseling service truly interested in families would not spurn my children; you would realize that separated and divorced families need guidance as much as intact ones, maybe more." (A little guilt was, I thought, good for his soul also.)

"Divorce never helps children! [He remained immutable. His convictions, like a suit of armor, proved to be a barrier impregnable by either logic or affront.] Why don't you think it over? Or better yet, make an appointment to see a marriage counselor. Trust me, your marriage is worth salvaging."

"Thank you, but we do not want to see a counselor who is interested only in our reconciliation. That is *not* why I came here." (I wanted him to know that I would not be a proselyte to his cause, no matter how he pleaded.)

"Don't decide now. Take home the forms and talk to your husband." (His tenacity was enviable.)

Herein I rest my case. There is no need to review Sheila's experience at the third of Westside's family counseling agencies, for the conversation was essentially a reproduction of the above two. It was clear, at least to me, that these public facilities had maintained a stalwart front against any pressure to reexamine their priorities and ideologies in light of changing social trends and attitudes. While the escalation of the nation's divorce rate had served in other communities as an incentive to extend family counseling to the separated and divorced, in Westside the same data were used as a justification for limiting services to those interested in reconciliation. To do otherwise was regarded as an endorsement of divorce, almost as if it would make the agencies parties to the divorce action. So intent were they on taking up the gauntlet for marriage and the family that they ignored all evidence that for some divorce was a healthy decision or that therapeutic intervention before or after divorce was a defensible treatment plan both in educative and preventive terms. In effect, they had disavowed separated and divorced families. While they alleged that "kids from broken homes have a hard time," they also turned their backs on these children, refusing to administer treatment until symptoms of disturbance became manifest. Only after the fact did these agencies open their doors to the children of divorce; only then did these children qualify for help in a *family* counseling service.

To my knowledge this policy still exists in 1981 as it did in 1975. No public service has of yet offered family counseling to the separated and divorced, although in 1979 one family agency did break with tradition by allocating space to members of a disbanded women's cooperative in order that they could continue to conduct their support groups and monthly seminars for separated and divorced women. The issue to be addressed is not whether saving marriages is a worthy goal, for it certainly is; the issue is whether the needs of some Westside families are being served at the expense of others. To this question there is no obvious answer, only evidence that some community agencies outside of Westside have chosen a different course of action.

For example, in 1974 the Mental Health Clinic at the Flushing Hospital in New York City responded to the increased incidence of divorce and separation in their community by designing a crisis-oriented program for parents and children involved in marital dissolution; in 1975 the South Hills Child Guidance Center in Pittsburgh established a county outreach program, the Center for Children in Family Crisis, for families undergoing marital transition; and around the same time, the Domestic Relations Division of the Hennepin County Family Court in Minneapolis initiated a special service for parents and children in separating and divorcing families.

In the main these and similar programs focus on early intervention as a method for preventing long-term problems. Through the provision of short-term groups (six-week sessions appear to be the norm) and individual counseling, therapists use clinical and educational techniques to help children and parents cope with the trauma of divorce, make informed decisions, and establish priorities for reorganizing their lives.

Still, it is difficult to formulate any conclusions as to the success or failure of these ventures. While some agencies, such as the Center for Children in Family Crisis, have received outside funding for programmatic evaluation, many others have not been so fortunate. Struggling to get maximum mileage from limited public monies, these agencies concentrate on the development and implementation of their programs, thereby relegating evaluative procedures to a lower level of priority. This is understandable but hardly instructive to those who regard these and like projects as possible models for dissemination.

Although this is not a weakness to be glossed over, it is also not one to be overemphasized. Naturally, hard data are needed before we can assess the actual achievements of these social service organizations or attempt to duplicate their efforts. Yet this should not be interpreted as a refutation of the contributions made by such agencies, for as pioneers, and pioneers they most certainly are, in the creation of programs for families in marital transition, they are to be commended. Nor should it be interpreted as a ploy for exonerating Westside's public mental health sector, for at the very least the absence of family-oriented services for the separated and divorced in Westside merits our further consideration, if not our reproach.

Why Westside has failed to follow the leadership of other communities remains unclear. Perhaps as a suburban, relatively affluent community, it sees itself as immune to the problems that beset urban areas. (It is notable that the majority of the aforementioned programs have been implemented in inner cities.) In part this is justifiable. For while we can document with national statistics the economic travails and even deprivations of single-parent families, in Westside poverty is not prevalent. And also while the separated and divorced of all socioeconomic strata share many of the same concerns and encounter many of the same problems, in middle-class families these difficulties are simply not as obvious. Those who are able, even barely, to afford babysitters, day-care centers, and lawyers, those who are able to reenter the labor market, even in jobs below their level of competency, and those who succeed in obtaining adequate, even if less than satisfactory, housing are not viewed as needy of special services; they do not stand as overt attestations to a community's negligence. No matter how slender an advantage they have over others in a like situation or how dramatic an upheaval has occurred in their lives—economically, socially, or psychologically—their problems are masked sufficiently to escape attention. Moreover, as a group they are unaccustomed to being dependent upon public monies and unfamiliar with the techniques necessary for negotiating within the public sector. Even if they had such savvy, it is unlikely that they would suddenly emerge as strong advocates, demanding their slice of the revenue pie. Divorce is still too linked to feelings of stigmatization and failure to permit individuals to stand up as forceful plaintiffs for their cause. Furthermore, the acceptance of public help is often regarded by the divorced as another indicator of failure. Silence may be nonproductive, but it does provide insulation, protecting the individual or family from the public eye.

If this kind of anonymity is valued by the middle classes, it is conceivable, as noted previously, that such individuals might not utilize *public* family counseling services even if they did exist in Westside. If this be true, then it matters little how much evidence we can marshall in corroboration of the needs of this resident group or of the scarcity of community resources. The most essential information remains conspicuously absent and will remain absent until after monies are allocated and programs are created. It is at this time that we would discover whether individuals would in fact make use of such public resources. This does not suggest that monies be withheld or services denied until guarantees of utilization are forthcoming; such assurances are all too rare in the real world. Nor does it suggest that there is nothing that can be done to reduce the risk of miscalculation. It does suggest, however, that questions pertaining to how new services can be structured and extant ones adapted to meet the needs of a different consumer population must first be addressed. We must explore ways in which public services can be dispensed without stigmatizing recipients. We must look within the private as well as the public sector for alternate options. We must examine utilization patterns and consumer satisfaction in existing programs. And above all we must concentrate on formulating more and more questions, not to delay action, but because unless we do question and probe, it is likely that our creations will be only replicas of what already exists, thereby maintaining the status quo at a costly price.

A LOOK AT THE PRIVATE SECTOR

That I had expected more from Westside's public sector, I do not deny. Nor do I deny that there was no real basis for my optimism. If I had read and heard about family counseling programs for the separated and divorced in other communities, all of these communities were geographically far removed from Westside. If respondents had described to me variant therapeutic experiences, some of which were family oriented, all of these individuals had received treatment in the private sector (see Chapter 7). In this way I appeased myself; in this way I prepped myself for the remainder of the investigation. My optimism returned. This time it was reserved for a different quarter—the private sector.

The principal question to be answered by both Sheila and myself was: Would families interested in obtaining divorce counseling have difficulty securing services in the private sector? Without any pamphlets or guides to direct the search, I began with the trusty Yellow Pages. Finding no heading for counseling, therapy, or divorce, I looked under "*Marriage* and Family Counselors." Somewhat curiously, it was here that individuals and centers advertised their divorce counseling services—but not many. I was perplexed. Different explanations came to mind as I tried to account for the seeming discrepancy between the number of individuals who had spoken of divorce therapy and the paltry showing in the Yellow Pages.

First, descriptions of services in the Yellow Pages were at best minimal and often nonexistent and therefore a poor indicator of available options. Second, some providers might deliberately avoid unorthodox labels, like divorce counselor, preferring to be associated with the more traditional specialty of marriage and family counselor. Third, some providers might not be divorce counselors, although they may function as one when a patient of theirs contemplates or undergoes a marital dissolution. Fourth, some providers do not advertise in the Yellow Pages, depending upon referrals for recruitment of patients.

The only way, of course, to learn whether or not my suppositions were correct was to contact the providers and facilities classified under the heading of "Marriage and Family Counselors." Because the list was a lengthy one, all names except those listed expressly as divorce counselors were selected at random and inquiries were made by telephone. In total, Sheila made 30 calls, asking the same question each time: "Do you offer conjoint and/or family therapy for separated and divorced families?" While on occasion she resorted to some of the divorce counseling jargon, she never referred to this mode of treatment by name. Still, over two-thirds of those contacted stated that counseling divorced couples and families was outside their area of expertise.

I have spent years training to be a marriage and family counselor. To get involved in divorce counseling would not only be a denial of my own beliefs, but would also be unfair to the patients. No counselor can completely detach himself from his own interests and feelings. I don't think I could help these people.

(Marriage and family counselor, Ph.D.)

For separated families there was more leeway. Those who specialized in the art of marriage counseling held out the carrot of reconciliation to Sheila or, for that matter, to any separating couples she might know. Others, who offered individual as well as family therapy, were to a significant degree more inclined to accept a separated individual for treatment than a separated couple. It was on this basis that they were willing to help separated and even divorcing individuals work through the problems engendered by a marital dissolution. Although none of the public family counseling services had presented this option, needless to say, there were only three such agencies, as compared to the 30 individual providers and centers contacted by Sheila in the private sector.

Yet there were some, albeit few in number, who regarded conjoint or family counseling for the separated and divorced as a worthwhile therapeutic experience. One therapist explained:

Divorce counseling can be an extremely positive experience. The couple can explore with the therapist their feelings about divorce as well as how the divorce will affect their lives and their children's lives. It is a sane and productive way to proceed. Too often people who divorce do not have the opportunity or time to plan ahead. Individual therapy helps, but when both spouses are present, they can discuss options and priorities with an objective third party. It is more than a time to air hostilities; it is also a time to reach decisions that in the long run can be very painful and costly if done without forethought and commitment on the part of both individuals. In particular, the benefit for the children is incalculable.

(Psychiatrist)

Another stated the following:

To undertake a joint treatment program a couple has to be able to reconcile their view of themselves as independent individuals with the fact that they have to interact with their former spouse as long as they have minor children. Those who have reached this state of maturity have the easiest time of it. Others come out of sheer desperation. They are less interested in reconciling these two components than in finding some way to escape the constant conflict that permeates their lives even though they live apart. They may be referred by a judge, a friend, a lawyer, or they may reach the decision themselves. Most, however, come because their children get into trouble or seem to be headed in that direction. When this happens, it sometimes acts as an inducement for even the most stubborn and self-righteous to think of somebody other than themselves.

(Psychologist)

That the usage of the word "family," as in "marriage and family counselor," only rarely indicated the provision of more broad-based services for the divorced family was one disappointing finding of the research; that many clinicians, in effect, had disenfranchised single-parent families, viewing them, if at all, in a classification apart from intact families, was another. Still, the prospects for obtaining help in the private sector were nary as bleak as it may sound. Moreover, Sheila's research and my interviews with mental health providers suggested that there was less of a discrepancy between the kinds of services actually utilized by respondents and those identified in the investigation. The majority of those who had had family therapy entered treatment for the purpose of reconciliation or for resolving marital conflicts. (Admittedly some did so only to placate their spouse or at the behest of their lawyer.) The second highest percentage of users defined their rationale as child oriented. Lastly, there were those who had chosen conjoint or family therapy for the purpose of working through the personal and practical issues of separation and divorce. If these usage patterns are applicable to others outside of this sample, we can hypothesize that only the latter group might encounter difficulties in identifying and procuring treatment, unless they confine themselves to the individuals and agencies who do advertise divorce counseling services. Although even in the 1981 edition of the Yellow Pages, divorce counseling appears as a novel clinical offering, lagging in numerical count behind all listings except holistic therapy, the newspapers regularly carry advertisements for divorce counseling. In addition, divorce support groups often serve as a source for referral.[14]

If I was reasonably confident that the majority of those interested in conjoint and family therapy would be spared the ordeal of a frenetic search for help, there was yet another issue to be addressed, an issue which pertained to the very nature of the therapeutic experience. In particular, I refer to the portraitures presented by some respondents of their therapists as prophets of doom—individuals who harped so on the problems of divorce that the patient's feelings of guilt and anxiety were exacerbated rather than resolved during treatment (see pp. 208-211). Having said this, I find myself in a quandary: While an indictment of such severity cannot be taken lightly, it is also one which is difficult to corroborate or to refute; in a sense it is the age-old dilemma of the chicken and the egg, the question being whether the guilt and anxiety over divorce originated apart from the therapy or was induced, or at least magnified, during therapy. And, too, was it the therapist's focus on the negative effects of divorce that led to this outcome or the therapeutic process itself, a process which requires the patient to engage in self-probing and analysis that at times can be painful and disruptive? On the one hand, there is ample documentation demonstrating that individuals undergoing a marital dissolution commonly experience guilt and anxiety, irrespective of whether or not they receive clinical treatment. Indeed, it is precisely these feelings as well as those of depression, loneliness, and inability to function which are most frequently cited as the reasons for seeking help. On the other hand, therapists must assume some responsibility for what occurs during treatment. If patients are to face up to their fears and not succumb to them, awareness of the repercussions of divorce is insufficient; more importantly, patients need to understand and learn how to handle these problems. Still, the frailty and intricacy of therapeutic encounters make it risky, if not impossible, to render any generalizations, let alone conclusions. Many variables, including when the couple enters therapy (e.g., before, at, or after the decision to divorce), what they expect to gain from the experience, the match between patients and therapist, and the economic, social, and personal aspects of their lives, influence not only outcomes but perceptions and evaluations of treatment.

Nonetheless, despite intervening factors and the complexity of assessing therapeutic relationships, respondents spoke often enough about the nightmarish aura of their treatments, as noted in Chapter 7, to make one pause for thought. And, in fact, some therapists with whom I spoke were so adamant in their denouncement of divorce that it was hard to believe that such feelings and biases could be concealed during treatment. For example, one marriage counselor described divorce as follows:

Divorce is a personal and a family tragedy. It is rare that the adults or the children of divorce escape from the experience unscathed. With intelligence and hard work some problems may be attended to, but very often the couple is so preoccupied with their own pain that they are of little help to themselves or to their children. They expect divorce to be a kind of emancipation, and when it brings on suffering, they are immobilized by shock. Unfortunately, by the time they get themselves together enough to do something constructive, the problems have deepened.

A psychologist offered this opinion:

Most marriages can and should be saved. Nobody says that marriage is a perfect institution or that it will guarantee personal happiness, especially on a continuous basis. But the alternatives are no better. Divorce doesn't make anyone happy and remarriages are less stable than first ones. Saving a marriage may take hard work and time, but that is minor in comparison to the benefits and to the time it takes to recover from a divorce. There are, of course, some marriages that can't be saved, but mostly this happens when one or both partners work toward its destruction instead of its improvement.

However, most therapists, be they psychiatrists, psychologists, social workers, or marriage counselors, did not inveigh against divorce, at least not during interviews. Their prognoses tended to be rather benign and their explications of the causes or effects of marital dissolution temperate and typically vague in character.

There are as many reasons behind a divorce as there are people who obtain them. Nobody likes divorce and nobody thinks it is a solution. But there are cases where the marriage is destructive to the couple and their children. Not all marriages are made in heaven; some come closer to being made in hell. But even when these unions are ended, the family suffers. Divorce is a painful experience; yet people usually recover. I try to help my patients understand that pain is to be expected, but it need not be a life sentence. The divorced need to learn that there will be problems but also that they can be dealt with.

(Psychologist)

When you are treating an individual or a couple who decides to divorce, it is your responsibility to level with them—to tell them that divorce is not easy, that recovery may be slow. You have to also point out the areas where problems are most likely to occur. But then, and this is the tricky part, you don't just leave them with this information. They have to know that they can deal with the pain and the problems and that you will help them. There is a very delicate balance to be sought between exposing problems to people and helping them to cope with these problems. You have to know when they can take certain information and when they can't and what kind of support they need.

(Marriage and divorce counselor)

This last quotation is perhaps best illustrative of the therapeutic approach in which attention to both the practical and emotional dimensions of divorce are integral to the treatment plan. That this kind of therapy was consistently rated above all others by respondents, we already know. That conjoint and family therapies were the modes of treatment most frequently associated with utilitarian ends, we already know. Yet regardless of these comparative data, we also know that *couples* who enter into therapy specifically to receive help in easing the adjustment to divorce and for guidance in their decision making (e.g., as to child custody, visitation privileges, child support, alimony) are a minority. Most who do elect conjoint or family therapy do so prior to separation, often terminating treatment upon reaching the decision to divorce or soon afterward. Thus it is not surprising that family and marriage counselors, even unbiased ones, cater to intact families, although the percentage of this group who decide to divorce during therapy is obviously on the rise. Further, since a goodly number of the separated and divorced who undergo family therapy do so because of child-related issues, the next item on Sheila's agenda was to survey mental health services for children and adolescents.

CHILDREN'S SERVICES

Of all the concerns expressed by separated and divorced parents (and there were many), none approached in intensity and depth of feeling their fear of the effects of divorce on their children. Almost any action, inaction, word, or gesture was regarded as a significant sign or clue as to how this unfathomable creature called "child" was reacting to the change in his or her life. Rarely, particularly in the initial stages of separation, did parents interpret the evidence positively. Good or bad, mild or wild, affectionate or indifferent, under the ever-watchful eye of a parent all children were viewed through the same portentous lens. And anticipating the worst, frequently parents saw the worst.[15]

I didn't know what was normal and to be expected and what was not. When 'Tommy' had trouble falling asleep, I thought it was because of the divorce, and when 'Ann' said she didn't like her teacher, I thought the same thing.

(38-year-old woman, 6 months separated)

But parents are not the only ones who spend long hours mulling over the fate of the children of divorce. Even before the late 1950s and early 1960s when the rising divorce rates and a national preoccupation with victims of all kinds and sizes led to an increased demand for information about the children of divorce, researchers had launched studies on the effects of "broken homes" and father absence on children. With few exceptions, the conclusions corroborated the instinctual fears of parents: These were, indeed, children to worry about.

It was, however, toward the middle of the 1970s that, metaphorically speaking, the dam broke. The issue went public as demographers pointed not only to the growing number of children living in single-parent homes, but predicted a continuation of the upward trend. Whereas before, popular offerings had been predominantly commonsensical guidelines for parents written by self-appointed advisers to the divorced, now the children of divorce became a fashionable topic, featured regularly in daily tabloids and supermarket magazines catering to a readership that extended far beyond the divorced. The logic of the marketing experts was inescapable: With divorce rates escalating and the number of children who would at some time be a member of a one-parent household predicted to reach 40% (Bane, 1976b), today's married might clearly be tomorrow's divorced; today's secure children might clearly be tomorrow's population at risk.

Thus the copy multiplied as the children of divorce became a subject worthy of headline billing. In 1975 we read "What Happens to the Children of Divorce?" (Fripp). In 1976 we had six chances to ponder the plight of these children in the series "Hapless Children of Broken Marriages: How Do They Cope?" (Duncliffe). In 1977, as interest in the fathers of divorce became more manifest, the media capitalized on the new angle in articles such as " 'Transparent' Fatherhood" (Goodman). And it did not let up. In 1978, as the demographic forecast raised to 45 the percentage of children who would reside in a one-parent family before the age of 18 (Glick, 1978), columnists returned to the basics in articles such as "Divorce and the Children" (Sifford, 1978c) and "Divorce: What About the Kids?" (McLaughlin, 1978). In 1979 the demographic news grew even more ominous as the proportion of children projected to be members of one-parent families by 1990 was raised to 50% (Glick, 1979). And so the presses kept running. In 1979 we read "How Kids Look at Divorce" and in 1980, "One-Parent Pupils—A Trouble and Growing Minority" (Pave).

These are but a few illustrations, all of which came from one metropolitan area. There were many more, even discounting the prodigious outpouring of scholarly articles on the subject. For example, in the same year that *Redbook*, "The Magazine for Young Women," told us the whole truth and nothing but the truth in an article unabashedly entitled,

"How Divorce Really Affects Children: A Major Report" (Streshinsky, 1976),[16] NBC televised "Children of Divorce" (January 19, 1976). By 1979, almost three years later to the day, the same network demonstrated that their interests had broadened and their concerns had deepened as they broadcast, "The American Family: An Endangered Species?" (January 2, 1979).[17] In 1980 the media's interest had still not abated as *Newsweek*'s February 11th cover sported the title (and a poignant picture) of one of its featured stories. You guessed it, "Children of Divorce" (Francke et al.).

One would presume, therefore, that with all the anxiety and concern for these children, public policymakers would be stumbling over each other, figuratively bumping heads in their scramble to create services and programs for this "needy" population. But this has not happened, particularly not in Westside. To the contrary, what is really conspicuous is the absence of any concerted effort. While some, like the Flushing Hospital Mental Health Clinic, the Hennepin County Family Court, and the Pittsburgh Center for Children in Family Crisis, have designed programs and services especially for children, in Westside whatever energy has been expended to create services for divorced families has been primarily for adults, albeit the record shows that even this population can scarcely be considered a major beneficiary of public generosity.

Various explanations for this development, or lack of it, ranging from the philosophical on down to the mundane, come to mind. It is no secret, for example, that the provision of public services for children has long been mired in an ideological quagmire. Although the issues are murky, two distinct schools of thought serve as sources of conflict and confusion. On the one side are the family-rights (really meaning parental control) advocates who repudiate outside intervention in domestic affairs except under extreme circumstances. Arguing that parents not only know what is best for their children, but almost invariably act in the child's best interests, they contend that any infringement on family turf violates the sanctity of home and family and undermines the stability of the conjugal unit (e.g., Lasch, 1977). On the other side are the children's rights advocates who decry society's neglect of its young, calling them anything from the forgotten minority to the disadvantaged. In waving a banner for the dependent and the voiceless, they urge a reversal of public priorities and an end to apathy (e.g., Keniston, 1977). The state must not refrain, they say, from trespassing on family ground whenever human entitlements and the safety of children are in jeopardy. Issues of supremacy and freedom for the family are not considered to be at stake, nor is the vitality of the family constellation. To the contrary, they theorize, a stronger, more responsible family will arise out of a greater social consciousness toward the young.

By accentuating polarities in thought and attitude, the two positions appear not only in their most simplistic form, but similarities between ideologies become inadvertently obscured. Thus it may not be evident that both sides believe that the family's well-being is essential to the health and solidarity of society. For this is neither a pro- versus antifamily debate nor an adult versus children debate. In the drama "The American Society," both sides cast the family in the lead role. It is in the production and direction of the script where they part company. The family-rights school sees little need for supporting actors, elaborate props, or a strong director. Stars of this caliber, they aver, can carry off the production without dependency upon other people or things. The children's rights school has assembled an array of props and hired a forceful director, for they maintain that even the most accomplished performers need assistance and guidance.

In translating this analogy we need to understand that neither group denies that the modern family has problems. Yet because they disagree as to the cause of its dilemmas, they are at odds over how to achieve remediation. Family-rights supporters fear that the allocation of public resources and increased government control over the family will demoralize and weaken this institution until it eventually abdicates responsibility for its own well-being, becoming ever more dependent on the government. While children's rights supporters also reject schemata for subjugating the family to intrusive government control, their stance permits more exceptions. They believe not only that some families require public supports and resources to survive, but that unintended consequences can result from according too much power to parents. In particular, they argue that families with unconditional control over their destiny may abuse and misuse their authority without due consideration for the rights of those under their aegis. To them the perils of a laissez-faire family policy may be greater than the risk of government intrusion (see Donzelot, 1980). Many, however, remain unconvinced.

The children's rights movement has also been assaulted on the grounds of producing unintended consequences evident in developments such as the recent upsurge of legal suits brought by children against their parents. Caution against this trend is urged by many, including Harvard law professor Frank E. A. Sander (Goodman, 1976), who forewarn that unless the courts impose restrictions on the cases which warrant legal redress, the judiciary will be pulled into a maelstrom of parent-child disputes, emerging as the final arbitrator for a host of conflicts in which there is *no* threat to the safety or rights of the child. In becoming overly preoccupied with the protection of children's rights the danger is, according to these critics, that we might jeopardize not only the freedoms of parents, but heedlessly create a new power play in which the child reigns with a heavy hand. In effect, one form of injustice will be replaced by another, no less dangerous.

Still other opponents of the children's rights platform do not concentrate on any particular issue, choosing instead to exploit the nation's paranoiac anxiety over the family's well-being. Thus, when Richard M. Nixon justified his presidential veto of the Child Development Bill of 1969 by proclaiming that the proposal would place "the vast moral authority of the government to the side of communal approaches to child-rearing over against the family-centered approach" (Woodward and Malamud), 1975, p. 56), his selection of words was determined with great care, calculated to raise the specter of an endangered family. It is this very sense of foreboding which permeates so many debates and policy decisions on expanding public services for children. Consequently, it is not, I believe, farfetched to suggest that one reason why public officials have refrained from sponsoring services for children of divorce stems from the apprehension that such interference will hasten, even invite, the collapse of the family.

Of course, there is no rigid boundary that separates the public sector and the family. The government has long been in the business of providing services and resources to children (and adults) and, indeed, has been increasingly, if not always wholeheartedly, moving further and further into the private domain of the family. But with respect to single-parent families they have so far tread softly. HEW's effort to locate fathers who have been delinquent in paying child support is a positive indicator of governmental interest, but it scarcely constitutes a major venture for redressing the economic and social disadvantages of the population of single-parent families. Moreover, this initiative is in keeping with the notion that the family, intact or separated, must provide for its own without reliance on public revenues.

Besides differing philosophies on the government's responsibility for the family, there are other reasons which might account for the absence of public programs in Westside for the children of separation and divorce. If, for example, we accept the theory that the mental and social stability of these children is dependent primarily upon their parents' coping ability, it makes sense to create services for the divorced rather than for their children. And also in times of fiscal restraint one way to exercise prudence is to use public monies for remedial, not preventive, services. In Westside such a position can be further defended by the population's high usage of private resources. The more willing the residents are to pay for mental health services, the less pressure there is for public assistance.

In point of fact, as Sheila learned when she contacted agencies in the public sector, all family counseling facilities in Westside did provide services for children and all children's facilities did provide services for adults in the family. Due to the uniformity of responses from children's agencies, a description of one encounter is representative of the group as a whole.

"If you do not offer counseling to separated and divorced families, do you have any group or individual services for children involved in a marital dissolution?" I asked.

"We are deeply concerned about the effect of divorce on children and have treated many children from broken homes, but until there is a clinical problem we do not become involved."

"I was thinking more along the lines of small groups for helping children understand and cope with whatever fears and concerns they might have as a result of a marital separation," I explained.

"This idea has been suggested by others, and it is a good one. Yet we have neither the staff nor the money to create such groups. Anyway the schools might be a better place for this kind of experiment."

Interestingly, the school system has been the only public institution in Westside to go on record in support of preventive programs for the children of divorce. What's more, they went a step further, piloting several short-term groups for children from single-parent homes on the elementary and secondary level. Community reception to these offerings, some of which were open also to parents, was anything but encouraging. For example, at the first meeting of a high school series on divorce given during the 1978-79 academic year only one student attended, despite media publicity. Perhaps the response of students and parents (see pp. 224-225) reflects the school system's own ambivalence to such intervention, limited as it may seem. More than a few have questioned the appropriateness of the system's involvement as well as its ability to shoulder an ever-growing number of responsibilities for roles and obligations once performed by family, community, and church. For this extension of services they have already been the recipients of praise from some and damnation from others (e.g., in the areas of sex education, racism, religion, health care). In addition, performance has generally fallen short of expectations. As the schools provide more and more services and make more and more promises, it is not surprising that the level of satisfaction has declined. It would be impossible, even if the schools did function according to the highest standard of accomplishment (whatever that may be), to fulfill the wants and desires of all. The latter keep multiplying at a rate which far surpasses any social institution's ability to keep pace.

I mention this only to caution the reader that in our zeal to find a sponsoring agent for a specific service or an advocate for a special population we should not lose sight of the real mission of any social institution. The school system's first priority, and in fact its mandate, is the education of the young. Thus, before any commitment is made to a district-wide program for the children of divorce, the system must not only justify its involvement from a social perspective but also from the perspective of its relationship to and benefit on schooling. This is no easy task.

In 1975 and again in 1979 school personnel defended the above-mentioned programs on the basis of the high percentage of learning and discipline problems among children from separated and divorced homes (a percentage purported to be in excess of 60% of the school population). Although Westside school officials are by no means the first, nor, I am sure, the last, to see a positive correlation between divorce and the onset of cognitive and behavioral problems (Benedek and Benedek, 1979; Hetherington et al., 1979; Pave, 1980b), neither their assessment nor for that matter anybody else's should be accepted as unequivocal. At the very least we need to consider for each child the measurement indices used in the identification of disturbances and the evidence in support of this particular cause-and-effect relationship.

Yet even if the noted disorders prove to be largely attributable to divorce and even if transitory or more long-term dysfunction proves to hinder the child's cognitive performance (and remember, both "even ifs" are blockbuster questions), it does not necessarily follow that the schools should be charged with effecting the "cure." Admittedly, if there was a rush of candidates all applying for the job of healer to the children of divorce, the school system would hold vantage points inaccessible to any other contender. It is not only the most visible community institution, but also the only one which is in daily contact with the largest percentage of the children of divorce. These are by no means small advantages, nor ones that proponents of school involvement have not played up for all they are worth. Still, visibility and accessibility are not synonymous with expertise. If some opine that classroom teachers can be trained to teach about divorce and even conduct support groups for children (Benedek and Bieniek, 1977), I remain dubious, even apprehensive, of this proposal. The myriad of implications and issues inherent in a venture of this nature does not lend itself to simple answers or quick decisions. To my mind alternative options must first be explored and numerous questions posed, otherwise the school system may find itself in the untenable position of trying to be all things to all people, and, as the proverb warns, emerge as a jack-of-all-trades and a master of none.

Perhaps until more is known about the effects of divorce on children and the merits of different preventive and remedial approaches, the schools would be wise to proceed gingerly. This does not mean that the schools do not need to understand the issues and problems related to separation and divorce from the perspectives of parents and children. This does not mean that the schools should not continue to make available counseling services for children manifesting signs of clinical disorders or dysfunction. Nor does it mean that the schools cannot assume a more proactive role, coordinating their services with those of public and private counseling agencies; in this way they would function as a broker of sorts, matching clients and providers. If in the process they manage to convince other public agencies (e.g., clinics, courts, hospitals) to create preventive programs for the children of divorce, they will have succeeded in extricating themselves from an assignment perhaps best left to those who do have the qualifications and facilities for sponsorship.

While I have dwelt on problems and advised caution, I have sidestepped the central question of whether or not the public school system is an appropriate agent for developing programs for the children of divorce. No artifice is intended. The truth is quite simple—I do not know the answer. Nor do I know if special programs are even needed, despite the fact that many interviewees, among others, have displayed no such incertitude, unhesitatingly granting their imprimatur. Perhaps Westside officials share my doubts. Would this not be another explanation for the city's failure to institute preventive mental health services for the children of divorce? I do not believe this to be the case, but it certainly cannot be dismissed without a fair hearing—one that, to my knowledge, has not been held.

In summarizing Sheila's research on Westside's public mental health facilities for children, we can state that city services are treatment oriented and nonspecific in design. It is therefore upon the identification of problems, not before, that family counseling services *and* child guidance centers open their doors to the children of divorce. Some children, of course, receive help earlier, for it is not uncommon for parents to declare that their children are in a state of psychological crisis, even if they are not. If we add all those who presume the existence of maladjustment and/or instability before the fact to all those who accurately discern symptoms of malfunction or distress, the potential population of clients becomes considerable.

Nevertheless, the majority of respondents utilized private resources for their children. And, as such, their greatest problem was related to the selection of a therapist, not to the availability or visibility of resources. In Westside there are child psychiatrists, psychologists, social workers, and guidance counselors galore. The trick, naturally, is in matching provider and client on personal as well as on financial indices. If we move, however, away from individual to group therapy, the options diminish dramatically. There are counseling groups for children and adolescents, but not many. A still rarer commodity is the group specifically designed for the children of divorce.

While we have noted a proliferation of support groups for separated and divorced adults, this trend has not been reproduced in the area of children's services. Even the 80,000-member (now over 90,000) Health Plan's sponsorship of seminar groups for those undergoing a marital dissolution (see p. 228) has been confined to adult members.[18] According to the law, children are not parties to a divorce action, and also, according to what we have observed in and around Westside, they are not parties of interest to those in the public and private sectors involved in the creation of thera-peutic services for the separated and divorced. Whether by happenstance or predetermination, the changes which have occurred in Westside's mental health system have been largely directed toward the adult population. Services for children remain primarily traditional in objective and design. Rightly or wrongly, individual therapy or counseling is the norm, with a noticeable dearth of alternatives in the area of prevention or short-term crisis intervention.

CONCLUSION

Despite the very high percentage of individuals from divorcing families who are consumers of mental health services, there is little to report in the way of innovation, especially in the area of children's services. The most prominent development has been the increase in the number of adult support groups in both the public and private sectors. Less conspicuous but also notable has been the concomitant rise of marriage and divorce coun-seling centers in cities and towns in the proximity of Westside. Since it is a matter of historical record that the origin of these services predates their arrival in Westside, we cannot issue any claims to novelty. Yet for West-sidians these developments did indeed indicate that a change had taken place, and a significant one at that.[19] In 1975 there were few options out-side of individual counseling available in Westside; further, such services were generally expensive and involved a long-term commitment to treat-ment. The group approach (and to some extent also the counseling center) offered an alternative that was less costly, less time consuming, and less pathologically oriented. While some exhorted consumer caution and others warned of more troublesome elements, their words were barely audible amid the chorus of hallelujahs.

Almost as if a new miracle drug had been invented, the ebullience for support groups seemed to mount daily. From the public and private sectors, from the media, from the universities, from professionals (e.g., clergymen, mental health providers, physicians), and from laypersons came benedic-tions and support. Curiously, despite all this ferment, few looked to the children of divorce as another target population. In other communities in which a similar movement had occurred, contiguous programs had been structured for adults *and* children, but not so in and around Westside. Here the drive began with adults and it has stayed that way.

Most assuredly, there is much controversy over the question of how divorce affects children. Some, like sociologist Robert Weiss, equivocate, stating that "there is for these children, loss along with the gain" (cited in McLaughlin, 1978, p. 21), and others, like clinical psychologist Lora Tessman, aver that the children of divorce are "transformed by 'a many-sided alchemy of fear and sadness'" (ibid.). With such differing opinions on how children react to divorce, one would hardly expect concordance on the methods of treatment—and there is none. Indeed, for the most part, whenever the subject of treatment or intervention surfaces, the experts remain noncommittal, hesitant either to advocate or, for that matter, repudiate any specific remedy. Somewhat paradoxically, the very same individuals are far more adventuresome when it comes to the adults of divorce. Here they do not fear to tread, often delivering lengthy treatises on their pet cure for the aches and pains of marital dissolution.

Consequently, it is no surprise that many communities have seen fit to target resources, particularly those in the public sector, to adults, leaving it essentially up to the parents to determine if, when, and what treatment is necessary for the children of divorce. This places the onus of responsibility as well as the burden of payment on parents, not an unpredictable development in light of the long-standing American tradition for parental control over the lives of children. In a sense, it is a "neat" solution: It accords the experts the freedom to engage in debate without jeopardizing their credibility or assuming accountability for the accuracy of their prognoses. And it encourages the utilization of resources in the private sector, a decided plus for all those who brood so over balancing federal, state, and local budgets. Perhaps it is even a good solution. For children who do manifest social and psychological disturbances there are public resources to which parents can turn; and for the others a cautious approach is at the least justifiable until such time when (and if) we do become more knowledgeable about the effects of divorce on children.

Yet the scent of change is in the air. As the professional and lay literature on the children of divorce becomes ever more voluminous and as researchers, clinicians, policymakers, the media, and laypersons continue to presage problems for these children, the incentive for reform and for profit also grows. The right ingredients are present in the right quantities: There is a demographic prediction for an increase in the number of children from divorced families; there is a guilt-plagued body of divorced parents agonizing over the fate of their children; and there is a national precedent for solving social and personal dilemmas through the creation of more and more services. If the call for solutions in the form of services and programs for the children of divorce has not yet reached the decibel level of a clamor in Westside, it is more audible today than six years ago. More than likely there will be some who will respond. Those who seek to help the children of divorce will come forth, devising programs and services for this population. The ambitious and inventive will also come forth, lured by the prospects of a financial windfall. That the children of divorce constitute a relatively untapped resource is clear; that prophecies of doom do not go long unheeded is clear; that the boom in divorce counseling centers and support groups for adults in Westside was a similar response to a similar set of circumstances is also clear. What will result is perhaps less clear. But at present the best bet is for more of the same. In substance, we can expect counseling centers in Westside to sponsor programs for children individually, in peer groups, and in conjoint sessions with their parents; we can expect support groups for the children of separation and divorce to be sponsored by public and private agencies and individual providers. New services and programs will compete with the few that already exist, augmenting the number of options available to children and parents, albeit some will undoubtedly be of questionable merit.

Indeed, of late, even some experts are calling for reform and some, like attorney Richard S. Benedek and psychiatrist Elissa P. Benedek (1979), have gone so far as to delineate model programs. Read their words carefully, for they will be followed, I believe, by others with similar concerns and plans.

The high incidence of divorce and rising divorce rate, coupled with the profound consequences of divorce, mandate that professionals take stock of the needs of the large and rapidly expanding number of children involved. Providing essential human services, such as those required to meet the needs of these children, is invariably expensive and ordinarily not politically attractive. Yet, in an even more compelling sense, failure to do so may ultimately prove to be far more costly.... We conclude that existing services are essentially inadequate for this purpose and that goal-directed, divorce-oriented programs, likely to reach all divorcing families, would offer the best prospects for dealing appropriately with their specific needs (p. 168).

Nonetheless, my use of words such as "boom" should not be translated literally either with respect to my projection for an increase in children's services or to extant adult services. These words have meaning only in a relative sense and are not to be interpreted as proof of abundance. In no way are separated and divorced adults being inundated by an excess of offerings—at least not in Westside. Nor does it appear that this will happen to their children. This is not necessarily a situation to bemoan, for we can marshall evidence to support a policy of financial prudence, particularly as it pertains to the expansion and adaptation of public services. Although respondents complained about the paucity of public mental health resources specifically for the separated and divorced, they also indicated a decided preference for services in the private sector. We can interpret this seeming contradiction as a sign of personal confusion and conflict, as a statement on

the inferior quality of public services in the community, or as a miscon-
struction on my part of what individuals were saying. Conversely, we can
come to an entirely different conclusion if we interpret these statements to
mean that individuals want and need greater access to mental health providers, but that they also expect public services to be dispensed and structured in the same manner as they are in the private sector. In short, they
should be personalized, anonymous, nonstigmatizing, and varied in kind,
yet be offered at little or no cost to the consumer.

Certainly this depiction has appealing aspects, utopian in concept and
expectation. Less certain is how such a proposal could be actualized, short
of totally revamping public services or setting up some form of voucher
system in which public funds would be allocated directly to individuals for
use in the public or private sector. In a time of budgetary constraints
and pressure for reduced or at least contained public expenditures, it
borders on the absurd to think that public officials can or would push
for such a proposal. It is implausible to think that they would even dream
up such a scheme, regardless of the availability of public funds. Thus,
if separated and divorced individuals are in fact asking for the public
to finance their treatment in the private sector or to scrap the existing
delivery system for a more quixotic version, they are likely to be disappointed. One does not have to be a sage to predict that the majority of
middle-class consumers in the mental health system will continue to negotiate within the private sector and at their own expense. Those able to
afford these services will, in Westside as in most communities, have little
difficulty identifying resources. If anything, they will find an oversupply of
providers, even though all will not be of equal personal or professional
repute. The treatment of choice will continue to be individual therapy, with
membership in support groups running in second place.

If my assumptions are correct, we will not see any dramatic upheaval in
the near future, at least not within the mental health system. Change will
most likely be reflected in an increase in the number of offerings rather than
in a transfiguration in the nature of treatment modes. More fundamental
change, if it occurs, will be made in incremental steps rather than by leaps
and bounds. The one idea for which there appears to be the most support
and greatest chance for approval is that of legal/psychiatric innovations,
especially in the more conservative realm of extralegal negotiation and
counseling. Here the high divorce and relitigation rates clearly call for less
expensive and less contentious methods for resolving interpersonal conflict
during and after divorce. Of course, this is not a therapeutic solution
strategy, not in the true sense of the term, and hence would not really
connotate a change in the mental health delivery system. For this we will
have to wait, perhaps a long, long time.

NOTES

1. The area office services three suburbs, one of which is Westside.

2. Note how on the basis of Sheila's question this individual quite naturally presumed that she was divorced.

3. Currently the four-page guide is being mailed annually to all residents serviced by the area office.

4. Convenience is often another feature advertised by these centers. For example, one such enterprise offers its clients seven-day service, 12 hours per day (9 A.M. to 9 P.M.).

5. As the lay and professional publications began to look ever more closely at the population of remarried persons, including within their purview the travails of stepparents, these counseling centers responded obligingly, extending their invitation to the remarried, be they stepparents or not.

6. Admittedly, sample members differed dramatically in their evaluations and descriptions of groups for the separated and divorced. Some exuded enthusiasm, going so far as to attribute their successful adjustment to group experiences. Others found them to be maudlin and excessively self-indulgent encounters, causing them to dwell on their problems, rather than aiding in the transition to a new way of life. And still others refused to even contemplate membership in a group, dismissing them as inappropriate or unsuitable. In part, these discrepant conclusions stem from the varying needs and goals of respondents. In addition, groups for the separated and divorced follow different prototypes (e.g., temporary crisis groups, consciousness-raising groups, social groups, information/advocacy groups). Since individuals often spoke exclusively of one kind of group, comparative analyses of fundamentally dissimilar experiences are invalid.

7. Federally funded by a Library Services Construction Act Grant, Title I, Special Project, this packet consists of pamphlets, films, program resource lists, program guidelines, publicity suggestions, and recommended literature for each topic. What is particularly appealing about this resource is the list of speakers and group leaders who had indicated their willingness to participate in programs and groups for single parents.

8. To my knowledge the results of the NIMH study mentioned above have not yet been released.

9. Naturally, there are incompetent and unscrupulous professionals who have legitimate credentials. An education and a license do not guarantee ability and adherence to ethical standards. All they do is provide consumers with more public and professional forums for appeal, although even here the route to redress is frequently slow and often unsatisfactory.

10. The publication of a 12-page pamphlet entitled "A Service of Affirmation When Parents Are Separating" by Forward Movement Publications and a two-column write-up on the service in the *New York Times* (Rozhon, 1980) suggest not only that others may be viewing divorce liturgies with far less skepticism than I, but, more interestingly, that these ceremonies are becoming increasingly fashionable. It should be noted that this service, in contrast to the Grollman and Sams one, is presented by its three Episcopalian authors (a marriage counselor, a priest, and a

social worker) as a kind of offering to the children of the divorcing couple. Reciting from the liturgy, parents assume responsibility for the separation and reaffirm the permanency of their love and responsibility for their offspring (ibid.). Be it in public or in private, it seems questionable that any such avowal can erase the personal guilt and fear that children may harbor (consciously or unconsciously) over the dissolution of their parents' marriage.

11. Twelve years ago divorce would have terminated a Methodist minister's career, but now a handbook is used to judge his or her fate. In April 1979 the Council of Bishops of the United Methodist Church voted to adopt a handbook on clergy divorce. As an indicator of progress, the 45 bishops of the Church are directed to use this handbook for individually evaluating the case of each divorced cleric. Only after consideration of his or her emotional state, whether he or she has sought professional counseling, and whether he or she has been guilty of immoral behavior or public scandal will a judgment be issued (Franklin, 1979, p. 9).

12. The acceptance of divorce should not be interpreted as a condonation of this act by the churches. In the foreword to "A Service of Affirmation When Parents Are Separating," it is significant that the authors felt impelled to state that the service "is in no way intended to suggest that the church can or should condone divorce. To the church, marriage is and will continue to be sacred and, by intention, lifelong" (cited in Rozhon, 1980, p. D14).

13. Lest the reader presume that the Family Dispute Service originated in 1977 in a state whose identity he or she may already have surmised, it should be noted that this service was in operation in 23 cities before it found its way to a city nearby Westside. With respect to this study, however, the establishment of the Family Dispute Service was indeed an innovation, for it provided Westside residents with another option for resolving divorce-related problems—an option nonexistent in 1975.

14. Utilization of one form of counseling does not preclude the use of another. Not uncommonly, individuals participate in short-term groups for the divorced at the same time that they are receiving individual therapy. Others follow up one experience with the other (e.g., from group to individual therapy or from individual to group therapy). As such, group leaders and sponsoring agencies may offer both modes of treatment or serve as referral agents for participants who are interested in variant forms of treatment.

15. In a study of 560 divorced parents conducted at the University of Minnesota Law School, Fulton (1979) reports that the majority of mothers *and* fathers who were interviewed two years after divorce felt that their children had been negatively affected by the marital dissolution (pp. 129-139). (It should be noted that for these families whose divorce decrees were granted in 1970 the average family income at the time of separation was $14,000.)

16. While it is hard to imagine how a study of 60 families in Marin County, California, could be ballyhooed by *Redbook* as a definitive report on the effects of divorce on all children, it most surely was.

17. Here the divorced constituted just one group, although a significant one, of an ever-growing 93% of families who, according to NBC, lived outside the norms of traditional family life.

18. Some of the children of separation and divorce have received individual and/ or group therapy at the Health Plan, and at times the participation of one or both parents has been an integral part of the treatment plan. Moreover, while there has been no formal program for these children like that offered to their parents, this is due to change in the near future. Under the NIMH grant mentioned previously, the Health Plan has received new funding to create services for children.

19. The idea of using short-term support groups for the separated and divorced arrived late in Westside. Yet any assessment of innovation is a relative one. Clearly, for Westsidians an advance had been made both with respect to the number and kind of options available for helping individuals to cope with marital dissolution.

CHAPTER 9

IN PURSUIT OF CHANGE: IMPLICATIONS FOR RESEARCH AND POLICY

Ever since Willard Waller's research in 1930, sociologists have relied upon the observations of the separated and divorced in order to understand the consequences of marital dissolution. My study has not deviated from this tradition. The stories which have appeared in this book are not of my making. Like a scribe, I have used the words of others, recording the concerns of separated and divorced women, their actions, reactions, and even inactions, their dependency upon other people and institutions, and their growths and triumphs. Even in the persona of Sheila Ash, the claim of originality founders, for the execution of roleplaying depends upon imitation far more than upon invention. All effort and craftsmanship must be channeled toward one end—the creation of a realistic reproduction. The more authentic the forgery, the greater the possibility of simulating the experiences of others. If Sheila accomplished this goal, and I believe she did, it was precisely because she was a credible replica of a separated woman.

And as the creation of Sheila was molded from the experiences of the women with whom I spoke, so too are the ideas presented in this chapter. If they have been somewhat recast, shaped in part by the information compiled during Sheila's investigation of Westside and in part by my knowledge of how institutions operate, how they change and stagnate, and how people act and interact in social settings, still I find myself playing the role of a scribe. The transcription is not verbatim, as these women (and men) spoke more in terms of needs and voids than of policy issues and strategies for effecting change. Nonetheless, whether by pronouncement or by allusion, it is their thoughts as well as their problems that underlie the questions I will pose and the guidelines I will set forth for further research and the development of social policy.

GUIDELINES FOR CHANGE

Had this chapter been written in 1975, its composition would have been strikingly different. At that time not only was I convinced that new services and programs for the divorced were essential, but also that I knew which ones should and could be promoted in Westside. While I recognized some of the difficulties in implementing my plans and even some of the drawbacks, they appeared insufficient in number or magnitude to suppress my visions of reform. Today I harbor no such ambition. I shall not, indeed cannot, provide Westside or any community with an agenda that would enable them to respond to the needs of separated and divorced individuals and their children.

I have come to believe that the problems of the separated and divorced are too complex, the population too diverse, and, above all, the potential for error too great to justify the advocacy of any particular preventive or remedial approach. That this change of mind and heart can be attributed largely to the successful implementation by others of several of the very reforms I so enthusiastically supported is an ironic twist. Yet, and herein lies the reason for my disenchantment, the impact of some of these changes was almost negligible and others potentially or actually damaging. For example, along with the recognition that divorce counseling could help individuals and families adjust to marital dissolution arose a whole industry of providers whose motives are not always above reproach and whose services should be scrupulously examined as to their legitimacy and value.

I regret the loss of my optimism, the end of my idealism, for there is perhaps no exhilaration so great as that which emanates from the conviction that one can "right" wrongs. Surely we need look back no further than the 1960s to recall how individuals and, in fact, a nation can become intoxicated by grandiose dreams and promises of a better tomorrow. If disillusionment and retrenchment replaced expectations for "The Great Society," the venture cannot be chronicled as a failure. Advances had been made, although for those whose eyes had seen the glory of a social reformation, it was hard to revel in less auspicious achievements.

It is all too easy to cite the legacy of the 60s as a rationale for inaction, to become so obsessed with the possibility of erring that we worship at the altar of the status quo. This, I think, would be a grave mistake, for the 1960s suggest the avoidance of extremes, not immobilization. On a smaller scale the same can be said for the creation of policies and programs for the separated and divorced. The realization that a major reform movement may be a fruitless, even retrogressive, initiative and that magic potions and instant bromides do not exist should not deflect attention from the problems of the separated and divorced, for they will not vanish of their own accord (at least not in the immediate future). We especially need to address issues related to inequity and negligence and to better understand the ways in which stigmatization and alienation are fostered. How we do this, I am not quite sure. I do believe that a responsible and responsive approach does not have to be a spectacular event. Our goal is not to institutionalize the fantasies of innovators or to enhance the image of politicians through the creation of any kind of Times Square program replete with blazing lights and public fanfare. Rather, we need to proceed cautiously, establishing priorities and weighing alternatives of both a formal and informal nature. I also believe that we must cease to think of the needs of separated and divorced women in a vacuum, as if they were an entity unto themselves. To identify the problems which they share with many, particularly other women, is not to deny that some of their problems are unique. To the contrary, it is to recognize that there are two dimensions—one being the commonalities that unite this group and others and speak for policies that are more encompassing in scope and objective; the second being those issues which pertain exclusively to the separated and divorced and speak for more circumscribed action on a local and national level.

Yet let there be no pretense. What follows is neither a prescription for reform nor an exhaustive review of the many issues raised in this book. My purpose is far more modest, for I have elected to concentrate only on *some* of the kinds of community services and programs that respondents regarded as essential to their adjustment and only on *some* of their suggestions for change. That I no longer entertain quixotic notions of myself as the grand reformer is but a partial explanation for this decision. There are two additional reasons for confining the scope of this analysis. First, I have selected issues and problems which relate solely to community resources and the provision of public and private services. From the outset this study was directed toward understanding the relationship between separated and divorced women and their community. It was anticipated that such information would reveal discrepancies between individual needs and local resources, thereby helping this community and others to define priorities and directions for change. It was never my intention to consider reforms that necessitated federal, or even state, intervention. Thus, although I may touch on ideas that require the support of higher levels of government, they are not my focal point. Secondly, I have selected areas in which the possibility for effecting change appears more likely, omitting from consideration those which would involve a major reorganization of either the structure or orientation of social service systems or the expenditure of much money.

One last word of caution—the following analysis is personalized and limited in scope; it is the product of one individual's experience with one group of people within the context of one community. As such it must be read and as such it must be understood.[1]

DISSEMINATION OF INFORMATION

How many married women are knowledgeable about their legal entitlements or about domestic law with respect to divorce procedures, requirements, and costs? How many married women who have never been employed or have been unemployed for years know how to initiate a job search and negotiate in the labor market? How many married women who do not use child-care services are aware of the different costs and options available to them? How many married women who have never searched for housing or applied for credit for themselves are acquainted with extant discriminatory practices or with the laws which purportedly have made such discrimination illegal? How many married women are cognizant of where and how singles socialize? How many married women who have never utilized mental health services are aware of the different methods of treatment and the various agencies and individual providers in the public and private sectors?

For those who have read this book these are merely rhetorical questions; for those who have not the answer to all the queries is the same: "not many." Still, this study reveals that the majority of separated and divorced women *do* succeed in obtaining the information that they need; however, it also reveals that the search for information is a time-consuming and taxing procedure, and, more significantly, that individuals' abilities to restructure their lives are dependent, at least in part, on the acquisition of new information. This suggests that increasing the availability and accessibility of such vital data would facilitate the coping process.

At first blush this seems to be a straightforward, simplistic idea. Certainly it does not belong in the same league as proposals for income redistribution or the revision of legal policies. But comparisons can be beguiling, causing us to underestimate complexities and difficulties. The reasons why I do not consider this an easy task to accomplish will become clearer in the course of this overview. This does not mean that we should scrap the idea, relegating it to the graveyard of castoff reforms—the burial place for all those ideas which never attained recognition in the social engineer's hall of fame. It does mean that we cannot back up an advocacy position solely by a documentation of need. While this is an important step, it is only a preliminary one, to be followed by a thorough examination of the obstacles to implementation and an assessment of potential outcomes. We cannot ignore the possibility that the creation of a process or an agency for disseminating information to separated and divorced individuals may do little but provide jobs for the planners and executers of the project.

With this caveat in mind, we begin with the recommendation for a *central dissemination agency*. Of course, there are numerous ways in which information can be disseminated, be it to a specific population or to the community at large. Yet it was of a central agency which respondents most often spoke, envisioning a place in which they could obtain answers to their questions as well as help in securing services. The agency was expected, therefore, to function as both an educational and an outreach facility. By now the justification for such a proposal should be fairly obvious. There is no agency in Westside with the data base or capacity to dispense information in the areas of particular concern to individuals undergoing or contemplating a marital separation and/or to act as a referral agent connecting consumers and providers. Because each of the community's social service organizations operates independently, the consumer is forced to research and negotiate with each facility separately. As such, the delivery of social services is not integrated, and linkages between services, where they do exist, are difficult to discern. Not until late 1978 was there even a listing of community resources (persons, programs, and services) other than a four-page brochure. Although the current directory (ca. 1978) provides a reasonably comprehensive guide to Westside's nonprofit resources, its usefulness as a reference has been restricted by its cumbersome and incomplete index and by the city's failure to effectively advertise and disseminate the guide to community residents (see p. 114).

That the separated and divorced need information in order to learn new skills and behaviors and assume new responsibilities is indisputable. In addition, I see no reason to quibble with the declaration by many that the procurement of information in Westside could stand considerable improvement. Clearly this was one conclusion of Sheila's investigation. However, I do question the likelihood of achieving this end through the creation of a centralized service, particularly if it is publicly sponsored.

From the singular standpoint of the quantity, not to mention diversity, of information which requires inclusion, we have the makings of a major project. The mechanics of designing a system for collecting, processing, and disseminating data in even one area of concern to this population would be a significant accomplishment. A more comprehensive incorporation would then qualify as an almost Sisyphean task, especially in an age that leans toward specialization and fragmentation. To be specific, we are talking of no less than compiling information on divorce law, employment, schooling, child care, housing, and credit in addition to that on social and psychological groups, programs, and services. While the Office for Children, for example, made a stab at presenting an overview of Westside's child-care resources, problems of updating and disseminating the data remain unresolved. Likewise, state employment agencies and public mental health services have experienced similar problems. If specialized organizations have failed to deal satisfactorily with this task on the one level related to their own area of expertise, how can we expect an agency that has to operate simultaneously on many levels to accomplish this goal?

Even if the difficulties posed by the collection, integration, and dissemination of information could be surmounted, local officials would still have to be persuaded to underwrite the project. In all probability we would first have to prove that there is a sufficient number of residents in need of this service to warrant city involvement, that, in fact, the target population extends far beyond separated and divorced women. We might argue further that the city would appreciate a more immediate return for its investment through the efficacious use of existing resources and in the long run would benefit from a reduction in the number of people dependent upon public services and revenues for their maintenance and well-being. In other words, we would maintain that increased consumer awareness leads to better and more efficient utilization of resources and ultimately, as individuals become more self-reliant and independent, to a declining need for public services. Unfortunately, this is mere conjecture.

We simply do not know or really understand why, when, or how individuals seek information and even less about how they process and use such data. Some individuals appear to acquire information almost by happenstance, often seemingly unaware of pertinent resources. Others are more methodical in both the pursuit and utilization of information, and still others actively ferret out information and then do not use it (Furman et al., 1965). Hence information and referral agencies (and systems) may be unable to maximize the utilization and delivery of services and may be even less effective at fostering individual independence.

Perhaps what is needed are more aggressive tactics. Agencies may have to, in a manner of speaking, take charge of the client. The agency (or agent) becomes the client's broker, assuming responsibility for helping the client secure necessary services (Rein, 1970). Of course, this approach surfaces other dilemmas, not the least of which include increased financing, more complex administrative structures, and the establishment of communication channels with interacting systems. Irrespective of these stumbling blocks, the notion of a broker agent appeals to some "experts" who contend that the separated and divorced are, at least for a time, incapable of acting and negotiating on their own behalf. Thus the agent who takes over, leading the individual by the hand through the bureaucratic maze, would appear to be a much needed support.

But one and one do not always equal two in the real world. Individuals who have trouble coping with divorce may not welcome, and may even resist, outside intervention in any form, particularly if it comes from agencies in the public sector. There is evidence in this study to suggest that middle-class individuals may not avail themselves of public services, despite all indicators that help is necessary and available. It was not that they had approached agencies and been turned off by a callous or indifferent reception or inadequate treatment (albeit some were); more frequently it was an a priori refusal based upon their perception of these agencies as caretakers for the indigent (see Chapter 8). Moreover, resentment and anger toward their ex-spouses served to intensify their resistance.

Whether the predicament faced by public service organizations in attracting a middle-class clientele can be described as an image problem or whether it is more basic, lying in the ways in which such services are currently structured and/or presented to the public, are questions for which there are no ready answers. We do know, however, that planners are not unlike tailors, for neither can "sell" their product if the fit is poor. In other words, this implies that planners must relate the structure and function of any agency to the individuals it seeks to service and to the community in which it is situated. This is easier said than done, for the difficulties of eliminating stigmatization and combating personal biases far outweigh those that pertain to the structure and nature of services.

With the recognition that further research and exploration must be directed toward these issues, two variant approaches for disseminating information will be presented, each of which attempts to deal with the problem of stigmatization in a different fashion.

One approach is to create an agency in which the dissemination of information would be nontargeted and dependent upon the consumer's request for service. Functioning somewhat like a public library, it would be open to all residents. While it is clear that stigmatization might not be an issue in such an agency, it is not so clear whether it would succeed in providing adequate information to users who also have to be their own sponsors in obtaining services. To some extent this would depend upon the quality of the data and, in particular, on the staff's ability to update and process information. Ultimately, however, the success or failure of such a venture would hinge on the consumer's decision to request service and his or her ability to translate information into action.

The second approach retains the idea of targeting services to the separated and divorced but posits that the stigmatization of consumers might be reduced and the utilization of information improved if group members themselves sponsored the service. Self-help support groups and organizations for single parents would be among the most likely choices. Not only are these groups familiar with the needs and concerns of this population, but their organizational values and goals are compatible with the objectives and priorities of an information-dissemination service. Furthermore, they can be expected to look beyond the public sector in the course of compiling information on community resources and making referrals to agencies and providers. This in itself has three advantages. One, it increases the chances of securing support (in the form of services, monies, or cooperation) from both the public and private sectors. Two, it encourages consumers to consider alternatives instead of following a predetermined utilization pattern. (Because public referral agencies usually have to adhere to set guidelines for eligibility and outreach, they rarely can offer their clientele a choice of options.) Three, such practices alleviate the pressure on public institutions to provide services for this population.

There is a Catch 22 that casts a cloud over these expectations and projections. Money, or more precisely the lack of it, is still the principal determinant of how many options an individual does or does not have. In point of fact, middle-class separated and divorce women may be the real victims of the social service system—as a group too frequently unable to afford private services and yet ineligible for public ones. Prior to divorce their husbands' incomes may disqualify them from obtaining public services, even though they may receive insufficient or no support from their spouses. In order to overcome this obstacle bureaucratic red tape in the form of papers to be filed, affidavits to be secured, and people to be seen can dissuade even the most hearty from pursuing this course of action. And it does not necessarily end with the granting of a decree, for those whose husbands are delinquent or negligent in paying alimony and/or child support must also furnish evidence to back up their charges. The bitter irony of the situation is that a woman who qualifies for public assistance on the basis of income received and/or earned may be disqualified on the basis of a husband who on paper is or should be contributing to her maintenance.

Undeniably, some middle-class women may have insufficient funds to use private resources and still be ineligible for or refuse to accept public help, be it money or services. Others will continue to rely upon public revenues. Nevertheless, the selection of a sponsoring agent for an information-dissemination service should not be contingent upon whether or not a specific group or organization can succeed in reducing dependency on public resources or in securing services for clients who have difficulty negotiating within the public sector. We already know that the provision of information does not ensure access to or the utilization of services, nor does it guarantee that individuals will be able to make it alone. Indeed, it will be recalled that we did not set out to discuss the attainment of these goals; rather, in response to one frequently expressed need of respondents, we focused on a much more limited objective—the creation of an information-dissemination agency or process. (In substance, this would not even include the responsibility for referral, although most individuals conceptualized it in this way.) Hence it is a system's or an organization's ability to accomplish this objective, above all others, which should guide us in the selection of a particular sponsor.

Overall, it appears that self-help support groups which initiate and manage their own services are more effective in compiling and disseminating information than are public agencies.[2] On the one hand, this is attributable to their personal knowledge of the needs of separated and divorced persons and their ability to outreach in a nonstigmatizing manner. Their interest in helping this population may be self-serving to the extent that it verifies their *raison d'être*, but it is also genuine, born as it is from experience. On the other hand, the success of these groups may be a byproduct of what can only be characterized as a national self-help movement. In recent years we have witnessed a veritable explosion in the growth of self-help groups. It has reached such epidemic proportions that it seems as if there is scarcely a problem, concern, call it what you may, that has not given rise to a special group, somewhere, at some time. In fact, a few days ago I heard about a woman who was planning to organize a support group for periodontal patients. Sounds incredible? Scan the newspapers and you will see otherwise. Or better yet, place an advertisement for, say, all guilty, nonworking mothers to join together to expunge their guilt. While there is an element of sarcasm here, the need for or the value of mutual support cannot be gainsaid. If nothing else, these groups provide companionship.

To understand the boom in self-help groups we need only look to the present women's movement.[3] The notion of sisterhood coupled with the recognition that women had long been the sufferers of inequality in the home, the schools, the marketplace, and society called for more than a minute of silent prayer; it called for action. If society, and in particular the democratic political system, was in no rush to redress injustices, then women would simply have to carry the gauntlet themselves. A discussion of the triumphs and failures of this movement is beyond the scope of this book. But it is worth mentioning that the increased pressure for women to band together, be it for reform or tender loving care, has undoubtedly helped to legitimatize the creation of women's groups of all kinds. It has also contributed to the febrile backlash of men who are not without their own list of inequities. The birth of groups like Fathers United for Equal Justice is as much attributable to women's increased proclivity to become self-advocates as it is to legal policies and norms favoring mothers' rights.

Nevertheless, it is not so much the etiology of these groups that concerns us as does their ability to outreach to the separated and divorced and provide them with the information they require for restructuring their lives. Here we have some evidence of success. The group that first comes to mind, perhaps because of their encyclopedic handbook, is Women in Transition in Philadelphia. But there are many others. For example, the Westside women's group was by far the most responsive and knowledgeable of the city's public and private resources contacted by Sheila (see Chapter 2). Yet to speak of the advantages of support groups as sponsors of information services without at least touching on their role as advocates for the separated and divorced is to negate their future and in part also that of their constituency. It is one thing to dispense help, another to invoke the help of others, and still another to obtain it. Movement in this direction is becoming increasingly discernible as more and more groups are publicizing the needs of their membership (see p. 62). If, in fact, they can marshall the support of those in the public and private sectors, they will have accomplished the ultimate goal—the phasing out of their own projects. Distant from the rumblings of politics, the antagonisms of labor and management, and bureaucratic face-saving, there is not only the increased freedom to create but also to terminate. In the words of Women in Transition (1975), "Our hope is that as agencies become more sensitive to the needs of all women, but especially those going through separation and divorce, programs like Women in Transition will no longer be necessary" (p. 3).

Before you raise your voice to acclaim support groups as the couriers of choice, there is more that I should tell you, for all the news is not good. The bad news is that there are drawbacks to the management of an information-dissemination service by such groups or organizations. For one, these groups often labor under the constant pressure of insufficient funding. If public agencies bewail monetary deficits, their woes are minor in comparison to small groups who neither are part of the tributary system through which money flows nor have the expertise and contacts necessary for securing grant monies.

From these funding difficulties comes the second piece of bad news, namely, the tenuousness of the membership's commitment. If the group has no source of outside revenue, or not enough to pay its administrators' salaries, the life expectancy of the group may be truncated. That the continuance of the group may become too great a price to pay in terms of other, more pressing commitments and responsibilities is one reason, as we have noted previously, why so many groups are short-lived (see pp. 62-63). There is only so much time in a day, only so much energy one can expend; even if they do not close shop, the members may be unable to devote the time required to the planning, implementation, and management of this or any project.

The third piece of bad news is that the population which they are to represent appears to have rather diverse and not uncommonly negative views of these groups, albeit often without a basis in either fact or experience. Several respondents, for example, voiced outright disdain for any so-called women's group, and others were suspicious of their motives. In point of fact, the Westside women's group, among others, suffered from an "image problem." In their effort to reach out to *all* women, they issued a mixed message, causing some to draw inaccurate conclusions about the nature and goals of the group. One woman who read in their newsletter two almost trivial comments, one about the Susan Saxe Defense Fund (1976) and another about lesbian mothers, inferred that the membership was comprised of radical, lesbian women. Naturally, this may say as much about the reader as it does about the printed material. And too, it says something about how people process information. But irrespective of personal distortions and biases, women's groups do have to address the very real problem of appealing to a heterogeneous clientele. Perhaps instead of relying upon promotional literature and word-of-mouth referrals to increase membership, they would do well, especially in middle- and upper-middle class communities, to work through more traditional channels (e.g., child-care centers, church and civic organizations, food collectives, PTA, workplaces). It is not, however, all that clear whether inaccurate or even negative preconceptions of a group would in actuality deter women from using an information-dissemination service. It is certainly imaginable that these conscientious objectors might utilize such a facility even though they would never contemplate membership in the group.

Paradoxically, the advantages of having a support group sponsor an information-dissemination agency (or process) can also become its gravest liabilities. Its distance from political and bureaucratic pressures may allow for the kind of creativity and flexibility infrequently found in public organizations, but it may also lead to insufficient financing and isolation from other public and private institutions. The benefits of easy phaseout are obvious when the program has accomplished its ends, but when the termination occurs too early and too abruptly, it can leave consumers without alternatives. Further, sponsorship by those who have first-hand knowledge of the target population's problems may reduce the likelihood of stigmatization, but the cost may be the sacrifice of objectivity. Personal biases, then, become impediments to action or rationales for inappropriate decision making.

If it is unclear at what time and under what circumstances a group's assets become its liabilities, it is clear that under scrutiny no organization, be it public or private, will emerge unblemished. While the recognition of such defects, and by extension the risks involved in selecting a specific sponsoring agent for a project, can cause us to inveigh against change, it can also have a totally different effect. In particular, we may realize that we are not judges of a contest in which there is but one choice and but one winner. By avoiding this kind of myopic mentality, sundry options begin to surface. For example, a support group may assume responsibility for the operation of an information-dissemination service that is funded by the city. The point to be made is not that this recommendation is in itself superior, but rather that we should cease to envisage choices as if they constituted polarities. Not only should we consider many different options but, more importantly, many different ways to combine and rearrange these options. Admittedly, one can argue that too many alternatives can be immobilizing, and so it can. But this does not negate the benefit to be gained from achieving a balance between too few and too many; for it is in this grey area that creative planning and decision making lie.

ALTERNATIVE DELIVERY OF PROFESSIONAL SERVICES

The number of suggestions made by respondents for changing the structure and delivery of professional services can be best described by the adjective "prodigious." For instance, with respect to the legal system, their proposals included the total delegalization of divorce, the replacement of domestic judges with a team composed of a lawyer (or judge), a psychiatrist, and an accountant, the substitution of extralegal arbitration for adversary proceedings, partnerships between mental health specialists and attorneys in the practice of family law, court collection of alimony and child support payments, and per-case legal fee schedules instead of hourly rates. And the legal system was not the only area of professional practice that came under their purview. In addition, they called for comprehensive health insurance coverage for divorce counseling and/or psychiatric treatment for the divorced and their families, the licensing of all mental health practitioners, ceilings on fees charged by mental health practitioners in accordance with training and experience, increased access for separated women to public agencies irrespective of their husbands' incomes, diagnostic and treatment centers for children in families undergoing a marital dissolution, survival training courses for the divorced taught by a team comprised of a lawyer, psychiatrist, financial planner, and employment counselor, the creation of publicly funded support groups with professionally trained staffs, and the development of a community-sponsored network of day-care centers for children of all ages and from all income brackets with a sliding fee schedule.

No shrinking violets were these women! The entire social service network became their prey as they methodically proceeded from system to system, analyzing its deficiencies, challenging its objectives, and designing remedial strategies.[4] Obviously they provided enough ideas to write several chapters on ways in which to revamp the structure of professional services. Yet I will address only the broader, more general topic of service delivery, thereby deliberately avoiding the more heady questions of how to effect major alterations in the nature and function of professional services. Why is it, you may ask, that I so wittingly circumvent the route set forth by respondents? The answer is simple: I, unlike my adventuresome sisters, am awed by both the theoretical and operational complexities inherent in any one of the undertakings they propose, for neither individuals nor systems are easily susceptible to change. Reforms that seek to restructure or adapt services can have negative repercussions on the system undergoing transformation, even to the extent of causing systemic dysfunction. Moreover, unless the values and goals of the system are already compatible with the proposed changes, it is doubtful that successful adaptation can be accomplished. And also reform efforts can fail to produce the anticipated ends for different reasons. For example, an innovation can scarcely be deemed a success if the clientele for whom it was created does not choose to avail itself of the service. Even the recommendations of respondents cannot always be taken at face value, for is there not evidence in this study that women who advocate more public mental health agencies and different eligibility standards are unlikely to use community services even if their demands are met?

Hence if I focus on suggestions which are not only of a less profound nature than many of those recommended by respondents but also ones in which change appears least apt to be disruptive to institutions and individuals, it is not so much due to timidity or to a repudiation of the merit of these women's observations as to a realistic appreciation of the formidable character of the reforms they so earnestly champion.

Still, the innovations which will be discussed are far from simplistic, either from the standpoint of planning or of implementation. They do constitute, however, a logical extension of the idea for centralizing information, for as we saw in the last section, it is exceedingly difficult to speak of or defend the need for increased consumer awareness (*vis à vis* new information) without at least considering issues related to service availability and utilization. In our pragmatic society knowledge in and of itself has limited saleability. As such, it becomes necessary to examine different ways in which services can be dispensed, bearing in mind the specific problems that respondents encountered in their negotiations and interactions with individual providers and social service organizations.

THE COMPREHENSIVE AGENCY

The comprehensive agency offers one variant approach to the delivery of professional services. Structurally such agencies are designed not only to house all services in one facility, but to provide consumers with a "total" care package. Although certain specialized services may be purchased and/ or financed outside the facility, in general the comprehensive agency does not have to depend upon others to supplement its care. Nor does it experience the problems of individual follow-through, access, and utilization which seem to plague referral agencies.

In effect, the comprehensive agency mimics the supermarket concept of shopping: Rather than having to identify and travel to different vendors, the consumer can do all his "purchasing" under one roof. The willingness of consumers to sacrifice personalized service and, at times, quality in exchange for convenience has been demonstrated again and again as food supermarkets keep expanding, forcing independent merchants out of business. The appeal of the comprehensive agency is not necessarily based, then, on the superiority of its service but rather on its convenience. Of course, it can be argued (and it often is) that such services not only eliminate individual problems of access and eligibility, but they also lower costs.[5]

If we look at the range of services used by separated and divorced families as well as those which they felt were needed but unavailable (or inaccessible), it appears that in order for a facility to present itself as a comprehensive agency for this population it would have to furnish legal, economic, social, and psychological services. Thus we can speculate that a "HMO" (Health Maintenance Organization) for the divorced would incorporate services for legal information, counseling, and referrals; employment counseling, training, and placement; information on community and work-based child-care options;[6] updated listings of available rentals and sales as well as of single parents interested in cooperative housing; information on antidiscrimination laws pertaining to employment, housing, and credit; and short- and long-term therapeutic and support services for children and adults.

It is doubtful that such a venture would have many supporters and even more doubtful that it would receive financial backing, particularly in the public sector.[7] Because many of these services already exist, in some form or other, in the public and private arenas, policymakers and planners are apt to regard a comprehensive agency as a wasteful duplication of resources. Even if superiority of access and utilization of services could be verified, proponents would remain on the defensive, for they would have to demonstrate that these advantages could not be achieved by an alternative approach such as improving coordination and collaboration among established facilities. The prospect for supporting such a case is at best slender. The negatives far outweigh the positives. Quite apart from economic considerations, there is the very real potential for resistance from the agencies and individual providers which the comprehensive service proposes to preempt or at least compete with for its clientele. Moreover, the resolution of these dilemmas would still leave unanswered the question of whether the target population would in fact utilize services provided in such a manner.[8] Along with convenience, access, and coordination come labeling and the risk of stigmatization, not an insignificant price to exact for convenience.[9]

What's more, the above-mentioned issues do not speak to the difficulties of designing, implementing, and running such a facility. In the past, failures of comprehensive agencies have been ascribed to many causes, including poor leadership, internal system problems, reliance upon singular approaches to conflict resolution, and outreach problems in attracting clientele. However, the most common cause of failure and conflict occurs because planners and entrepreneurs operate under what Sarason (1972) calls the "myth of unlimited resources" (p. 101). If agencies persist in striving for comprehensive delivery, ignoring the harbingers of economic scarcity, all may stand to be losers. The organizations may lose, because in a struggle for funding, which pits agency against agency, some will not survive the competition and others will have to redefine the quantity or quality of their services. The clients may lose, because service delivery may become so compromised or so fragmented that adequate care is no longer obtainable.

Nonetheless, the actual idea of a comprehensive service program for the women (and men) of separation and divorce should not yet be abandoned. That we may not achieve this goal through the creation of a formalized agency does not imply that the concept is a poor one or the end unattainable. To the contrary, it may suggest that we need to develop alternative delivery strategies and/or structures. One such approach is to be found in the model created by the aforementioned Women in Transition.[10]

The services provided by this group and others like it are not publicly owned and operated; they are not agencies; they are not housed in impressive edifices. Yet within the confines of an informal and sheltered environment, they have demonstrated the capacity of relatively small groups to design programs which encompass many of the services cited for inclusion in a comprehensive agency (see p. 272).[11] Admittedly the programs of which I speak are smaller in scale and less sweeping in scope, for they are not facsimiles of the supermarket paradigm. Thus members may have to utilize resources in the public and private sectors to supplement the groups' offerings. But if they do not peddle a total care package, there are other advantages which in the long run may prove more beneficial from both the perspective of individual users and service planners. For example, small group comprehensive services are frequently more economical, flexible, personalized, and less stigmatizing than are institutionalized ones. These attributes, in themselves meritorious, assume even greater value when the program is to be targeted to a specific population rather than to the general public.[12]

THE DEMONSTRATION PROGRAM

Demonstration programs present yet another approach to reforming the delivery of professional services. More glamorous in theory than comprehensive agencies, such programs hold out the promise of being innovative in design and function, of reaching populations neglected by existing social service organizations, and of promoting the dissemination of their programs. Unfortunately, their track record is far less glamorous. Innovative concepts are frequently not operational because planners rely upon traditional structures or mechanisms for dispensing services. New populations are frequently not serviced because, in an effort to prove the superiority of their program, planners confine recruitment to those clients who are considered good risks. Thus, as Martin Rein notes (1970), "programs designed to reach the unreached have only augmented their numbers" (p. 64). And dissemination plans frequently fall short of projections because planners do not accept the fact that programs that are successful in one locale may not be successful in another. Without understanding the obfuscations of transposition, they fail to realize that "there is no single innovation that will work in all local settings, for those settings are not only different and unpredictable in specifics, but they are also constantly changing" (House, 1974, p. 245).

Few would dispute the importance of nurturing the development of new ideas and new ways for redressing social dilemmas, nor would many dispute that small-scale programs proffer an economically feasible route, affording more social innovators more opportunities for experimentation. Yet there appears to be a discrepancy between the potential and the actual capacity of these programs to effect change. The word "demonstration" harbors one clue, exposing as it does a fundamental contradiction between the theoretical and practical application of this approach to social reform. "Demonstration" implies a different purpose than does research or experimentation (although these programs are sometimes called "demonstration-research" projects). In essence, it suggests that the objective of the venture is not to test the program's effectiveness, but that it is for show, to illustrate *proven* merit. Accepting its value without (or almost without) question, the planners and implementers are left with two tasks, neither of which has much to do with research. One, they need to orchestrate the project so that it will appear in its most favorable light. (This may lead to a restrictive selection of clients.) Two, they become its sales agents, aiming for the wider distribution of their "product."

Seen in this way, it becomes clearer why many demonstration programs neither serve as models of innovation nor advance our understanding of why certain reforms succeed or fail. It also helps to explain why costs often exceed the expenditures anticipated for planning and implementation. How can it be otherwise when the ambitions of planners extend far beyond the development of a program? Promotion, marketing, and all the other trappings of hype do not come cheaply.

This is not to say that there is no need for demonstration programs, for the basic premises underlying the idea are sound and worthy of support; rather, my point is that we should pay more attention to the experimental side of these proposals, playing down the demonstration-dissemination end.[13]

Demonstration or experimental programs for the separated and divorced can include such diverse pilot projects[14] as legal clinics for women,[15] the development of training programs for paralegal *counselors*,[16] postdivorce counseling and arbitration centers,[17] employment training and placement services for displaced homemakers, housing compounds for single-parent families,[18] and women's all-purpose banks.

Alternatively, pilot projects can have more comprehensive goals, essaying to accomplish a variety of objectives simultaneously. Again Women in

Transition furnishes an illustration. In addition to serving as a resource center, support group, and referral agent for the separated and divorced, group leaders have also adopted an advocacy stance on behalf of this population. Of all the group's multifarious functions, the role of advocate holds the most hope for effecting reform, for without increasing a community's awareness of the needs of a particular resident group, it is unlikely that a supportive climate for change will evolve (Chin and Benne, 1969).

Yet if we accept the statement of Women in Transition, as cited previously (p. 270), their goal is not to disseminate their program, but to have it subsumed by extant social service agencies. Thus their success is to be measured by their demise. It is in this variation on the advocacy theme that the group strays from the standard format of demonstration programs and from the aspirations of other promoters. This does not mean that the group has spurned the glories to be accrued from dissemination; to the contrary, they may be aiming toward an even higher order of accomplishment. After all, if social service organizations were to adopt the model of Women in Transition, their program would have achieved the supreme end of dissemination worshippers. Nonetheless, perhaps I am being overly suspicious. The apparent accomplishment of this group effort does justify consideration by others. If this culminates in alterations in the structure and delivery of community services where they are warranted and necessary, then their achievement is indeed to be trumpeted. However, I cannot resist sounding a note of caution: No program can be transferred intact from one setting to another, no matter how appealing it may seem or how successful it has been. Duplication should be restricted to the adoption of general objectives (e.g., the dissemination of information in areas such as law, employment, child care, housing, and psychosocial support services), not the acceptance of an a priori design. Even social service organizations should strive to respond organically to the needs of their members, a goal that they are unlikely to attain by rigidly following a prescribed format. But the accomplishment of this end, or any reform end, will require more than careful planning. To be precise, it will require money—a commodity which appears to be in short supply.

Women in Transition was one of the fortunate few—their program was funded by local and national foundations. Many others have not been (and will not be) so fortunate. As we have seen, public agencies labor continuously under the threat of reduction or even loss of monies, and certainly the high cost factor of a comprehensive agency has time and again served to thwart the plans of its supporters. And so, too, demonstration and experimental programs may live on only in the minds of their creators if the hope for or the promise of funding does not materialize. The facts are harsh. The golden 60s vanished into the annals of history, to be replaced by the prudent 70s. As private foundations and government funding agencies pulled in the reins, good ideas and lofty goals were frequently insufficient enticements to exact funding. Whether the coffers had been emptied in the 60s, or at least depleted, whether the national mood of optimism had given way to caution, even pessimism, or whether liberal movements are foreordained to be followed by conservative periods, the bottom line was that the money no longer flowed so freely. The story of the 80s has yet to be written; but if we believe the scuttlebutt circulating among the so-called informed, it appears as if we had better brace ourselves for a period of austerity unknown in recent decades. Be they right or wrong, a return to the 60s is not in the cards. Competition for scarce resources will continue to be the name of the game that planners of demonstration and experimental programs as well as all others must be willing to play. In the private and public sectors the contenders will have to wage their campaigns, struggling to convince funding agencies that the needs of a particular population justify the allocation of funds; thus single-parent families will be one of many groups, all of whom will claim priority and special consideration. As a consequence, the search for funding cannot be limited to a singular source; every conceivable resource—local, state, and national, public and private—must be investigated.

Since my interest lies in that narrow realm of the community, I will speak only of alternative forms of community sponsorship and, of course, only as they relate to the separated and divorced. Obviously, the direct allocation of public funds to individuals, groups, or organizations for the creation of pilot programs for separated and divorced women (and/or men) is one possibility. But community involvement can come wrapped in a variety of packages and appear in a variety of guises. For example, the community can provide incentives for program formation by publicly acknowledging the needs of this population, albeit this may not succeed in generating more substantial support from the public or private sectors or concerned citizens. The community can also provide resources in the form of personnel (e.g., for project staffing, for project planning, for writing grant proposals). The provision of space would constitute another contribution, one for which Westside officials have already set a precedent by permitting Widowed-to-Widowed to house their office in City Hall. Additionally, the community can become an active participant in the search for funding by urging social service agencies or businesses to back special programs or projects for the separated and divorced.

While these kinds of community commitments may not satisfy funding needs, we should neither discount the value of such benefactions nor overlook the possibility that total community funding could have a deleterious influence. Monies are rarely bestowed without stipulations, some of which can retard the innovational process or undermine the goals of planners. Moreover, city ownership increases the risk that middle- and upper-middle-class residents will boycott the enterprise, viewing it as an offering to the poor. Despite the intrinsic appeal of community financing, in the final analysis, relegating city or town involvement to a subsidiary position may prove to be both judicious and advantageous.

Funding is not the only problem faced by planners of demonstration projects; it may not even be the most formidable one. Unless planners can gain entrance to and acceptance within the social service system, their programs have little chance of succeeding. And herein is the rub; for while their strengths lie in their willingness to experiment, to stray from the path of orthodoxy, their creation and survival are largely dependent upon the support of the very systems that they propose to change or challenge. If these systems respond by denying the "upstart" access to information, expertise, and especially referral courtesies for their clientele, the resultant isolation becomes terrifically costly. Even those who go it alone are in trouble: Unable to provide the kind of comprehensive service that is contingent upon cooperation and collaboration among agencies, some clients may receive inadequate coverage and others may "abandon ship."

Still, the identification of methods for attracting consumers remains the most troublesome dilemma confronting planners of *any* program for the separated and divorced. We really do not know how to advertise, structure, and locate programs that will promote participation and limit stigmatization. We do not even know if the desired goal for reciprocity among agencies will facilitate or impede outreach efforts. In part, our lack of knowledge may be attributable to the fact that, despite pontifications and research, we do not in actuality know what kind of programs are needed or what kind of changes can and should be made within the existing social service system. At the least, this should make us pause for thought.

But, dear reader, before you become absorbed in meditation, I ask that you consider, if only briefly, the children of separation and divorce, for in discussing different forms of service delivery, I have focused almost exclusively on their parents. In the way of an explanation, two observations are to be noted: First, this is a study about and for adults, and second, and more to the point, most of the programs and projects which have been created and others which have been recommended are primarily for adults. In general, planners have operated under the premise that the children of divorce will fare better if their parents are able to cope with the changes caused by a marital dissolution. Although the postulate is probably accurate, the theory is a bit too "neat." In presenting a narrow and inchoate view of the circumstances surrounding separation and divorce, it diverts our attention from other critical questions and problems. Lest we forget, it should be stated that even well-adjusted parents engage in interpersonal and family conflicts (before and after divorce) that may have a negative effect on their children; even children whose parents experience minimal adjustment difficulties may manifest separation-related problems; and even children whose parents never structure a workable relationship may manage to "overcome." As important as parental adjustment is for children, it does not necessarily eliminate or resolve other needs and conflicts, nor does parental maladjustment doom the child to a life of abnormality.

While it may be true that the children of divorce have not received their just desserts, at present we are not in a position to draw such a conclusion. Surprisingly, we know precious little about the needs or problems of children in single-parent homes. If public interest is at an all-time high and more and more researchers are studying this population, to date, their contributions can be most generously described as meager. Moreover, most research continues to be directed toward the pathology of single-parent homes (Halem, 1980). And even when investigators are not focusing on abnormality, their qualitative and quantitative data are inconclusive and often contradictory. Some scholars argue that permanent psychological damage can occur to children, whereas others contend that children are extremely resilient, recovering from the experience without noticeable effects. Perhaps researchers have become so preoccupied with uncovering evidence on the effects of divorce on children that they have failed to consider the far more fundamental question of whether divorce is a crisis situation or a chronic state of stress. If an answer to this query is to be found, we must provide support for longitudinal studies that look at the separation process over time (Brandwein et al., 1974; Heclo et al., 1973; Price-Bonham and Balswick, 1980). So far the most concrete step in this direction has been the previously cited five-year Children of Divorce Project in Marin County, California (see Wallerstein and Kelly, 1980). Although its small sample, among other methodological limitations, prevents us from generalizing its results to the population as a whole, this study constitutes an important beginning; for we cannot address the issue of whether or not additional services for children are necessary, let alone how children's services should be structured and delivered, until we look more closely and for longer periods of time at the children of divorce.

This cautionary advice pertains equally to the adults of divorce; of this we need to be aware, particularly as we turn to the subject of networks—the last and most ambitious of the change proposals to be discussed.

A NETWORK OF SOCIAL SERVICES FOR SINGLE-PARENT FAMILIES[19]

The term *network* is used to designate...the interaction of social service organizations.... The term can be used to describe how a variety of community agencies, each performing different functions such as control, socialization, guidance, accommodation to and prevention of dependency and ill health, share either potentially, concurrently, or serially the same population (Rein, 1970, pp. 47-48).

Fact: In keeping with the national trend, the population of single-parent families in Westside is on the upswing. Fact: The majority of respondents believe that the community has been delinquent in understanding and addressing their problems. Fact: Despite the number and variety of social service organizations in Westside, for the most part resources are not targeted either individually or as a whole to separated and divorced families.[20] Question: Would the creation of a network of community social services be an effective response to the identified needs and concerns of single-parent families in Westside?[21]

THE CASE FOR A NETWORK IN WESTSIDE

The data from this study present two rationales, albeit tenuous and debatable ones, for the development of a network. First, informal networks, linking individuals to other individuals and to specific services, already exist within the community of Westside. Respondents attested to the different ways in which they provided support and information to each other via personal contacts and group memberships (e.g., PWP, Solo, support groups). In effect, each member of the network became a quasi-researcher, identifying and evaluating resources and then communicating his or her findings to others. Dissemination of information, consultation, referral, and exchange of services (e.g., babysitting, carpooling, housekeeping) were major functions of the informal network. But the most essential component lay in the more elusive and intimate realm of personal relationships. More than practical assistance, the support and friendship of others were considered indispensable to people's ability to cope with and adjust to marital dissolution.

Not all of the separated and divorced are members of informal networks, and some require more guidance and services than can be obtained in this manner. Nevertheless, the existence of informal networks suggests not only that the separated and divorced need such information and support, but also that they will accept help when it is visible, accessible, and nonstigmatizing. It is, however, conceivable that this delivery system cannot be institutionalized nor its components reproduced within structured settings, for its appeal may be dependent upon its informality.

Data collected from Sheila's investigation of Westside supply the second rationale for the creation of a social service network. This research furnished evidence that existing community resources have *potential* for meeting at least some of the needs of single-parent families. Yet, important as the discovery of potentiality may be, especially in an era of fiscal prudence, it must be emphasized that it is only a latent possibility of which I speak. Moreover, this finding was further qualified by the observation that in some facilities organizational restructuring or adaptation would first be required, in others an adjustment of service priorities and even ideologies, and in still others the development of different outreach procedures.

To note that the accomplishment of these changes would be a tall order is a gross understatement. We do not know enough about the mechanics of change and the supports necessary to sustain its momentum to be able to fashion a blueprint for action. Nor can we issue a fiat mandating the compliance of individuals and agencies. What's more, there is no guarantee that if change does occur along the lines we suggest, that it will, in fact, meet the needs of single-parent families. Not only do needs change over time, but the likelihood remains high that there will be oversights both in the planning and implementation of reforms.

All this is by way of saying that the limitations of any change venture must not be given short shrift. Reform movements have frequently gone awry precisely because too little attention was paid to problems and long-range consequences. This, of course, has been neither the sole cause of aborted change efforts nor the sole dilemma confronting reformers. Still, the ambiguities, contradictions, and difficulties inherent in any reform initiative should not be played down. It is therefore imperative that we look at the potential for failure even as we dream of the glories of success. Of this the history of social innovation warns.

Perhaps nowhere else in this chapter is it so important that the reader understand my skepticism and agree to the terms it sets forth. This does not mean that you have to accept my arguments. It does mean that you have to recognize my position and the restrictions it imposes. Let me be very specific: The following overview of a social service network for the separated and divorced, despite rather explicit attention to strategies for planning and implementation, does not constitute an endorsement of this project either in its own right or in comparison to other proposals previously reviewed. It is merely another idea, one which merits consideration, but which also needs to be subjected to further research and analysis.

THE IDENTIFICATION OF A SPONSORING AGENT

Those who have experienced a marital dissolution may be the most obvious and indeed the best source of information on divorce. Their appraisals of existing resources and their suggestions for change may even proffer a realistic agenda for reform. Whether they can take the next step—the translation of knowledge into action—is an entirely different matter.

We do know that members of this population have already been major contributors to the cause of reform. Certainly, programs such as Parents Without Partners and Women in Transition attest to their ingenuity and ability. That these same energies and talents could be mobilized behind a plan to fashion a network of social services is conceivable; but it is also unlikely. For my research indicates that an undertaking of this nature would require, at a minimum, the influence and connections of a major institution (or system). Moreover, such an institution must be able to perform a variety of roles, foremost of which would be to function as a catalyst, occasioning changes within and among the community's social service systems.[22]

There are at least four guidelines to be used in determining whether a particular institution or system possesses the qualifications to carry forth this proposal. First, and most fundamental, top management must evince more than a concern for the unmet needs of single-parent families; a willingness to assume a leadership role in initiating and overseeing such a change venture must be clearly evident.

Second, both management and staff must have a broad understanding of the needs and problems of single-parent families as a group and of its members as individuals, including an awareness of how needs and concerns change over time. In addition, they must recognize that the emotional impact of divorce directly influences the ways in which individuals perceive external events and the ways in which they act or react. For example, failure to obtain a job or credit may be interpreted as a rejection of self. Although economic issues, or, for that matter, any issue, cannot be dissociated from their psychological counterparts, this does not suggest that the separated and divorced are a population of psychological cripples. It does suggest that they may be especially vulnerable and more likely to indulge in self-depreciation than at other times in their lives. The importance attributed to psychological factors would seem to imply that the sponsoring agency should have special expertise in the area of mental health. This deduction is further supported by the fact that mental health organizations (e.g., Flushing Hospital Mental Health Clinic in New York City, the Pittsburgh Center for Children in Family Crisis) have been the principal organizers of special programs for separated and divorced families. However, no such inference is intended. Court-connected services, among others, may be just as appropriate a choice, if not more so. The essential point is to identify an institution sensitive to the diverse needs of this population and capable of structuring solutions that deal concurrently with specific problems and their psychological ramifications (and manifestations).

Third, the institution should have the functional capacity to provide at least some of the special services recommended by respondents (e.g., information dissemination, referral, consultation, and planning). Moreover, there should be established linkages between this system and other community services; for if channels of communication do not already exist, it is doubtful whether joint planning and interactions within the larger system of community services could be effected.

Fourth, the institution should be philosophically receptive to citizen participation in decision-making processes. The active involvement of concerned and affected residents is one method for reducing stigmatization of prospective clients and for ensuring that the program will be responsive to the needs of the population it services rather than those of its creators.

In short, the role of the selected institution is that of a "broker..., connecting various strands" of the social service delivery system "which are otherwise disconnected" (Schon, 1971, p. 199). The dissemination of information and referral to other agencies become two subsidiary tasks of the greater effort to maximize interconnectedness and communication between all members of the community social service system. From this viewpoint the institution would act primarily as a facilitator, not as a principal sponsor or owner of the different resources.

The difficulty and complexity of this role necessitates assertive but circumspect leadership. It is conceivable that such a leadership posture could best be assumed by a new organization, created solely to spearhead this process. It is also conceivable that the agency, new or old, may not become involved with the creation of any definitive programs, choosing to concentrate, at least initially, on the development of a process. But regardless of the ultimate shape that the initiative assumes, the facilitating institution must be concerned with devising mechanisms for increasing consumer access to existing services, resolving intersystem conflicts, and ensuring that resources are allocated in response to the needs of this and/or other populations. It is quite possible that this would be only a provisional position; with the implementation of an effective intersystem process, the directorship role would be phased out.

Although collaborative projects like this one are intellectually seductive, they often require more extensive commitments to planning and oversight than do projects sponsored and owned by one system. Existing channels of communication must be identified and new ones developed; an information-processing system must be designed that encourages each system to contribute its resources to the project in a complementary, nonthreatening way; staff must be selected who are capable of functioning in linking, if not interface, roles; and periodic joint planning sessions between participating systems must be part of the commitment of each system from the planning through the execution and evaluation stages.

Yet these tasks pertain almost exclusively to the demands placed upon the cooperating agencies. They say nothing about the procedures for eliciting citizen involvement or the nature of their obligation. One method for integrating citizen participation into the ongoing operation of the network would be to establish a community board either prior to or during the first phase of the project. However, the mandate for citizen participation requires more than the formation of a community policymaking body; the mandate for serving the needs of single-parent families requires more than citizen participation. The achievement of both mandates calls for a board capable of playing a meaningful role in the planning *and* operation of the network, a role which, in this case, cannot be assumed unless the board members are aware of the needs and problems of separated and divorced families. Hence the determination of the board's composition is of considerable importance. The inclusion of individuals representative of the different areas of concern to this population (e.g., lawyers, accountants, bankers, psychiatrists) as well as interested residents (e.g., members of the target population) would, in effect, make the board a miniature network, with linkages to a variety of resources. Its very existence would constitute one mechanism for creating bonds between separated and divorced individuals and their community.[23] While initially the board might serve primarily in an advisory capacity, ideally its functions would be expanded to incorporate group involvement in the formulation of programs and eventually even to undertake responsibility for and ownership of the process.

SOME LAST WORDS ON NETWORKS

The development of a network for single-parent families could certainly be described as a concerted and broad-based effort to respond to the problems of this resident group. It could also be described as a high-risk undertaking. The task of redirecting priorities and restructuring the delivery of services in one system is in itself, as I have noted previously, a formidable job. But change strategies that depend upon coordinating the activities of many systems give rise to a whole new set of problems, some of which, at least in theory, appear insuperable. Further, and perhaps more significant, we cannot state with any degree of surety that a network would be an efficacious or even an appropriate approach to redressing the problems raised in this book. Indeed, by institutionalizing a functional delivery system for single-parent families we may inadvertently prolong this population's dependency upon its community. And, as Daniel Patrick Moynihan (1973) states, dependency has both negative connotations and repercussions.

This is not to say that dependent people are not brave, resourceful, admirable, but simply that their situation is never enviable, and rarely admired. It is an incomplete state in life: normal in the child, abnormal in the adult. In a world where completed men and women stand on their own feet, persons who are dependent—as the buried imagery of the word denotes—hang (p. 17).

Or, by increasing this population's visibility and publicizing their need for special services, we may create a milieu in which stigmatization is exacerbated. Alternatively, despite good intentions, evidence of inequities and unmet needs, and innovative problem-solving techniques, the venture may fail to produce the anticipated ends, either because of individual refusal to utilize these public resources or because in the interim changes in social climate and/or the installation of new services have rendered the network largely superfluous.

CONCLUSION

Although coping differences are often noticeable among those who initiate divorce proceedings, those who at least suspect a marital problem, and those who are caught unaware, all individuals report a need to reach out for support and help during separation and divorce. Even when individuals reach a point of adjustment in which they can initiate changes and make future plans independently, society's treatment of the separated and divorced often makes growth more difficult. The structured discriminations of social institutions and the more subtle biases of "friends," neighbors, and acquaintances cannot be stayed while individuals concentrate on reordering their personal lives, for the success or failure of these negotiations rebounds on their ability to cope. The problems encountered by single-parent families are not limited to a particular economic, social, geographic, or racial group.

Still, no singular solution is likely to resolve the needs of this population. Increased information, technology, and even concern may be an insufficient basis either for transforming the structure and function of social services or for expunging social prejudices toward those with uncoupled status. The very attitudes, values, and norms that shape society's priorities and goals may first have to undergo metamorphosis. For as long as separation and divorce are referred to as family breakdowns rather than as marriage breakdowns, as long as a family is conceptualized as two married adults and their children, and as long as remarriage is viewed as a return to a state of stability, we will continue to stigmatize those who separate and divorce. We will continue to look at single-parent families as incomplete units, not as an alternative form of family structure. We will continue to direct community support services primarily toward intact families, thereby proving that in heart and mind we support the "right" cause. And we will continue to fear that any intervention strategies and targeted policies will "desacralize" the institution of marriage and hasten its demise.

To break the cycle—a cycle which has fostered alienation and deprivation—should we champion the institutionalization of new services for separated and divorced individuals and their families? Should we champion the creation of new public policies and laws? The answer, my friends, is not "blowin' in the wind." Perhaps there is no answer, only different "truths" and different risks. If inaction has begotten injustice, is it not possible that the antithesis—a concerted public effort to redress wrongdoing—would, for different reasons and in different ways, also do harm? Instead of an intractable reliance upon formalized approaches to rectifying social problems, this may be the time for a reappraisal of our theories and methods. Instead of structuring solutions that encourage dependency upon society, we may need to consider alternative approaches that encourage individual responsibility and self-actualization. Indeed, the needs of this population may be crisis oriented. A population in a state of transition may be temporary and intermittent clients of community support services, not permanent and dependent victims of social disintegration.

NOTES

1. Nonetheless, this does not mean that Westside is a maverick among American communities or that the women with whom I spoke are anomalous to their sisters in other towns and states. The literature on divorce attests far more to the similarities than to the differences between this community and others, between these women and others.

2. Since self-help groups have initiated far more programs for separated and divorced individuals than have public agencies, this comparison is somewhat specious. Moreover, most public and private services have not established evaluation systems for measuring either their successes or failures. As a result there is a paucity of data to back up any assertions of success, although the literature is filled with citations from individual users affirming the superiority of self-help groups. What we are left with, then, is only a premise which posits that these groups have a better track record in taking care of their own.

3. We must remember that the 19th century played host to a women's movement that was, if anything, even more vitriolic in its criticism of society's treatment of its female population than is the present movement.

4. The number of recommendations which directly or indirectly speaks to the need for psychiatric services is especially noteworthy. Even in discussing the legal system, respondents repeatedly presented ideas which would necessitate the collaboration of the law and psychiatry. For example, to some, who decried the callousness and insouciance of their lawyers, the solution was to create a new form of legal practice in which a mental health professional and a lawyer would function as a team. And to others, who were less than satisfied with the performance of the judges who issued their decrees, the answer resided in a three-person team, one of whom would be a psychiatrist. I, however, hesitate to read too much into these and similar proposals. It is unclear whether the emotional texture of divorce leads

inevitably, or at least frequently, to the conclusion that therapeutic guidance or intervention is warranted or whether the connection between divorce and psychic trauma has come to be accepted as a scientific truth. The first emanates from personal need or the perception of need. The second is more complex, as it has less to do with the realities of divorce and more to do with the blanket acceptance that divorce and psychiatric maladjustment are intimately intertwined. The latter premise also suggests that the disturbance is not crisis oriented and thus short-lived but of a more profound nature.

5. This point is debatable, particularly if we use the supermarket analogy as a basis of comparison. Increasingly it is becoming obvious to intelligent consumers that the supermarket is not a bargain center. While many still depend on its services because it does offer convenience and saves time, they do so with the full awareness that they may not be saving money on at least some items and may in fact be paying a premium price for others.

6. While day care in the workplace is not a new idea, it is only recently that it has come back into vogue. By no means yet a widespread practice, there is evidence that it will continue to increase in popularity. In the Westside area there is already positive feedback from employers and employees that such operations have proved to be mutually advantageous. If they are less useful to parents with school-age children, they still service the preschool set, the population most difficult to obtain care for and the one whose mothers are entering the work force at a rate higher than any other group of working mothers.

7. Probably its best chances for materialization lie in the private sector, where some enterprising group or individual might see in this proposal an opportunity for profit. The financial success of divorce counseling agencies and divorce resource centers suggests that the same population that utilizes these services might also be attracted to a multipurpose facility.

8. While Health Maintenance Organizations (HMO) may be viewed as the most conspicuous example of a comprehensive agency which has, in a manner of speaking, made it, we cannot ignore the fact that the goals of HMO(s) are far more circumscribed, relating as they do exclusively to the delivery of health care. That various HMO(s) have succeeded in attracting a middle- and upper-middle class clientele may be attributable not only to their ability to offer quality medical care at a lower cost but to their dissociation from the stigma of clinics. However, it would take more than a leap of faith to draw an analogy between such health agencies and an umbrella agency created solely for separated and divorced families.

9. Perhaps stigmatization could be avoided or at least mitigated if services were targeted to a more general population (e.g., women, single parents, or even the community at large). If structured as an agency for all community residents as part of or in conjunction with an information-dissemination service, residents could avail themselves of only those services relevant to their own needs. (For example, the unemployed, married and single, might utilize the employment services.) Nevertheless, it is conceivable that by creating an agency with such a broad-based appeal, the demand for services would expand at a rate that would exceed the agency's capacity to provide help on any level. In a sense the problems experienced by the state employment service, referred to previously, would be reproduced on the local

level in all areas in which client demand and need were high. (We would, for instance, expect the agency to encounter difficulty in the areas of legal and therapeutic services.)

10. Another approach is through court-sponsored programs. Although existing projects (e.g., the Hennepin County Family Court in Minneapolis) are not currently designed as comprehensive service programs, their efforts to respond to at least some of the legal and psychosocial concerns of divorcing families are noteworthy. Through educational and therapeutic techniques they focus on individual patterns of coping, as well as interpersonal dynamics within the family setting. The objective is to make divorce a less debilitating experience by demystifying the divorce process and emphasizing constructuve adaptation to a marital dissolution. Some, like Benedek and Benedek (1979), believe that court-connected services have the most potential for providing divorcing families with comprehensive programs (pp. 161-163; 166-168).

11. Some groups have more limited goals, the most typical of which is the provision of social and psychological supports. Other women's groups have chosen to focus on different issues. For example, in 1972 the Women's Divorce Co-operative in Seattle, Washington, initiated a project to help women become more informed users of the legal system and even to represent themselves in court.

12. Although I have expressed reservations about the sponsorship of large-scale programs by support groups, noting both the limitations of group control and the negative attitudes of some respondents toward women's groups, in general I am more inclined to favor the management of services for the separated and divorced by such groups than by public agencies. If this is a personal bias, it is of recent origin. I began this study without any preconceived notions on the nature or function of women's groups and, in fact, did not have any familiarity with these groups either through personal contact or from other means.

13. Experimentation both inside and outside of institutional settings is to be considered. In addition, programs need not be designed solely to test the effectiveness of new ideas but also to better understand the problems affecting existing programs and institutions.

14. The following projects are a sampling of the recommendations of respondents, not a listing of untried innovations. Indeed, many of their proposals have already been suggested by others, and some have been put into practice with varying degrees of success. Moreover, inclusion of a suggestion should not be construed as a sign of *my* endorsement.

15. It is unrealistic to expect existing legal clinics to meet the needs of an expanded clientele. Too frequently such clinics are understaffed and unable to meet current demand for services, even with narrowly defined eligibility criteria. A more efficacious response would be for such services to assume increased responsibility for disseminating routine legal information and for referring consumers to appropriate resources. Staffing for the program might have to depend upon the use of law students and/or paralegal trainees enrolled in school-sponsored internships or practicums. (Note that these clinics target their services to the poor and are not to be confused with other so-called "legal clinics" which are open to the general public [see Chapter 2]).

16. In this context the term "paralegal" refers to an individual trained in both divorce counseling and domestic law. In all probability, this individual would be the first point of contact for people seeking legal counsel and would continue to function as a sort of middleman (sic) between the client and the lawyer, answering routine questions, explaining procedural steps, and, when necessary, providing support and comfort. This recommendation is regarded by some respondents as one way to alleviate the tension between lawyers and clients, while at the same time making legal services more responsive to individual needs.

17. There are essentially two ideas here: Postdivorce counseling refers to the use of therapeutic techniques for resolving interpersonal conflicts and problems. Arbitration is more specifically a strategy for resolving a particular issue of contention (e.g., custody, child support, visitation, alimony). It may, of course, also "educate" individuals on how to approach and resolve interpersonal problems, but it is neither fundamentally therapeutic in design nor educational in purpose.

18. While I know of others who wholeheartedly endorse such a venture, I am not among this group. The advantages to be gained from being part of a like population and having access to special services (e.g., day care, food cooperatives) seem insufficiently compelling to offset other problems inherent in this plan. In the final analysis, artificial environments may impede individual efforts to reintegrate themselves into the larger community. Thus by isolating a population we may foster not only stigmatization, but also encourage dependency and inaction. In a sense this compound is similar in concept to that of communities for the elderly. But unlike the elderly, who cannot be rejuvenated, single parents do not have to remain in a closed, protected environment. Their chances for growth far exceed the likelihood of progressive debilitation. Further, other experiences with project living (e.g., elderly, low-income housing) fail to furnish enough evidence of success to warrant the duplication of this model for other populations. (Indeed, many elderly citizens do not advocate communal enclaves, finding life in a mixed community to be more satisfying than that of a segregated one so long as the community provides supports and necessary services to meet their needs.)

19. For some of the ideas appearing in this section, I am indebted to my friend and colleague Barbara Ann Intrilligator. In 1975 she and I worked together to develop a proposal for a network of social services for single-parent families.

20. However, in the years 1975 through 1980, changes had occurred. In 1975 there was no public counseling agency that offered services to this population, but by 1979 even some of the more provincial counseling services had begun to organize support groups for separated and divorced women (notably not for men). While there has not been any dramatic shift in the delivery of services and the divorced have not yet been identified as a primary target for public resources, we still cannot ignore the changes which have occurred and others which appear to be in the offing.

21. In substance, the idea for a network could be classified under alternative delivery of professional services. But because of its comprehensive nature and intricate design, I have chosen to present this proposal separately. It should also be noted that I have, in considering this proposal, broken my oath*not to discuss reforms that require significant investments of time and money.

22. Although independent groups, like PWP and Women in Transition, may

ultimately succeed in impacting on the ways in which community agencies deliver services and fashion policies, the too early assumption of a leadership role would in all likelihood be met with resistance by public agencies who are, in general, suspicious of special interest groups.

23. This does not mean that group membership should be static; membership on the board or in specific task groups can vary in relationship to need requirements. In Bennis's (1969) definition of a problem-oriented task force, he envisions the group as being composed of "relative strangers who represent a diverse set of professional skills" and "evolve in response to a problem rather than to programmed role expectations" (p. 578).

APPENDIX A _____

RESEARCH METHODOLOGY[1]

The original intention was to select a sample of Westside women between 28 and 38 years of age with the following characteristics: Participants were separated pending divorce,[2] with two to three dependent children under age 18, with postsecondary education, and with former husbands of similar educational backgrounds. In addition, prior to separation all participants were to have lived in single-family residences and had joint family incomes ranging from $15,000 to $50,000. Specificity on age and education was determined largely by the decision to select a sample of whom Sheila Ash could be representative.

Preliminary canvassing of the community revealed only two Westside groups for separated and divorced women, both of which were affiliated with religious institutions. In order to recruit a larger sample, two organizations for single parents located in communities peripheral to Westside were identified. Initial contact was made with representatives of both organizations and permission was obtained to administer an information-generating questionnaire to their members. We also identified three informal support groups for separated and divorced individuals whose members were willing to participate in the study. Further, two attorneys, who were interested in the problems confronting individuals during separation and divorce, agreed to send questionnaires to some of their clients with a cover letter explaining the study as well as their own interest.

The content of the self-administered questionnaire was developed by researching the literature on separation and divorce. The questionnaire was then pretested on a group of 52 separated and divorced individuals.[3] The refined questionnaire was distributed by mail and in person to 431 individuals. The groups to whom questionnaires were distributed had the following limitations: First, group memberships were comprised of separated *and* divorced individuals; second, each attorney's clientele was biased by a required financial selectivity; and third, both informal and organized groups for the separated and divorced have a self-selection bias in their memberships. Although all field research studies have built-in biases, the size of the questionnaire population (250) enabled us to minimize experimental biases in the selection of a representative sample.

From the questionnaire sample 40 male and female respondents were identified as meeting the criteria specified for individual selection (see p. 293). Twenty-five women were interviewed.

Because interviewees were at different stages in the separation process, to make generalizations from interview data it was necessary to consider the length of time individuals had been separated as well as individual variations in coping with the transition from marriage to separation. Moreover, a comparison group of separated males was identified, but due to time constraints we were unable to extend our interviewing schedule to this group. Questionnaire data on selected males were, however, incorporated into the study.

Interviews were informal and open-ended. All interviews were tape-recorded and later transcribed. In this sample 21% of the participants were Roman Catholic, 39% were Protestant, and 40% were Jewish. (This parallels the religious distribution of Westside residents.) All participants were white. (Less than 1% of Westside is nonwhite.)

This initial study was conducted in a three-month period between March and May 1975.

NOTES

1. This exploratory project was conducted with a friend and colleague, Barbara Ann Intrilligator.

2. Legal terminology distinguishes between three possible dissolutions of the marital status: (1) A *legal separation* is obtained through the court; there are no additional proceedings for finalization by a divorce decree; (2) *separated pending divorce* is the initial decree (libel) prior to the finalization of divorce proceedings; (3) *divorce* is the final stage in the dissolution of the marriage and usually takes about one year in this state.

Annulment is another form of dissolution, but because its grounds depend upon "proof" of misrepresentation prior to marriage, it has not been included in the above list.

3. Since 21 of the 52 respondents were divorced, their questionnaire forms were eliminated from consideration.

APPENDIX B

QUESTIONNAIRE

1. Year of birth _____ 2. Sex: M   F

3. In what city or town do you live? _____

4. How many years have you lived there? _____

5. Circle last year of education completed.
   6, 7, 8, 9, 10, 11, 12; College 1, 2, 3, 4; Graduate work, 1, 2, 3, 4

   Other vocational education or training _____

6. What degrees, certificates, or licenses do you have? _____

   _____

7. How many years were you married? _____

   How many times were you married? _____

8. Are you presently?

   _____ separated pending divorce

   _____ legally separated

   _____ divorced

   _____ other

9. Number of children _____

10. Husband's/wife's profession _____

    Husband's/wife's age _____

    Husband's/wife's educational background _____

11. Personal data about children:

    a. _____   _____   _____   _____
       SEX   AGE   GRADE IN   PRIVATE/PUBLIC
                                 SCHOOL

b. _____   _____   _____   _____

c. _____   _____   _____   _____

d. _____   _____   _____   _____

e. _____   _____   _____   _____

12. Custodial arrangement: Please state who has custody of your children and describe the nature of the custodial arrangement: _____

_____

13. Family income prior to separation:

_____ under 5,000   _____ 30,000 to 35,000

_____ 5,000 to 10,000   _____ 35,000 to 40,000

_____ 10,000 to 15,000   _____ 40,000 to 45,000

_____ 15,000 to 20,000   _____ 45,000 to 50,000

_____ 20,000 to 25,000   _____ 50,000 and over

_____ 25,000 to 30,000

14. Do you receive child support?   _____ yes   _____ no

If yes, how much? _____

15. Current family income:

_____ under 5,000   _____ 30,000 to 35,000

_____ 5,000 to 10,000   _____ 35,000 to 40,000

_____ 10,000 to 15,000   _____ 40,000 to 45,000

_____ 15,000 to 20,000   _____ 45,000 to 50,000

_____ 20,000 to 25,000   _____ 50,000 and over

_____ 25,000 to 30,000

16. Do you have any additional personal income (check any)?

_____ employment

_____ inheritance

_____ personal savings

_____ personal investments

_____ other (please explain)

17. Has your financial status changed since separation?

_____ better

_____ same

_____ worse

18. Have you had any difficulty with (check any):

_____ purchasing power

_____ establishing credit

_____ maintaining credit

19. Are you planning to go or have you gone back to school?

_____   yes   _____   no

If yes, what kind of program? _____

If yes, what is the reason for returning to school?

_____ to meet new people

_____ to learn new skills

_____ to train for a particular occupation or profession

_____ leisure time activity

_____ other

20. Employment status:

_____ employed full-time

_____ employed part-time

_____ unemployed, seeking work

_____ unemployed

21. If not presently employed, state your last year of employment.

_____

22. Please list current or previous employment:

a. _____

   Job title/Occupation   skills

   _____

   Length of employment   location

b. _____

   _____

c. _____

   _____

23. Are you seeking _____ full   _____ part-time employment now?

If yes, what kind? _____

24. In seeking employment, have you used (check any):

_____ job placement services

_____ training programs

_____ on-the-job training or retraining

_____ friends

_____ newspaper classified

_____ other aids (please explain) _____

_____

25. Do you have any of the following employment-related problems?

_____ transportation

_____ babysitting, day care

_____ children's schooling

_____ housekeeping

_____ health

_____ other (please explain) _____

_____

26. If you have any of these employment-related problems, please list the agencies which have been helpful:

a. _____ I have _____ have not used any agencies

b. If transportation, _____
   NAME

c. If child care, _____
   NAME

d. If children's schooling, _____
   NAME

e. If housekeeping, _____
   NAME

f. If health, _____
   NAME

g. If other, _____
   NAME

27. Change in residence:

a. Have you moved since your separation or divorce?

_____ yes _____ no

If yes, please explain: _____

_____

  b. Have your children changed schools? _____ yes _____ no

    If yes, is the reason related to the move? _____

    Other reason _____

28. Have you or your children received support from (please specify whether for you or your children):

  _____ clergy

  _____ family physician

  _____ psychiatrist

  _____ psychologist

  _____ social worker

  _____ attorney

  _____ personal friend(s)

  _____ family

  _____ neighbors

  _____ others, specify _____

29. Have you had difficulty in maintaining relationships with:

  _____ family

  _____ friends

  _____ children

  _____ neighbors

  _____ employers

  _____ coworkers

  _____ storekeepers

  _____ ex-spouses

  _____ others, specify _____

30. Have your children had difficulty maintaining relationships with:

  _____ school friends

  _____ relatives

  _____ neighbors

  _____ noncustodial parent

  _____ stepparent

  _____ siblings

  _____ teachers

  _____ others, specify _____

31. Which of the following areas have you found most difficult to handle during your separation or divorce (check and order)?

_____ housing

_____ employment

_____ meeting new people

_____ child care

_____ legal problems

_____ adjustment (personal)

_____ relationship with children

_____ identifying community resources

_____ other, specify

_____ other, specify

_____ other, specify

32. Would you be available for a personal interview? We will ensure confidentiality and anonymity. _____ yes _____ no

If yes, please give your telephone number _____

APPENDIX C

ANNOTATED LAWS OF _____

C. 151B

§4. Unlawful Practices

[No change in opening paragraph.]

[Subsection 1 is amended to read as follows:]

1. For an employer, by himself or his agent, because of the race, color, religious creed, national origin, sex, age, or ancestry of any individual, to refuse to hire or employ or to bar or to discharge from employment such individual or to discriminate against such individual in compensation or in terms, conditions or privileges of employment, unless based upon a bona fide occupational qualification. (Amended by 1965, 397, § 4, approved May 3, 1965, effective 90 days thereafter.)

[The following subsection is added:]

1A. It shall be unlawful discriminatory practice for an employer to impose upon an individual as a condition of obtaining or retaining employment any terms or conditions, compliance with which would require such individual to violate, or forego the practice of, his creed or religion as required by that creed or religion including but not limited to the observance of any particular day or days or any portion thereof as a sabbath or holy day and the employer shall make reasonable accommodation to the religious needs of such individual. No individual who has given notice as hereinafter provided shall be required to remain at his place of employment during any day or days or portion thereof that, as a requirement of his religion, he observes as his sabbath or other holy day, including a reasonable time prior and subsequent thereto for travel between his place of employment and his home, provided, however, that any employee intending to be absent from work when so required to his or her creed or religion shall notify his or her employer not less than ten days in advance of each absence, and that any such absence from work shall, wherever practicable in the judgment of the employer, be made up by an equivalent amount of time at some other mutually convenient time. Nothing under this subsection shall be deemed to require an employer to compensate an employee for such absence. "Reasonable Accommodation", as used in this subsection shall mean such accommodation to an employee's or prospective employee's religious observance or practice as shall not cause undue hardship in the conduct of the employer's business. The employee shall have the burden of proof as to the required practice of his creed or religion.

Undue hardship, as used herein, shall include the inability of an employer to provide services which are required by and in compliance with all federal and state laws, including regulations or tariffs promulgated or required by any regulatory agency having jurisdiction over such services or where the health or safety of the public would be unduly compromised by the absence of such employee or employees, or where the employee's presence is indispensable to the orderly transaction of business and his or her work cannot be performed by another employee of substantially similar qualifications during the period of absence, or where the employee's presence is needed to alleviate an emergency situation. The employer shall have the burden of proof to show undue hardship. (Added by 1973, 929, approved Oct. 17, 1973, effective 90 days thereafter.)

[Subsection 2 is amended to read as follows:]

2. For a labor organization, because of the race, color, religious creed, national origin, sex, age, or ancestry of any individual to exclude from full membership rights or to expel from its membership such individual or to discriminate in any way against any of its members or against any employer or any individual employed by an employer, unless based upon a bona fide occupational qualification. (Amended by 1965, 397, § 5, approved May 3, 1965, effective 90 days thereafter.)

[Subsection 3 is amended to read as follows:]

3. For any *employer or employment agency** to print or circulate or cause to be printed or circulated any statement, advertisement or publication, or to use any form of application for employment or to make any inquiry or record in connection with employment, which expresses, directly or indirectly, any limitation, specification or discrimination as to race, color, religious creed, *national origin, sex, age, or ancestry* or any intent to make any such limitation, specification or discrimination, or to discriminate in any way on the ground of race, color, religious creed, national origin, sex, age, or ancestry, *unless based upon a bona fide occupational qualification*. (Amended by 1965, 397, § 6, approved May 3, 1965, effective 90 days thereafter.)

3A. For any person engaged in the *insurance* or *bonding business*, or his agent, to make any inquiry or record of any person seeking a bond or surety bond conditioned upon the faithful performance of his duties or to use any form of application, in connection with the furnishing of such bond, which seeks information relative to the race, color, religious creed, national origin, sex or ancestry of the person to be bonded. (Amended by 1971, 874, § 1, approved Oct. 13, 1971, effective 90 days thereafter.)

3B. For any person engaged in the *business of granting mortgage loans* to discriminate against any person in the granting of any mortgage loans, including but not limited to the interest rate, terms or duration of such mortgage loan, because of his race, color, religious creed, national origin, sex, or ancestry. (Amended by 1971, 874, § 2, approved Oct. 13, 1971, effective 90 days thereafter.)

[No change through subsection 5.]

---

*Italics have been added by the author.

[Subsection 6 is amended to read as follows:]

6. *For the owner, lessee, sublessee, licensed real estate broker, assignee, or managing agent of publicly assisted or multiple dwelling or continuously located housing accommodations* or other person having the right of ownership or possession or right to rent or lease, or sell or negotiate for the sale of such accommodations, or any agent or employee of such a person:—*(a) to refuse to rent or lease or sell or negotiate for sale* or otherwise to deny to or withhold from any person or group of persons such accommodations because of the race, religious creed, color, national origin, *sex, age, ancestry or marital status* of such person or persons or because such person is a veteran or a member of the armed forces, or because such person is blind; *(b)* to discriminate against any person because of his race, religious creed, color, national origin, sex, age, ancestry or marital status or because such person is a veteran or a member of the armed forces or because such person is blind in the terms, conditions or privileges of such accommodations or the acquisitions thereof, or in the furnishing of facilities and services in connection therewith; or *(c)* to cause to be made any written or oral inquiry or record concerning the race, religious creed, color, national origin, sex, age, ancestry or marital status of the person seeking to rent or lease or buy any such accommodation, or concerning the fact that such person is a veteran or a member of the armed forces or because such person is blind. The word ''age'' as used in this subsection shall not apply to persons who are minors nor to residency in state-aided or federally-aided housing developments for the elderly nor to residency in self-contained retirement communities constructed expressly for use by the elderly and which are at least twenty acres in size and have a minimum age requirement for residency of at least fifty-five years. (Amended by 1969, 90, approved March 19, 1969, effective 90 days thereafter; 1971, 661, approved August 12, 1971, effective 90 days thereafter; 1972, 185, approved April 20, 1972, effective 90 days thereafter; 1973, 187, § 1, approved Apr. 17, 1973, effective 90 days thereafter; 1973, 1015, § 1, approved Nov. 8, 1973, effective 90 days thereafter.)

[Subsection 7 is amended to read as follows:]

7. For the *owner, lessee, sublessee,* real estate broker, assignee or managing agent of other *covered housing* accommodations or of land intended for the erection of any housing accommodation included under subsections 10, 11, 12 or 13 of section one, or other persons having the right of ownership or possession or right to rent or lease, or sell, or negotiate for the sale or lease of such land or accommodations, or any agent or employee of such a person:—*(a) to refuse to rent or lease or sell* or negotiate for sale or lease or otherwise to deny to or withhold from any person or group of persons such accommodations or land because of the race, color, religious creed, national origin, sex, age, *ancestry or marital status* of such person or persons; *(b)* to discriminate against any person because of his race, color, religious creed, national origin, sex, age, ancestry or marital status in the terms, conditions or privileges of such accommodations or land or the acquisition thereof, or in the furnishing of facilities and services in connection therewith; or *(c)* to cause to be made any written or oral inquiry or record concerning the race, color, religious creed, national origin, sex, age, ancestry or marital status of the person seeking to rent or lease or buy any such accommodation or land; provided, however, that this subsection shall not apply to the leasing of a single apartment or flat in a two family dwelling, the other occupancy unit of which is occupied by the owner as his resi-

dence. The word "age" as used in this subsection shall not apply to persons who are minors, nor to residency in state-aided or federally-aided housing developments for the elderly nor to residency in self-contained retirement communities constructed expressly for use by the elderly and which are at least twenty acres in size and have a minimum age requirement for residency of at least fifty-five years. (Amended by 1971, 661, approved August 12, 1971, effective 90 days thereafter; 1973, 187, § 2, approved Apr. 17, 1973, effective 90 days thereafter; 1973, 1015, § 2, approved Nov. 8, 1973, effective 90 days thereafter.)

[The following subsections are added:]

8. For the owner, lessee, sublessee, or managing agent of, or other person having the right of ownership or possession of or the right to sell, rent or lease, *commercial space*: (1) To refuse to sell, rent, lease or otherwise deny to or withhold from any person or group of persons such commercial space because of the race, color, religious creed, national origin, *sex, age, ancestry or marital status* of such persons or persons. (2) To discriminate against any person because of his race, color, religious creed, national origin, *sex, age, ancestry or marital status* in the terms, conditions or privileges of the sale, rental or lease of any such commercial space or in the furnishing of facilities or services in connection therewith. (3) To cause to be made any written or oral inquiry or record concerning the race, color, religious creed, national origin, sex, age, ancestry or marital status of a person seeking to rent or lease or buy any such commercial space. The word "age" as used in this subsection shall not apply to persons who are minors, nor to residency in state-aided or federally-aided housing developments for the elderly nor to residency in self-contained retirement communities constructed expressly for use by the elderly and which are at least twenty acres in size and have a minimum age requirement for residency of at least fifty-five years. (Added by 1965, 213, § 2, approved March 29, 1965, effective 90 days thereafter; amended by 1971, 661, approved August 12, 1971, effective 90 days thereafter; 1973, 187, § 3, approved Apr. 17, 1973, effective 90 days thereafter; 1973, 1015, § 3, approved Nov. 8, 1973, effective 90 days thereafter.)

9. For an employer, himself or through his agent, in connection with an application for employment, or the terms, conditions, or privileges of employment, or the transfer, promotion, bonding, or discharge of any person, or in any other matter relating to the employment of any person, to request any information, to make or keep a record of such information, to use any form of application or application blank which requests such information, or to exclude, limit, or otherwise discriminate against any person by reason of his or her failure to furnish such information through a written application or oral inquiry or otherwise regarding: *(i)* an arrest, detention, or disposition regarding any violation of law in which no conviction resulted, or *(ii)* a first conviction for any of the following misdemeanors: drunkenness, simple assault, speeding, minor traffic violations, affray, or disturbance of the peace, or *(iii)* any conviction of a misdemeanor where the date of such conviction or the completion of any period of incarceration resulting therefrom, whichever date is later, occurred five or more years prior to the date of such application for employment or such request for information, unless such person has been convicted of any offense within five years immediately preceding the date of such application for employment or such request for information.

No person shall be held under any provision of any law to be guilty of perjury or of otherwise giving a false statement by reason of his failure to recite or acknowledge such information as he has a right to withhold by this subsection.

Nothing contained herein shall be construed to affect the application of section thirty-four of chapter ninety-four C, or of chapter two hundred and seventy-six relative to the sealing of records. (Added by 1969, 314, approved May 19, 1969, effective 90 days thereafter; amended by 1972, 428, approved June 15, 1972, effective 90 days thereafter; 1974, 531, approved July 12, 1974, effective 90 days thereafter.)

9A. For an employer himself or through his agent to refuse, unless based upon a bonafide occupational qualification, to hire or employ or to bar or discharge from employment any person by reason of his or her failure to furnish information regarding his or her admission, on one or more occasions, voluntarily or involuntarily, to any public or private facility for the care and treatment of mentally ill persons, provided that such person has been discharged from such facility or facilities and can prove by a psychiatrist's certificate that he is mentally competent to perform the job or the job for which he is applying. No application for employment shall contain any questions or requests for information regarding the admission of an applicant, on one or more occasions, voluntarily or involuntarily, to any public or private facility for the care and treatment of mentally ill persons, provided that such applicant has been discharged from such public or private facility or facilities and is no longer under treatment directly related to such admission. (Added by 1973, 701, § 1, approved Aug. 27, 1973; by § 2 it takes effect Jan. 1, 1974.)

10. For any person furnishing credit, services or renting accommodations to discriminate against any individual who is a recipient of federal, state or local public assistance, including medical assistance, or who is a tenant receiving federal, state or local housing subsidies, including rental assistance or rent supplements, solely because the individual is such a recipient. (Added by 1971, 726, approved August 31, 1971, effective 90 days thereafter.)

11. For the owner, sublessee, real estate broker, assignee or managing agent of publicly assisted or multiple dwelling or contiguously located housing accommodations, or other person having the right of ownership or possession or right to rent or lease such accommodations, or any agent or employee of such a person, to refuse to rent or lease or otherwise to deny to or withhold from any person such accommodations because such person *has a child or children* who shall occupy the leased or rented premises with such person; provided, however, that this subsection shall not apply to dwellings containing three apartments or less, one of which apartments is occupied by an elderly or infirm person for whom the presence of children would constitute a hardship. For the purposes of this subsection an "elderly person" shall mean a person sixty-five years of age or over, and an "infirm person" shall mean a person who is disabled or suffering from a chronic illness. (Added by 1971, 874, § 3, approved Oct. 13, 1971, effective 90 days thereafter.)

11A. For an employer, by himself or his agent, to refuse to restore certain female employees to employment following their absence by reason of a maternity leave taken in accordance with section one hundred and five D of chapter one hundred and forty-nine or to otherwise fail to comply with the provisions of said section.

(Added by 1972, 790, § 2, approved July 19, 1972, effective 90 days thereafter.)

12. For any retail store which provides credit or charge account privileges to refuse to extend such privileges to a customer solely because said customer had attained age sixty-two or over. (Added by 1972, 542, approved June 29, 1972, effective 90 days thereafter.)

13. For any person to directly or indirectly induce, attempt to induce, prevent, or attempt to prevent the sale, purchase, or rental of any dwelling or dwellings by:

a) implicit or explicit representations regarding the entry or prospective entry into the neighborhood of a person or persons of a particular age, race, color, religion, national or ethnic origin, or economic level, or implicit or explicit representations regarding the effects or consequences of any such entry or prospective entry;

b) unrequested contact or communication with any person or persons, initiated by any means, for the purpose of so inducing or attempting to induce the sale, purchase, or rental of any dwelling or dwellings when he knew or, in the exercise of reasonable care, should have known that such unrequested solicitation would reasonably be associated by the persons solicited with the entry into the neighborhood of a person or persons of a particular age, race, color, religion, national or ethnic origin, or economic level;

c) implicit or explicit false representations regarding the availability of suitable housing within a particular neighborhood or area, or failure to disclose or offer to show all properties listed or held for sale or rent within a requested price or rental range, regardless of location; or

d) false representations regarding the listings, prospective listing, sale, or prospective sale of any dwelling. (Added by 1972, 786, §2, approved, with emergency preamble, July 19, 1972, effective 90 days thereafter.)

14. *For any person furnishing credit or services to deny or terminate such credit* or services or to adversely affect an individual's credit standing because of such *individual's sex or marital status.*

Any person who violates the provisions of this subsection shall be liable in an action of contract for actual damages; provided, however, that, if there are no actual damages, the court may assess special damages to the aggrieved party not to exceed one thousand dollars; and provided further, that any person who has been found to violate a provision of this subsection by a court of competent jurisdiction shall be assessed the cost of reasonable legal fees actually incurred. (Added by 1973, 168, approved and effective by act of Governor, Apr. 11, 1973; amended by 1973, 325, approved May 29, 1973, effective 90 days thereafter.)

[No change in balance of section as appearing in bound volume.]

[The two following paragraphs are added:]

Notwithstanding the foregoing provisions of this section, *(a)* every employer, every employment agency, including the division of employment security of the department of labor and industries, and every labor organization shall make and keep such records relating to race, color or national origin as the commission may prescribe from time to time by rule or regulation, after public hearing, as reasonably necessary for the purpose of showing compliance with the requirements of this chapter, and *(b)* every employer and labor organization may keep and maintain such records and make such reports as may from time to time be necessary to comply, or show compliance with, any executive order issued by the President of the

United States or any rules or regulations issued thereunder prescribing fair employ- ment practices for contractors and subcontractors under contract with the United States, or, if not subject to such order, in the manner prescribed therein and subject to the jurisdiction of the commission. Such requirements as the commission may, by rule or regulation, prescribe for the making and keeping of records under clause *(a)* shall impose no greater burden or requirement on the employer, em- ployment agency or labor organization subject thereto, than the comparable re- quirements which could be prescribed by Federal rule or regulation so long as no such requirements have in fact been prescribed, or which have in fact been pre- scribed for an employer, employment agency or labor organization under the authority of the Civil Rights Act of 1964, from time to time amended. This para- graph shall apply only to employers who on each working day in each of twenty or more calendar weeks in the annual period ending with each date set forth below, employed more employees than the number set forth beside such date, and to labor organizations which have more members on each such working day during such period.

Period Ending	Minimum Employees or Members
June 30, 1965	100
June 30, 1966	75
June 30, 1967	50
June 30, 1968 and thereafter	25

(Added by 1966, 361, approved June 9, 1966, effective, by act of Governor, July 13, 1966.)

Nothing contained in this chapter or in any rule or regulation issued by the commission shall be interpreted as requiring any employer, employment agency or labor organization to grant preferential treatment to any individual or to any group because of the race, color, religious creed, national origin, sex, age or ancestry of such individual or group because of imbalance which may exist between the total number or percentage of persons employed by any employer, referred or classified for employment by any employment agency or labor organization, admitted to membership or classified by any labor organization or admitted to or employed in, any apprenticeship or other training program, and the total number or per- centage of persons of such race, color, religious creed, national origin, sex, age or ancestry in the ——— or in any community, section or other area therein, or in the available work force in the ——— or in any of its political subdivisions. (Added by 1966, 361, approved June 9, 1966, effective, by act of Governor, July 13, 1966.)

APPENDIX D_____

RÉSUMÉ

Sheila Ash

26 Barron Road   Date of Birth: May 15, 1942
City, State (zip code)[1]   Telephone: _____

EDUCATION
9/60-6/64   • *UNIVERSITY OF MICHIGAN,
                            ANN ARBOR*
                            Received Bachelor's degree in June, 1964.
                            Majored in Elementary Education with a
                            minor concentration in English. Graduated
                            cum laude. Elected to Kappa Delta Pi, Edu-
                            cational Honor Fraternity.

9/56-6/60   • *MARTIN VAN BUREN HIGH SCHOOL,
                            QUEENS, NEW YORK*
                            Academic program with honors. Graduated
                            with a 91% average. Active on school news-
                            paper, yearbook, and student council.

EXPERIENCE
9/65-6/68   • *LES ENFANTS NURSERY SCHOOL,
                            CITY, STATE*
                            Taught three- and four-year-olds. Attempted
                            to incorporate philosophy of open classroom
                            with special learning characteristics of this
                            age group.

9/64-6/65   • *P.S. 109, NEW YORK, NEW YORK*
                            Taught grade two. Instituted program utiliz-
                            ing audiovisual aids in the instruction of
                            reading and creative writing. Individualized
                            mathematics and spelling program.

ADDITIONAL EXPERIENCE

- Tutored children with learning disabilities
- Supervised volunteer workers for local charity drives
- Coordinated political campaigns for local candidates
- Organized children's play group
- Assisted in planning and initiating outreach center for school dropouts
- Sold advertising space for local newspaper

INTERESTS AND HOBBIES

- Art—Amateur showing at local community center
- Sports—Bowling team, golf, swimming, tennis
- Travel

PERSONAL DATA[2]

Two children: Peter (July 1, 1969)
Laurie (August 21, 1972)

---

1. For publication, all cititations of city and state as well as the name of the nursery school where Sheila worked have been deleted or coded.

2. It is no longer standard practice to list information on family, marital status, etc.

APPENDIX E

UNSOLICITED LETTER OF INQUIRY[1]

26 Barron Road
City, State (zip code)
April 1, 1975

_____, Inc.
Office of Personnel
20 Walnut Street
City, State (zip code)

Gentlemen:

I am an intelligent and sensitive individual who is ready to resume a professional career. I am writing to you because I think that your company might provide me with the opportunity to develop a creative position. My skills in planning, administration, and teaching are applicable to a variety of settings within your company.

My background in education and English as well as my active roles in community organization would qualify me for job openings in editing, curriculum development and innovation, and public relations.

Due to family responsibilities, I am presently interested in a part-time position. However, I would anticipate this becoming a full-time commitment within a year.

I am available for a personal interview at your convenience. My résumé is enclosed and references will be sent upon request.

Thank you for your consideration. I look forward to hearing from you.

Sincerely yours,
Sheila Ash

---

1. This is one of several letters used for Sheila's job search.

APPENDIX F

RESPONSE LETTER[1]

May 5, 1975

Ms. Sheila Ash
26 Barron Road
City, State (zip code)

Dear Ms. Ash:

Thank you for your recent reply to our advertisement for the position of Director of Development.

An unusually large number of individuals have responded, many with impressive credentials. Since it is not possible for us to interview every applicant personally, it has been necessary for us to select for further consideration only a few individuals who are especially qualified.

We have reviewed your application carefully and find that your experience and qualifications do not meet our requirements as closely as a number of others.

We appreciate your interest in writing to us and wish you success in finding a position that will fulfill your objectives.

Sincerely,

Name
Director of Personnel

AN INDEPENDENT NONPROFIT EDUCATIONAL INSTITUTION

---

1. This letter has been retyped in order to delete all identifying material on institution and individual respondent.

APPENDIX G ———————————

RESPONSE LETTER[1]

April 9, 1975

Ms. Sheila Ash
26 Barron Road
City, State (zip code)

Dear Ms. Ash:

Thank you for your recent letter. I am sorry to say that we rarely have positions suitable for someone with teaching background, since _____ does not publish elementary or high school texts.

May I suggest that you look in your library for *Literary Market Place*, a directory of publishing which lists American publishers and their areas of specialization. It may lead you to the publishers who do draw on teaching experience.

We wish you quick success finding a position to your liking.

Sincerely,

Name
Personnel Department

---

1. This letter has been retyped in order to delete all identifying material on publishing company and individual respondent.

BIBLIOGRAPHY

Bibliographical citations marked with an asterisk have been altered to protect the anonymity of the community. The author will provide reference data upon request.

Addeo, Edmond, and Burger, Robert. *Inside Divorce: Is it Really What You Want?* Radnor, PA: Chilton, 1975.

Albrecht, Stan L. "Reactions and Adjustments to Divorce: Differences in the Experiences of Males and Females." *Family Relations* 29:1 (January 1980): 59-68.

Alexander, Franz G., and Selesnick, Sheldon. *The History of Psychiatry*. New York: Harper and Row, 1966; reprint edition, New York: New American Library, Mentor Books, 1966.

Alter, Eleanor. Quoted in Daniel D. Molinoff, "Life With Father." *New York Times Magazine*, 22 May 1977, p. 17.

Anthony, E. James. "Children at Risk from Divorce: A Review." In *The Child in His Family: Children at Psychiatric Risk*, vol. 3, pp. 461-477. Edited by E. James Anthony and Cyrille Koupernik. New York: Wiley, 1974.

*Auerback, Susan. "Private Day Care Offers Nine to Five Mom." *The Westside Times*, 19 March 1975, pp. 1, 10.

Baguedor, Eve. *Separation: Journal of a Marriage*. New York: Warner, 1972.

Bahr, Stephen J. "The Effects of Welfare on Marital Stability and Remarriage." *Journal of Marriage and the Family* 41:3 (August 1979): 553-560.

Bane, Mary Jo. *Here to Stay: American Families in the Twentieth Century*. New York: Basic, 1976a.

———. "Marital Disruption and the Lives of Children." *Journal of Social Issues* 32:1 (1976b): 103-107.

Baum, Charlotte. "The Best of Both Parents." *New York Times Magazine*, 31 October 1976, pp. 44-48.

Beck, Rochelle. "The White House Conference on Children: An Historical Perspective." *Harvard Educational Review* 43:4 (November 1973): 653-668.

Benedek, Elissa P., and Bieniek, C. M. "Interpersonal Process Recall: An Innovative Technique." *Journal of Medical Education* 52 (1977): 939-941.

Benedek, Richard S., and Benedek, Elissa P. "Children of Divorce: Can We Meet Their Needs?" *Journal of Social Issues* 35:4 (1979): 155-169.

Bennis, Warren G. "Changing Organizations." In *The Planning of Change*, 2nd edition, pp. 568-579. Edited by Warren G. Bennis, Kenneth D. Benne, and Robert Chin. New York: Holt, Rinehart and Winston, 1969.

Benzaquin, Paul. "Female Divorce Lawyer Enjoys Her Work." *Boston Sunday Globe*, 7 December 1975, p. E5.

Bloom, B. L., Asher, S. J., and White, S. W. "Marital Disruption as a Stressor: A Review and Analysis." *Psychological Bulletin* 85 (1978): 867-894.

Blum, Sam. "The Re-Mating Game." *New York Times Magazine*, 29 August 1976, pp. 10-11, 16, 18, 20, 22.

Bodenheimer, Brigitte M. "The Rights of Children and the Crisis in Custody Litigation: Modification of Custody In and Out of State." *University of Colorado Law Review* 46 (1975): 495-508.

Bohannan, Paul, ed. *Divorce and After: An Analysis of the Emotional and Social Problems of Divorce*. Garden City, NY: Doubleday, 1970; Anchor, 1971.

_____. "Some Thoughts on Divorce Reform." In *Divorce and After: An Analysis of the Emotional and Social Problems of Divorce*, pp. 283-299. Edited by Paul Bohannan. Garden City, NY: Doubleday, 1970; Anchor, 1971.

Bradbury, Katherine; Danziger, Sheldon; Smolensky, Eugene; and Smolensky, Paul. "Public Assistance—Female Headship and Economic Well-Being." *Journal of Marriage and the Family* 41:3 (August 1979): 519-535.

Brandwein, Ruth A., Brown, Carol A., and Fox, Elizabeth Maury. "Women and Children Last: The Social Situation of Divorced Mothers and Their Families." *Journal of Marriage and the Family* 36:3 (August 1974): 498-532.

Brozan, Nadine. "Personal Side to Single-Parent Issues." *New York Times*, 27 June 1980a, p. A20.

_____. "Women Now Hold 30 Percent of 2d Jobs." *New York Times*, 24 June 1980b, p. B6.

Caldwell, Jean. "Displaced Homemaker's Plight." *Boston Globe*, 7 January 1980, pp. 13, 15.

Campbell, A., Converse, P. E., and Rodgers, W. *The Quality of American Life: Perceptions, Evaluations and Satisfactions*. New York: Sage, 1976.

Carter, Hugh, and Glick, Paul C. *Marriage and Divorce: A Social and Economic Study*. Cambridge, MA: Harvard University Press, 1976.

Cassetty, J. *Child Support and Public Policy: Securing Support from Absent Fathers*. Lexington, MA: Heath, 1978.

Cerra, Frances. "Helping Unemployed Teachers Make a New Start." *New York Times*, 15 March 1980a, p. 16.

_____. "Study Finds College Women Still Aim for Traditional Jobs." *New York Sunday Times*, 11 May 1980b, p. 46.

Chambers, David L., and Adams, T. K. *Making Fathers Pay: The Enforcement of Child Support*. Chicago, IL: University of Chicago Press, 1979.

Chesler, Phyllis, and Goodman, Emily Jane. *Women, Money and Power*. New York: William Morrow, 1976.

Chin, Robert, and Benne, Kenneth D. "General Strategies for Effecting Changes in Human Systems." In *The Planning of Change*, 2nd edition, pp. 32-57. Edited by Warren G. Bennis, Kenneth D. Benne, and Robert Chin. New York: Holt, Rinehart and Winston, 1969.

Chiriboga, D. A., and Cutler, L. "Stress Responses Among Divorcing Men and Women." *Journal of Divorce* 1:2 (1977): 95-106.

Christensen, Kathryn. "Business Bias Bands Those Outside 'Norm' All Together." *Boston Globe*, 26 May 1976, p. 2.

Cohen, Richard. "Fog at the Scene of the Crime." *Boston Globe*, 16 June 1980, p. 14.

Cole, K. C. "The Travails of a Part-Time Stepparent." *New York Times*, 14 May 1980, p. 61.

Corbett, Mary Ellen. "Ageism Problem Realized." *Herald Advertiser*, 25 August 1975, p. A31.

Dancey, Elizabeth (pseud.). "Who Gets the Kids." *Ms*, September 1976, pp. 70-85.

Degler, Carl. *At Odds: Women and the Family in America From the Revolution to the Present*. New York: Oxford University Press, 1980.

Derdeyn, Andre P. "Child Custody Consultation." *American Journal of Orthopsychiatry* 45:5 (October 1975): 791-801.

———. "A Consideration of Legal Issues in Child Custody Contests." *Archives of General Psychiatry* 33 (February 1976): 165-171.

Dewan, George. "Women Lag in Getting Credit in Their Own Names." *Boston Globe*, 10 April 1978, p. 33.

Dietz, Jean. "Women Bankers Seek Freedom." *Boston Globe*, 13 February 1976, p. 32.

"The Divorce Experience." A program developed by Hennepin County Family Court Services, Minneapolis, MN.

"Divorced Father Is Told to Keep Dates or Pay." *New York Sunday Times*, 25 November 1979, p. 28.

Dodd v. Dodd (pseud.). *New York Law Journal*, February 27, 1978, p. 13.

Donzelot, Jacques. *The Policing of Families*. Translated by Robert Hurley. New York: Pantheon, 1980.

Downey, C. E. "A Way to Afford Your Day in Court." *Money*, August 1975, pp. 79-82.

Droppler, George F. *America Needs Total Divorce Reform—Now!* New York: Vantage, 1973.

Dullea, Georgia. "A Disco for Singles—and Their Children." *New York Sunday Times*, 12 March 1978, p. 62.

———. "For Women It's Being There." *New York Times*, 20 June 1980a, p. A18.

———. "Is Joint Custody Good for Children?" *New York Times Magazine*, 3 February 1980b, pp. 32-37, 40, 46.

Duncliffe, Bill. "Hapless Children of Broken Marriages: How Do They Cope?" *Boston Herald American*, 9, 10, 11, 12, 13, 14 May 1976.

Eckhardt, Kenneth W. "Deviance, Visibility and Legal Action: The Duty to Support." *Social Problems* 15:4 (1968): 470-477.

Ehrlich, Thomas. "Legal Pollution." *New York Times Magazine*, 8 February 1976, pp. 17-24.

Ellsworth, P. E., and Levy, Robert J. "Legislative Reform of Child Custody Adjudication: An Effort to Rely on Social Science Data in Formulating Legal Policies." *Law and Society Review* 4 (1969): 167-233.

Espenshade, Thomas J. "The Economic Consequences of Divorce." *Journal of Marriage and the Family* 41:3 (August 1979): 615-625.

Farrell, David. "Liberated Husbands Nicking State for $50 Million a Year." *Boston Sunday Globe*, 19 December 1976, p. A5.

Felder, Raoul L. *Divorce: The Way Things Are, Not the Way Things Should Be.* New York: World Publishing, 1971.

Ferris, Abbott. *Indicators of Trends in the Status of Women.* New York: Russell Sage Foundation, 1971.

Fisher, Ester O. *Divorce: The New Freedom: A Guide to Divorcing and Divorce Counseling.* New York: Harper and Row, 1974.

Fitzgerald, R. V. *Conjoint Marital Therapy.* New York: Jason Aronson, 1973.

Foote, Caleb, Levy, Robert J., and Sander, Frank E. A. *Cases and Materials on Family Law*, 1st edition. Boston, MA: Little, Brown and Company, 1966.

———. *Cases and Materials on Family Law*, 2nd edition. Boston, MA: Little, Brown and Company, 1976.

Foreman, Judy. "Helping Divorcees to Cope...." *Boston Sunday Globe*, 19 November 1978a, p. B7.

———. "Recovering From the Trauma of Divorce." *Boston Sunday Globe*, 19 November 1978b, pp. B1, B7.

Foster, Henry H., Jr. *A "Bill of Rights" for Children.* Springfield, IL: Charles C. Thomas, 1974.

Foster, Henry H., Jr., and Freed, Doris J. "Divorce Reform: Breaks on Breakdown." *Journal of Family Law* 13:3 (1973-1974): 443-493.

Fox, W. "Alimony, Property Settlement, and Child Custody Under The New Divorce Statutes: No-Fault Is Not Enough." *Catholic University Law Review* 22 (1973): 365-384.

Francke, Linda Bird; Sherman, Diane; Simons, Pamela Ellis; Abramson, Pamela; Zabarsky, Marsha; Huck, Janet; and Whitman, Lisa. "The Children of Divorce." *Newsweek*, February 11, 1980, pp. 58-59, 61-63.

Franklin, James L. "Methodist Handbook on Clergy Divorce." *Boston Sunday Globe*, 22 April 1979, p. 9.

———. "Remarriage and the Religion Factor." *Boston Globe*, 11 March 1978, p. 9.

———. "Vatican Lifts Ban on Divorce—Remarriage." *Boston Globe*, 11 November 1977, p. 8.

Freed, Doris, and Foster, Henry H., Jr. "The Shuffled Child and Divorce Court." *Trial* 10 (May-June 1974): 26-41.

Fripp, Bill. "Aid for Couples in Distress." *Boston Globe*, 31 March 1977, p. 15.

———. "What Happens to the Children of Divorce?" *Boston Globe*, 22 November 1975, p. 10.

Fulton, Julie A. "Parental Reports of Children's Post-Divorce Adjustment." *Journal of Social Issues* 35:4 (1979): 126-139.

Furman, Sylvan S. et al. "Social Class Factors in the Flow of Children to Out-patient Psychiatric Facilities." *American Journal of Public Health* 55 (1965): 387-397.

Gatto, Patricia. "Single Women Buying Homes." *Boston Globe*, 1 August 1979a, pp. 13, 18.

_____. "They Need to Know They Are Not Alone." *Boston Globe*, 13 March 1979b, pp. 1, 10.

Gebhard, Paul. "Postmarital Coitus Among Widows and Divorcees." In *Divorce and After: An Analysis of the Emotional and Social Problems of Divorce*, pp. 89-106. Edited by Paul Bohannan. Garden City, NY: Doubleday, 1970; Anchor, 1971.

Gettleman, Susan, and Markowitz, Janet. *The Courage to Divorce*. New York: Simon and Schuster, 1974.

Glick, Paul C. "Children of Divorced Parents in Demographic Perspective." *Journal of Social Issues* 35:4 (1979): 170-182.

_____. "Social Change and the American Family." *The Social Welfare Forum, 1977*. New York: Columbia University Press, 1978.

Glick, Paul C., and Norton, Arthur J. "Marrying, Divorcing, and Living Together in the U.S. Today." *Population Bulletin*, Vol. 32, No. 5. Washington, DC: Population Reference Bureau, 1977.

Glick, Paul C., and Spanier, Graham B. "Married and Unmarried Cohabitation in the United States." *Journal of Marriage and the Family* 42:1 (February 1980): 19-30.

Goldstein, Joseph, Freud, Anna, and Solnit, Albert J. *Beyond the Best Interests of the Child*. New York: Free Press, 1973.

Goode, William J. *Women in Divorce*. Chicago, IL: Free Press, 1956, as *After Divorce*; reprint edition, New York: Free Press, 1965.

Goodman, Ellen. "New Rights for Children." *Boston Globe*, 9 November 1976, p. 21.

_____. "The Plight of Displaced Homemakers." *Boston Globe*, 25 July 1978, p. 15.

_____. " 'Transparent' Fatherhood." *Boston Globe*, 7 January 1977, p. 25.

Gordon, Henry A., and Kammeyer, Kenneth C. W. "The Gainful Employment of Women with Small Children." *Journal of Marriage and the Family* 42:2 (May 1980): 327-336.

Griffin, John. *Black Like Me*. Boston, MA: Houghton Mifflin, 1961.

Grossman, Allyson S. "Almost Half of All Children Have Mothers in the Labor Force." *Monthly Labor Review* 100 (June 1977): 41-44.

_____. "Divorced and Separated Women in the Labor Force—An Update." *Monthly Labor Review* 101 (October 1978): 43-45.

Grunwald, Beverly. "Getting Around." *Women's Wear Daily*, 1 April 1976, pp. 24-25.

Haddad, W. F., and Roman, M. *The Disposable Parent: The Case for Joint Custody*. New York: Holt, Rinehart and Winston, 1978.

Halem, Lynne Carol. *Divorce Reform: Changing Legal and Social Perspectives*. New York: Free Press, 1980.

"Halting Colorado's Do-It-Yourself Divorce." *New York Times*, 24 April 1977, p. 58.

Hartman, Curtis. "First Thing We Do, Let's Kill All the Lawyers." *Boston Magazine*, March 1978, pp. 63-65, 106-109.

Hatherley, John Edward. "The Role of the Child's Wishes in California Custody Proceedings." *University of California, Davis Law Review* 6 (1973): 332-353.

*_____. "Health Plan Newsletter." Vol. 7, No. 2, Spring, 1977.

Heclo, Hugh et al. "Single Parent Families: Issues and Policies." Washington, DC: U.S. Department of Health, Education, and Welfare, 1973.

Herman, Robin. "Major Changes in Divorce Law Voted in Albany." *New York Times*, 4 June 1980, pp. 1, B2.

Herzog, Elizabeth, and Sudia, C. E. *Boys in Fatherless Families*. Washington, DC: U.S. Department of Health, Education, and Welfare, Children's Bureau, No. (OCD), 1971, pp. 72-33.

Hetherington, E. Mavis, Cox, Martha, and Cox, Roger. "The Aftermath of Divorce." In *Mother-Child, Father-Child Relations*, pp. 149-176. Edited by J. H. Stevens, Jr. and Marilyn Mathews. Washington, DC: National Association for the Education of Young Children, 1978.

_____. "Divorced Fathers." *Psychology Today* 10:11 (April 1977): 42-45.

_____. "Play and Social Interaction in Children Following Divorce." *Journal of Social Issues* 35:4 (1979): 26-49.

Hinds, Michael de Courcy. "For Men, It's Opening Lines." *New York Times*, 20 June 1980, p. A18.

Hofferth, Sandra L. "Daycare in the Next Decade: 1980-1990." *Journal of Marriage and the Family* 41:3 (August 1979): 649-658.

Hoffman, Blair W. "Restrictions on a Parent's Right to Travel in Child Custody Cases: Possible Constitutional Questions." *University of California, Davis Law Review* 6 (1973): 181-194.

Hoffman, L. W., and Nye, F. Ivan. *Working Mothers*. San Francisco, CA: Jossey-Bass, 1974.

House, Ernest R. *The Politics of Educational Innovation*. Berkeley, CA: McCutchan, 1974.

"Housing Bias Not Eliminated—Rights Panel." *Boston Globe*, 13 April 1979, p. 8.

"How Kids Look at Divorce." *Boston Sunday Globe*, 29 July 1979, pp. 49, 54-55.

Hunt, Morton. *The World of the Formerly Married*. New York: McGraw-Hill, 1966.

Hunt, Morton, and Hunt, B. *The Divorce Experience*. New York: McGraw-Hill, 1977.

Hutchison, Ira W., and Hutchison, Katherine R. "The Impact of Divorce Upon Clergy Career Mobility." *Journal of Marriage and the Family* 41:4 (November 1979): 847-855.

Hutson, Ron. "The Sign's Still Out: No Children." *Boston Sunday Globe*, 3 September 1978, p. 14.

Hyatt, James C. "Staying Together." *Wall Street Journal*, 27 June 1978, p. 48.

"Increase Foreseen in Wives at Work." *New York Times*, 29 September 1979, p. B9.

Jancourtz, Isabella. "Divorce Handbook," 2nd edition. Weston, MA, 1975.

Janney, Mary D. "How Schools Can Prepare Girls for Careers." *Boston Globe*, 9 November 1975, p. C11.

"Jewish 'Singles' A New Problem After Years of Focus on Family." *New York Sunday Times*, 2 May 1976, p. 60.

Johnson, Sharon. "Renters' Plight: No Children Allowed." *New York Times*, 12 July 1980, p. 42.

Kahn, Robert, and Kahn, Lawrence. *The Divorce Lawyer's Casebook*. New York: St. Martin's, 1972.

Kamerman, Sheila B., and Kahn, Alfred J. "The Day-Care Debate: A Wider View." *The Public Interest* 54 (Winter 1979): 76-93.

Kanowitz, Leo. *Sex Roles in Law and Society: Cases and Materials*. Albuquerque: University of New Mexico Press, 1973.

_____. *Women and The Law: The Unfinished Revolution*. Albuquerque: University of New Mexico Press, 1969.

Karagianis, Maria. "Changing Trends in Couple Counseling." *Boston Globe*, 8 September 1975, pp. 30, 33.

Kaufman, Louis. "Men Protest Divorce Laws." *Boston Globe*, 20 May 1979, p. 87.

Kay, Herma Hill. "Making Marriage and Divorce Safe for Women." *California Law Review* 60 (1972): 1683-1700.

Keniston, Kenneth, and the Carnegie Council on Children. *All Our Children*. New York: Harcourt, Brace, Jovanovich, 1977.

Kiester, Edwin, Jr. "How Divorce Counselors Sweeten the Sour Taste of Separation." *Today's Health*, November 1975, pp. 46-50.

Kirchheimer, Anne. "Daycare: The Choices are Few." *Boston Globe*, 25 March 1979a, pp. B1, B6.

_____. "The Family in the '80s: Fatherhood in Transition." *Boston Globe*, 18 March 1980, p. 41.

_____. "Single, Searching, Scared...." *Boston Sunday Globe*, 12 August 1979b, pp. A1, A6.

Konut, Nester C. *Therapeutic Family Law: A Complete Guide to Marital Reconciliation*, 2nd edition. Family Law Publications. Chicago, IL: Adams, 1968.

*Kowal, Loretta. "A New Kind of Family Makes Waves in—." *Westside Times*, 24 September 1975, p. 22.

Krantzler, Mel. *Creative Divorce: A New Opportunity for Personal Growth*. New York: M. Evans, 1973.

*Kravitz, Barbara K., ed. *The Villages of Westside*. Westside,—: Westside Times, 1977.

Kreps, Juanita, and Clark, Robert. *Sex, Age, and Work: The Changing Composition of the Labor Force*. Baltimore, MD: Johns Hopkins Press, 1975.

Kressel, Kenneth. "Patterns of Coping in Divorce and Some Implications for Clinical Practice." *Family Relations* 29:2 (April 1980): 234-240.

Kriesberg, Louis. *Mothers In Poverty: A Study of Fatherless Families*. Chicago, IL: Aldine, 1970.

Lake, Alice. "Divorcees: The New Poor." *McCalls*, September 1976, pp. 18, 20, 22, 24, 152.

Lasch, Christopher. *Haven in a Heartless World: The Family Besieged*. New York: Basic, 1977.

Laws, Judith Long. *The Second X: Sex Role and Social Role*. New York: Elsevier, 1979.

LeMasters, E. E. et al. "Eighty Divorced Men." School of Social Work, University of Wisconsin, 1968.

Lewis, Melvin. "The Latency Child in a Custody Conflict." *Journal of the American Academy of Child Psychiatry* 13:4 (Autumn 1974): 635-647.

Lipson, Benjamin. "Insurance After Divorce: Coverage Isn't the Same." *Boston Globe*, 7 April 1980, pp. 20-21.

Longcope, Kay. "The Reality of the Divorced Clergy." *Boston Sunday Globe*, 22 February 1976, pp. B1, B4.

McConnell, Adeline. "Old Friends Take on a New Look." *Boston Globe*, 2 April 1979, p. 25.

McCormack, Patricia. "Women Polled on Views of Credit Use." *Boston Globe*, 27 November 1978, p. 35.

McLaughlin, Jeff. "Divorce: What About the Kids?" *Boston Globe*, 7 November 1978, p. 21.

McLaughlin, Loretta. "A Commercial Counseling Shop." *Boston Globe*, 27 May 1976, p. 43.

McManus, Otile. "Separation—the Dollar Drain." *Boston Sunday Globe*, 6 February 1977, pp. B1, B5.

Mariano, John H. *The Use of Psychotherapy in Divorce and Separation Cases*. New York: American, 1958.

Marris, Peter. *Loss and Change*. New York: Pantheon, 1974.

Martin, Peter. "Names . . . Faces." *Boston Globe*, 19 June 1978, p. 3. Quoted from paper presented at the meeting of the American Medical Association 1978.

Masnick, George, and Bane, Mary Jo. *The Nation's Families: 1960-1990*. Cambridge, MA: The Joint Center for Urban Studies of MIT and Harvard University, 1980.

Mendes, H. A. "How Fathers Obtain Custody—A Review of Research." *Conciliation Courts Review* 17:1 (1979): 27-30.

Metz, Charles V. *Divorce and Custody for Men: A Guide and Primer Designed Exclusively to Help Men Win Just Settlements*. Garden City, NY: Doubleday, 1968.

Miller, Arthur A. "Reactions of Friends to Divorce." In *Divorce and After: An Analysis of the Emotional and Social Problems of Divorce*, pp. 63-86. Edited by Paul Bohannan. Garden City, NY: Doubleday, 1970; Anchor, 1971.

Miller, Margo. "What To Look For in a Lawyer and Where." *Boston Globe*, 12 June 1978, pp. 17, 20.

Mills, Kay. "Single Parent Families Top Average Investor." *Boston Globe*, 12 March 1976, p. 33.

Milne, A., ed. *Joint Custody: A Handbook for Judges, Lawyers and Counselors*. Portland, OR: Association of Family Conciliation Courts, 1979.

Moffett, Robert K., and Scherer, Jack F. *Dealing With Divorce*. Boston, MA: Little, Brown and Company, 1976.

Molinoff, Daniel. "Can a Lawyer Really Be Objective With Divorce Clients?" *Boston Sunday Globe*, 18 December 1977a, p. A21.

_____. "Life With Father." *New York Times Magazine*, 22 May 1977b, pp. 12-17.

Morris, Bailey. "Day Care Lack a Roadblock to Advancement." *Boston Sunday Globe*, 30 March 1980a, p. B3.

_____. "More Firms Offer Day-Care Services." *Boston Sunday Globe*, 6 April 1980b, p. B2.

"Mother's Day in Court." *New York Times*, 11 May 1980, p. 20E.

Mott, Frank L., and Moore, Sylvia F. "Marital Disruption: Causes and Consequences." In *Years for Decision*, vol. 4, pp. 207-256. Edited by Frank L. Mott. U.S. Department of Labor, Research, and Development. Monograph 24. Washington, DC: U.S. Government Printing Office, 1978.

Moynihan, Daniel P. *The Politics of a Guaranteed Income: The Nixon Administration and the Family Assistance Plan*. New York: Vintage, 1973.

Nagel, Stuart S., and Weitzman, Lenore J. "Women As Litigants." *Hastings Law Journal* 23 (November 1971): 171-198.

"Names...Faces." *Boston Globe*, 19 June 1978, p. 3.

National Association for Divorced Women Bulletin. New York, n.d.

NBC Reports. "The American Family: An Endangered Species?" 2 January 1979.

NBC Reports. "Children of Divorce." 19 January 1976.

Nemy, Enid. "Stress in the Lives of Women: Seminar Examines Its Causes." *New York Times*, 23 October 1979, p. B10.

Newcomb, Paul R. "Cohabitation in America: An Assessment of Consequences." *Journal of Marriage and the Family* 41:3 (August 1979): 597-603.

Norton, Arthur J., and Glick, Paul C. "Marital Instability: Past, Present, and Future." *Journal of Social Issues* 32:1 (1976): 5-20.

Osgood, Viola. "U.S. Move Balances Job-Family Juggling." *Boston Globe*, 22 March 1978, p. 17.

Pave, Marvin. "Ex-Teachers to Study for Hi-Tech Jobs." *Boston Sunday Globe*, 30 March 1980a, p. 55.

_____. "One-Parent Pupils—A Troubled and Growing Minority." *Boston Globe*, 29 July 1980b, pp. 1, 21.

Permanent Commission on the Status of Women. "Marital Dissolution: The Economic Impact on Connecticut Men and Women." Hartford, CT, November 1979.

Plateris, Alexander. Personal communication, April 23, 1976. Marriage and Divorce Statistics Branch, U.S. Division of Vital Statistics.

Price-Bonham, Sharon, and Balswick, Jack O. "The Noninstitutions: Divorce, Desertion, and Remarriage." *Journal of Marriage and the Family* 42:4 (November 1980): 959-972.

Quinn, Jane Bryant. "Equal Credit Some Progress." *Boston Globe*, 18 May 1979, p. 34.

Raschke, Helen J. "The Role of Social Participation in Postseparation and Postdivorce Adjustment." *Journal of Divorce* 1 (Winter 1977): 129-139.

Rein, Martin. *Social Policy: Issues of Choice and Change*. New York: Random House, 1970.

Reinhold, Robert. "Census Study Backs Divorce Trend Rise." *New York Times*, 2 July 1979, p. A14.

Roncek, Dennis W., Bell, Ralph, and Choldin, Harvey M. "Female-Headed Families: An Ecological Model of Residential Concentrations in a Small City." *Journal of Marriage and the Family* 42:1 (February 1980): 157-169.

Rosen, Bernard C., and Aneshensel, Carol S. "Sex Differences in the Educational-Occupational Expectation Process." *Social Forces* 57 (September 1978): 164-186.

Ross, Heather L., and Sawhill, Isabel V. *Time of Transition: The Growth of Families Headed by Women.* Washington, DC: Urban Institute, 1975.

Ross, Nancy L. "New U.S. Report Cites Prejudice of Lenders Toward Minorities." *Boston Globe*, 23 June 1980, p. 17.

Rothenberg, Charles. *Matrimonial Litigation Strategy and Techniques.* New York: Practicing Law Institute, 1974.

Rothman, Sheila. "The Other People's Children: The Day Care Experience in America." *The Public Interest* 30 (Winter 1973): 11-27.

Rowe, Richard R. "Child Care in Massachusetts: The Public Responsibility." Harvard University Program in Public Psychology, 1972, pp. 3-27.

Rozhon, Tracie. "A Divorce Ceremony, for Children's Sake." *New York Times*, 15 August 1980, p. D14.

Rule, Sheila. "Albany Senate Acts to Ease Financial Burden for Some Divorced Men." *New York Times*, 19 March 1978, p. 45.

Ryan, Michael. "Uncoupling Catholics." *Boston Magazine*, April 1975, pp. 46-49, 72, 75.

Sarason, Seymour. *The Creation of Settings and Future Societies.* San Francisco: Jossey-Bass, 1972.

Sardoff, Robert L. *Forensic Psychiatry: A Practical Guide for Lawyers and Psychiatrists.* Springfield, IL: Charles C. Thomas, 1975.

Schon, Donald. *Beyond the Stable State.* New York: Norton, 1971.

Sheffner, David J., and Suarez, John M. "The Post Divorce Clinic." *American Journal of Psychiatry* 132:4 (April 1975): 442-444.

Sherisky, Norman, and Mannes, Marya. *Uncoupling: The Art of Coming Apart.* New York: Viking Press, 1972.

Sherman, Charles. *How To Do Your Own Divorce in California.* Berkeley, CA: Nolo Press, 1972.

Sherwin, Robert V. *Compatible Divorce.* New York: Crown, 1969.

Sifford, Darrell. "Bouncing Back From a Divorce." *Boston Globe*, 27 November 1978a, pp. 19, 21.

_____. "Divorce and the Children." *Boston Globe*, 2 September 1978c, p. 15.

_____. "On the Rebound? How to Act at a Singles Bar." *Boston Globe*, 28 November 1978b, pp. 21, 28.

Smith, Ralph E., ed. *The Subtle Revolution: Women at Work.* Washington, DC: Urban Institute, 1979.

Smith, Shirley. "Woman Alone." *Boston Globe*, 2, 3, 4, 5, 6, 8, 9, 10 January 1979.

Spanier, Graham B., and Anderson, Elaine A. "The Impact of the Legal System on Adjustment to Marital Separation." *Journal of Marriage and the Family* 41:3 (August 1979): 605-625.

Spanier, Graham B., and Casto, R. "Adjustment to Separation and Divorce: An Analysis of 50 Case Studies." *Journal of Divorce* 2 (Spring 1979): 241-253.

Stack, James. "No-Fault Divorce Law Has Problems." *Boston Sunday Globe*, 2 April 1978, p. 4.

Stocker, Carol. "Extended Families Offer Salvation." *Boston Globe*, 10 July 1980a, pp. 37-38.

_____. "Wanted: A Job for a Mother." *Boston Globe*, 17 March 1980b, pp. 25, 27.

Streshinsky, Shirley. "How Divorce Really Affects Children: A Major Report." *Redbook*, September 1976, pp. 70, 132, 134, 136.

"Those #*X*!!! Lawyers!" *Time Magazine*, April 10, 1978, pp. 56-66.

Tubbs, Ace L. *Divorce Counseling: A Workbook for the Couple and Their Counselor.* Danville, IL: Interstate Printers and Publishers, 1973.

Unco, Inc. *National Day Care Consumer Study: 1975*, 4 vols. Unco, 1975.

U.S. Bureau of the Census. "Household and Family Characteristics: March 1978." *Current Population Reports*. Series P-20, No. 340. Washington, DC: Government Printing Office, 1979.

_____. "Household and Family Characteristics: March 1979." *Current Population Reports*. Series P-20, No. 352. Washington, DC: Government Printing Office, 1980.

_____. "Marital Status and Living Arrangements: March 1977." *Current Population Reports*. Series P-20, No. 323. Washington, DC: Government Printing Office, 1978a.

_____. "Money Incomes and Poverty Status of Families and Persons in the United States: 1977 (Advanced Report)." *Current Population Reports*. Series P-60, No. 116. Washington, DC: Government Printing Office, 1978b.

U.S. National Center for Health Statistics. "Advanced Data from Vital and Health Statistics." No. 58. Washington, DC: Government Printing Office, February 14, 1980a.

_____. "Provisional Statistics." Department of Health and Human Services. Vol. 29, No. 2. Washington, DC: Government Printing Office, May 13, 1980b.

_____. "Advance Report: Final Statistics, 1978." Department of Health and Human Services. Vol. 29, No. 6, Supp. (1). Washington, DC: Government Printing Office, September 12, 1980c.

_____. "Provisional Statistics: Annual Summary for the United States, 1979." Department of Health and Human Services. Vol. 28, No. 13. Washington, DC: Government Printing Office, November 13, 1980d.

"Unmarried Couples Rate Up." *Boston Globe*, 28 June 1979, p. 8.

Van Gelder, Lawrence. "Role of Pension in Divorce Cases Becomes Focus of Legal Debate." *New York Times*, 5 March 1979, pp. A1, B9.

Victor, Ira, and Winkler, Win A. *Fathers and Custody*. New York: Hawthorn, 1977.

Waldman, W. E., and Grover, K. R. "Children of Women in the Labor Force." *Monthly Labor Review* 94 (1972): 19-25.

Waller, Willard. *The Old Love and the New: Divorce and Readjustment*. New York: Liveright, 1930.

Wallerstein, Judith S., and Kelly, Joan B. "The Effects of Parental Divorce: The Adolescent Experience." In *The Child in His Family: Children at Psychiatric*

Risk, vol. 3, pp. 479-505. Edited by E. James Anthony and Cyrille Koupernik. New York: Wiley, 1974.

_____. "The Effects of Parental Divorce: Experiences of the Pre-School Child."
Journal of the American Academy of Child Psychiatry 14:4 (Autumn 1975):
600-616.

_____. "The Effects of Parental Divorce: Experiences of the Child in Early
Latency." *American Journal of Orthopsychiatry* 46:1 (January 1976a):
20-32.

_____. "The Effects of Parental Divorce: Experiences of the Child in Later
Latency." *American Journal of Orthopsychiatry* 46:2 (April 1976b):
256-269.

_____. *Surviving the Break-up: How Children Cope with Divorce.* New York:
Basic, 1980.

Walters, J., and Stinnett, N. "Parent-Child Relationships: A Decade Review of
Research." *Journal of Marriage and the Family* 33 (1971): 70-111.

Washburn, Gary. "Report Cites Women Housing Bias." *Boston Globe*, 18 March
1976, p. 22.

Watson, Andrew S. "The Children of Armageddon: Problems of Custody Following
Divorce." *Syracuse Law Review* 21 (1970): 55-86.

Weiss, Robert. *Marital Separation.* New York: Basic, 1975.

Weitzman, Lenore J. "Legal Regulation of Marriage: A Proposal for Individual
Contracts and Contracts in Lieu of Marriage." *California Law Review* 62
(1974): 1169-1288.

Westinghouse—Westat. *Day Care Survey—1970: Summary Report and Basic
Analysis.* Bladensburg, MD: Westinghouse Corporation and Westat Research, Inc., 1971.

Westman, Jack C., and Cline, David. "Divorce is a Family Affair." *Family Law
Quarterly* 5:1 (March 1971): 1-10.

*"What's in a Family?" letter to the editor. *Westside Times*, 17 September 1975,
p. 4.

Wheeler, Michael. "The Bonds of Acrimony." *New York Times*, 19 April 1980a,
p. 23.

_____. *Divided Children: A Legal Guide for Divorcing.* New York: Norton,
1980b.

"Who's Minding the Kids?" *Boston Sunday Globe*, 11 May 1980, p. A6.

Wilkerson, Albert E., ed. *The Rights of Children: Emergent Concepts in Law and
Society.* Philadelphia, PA: Temple University Press, 1973.

Winfrey, Carey. "Pay Deductions for Child Support Urged in Study." *New York
Times*, 31 December 1979, p. A12.

Winston, M. P. *Nonsupport of Legitimate Children by Affluent Fathers as a Cause
of Poverty and Welfare Dependence.* Santa Monica, CA: Rand Corp., 1971.

*Wise, Barbara. "—is Common Ground for Single Parents." *Westside Times*, 10
May 1978, p. 4.

"Women and Credit: What Does the Law Provide?" *Boston Sunday Globe*, 8 June
1980, p. D1.

Women in Transition, Inc. *Women in Transition: A Feminist Handbook on Separation and Divorce.* New York: Charles Scribner's Sons, 1975.

Woodward, Kenneth L., and Malamud, Phyllis. "The Parent Gap." *Newsweek*, September 22, 1975, pp. 48-56.

Woolsey, Suzanne H. "Pied Piper Politics and the Child-Care Debate." *Daedalus* 106:2 (Spring 1977): 127-145.

Zack, Ellen. "How To . . . Retain a Lawyer." *Boston Globe*, 14 November 1975, p. 12.

Zenor, Donna L. "Untying The Knot: The Course and Patterns of Divorce Reform." *Cornell Law Review* 57 (April 1972): 649-667.

INDEX

Volunteer work, 82

Weiss, Robert, 200; *Marital Separation,* 227

Women: and absence of credit history, 94-97; alienation from legal system, 63-64; and credit discrimination, 131-33; custody suit advantage of, 37; economic status of, 59; and friendship, 151-52; as household heads, 76, 113, 195; and housing discrimination, 122-28; in labor force, 77, 78; as lawyers, 66, 67; as single parents, 80; socialization of, 23, 26, 85; use of psychological counseling, 203, 216

Women in Transition (Philadelphia), 269, 270; handbook, 227; as model program, 275, 277, 283

Women's groups. *See* Advocacy groups; Support groups

Women's movement: relationship to self-help movement, 269

Work. *See* Employment; Volunteer work

ABOUT THE AUTHOR

LYNNE CAROL HALEM, a specialist in family policy, holds a doctorate from Harvard University and is a staff member and joint partner of HHI Associates, Andover, Massachusetts, a consulting firm providing services in health, education, and social welfare. She is the author of *Divorce Reform: Changing Legal and Social Perspectives.*